The Story of Bahá'u'lláh

The Story of Bahá'u'lláh

Promised One of All Religions

Druzelle Cederquist

BAHÁ'Í PUBLISHING
WILMETTE, ILLINOIS

Bahá'í Publishing
401 Greenleaf Avenue, Wilmette, Illinois 60091-2844

Printed in the United States of America

20 19 18 7 6 5

ISBN 10: 1-931847-13-4 (softcover)
ISBN 13: 978-1-931847-13-1 (softcover)

Library of Congress Cataloging-in-Publication Data
Cederquist, Druzelle, 1949–
The story of Bahá'u'lláh, promised one of all religions / Druzelle Cederquist.
p. cm.
Includes bibliographic references (p.) and index.
ISBN 1-931847-13-4 (sc: alk. paper)
1. Bahá'u'lláh, 1817–1892. I. Title.
BP392.C43 2005
297.9'3'092—dc22
[B]
2004054411

Cover design by Robert A. Reddy
Book design by Suni D. Hannan
∞This book is printed on acid-free paper.

For the teachers in my life,
To whom I am eternally grateful

Turn ye away from all that is on earth and seek none else but Me.
I am the Sun of Wisdom and the Ocean of Knowledge.
I cheer the faint and revive the dead.
I am the guiding Light that illumineth the way.
I am the royal Falcon on the arm of the Almighty.
I unfold the drooping wings of every broken bird and start it on its flight.

—*Bahá'u'lláh*

Contents

Acknowledgments xi
Note to the Reader xv
Map of Persia in the Time of Bahá'u'lláh xvi
Map of the Exiles of Bahá'u'lláh xvii

The Story of Bahá'u'lláh

Part 1: The Dawn

1 Shaykh Maḥmúd's Secret Plan 3
2 The Puppet Show and the Dream 6
3 The Home of Love 10
4 Father of the Poor and Mother of Consolation 13
5 No Time to Lose 17
6 The Quest 23
7 Witnesses of the Dawn 27
8 Noble Descendant of a Noble Father 32
9 The Mujtahid and the Dervish 36
10 Awake, Awake! 40
11 The Scholar and the Governors 44
12 The Open Mountain and the Grievous Mountain 50
13 Rage and a Secret Rescue 53
14 The Blast of the Trumpet 57
15 The Sermon of Wrath and a Royal Command 62
16 Bandar-Gaz and the Black Standard 64
17 Danger at Amul 68
18 Courage at Ṭabarsí 72
19 Embattled 76
20 No Peace in the City of Tabríz 80
21 A Promise Kept in Karbala 86
22 A Plot against the Shah 90
23 Prisoner 94
24 The Black Pit 96

25 Cruel Days 100
26 The Mystery of God and His Treasure 105
27 Banished 110
28 Terrible Journey 114

Part 2: The Sun in Its Splendor

29 Baghdad 121
30 Thousands of Oceans of Light 124
31 The Dark Campaign 128
32 Alone in the Wilderness 131
33 The Nameless One 135
34 A Joyful Naw-Rúz 140
35 Purity within Purity 144
36 Unlocking the Doors of Heaven 148
37 The Shaykh and the Assassin 153
38 The Eldest Uncle's Questions 157
39 A Paradox Resolved 163
40 The Garden of Paradise 167
41 One Hundred and Ten Days 172
42 The Sultan's Command 175
43 The Poisoned Cup 178
44 The Most Great Separation 182
45 He Who Feareth No One 186
46 O Kings of the Earth! 190
47 Destination Unknown 194
48 The Most Great Prison 198
49 Seeking a Glimpse of the Lord 201
50 For the Healing of All the World 204
51 Into the Mouth of the Serpent 209
52 The Greatest Gift 213
53 The Whisperings of Satan 218
54 The Keys of My Mercy 222

55 The Governor and the Master of Acre 226
56 Two Birds of the Nest of Thy Love 229
57 The Hand of God 234
58 Oasis 238
59 The King of Martyrs and the Beloved of Martyrs 242
60 Blessed Is the Place 246
61 To Conquer the Cities of the Hearts 250
62 The Master 254
63 O Most Exalted Leaf! 258
64 These Fruitless Strifes, These Ruinous Wars 263
65 The King of Days 267
66 The Holy Mountain and the Martyrs of Yazd 273
67 A Pattern for the Future 278
68 The Sun of Bahá Has Set 284
69 An Excellent and Priceless Heritage 287
Appendix 1: A Brief Chronology of Events in the Life of Bahá'u'lláh 291
Appendix 2: A Note about the Wives of Bahá'u'lláh and Bahá'í Marriage 293
Appendix 3: Islam and its Two Major Branches, Shia and Sunni 294
Appendix 4: Millennial Christians 296
Appendix 5: Mírzá Yaḥyá 300
Notes 303
Glossary 319
Bibliography 335
Index 341

Acknowledgments

A historical biography such as this must of necessity stand on the shoulders of other scholars and writers, to whom I am greatly indebted.

Adib Taherzadeh's four-volume series, *The Revelation of Bahá'u'lláh,* offered a most excellent and invaluable resource, not only for information but also for insight and inspiration. This series, as well as his later work titled *The Covenant of Bahá'u'lláh,* provided the backbone for my own work. I am grateful to David Ruhe, who, in addition to providing the books *Robe of Light* and *Door of Hope,* was generous in sharing his unpublished manuscripts on the life of Bahá'u'lláh and in taking time to read an early version of my manuscript. His artist's eye, as well as his love of the history of the Holy Land, were sources of unique detail that I appreciated.

Other books that helped bring to life many stories in the life of Bahá'u'lláh were H. M. Balyuzi's thorough history, *Bahá'u'lláh: The King of Glory,* as well as William Sears's captivating works *Release the Sun,* which summarizes the early history of the Bahá'í Faith, and *Thief in the Night,* which summarizes prophecies about Bahá'u'lláh. I found Mary Perkins's two volumes *Hour of the Dawn* and *Day of Glory* greatly helpful in their concise telling of the history of both the Báb and Bahá'u'lláh.

I want to express my appreciation to Geoffry Marks for *Call to Remembrance: Connecting the Heart to Bahá'u'lláh,* which gives an illuminating selection of Bahá'u'lláh's writings that highlights the episodes of His life. I also found helpful the lucid explanation of Bahá'í governance and community life found in *The Bahá'í Faith: The Emerging Global Religion,* by William S. Hatcher and J. Douglas Martin. My thanks go to Janet Ruhe-Schoen for kindly sharing an unpublished edition of her manuscript titled "The Nightingale, Bahá'u'lláh."

An especially useful resource entitled *A Basic Bahá'í Chronology,* compiled by Glenn Cameron and Wendi Momen, saved hours of research, for which I am most assuredly grateful. I am also appreciative of Moojan and Wendi Momen for their assistance with points of Islam. Thanks must also go to George Ronald for their generous permission to use the map drawn by Moojan Momen on page 121 of *A Basic Bahá'í Dictionary,* which locates key places mentioned in the text but not found on larger maps.

Special thanks go to Carrie Kneisler for permission to use her map of Bahá'u'lláh's exiles. I am also grateful to Robert Stockman, who, amid his many educational pursuits, generously and consistently facilitates communication among scholars. It was also through a course of the Wilmette Institute, of which he is the primary facilitator, that I discovered another informative resource on Islam, *Living Religions* (fifth edition), by Mary Pat Fisher.

I am particularly indebted to those whose work has shed additional light on the women in Bahá'u'lláh's family. As Adib Taherzadeh notes, the lives of women in nineteenth-century Persia were considered beyond the reach of historians (usually male), whose inquiries would have been considered an unethical trespass into private domain. As a result, records of such women's lives during the time of Bahá'u'lláh are sparse. A welcome book that helps to fill this void is *The Chosen Highway,* by Lady Blomfield, who traveled twice to the Holy Land, where she listened to the stories of Bahá'u'lláh's daughter and 'Abdu'l-Bahá's wife, among others. Her work serves as a precious link to those family members whose days were intimately connected with the days of Bahá'u'lláh.

More recent books that offer additional insights into these lives are *Munírih Khánum: Memoirs and Letters,* translated by Sammireh Anwar Smith; *Ásíyih Khánum: The Most Exalted Leaf entitled Navváb,* by Baharieh Rouhani Ma'ani; and *Bahíyyih Khánum: The Greatest Holy Leaf,* compiled by the Research Department at the Bahá'í World Center. My thanks go to Derek Cockshut for sharing previously unpublished details about the women in Bahá'u'lláh's household.

Naturally, one cannot write about Bahá'u'lláh without reference to the writings of Shoghi Effendi, especially his masterful history of the Bahá'í Faith, *God Passes By,* and his equally powerful translation of *The Dawn-Breakers: Nabíl's Narrative of the Early Days of the Bahá'í Revelation,* written by the first historian of the Bahá'í Faith, Nabíl-i-A'ẓam, who lived during the time of Bahá'u'lláh. I am also very appreciative of the staff of the Research Department of the Bahá'í World Center, who answered a handful of questions not covered in other sources, and to the Universal House of Justice for shedding light on certain complex subjects.

I am additionally grateful to a number of people who assisted my research into the broader scope of world events that occurred during the lifetime of Bahá'u'lláh. The reference librarians at Poughkeepsie's Adriance Memorial Library and at the Vassar College Library were a great help in locating sources for specific nuggets of information that I was very pleased to find. William Collins generously shared information from his research on millennial Christians, including a particularly useful article titled "Millennialism, the Millerites, and Historicism," published in the fall 1998 issue of *World Order* magazine. Other valuable sources on this topic were *Year of the Lord,* by Charles W. Meister, and *The Prophecies of Jesus,* by Michael Sours. Thanks also go to David Freeth, whose appreciation of a passage from the Koran (8:30) stuck with me.

Elizabeth Warnock Fernea's *Guests of the Sheik: An Ethnography of an Iraqi Village* contains an intimate account of her time among the women of Iraq, and her details about life in Iraq yielded useful additions to the descriptions of Bahá'u'lláh's years in Baghdad. Similarly, I found Russell Freedman's works entitled *Lincoln: A Photobiography* and *Indian Chiefs* helpful not only for their detail but also for their example of sensitive storytelling. Other useful resources were *Harriet Tubman,* by M. W. Taylor, and Dee Brown's *Wounded Knee: An Indian History of the American West,* adapted by Amy Ehrlich for young readers.

Details in Suzanne Sprague's 1999 radio program "From Seneca Falls to Ally McBeal: 150 Years of Women's Rights," aired on radio station KERA in Dallas, helped me relate the initiators of the women's movement in this country with an equally courageous proponent of women's equality in the early history of the Bahá'í Faith. Concerning women and resolving conflict, Leila Rassekh Milani's article "Women as Decision Makers: A Case for Inclusion," in the summer 2001 issue of *World Order* magazine highlights the United Nations' recognition of the vital role played by contemporary women in conflict resolution.

I have an especially warm spot in my heart for those who lent their support to the writing process itself, particularly when the goal seemed a long way off. Among them is the International Women's Writing Guild, whose conferences introduced me to the value of writer networking, and whose work continues to provide great support for women writers. I would also like to acknowledge the Taconic Writers, in which I met a good group of talented people. Most especially my heartfelt gratitude goes to our Tuesday morning group of writers: Angela, Amy, Elaine, Jeanne-

Marie, Karen, Liz, and Margaret. I cannot imagine how I would have written this book without their wit and humor, their hard questions and loving support over many cups of coffee.

My deep gratitude goes as well to my editors, Terry Cassiday and Christopher Martin, whose well-honed editing skills drew out the best from the book and me, and whose technical expertise was consistently accompanied by a warmth of spirit that lent unfailing support throughout the process. I could not have asked to work with better people. The best in this book is a reflection of their efforts; any weaknesses are my own. I am especially grateful to Ladan Cockshut, the first editor who thought my rough manuscript had merit and brought it to the attention of others.

My acknowledgments would not be complete without the mention of my family. Well-earned thanks go to my husband, Robert, whose support came in innumerable ways—from his own knowledge and love of history to his many skills on the home front and with the computer. He quietly made possible that which seemed, at times, insurmountable. Finally many thanks go to our sons, Aaron and David, who were in great part the first motivators for my writing a story of Bahá'u'lláh that could be enjoyed by readers young and old. My hope is that it may be so, and that this book may convey a measure of my love for the myriad stories that not only recount the life of Bahá'u'lláh but also tell of the heroes and heroines whose lives were inextricably interwoven with that of the Promised One Who was known as Bahá'u'lláh, the Glory of God.

Note to the Reader

The system of transliterating Persian and Arabic terms that is followed in this book is one of several that are currently in use. It has been chosen because Shoghi Effendi, Guardian of the Bahá'í Faith, advocated its use for the sake of consistency.

However, place names and other terms that have well-established English equivalents (e.g., Baghdad, Karbala, Tehran, muezzin, howdah, etc.) are not transliterated unless they occur as part of a quotation that employs the Bahá'í system (Ba<u>gh</u>dád, Ṭihrán). The same is true for titles such as sultan and shah, which appear without diacriticals unless they occur as part of a transliterated quotation or part of a transliterated name (Náṣiri'd-Dín <u>Sh</u>áh, Sulṭán 'Abdu'l-'Azíz).

Map of Persia in the Time of Bahá'u'lláh

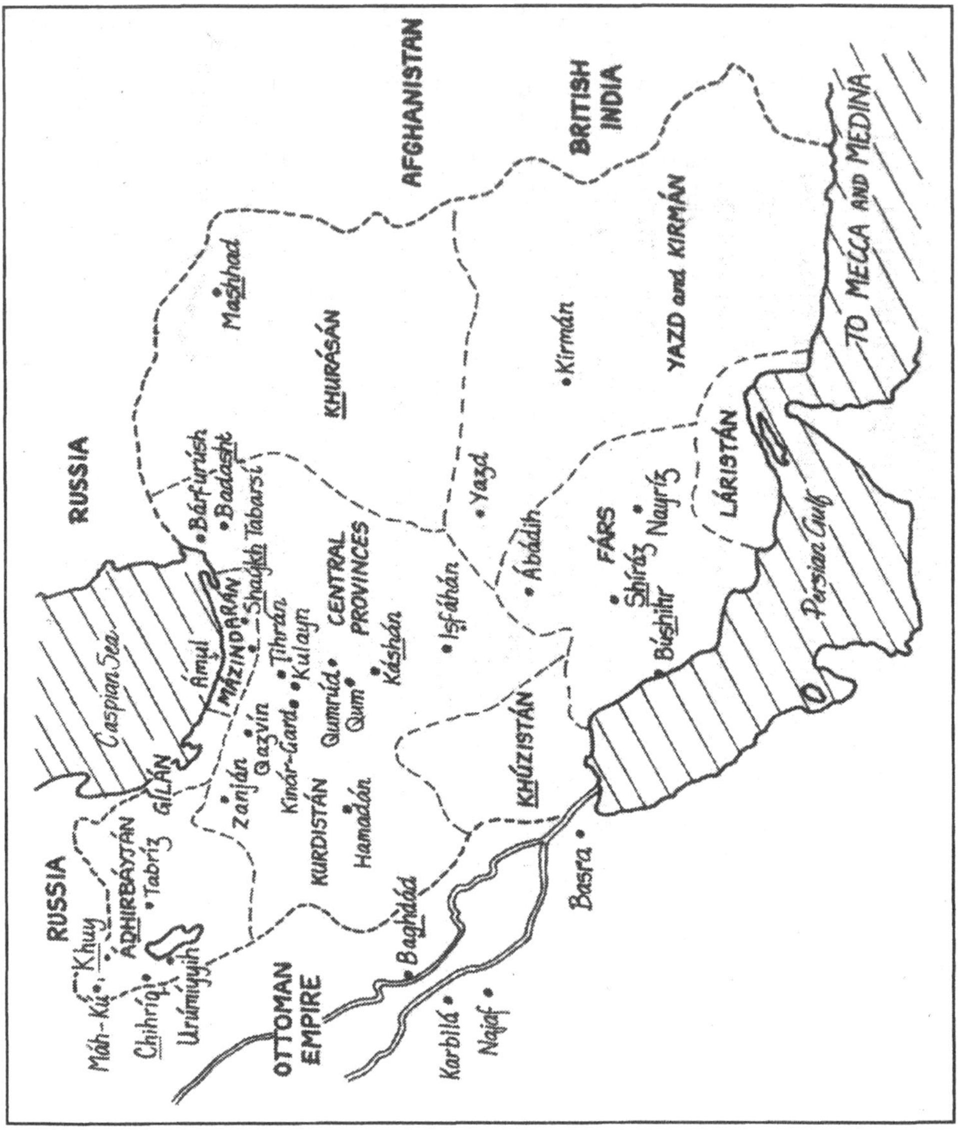

Map of the Exiles of Bahá'u'lláh

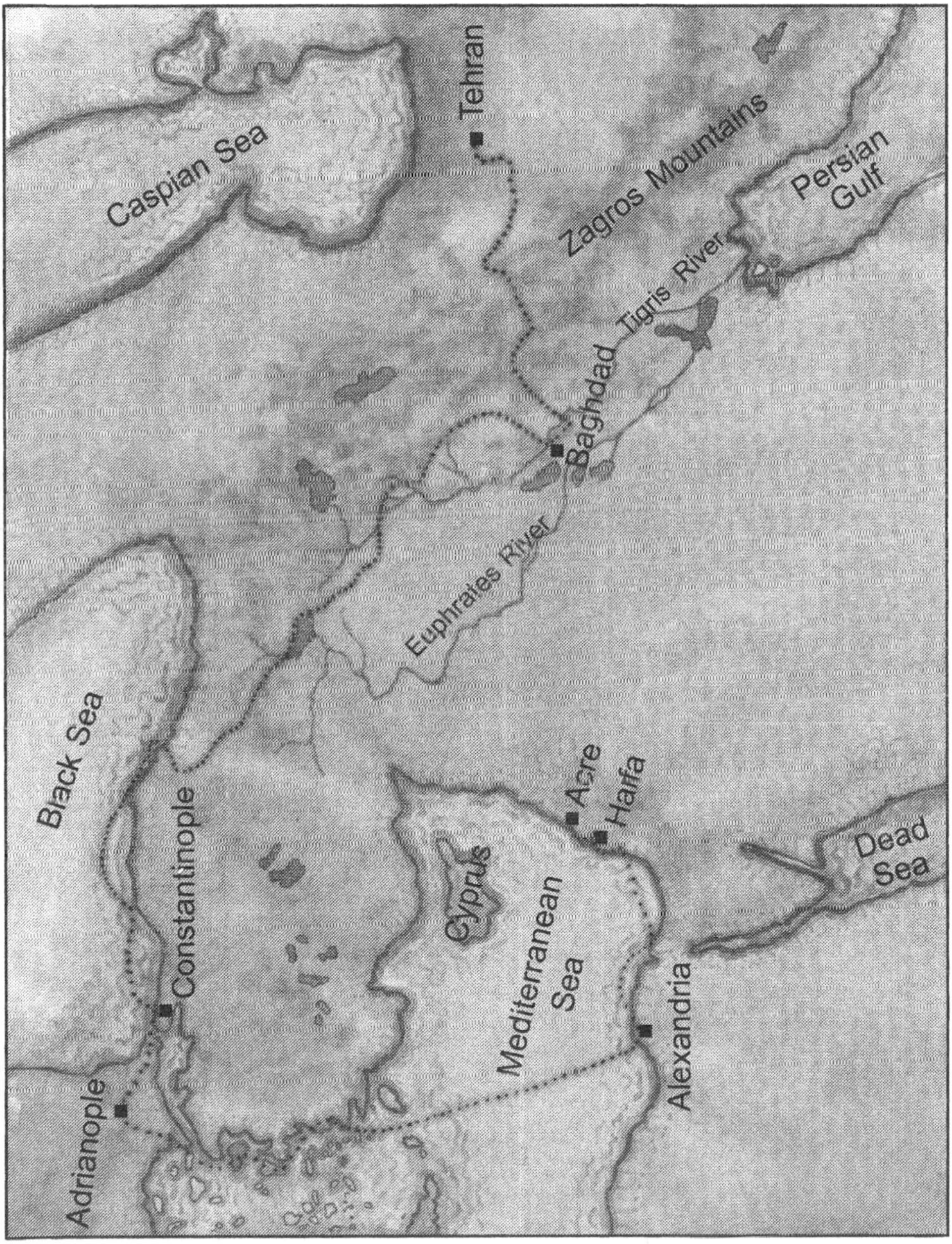

Part 1
The Dawn

1

<u>Sh</u>ay<u>kh</u> Maḥmúd's Secret Plan

<u>Sh</u>ay<u>kh</u> Maḥmúd walked north along the streets of Acre with a determined stride. A gentle sea breeze off the Mediterranean ruffled his white beard and his long black aba, but the <u>sh</u>ay<u>kh</u> was too angry to notice. The Persian government and the Ottoman Empire might be afraid to execute an enemy of Islam, but he, <u>Sh</u>ay<u>kh</u> Maḥmúd, was not.

As the brick prison barracks came into view, <u>Sh</u>ay<u>kh</u> Maḥmúd clutched the cold metal dagger more tightly beneath his cloak. The task was simple and would surely please God. He would eliminate the heretic who dared to claim he was God's chosen Messenger.

"Tell the prisoner I wish to see Him," <u>Sh</u>ay<u>kh</u> Maḥmúd told the guards at the prison gate. Although the prisoner was not allowed visitors, the guards obeyed, for the <u>sh</u>ay<u>kh</u> was a highly respected Muslim teacher and leader in Acre.

The guards delivered the <u>sh</u>ay<u>kh</u>'s message, but the prisoner answered calmly, "Tell him to cast away the weapon and then he may come in."[1]

<u>Sh</u>ay<u>kh</u> Maḥmúd was startled when he heard the reply. How could the prisoner know about the dagger? It was still well hidden, and he had told no one of his plan. Puzzled and upset, the <u>sh</u>ay<u>kh</u> returned home.

But <u>Sh</u>ay<u>kh</u> Maḥmúd was not a man to be thwarted when he set his mind to do something—and he was physically strong. He did not need a weapon. His own two hands were strong enough to accomplish the task. The determined <u>Sh</u>ay<u>kh</u> Maḥmúd returned once again to the prison. Once again he asked to see the prisoner.

This time the reply came, "Tell him to purify his heart first and then he may come in."[2]

The <u>sh</u>ay<u>kh</u> was astonished to hear such an answer. What magic did this prisoner possess that he could read the inner secrets of his heart! Once again he left the prison, more deeply disturbed this time, his mission still unaccomplished.

Later the troubled <u>Sh</u>ay<u>kh</u> Maḥmúd fell into a deep sleep. He dreamed about his father, who was long dead, and about a wise old <u>sh</u>ay<u>kh</u> who had visited his father when Maḥmúd was a boy of ten. The <u>sh</u>ay<u>kh</u> had told Maḥmúd to watch for the coming of the Lord—the "Promised One" sent by God. He would come to Acre, the shaykh had said, when little Maḥmúd was a grown man. He would speak Persian and dwell in an upper room at the top of a long flight of stairs.

When Shaykh Maḥmúd awoke, his dream lingered with him, vivid and clear. As he pondered the words of the wise old shaykh, questions deep within him and long forgotten began to stir. Shaykh Maḥmúd decided to return once more to the prison gate. Again he took no weapon, but this time the malice in his heart had given way to a new desire—a deep longing to discover the truth. This time, when Shaykh Maḥmúd asked to see the prisoner, the prisoner gave His consent.

The shaykh walked up a long flight of stone stairs that led to the prison cells. He spoke first with the prisoner's eldest son, who prepared him to meet with his father. Finally, Shaykh Maḥmúd stood at the threshold of the prisoner's cell and was given permission to enter.

The man who stood before him was of middle age and average height, with jet-black hair and beard. As a prisoner He had survived the Black Pit of Tehran and the mountainous winter journey into exile. He had endured the torture of the bastinado—the soles of His feet beaten until they bled—and the weight of a hundred-pound chain that left its scars upon His neck. He had faced down assassins and their guns in Baghdad, but His hand was no longer steady, and His writing wavered now from the poison that had been meant to end His life.

Shaykh Maḥmúd did not know about all these things, but one thing he realized at once. This prisoner was not at all what he had imagined Him to be. When He moved, it was with a natural grace and majesty that made Shaykh Maḥmúd feel like a humble subject in the presence of his king. When He spoke, He spoke with the assurance of a king and more—with a love that penetrated every word. This was the One called *Bahá'u'lláh*—"the Glory of God."

The gentle sound of waves lapping against the city wall drifted in through the prison window. Acre was a prison-city on the shores of the Holy Land, and Bahá'u'lláh had been sent there in 1868 to die. Bahá'u'lláh, Who was the noble son of a noble family, Who was called "father" by the poor for His loving-kindness and generosity, Whose wisdom and courage were recognized even by His enemies—Bahá'u'lláh had been sent to Acre to die.[3]

Yet when offered a chance to escape His fate, He had refused to run away. "Who is to be preferred," Bahá'u'lláh later wrote, "he that hath sheltered himself behind curtains, or he that hath offered himself in the path of God?"[4]

Although Bahá'u'lláh had committed no crime, in the eyes of His accusers He had committed the greatest crime. He claimed to be a divine Messenger, chosen by God to speak to the world as the great Prophets before Him—Abraham, Moses, Krishna, Buddha, Zoroaster, Christ, and Muḥammad—had done. He claimed to fulfill the prophecies of old and to bring new guidance from God.

"This thing is not from Me," Bahá'u'lláh had written to the shah of Persia, "but from One Who is Almighty and All-Knowing."[5]

His accusers were outraged. "Blasphemy!" they called it. How dare He—Who had never even received religious training—claim to speak with divine authority!

"And if My sin be this," Bahá'u'lláh further wrote, "that I have exalted the Word of God and revealed His Cause, then indeed am I the greatest of sinners! Such a sin I will not barter for the kingdoms of earth and heaven."[6]

When Bahá'u'lláh spoke, people were drawn to listen. With the eloquence of His arguments He stirred their thoughts and inspired their hearts as no one else. Many were convinced that He spoke the truth. Bahá'u'lláh's enemies could not bear it. They wanted His name, His life, and His Cause erased from the face of the earth. In 1868 they used their sovereign powers to exile Bahá'u'lláh to Acre in Palestine, far from His Persian homeland. There He would surely die, they thought, disgraced and entirely forgotten.

But the Koran warns, "They plotted—but God plotted: and of plotters is God the best!"[7] The rulers who imprisoned Bahá'u'lláh thought of themselves as mighty kings who commanded the peoples of the world. They forgot that the sovereignty of kings is not the sovereignty of God, Who claims for His domain the hearts of all humankind. Blinded by their ambitions, they could not know that one day, when their own names lay forgotten as dust, the name of Bahá'u'lláh would be cherished in every land.

From his first moment in Bahá'u'lláh's presence, Shaykh Maḥmúd felt the power and majesty of the Messenger of God. The shaykh could scarcely look upon Bahá'u'lláh's face, so radiantly did it shine with the light of His spirit. Here was a splendor that needed no royal robes or trumpets to herald it. Here was a majesty that belonged to no one else on earth.

The shaykh's own position as a respected religious leader paled, all at once, to insignificance. Moved by a deep sense of reverence and a joy that flooded his being, Shaykh Maḥmúd lay face down, prostrate at the feet of Bahá'u'lláh. How else could he express the feelings that overwhelmed him—the awe and wonder and gratitude? How could he explain the certain knowledge that filled his heart? He was but a candle in the presence of the sun. The Lord had indeed come to Acre.

The story of Bahá'u'lláh—"the Glory of God"—begins in the early nineteenth century, not in the prison-city of Acre, but to the east, in another walled city that stands near the foot of the tallest mountain in Persia—the city of Tehran.

2

The Puppet Show and the Dream

"Alláh-u-Akbar!" (God is Most Great!) From the high, slender towers of the mosques of Tehran came the familiar Arabic call to prayer.

The call that had wakened Muslims for more than a thousand years floated out over the sleeping city. The sound of it gently traced the edges of blue-and-gold-domed mosques and flat-roofed houses, reaching with delicate fingers into the last dreams of night.

Long ago Tehran had been a quiet village where travelers rested in shady groves of fruit trees and nomads stopped to graze their sheep. Now it was the capital of Persia and home to 160,000 people—merchants and peasants, landowners and servants, and the shah who ruled over all of them.

Each dawn, as the first rays of sunlight washed the sky, the people of Tehran woke with the call to prayer. Getting up, they washed hands and face—the ablutions required before prayer—with pitchers of cold water. Then, with prayer rug unrolled, each believer turned to God to begin the day as the Prophet Muḥammad had taught His followers generations before.

In a mansion on the eastern edge of the city, young Ḥusayn-'Alí awoke, excited at the prospect of another day of celebration. Ḥusayn-'Alí's older brother had gotten married earlier in the week. Because their family was noble and wealthy, the marriage celebration, by Persian custom, continued for seven days and nights. Friends and relatives came from near and far. In an era when travel and communication were slow and entertainment did not come every day, people found great pleasure in attending such a festive gathering.

All week Ḥusayn-'Alí had enjoyed plates of delicious Persian food—rice cooked with almonds and dates, skewers of roasted meat and vegetables, sweet pastries, juicy melons, and icy fruit sherbets. He had enjoyed the music and other entertainment arranged for this special occasion.

Today, on the last day of the festivities, Ḥusayn-'Alí watched as a tent was pitched in the open courtyard and a stage was made ready. In a short time, much to His delight, the wedding guests were invited to come to a puppet show. As Ḥusayn-'Alí watched, a puppet figure wearing a crown and majestic robes appeared—the king! The miniature king was surrounded by a procession of advisors, princes, and ministers of state—all finely dressed and all puppet-sized.

As the play continued, a puppet thief was brought before the king. The king ordered the thief beheaded, and an executioner carried out the king's command. News was brought to the miniature king of a rebellion in his land. The king ordered his regiments and artillery to battle the rebels, and soon the sounds of an imaginary battle could be heard offstage.

Ḥusayn-'Alí watched it all, entranced by the small figures and the story they played out. When the drama finally ended and the audience of guests had gone, young Ḥusayn-'Alí saw a man leave the tent with a box under his arm.

"What is this box?" Ḥusayn-'Alí asked him.

"All these lavish trappings," the man replied, "the king, the princes and the ministers, their pomp and glory, their might and power, everything you saw, are all now contained within this box."[1]

To Ḥusayn-'Alí, the puppeteer's answer held truth for more than his puppets. People themselves, He had noticed, seemed to treat the world as though it were the tent with a puppet stage and their lives the stories on that stage. Those who gained wealth, fame, or authority in the world felt the drama's best parts belonged to them. Yet wealth and poverty, honor and dishonor, often changed hands in the world, and many held tight to selfish ambitions, eager to gain a better part.

Why should they take pride, Ḥusayn-'Alí wondered, in such self-centered aims and accomplishments? How could they forget the truth that surrounded them? Whenever a life ended in this world, the body of that person—rich or poor, powerful or not—was laid to rest in the earth, like the puppets returned to their box. Only the soul of each one continued its journey in the next world. Only the invisible qualities of each soul—generosity, kindness, courage—were carried into the life hereafter. Every selfish ambition was left, at last, buried in the dust of the world that had spawned it. Ḥusayn-'Alí understood this with a certainty He could not explain.

These were unusual thoughts for a youth to ponder, but Ḥusayn-'Alí often thought about things that other youth did not, and could answer questions that even adults could not answer. It was simply His nature—a unique nature that was evident from His earliest days.

Ḥusayn-'Alí was born November 12, 1817, at dawn when the birds begin their songs. He was born in the land of Persia, in the city of Tehran. According to the Muslim calendar used in Persia, the day of His birth was the second day of the month of Muḥarram in the year 1233 A.H.

At that time, Fatḥ-'Alí S͟háh ruled Persia, and King George III was king of England. James Monroe was president of the United States, which had only nineteen states, Abraham Lincoln was a boy of eight, living in Indiana, and Frederick Douglass was a baby, born into slavery in the state of Maryland.[2]

Ḥusayn-'Alí was the third-born child of the honorable Mírzá 'Abbás Buzurg, a vizier (minister of state) of the shah, and his noble wife K͟hadíjih K͟hánum.* Only later, when the time was right, would He take the title "Bahá'u'lláh," meaning in Arabic "the Glory of God."

Early on, His parents recognized that Ḥusayn-'Alí was an unusual child. His mother often wondered how a baby could be so happy and content all the time. "This child never cries!" she would exclaim.[3]

But what truly astonished them as they watched their young son grow was His extraordinary knowledge and wisdom. His simple education was no different from that given to other sons of the Persian nobility. Tutors came to His home to teach reading, writing, and Persian culture, just as

---

* Mírzá and K͟hánum are honorific titles. "Mírzá" is a contraction of amír-zádih meaning "son of a prince, ruler, commander, or governor." When used before a name, it conveys the honorific sense of "Mister." "K͟hánum," meaning literally "lady" or "wife," when placed after a woman's given name is a courtesy title meaning "gentlewoman."

they did for the other boys. Ḥusayn-'Alí learned to read the great Persian poets—'Attar, Hafez, Rumi—as the other boys did, and to recite from the Koran, the holy book of Islam. He did not study science, for science was viewed with suspicion in nineteenth-century Persia, nor did He study philosophy or religion. Those were left to the *mullás* and *mujtahids*—Muslim scholars who spent long years studying the teachings, laws, and traditions of Islam.

Yet Ḥusayn-'Alí showed a lively interest in spiritual topics, and from His boyhood He displayed a profound understanding of spiritual truth. His understanding was innate and reached far beyond the knowledge of His teachers. Although Ḥusayn-'Alí was never arrogant or boastful about the knowledge that came so easily to Him, neither was it something He could hide.

As Ḥusayn-'Alí grew into a youth, His father could find Him, from time to time, deep in conversation with the most learned of men. They welcomed Him into their company despite His young age. His understanding of the Prophets and Their teachings, of the nature of God and the human spirit, added much to their discussions. By the time He was fourteen years old, Ḥusayn-'Alí's innate knowledge and wisdom were recognized by all who knew Him.

"Such intelligence! And such perception! He is as a flame of fire," Mírzá Buzurg said. "Even at this young age He surpasses mature men."[4]

He wondered how his young son could know these things. Did His gift have something to do with the noble ancestors of their family lineage? Through His father, Ḥusayn-'Alí was a descendant of the great Persian kings of old as far back as Yazdigird the Sassanian. He was also a descendant of two holy Prophets: the Persian Prophet Zoroaster, Who taught His followers about the battle between good and evil; and Abraham,* Who taught the Jews to worship one God.

Mírzá Buzurg pondered these things about his young son. One night he dreamed a strange dream. In his dream he saw an ocean stretching in every direction as far as the eye could see. In the center of the ocean swam Ḥusayn-'Alí, strong and peaceful, with His long, jet-black hair

---

* Bahá'u'lláh was descended through Abraham's wife Keturah and through the line of Jesse, father of David.

floating on top of the waves. His body seemed to glow with light, attracting fish from every direction. As the fish gathered around Him, each clung tightly to one of His hairs; but the fish did not bother Ḥusayn-'Alí. He swam freely wherever He wished, while the fascinated fish swam with Him.

When he awoke, Mírzá Buzurg remembered the dream clearly. It seemed strange yet wonderful, as some dreams do. But what did it mean? He would need to call on a soothsayer who was wise in the language of dreams to find out.

3

The Home of Love

In the twisting maze of narrow streets, the early morning market of Tehran stirred to life. Watchmakers and leather workers, potters and tailors, opened their doors to begin the day's work. Soon the steady rhythm of blacksmiths swinging their heavy hammers onto red-hot iron rang throughout the market. Here and there an overloaded donkey brayed loudly, or a mean-tempered camel spit his displeasure.

Before long, loud-voiced merchants would bargain with their customers over piles of melons and mounds of fragrant spices. They would haggle over the prices of dates from the palm groves near the Persian Gulf and rice from the warm coast of the Caspian Sea. Already, the smell of animals mingled with the more delicate scents of oranges and cinnamon, of hot tea and freshly baked bread.

But today Mírzá Buzurg was not interested in the hustle and bustle of the outside world. His attention was turned to the world of dreams. Mírzá Buzurg's dream about his extraordinary young son was a puzzle that he longed to unlock. He had summoned a soothsayer to his home for this purpose.

When the soothsayer came, he listened closely to every detail of Mírzá Buzurg's dream. Finding the truth of a dream could seem like winding through the maze of a marketplace, but the soothsayer was experienced in interpreting the language of dreams. Soon it was Mírzá Buzurg's turn to listen as the soothsayer spoke.

The ocean was the world, he explained. The fish that gathered around Ḥusayn-'Alí were the peoples of the world. Ḥusayn-'Alí would cause great confusion and turmoil amongst them, but no one could stop Him or stand in His way.

"Single-handed and alone," the soothsayer promised, "your son will achieve supreme ascendancy over it [the world of being]. Wherever He may please, He will proceed unhindered."[1]

Not even the soothsayer could tell the exact path of events that would unfold Ḥusayn-'Alí's future. But Mírzá Buzurg's heart was deeply moved. The soothsayer's words confirmed his own thoughts about the boy Who was wise beyond His years. The finest qualities of those kings and Prophets who were their forbearers was reflected in the brilliance of His spirit. Now more than ever Mírzá Buzurg was determined to protect and care for his beloved son. Everything that was his—wealth, position, and honor—he valued only for this purpose.

Mírzá 'Abbás Buzurg, who served as a vizier of the shah, was himself a man of both talent and good character. Unlike many officials who were easily influenced by anyone willing to pay a price, Mírzá Buzurg was a just man who decided matters fairly. Although wealthy, with mansions in both the city and the country, Mírzá Buzurg showed compassion toward the poor and always gave generously to those in need. He was a highly regarded calligrapher who created beautiful designs from the graceful lines of Persian script. The shah himself had honored Mírzá 'Abbás by giving him the title *Buzurg,* which means "Great One." He was known throughout Persia and respected by his countrymen.

Ḥusayn-'Alí, Who loved His father dearly, called him "Master" to express His own deep respect for one whose source of nobility reached far deeper than mere title. It was the custom in Persia that sons follow their fathers in skill or profession. Other people expected Ḥusayn-'Alí to hold an important government office when He came of age. No one doubted that Ḥusayn-'Alí, like His father, would continue to be welcomed at the royal court. Like the other boys of noble families, He had learned the etiquette that governed behavior at the royal court, but such a life and career did not attract Ḥusayn-'Alí.

He saw that many of Tehran's privileged, unlike His own father, were less concerned with justice or the needs of the poor than with their own enjoyment. How they vied with one another in their feasts and lavish lifestyles, in acquiring "heaped-up treasures" and "gorgeous finery"! How they schemed and maneuvered for the power and prestige they so coveted! But Ḥusayn-'Alí remembered the puppet show and how the puppets, with all their pomp and glory, were put away in a box at the end of the play.

For Himself, Ḥusayn-'Alí much preferred to mount His horse and ride out of the city gates into the countryside and the mountains beyond. Among the tall trees and rocky paths He heard no scheming or gossiping tongues, only the gentle rustling of leaves, the soft splashing of meandering streams, and the sweet warbled songs of birds. Here paused and darted the swift, black-eyed gazelles, whose graceful beauty had been captured by Persian poets for a thousand years. Here Ḥusayn-'Alí felt a deep contentment that He did not find at the court of the shah.

"'The country is the world of the soul,'" He would remark in His later years, "'the city is the world of bodies.'"[2]

When Ḥusayn-'Alí rode out of the city and through the Persian countryside, He would pass the simple stone and mud-plastered homes of humble farmers and villagers. Often He would stop to talk with the people who lived there and ask about their concerns. How were their families faring? Did they have enough to eat? Was anyone sick, in need of a doctor or medicine? Wherever there was a need, He would see to it that help was given. Sometimes a dispute needed mediating or an injustice needed attention. Here, too, Ḥusayn-'Alí gave assistance. Even as a youth, He was not afraid to speak up at the shah's courts in defense of the weak and innocent.

So it was that Ḥusayn-'Alí, who cared sincerely about all people, followed in the spirit of His father's footsteps. In deed as well as in name, He grew up as the noble son of a noble father. Mírzá Buzurg, for his part, never forgot his dream and the soothsayer's words. Although he could not know the future, Mírzá Buzurg felt sure that whatever unfolded, his unique son would be at the center of it. The words he carved above the door of their country mansion in Tákur hinted at the mystery he felt:

> When thou enterest the sacred abode of the Beloved say:
> "I am at thy command.
> This is the home of Love; enter with reverence.
> This is holy ground; remove thy shoes when thou enterest here."[3]

On November 12, 1833, when Ḥusayn-'Alí turned sixteen, the heavens themselves seemed to celebrate. It was as if the great bowl of night turned upside-down. Stars began spilling to earth as thick and fast as snowfall. More than thirty-four thousand stars fell in one hour, and the starfall continued all night. It was a meteor shower that set the night ablaze with light as though it were day.

People who witnessed the meteor shower were amazed. Some were delighted with its beauty. Others were terrified, for it looked like the end of the world. Those who saw it most clearly lived in North America, halfway around the world from Persia. There many Christians recalled the words of Christ in the Bible telling His disciples about the signs of His return, when "the stars shall fall from heaven." It would be a time of "great tribulation," He had told them.[4] Many Christians expected a fierce and mighty change, like a great storm, to sweep the world at the time of Christ's return, and they wondered, as they gazed up at the starfall, what would happen next.

4

Father of the Poor and Mother of Consolation

Horsemanship, hunting, and expert use of a sword—these were skills that Persians had prized from their earliest days as conquering warriors. Half a century before Christ, Persia had been the center of an empire that stretched from Africa as far as India. Cyrus the Great, king of Persia, had called it "the Kingdom of the Whole World."[1] Those days of glory had long passed for Persia, but they were not forgotten.

Ḥusayn-'Alí did not care for hunting or swordplay, but His skill with horses was unquestionable. Whatever horse carried Him seemed to sense the command of a loving spirit and to grow gentle in His hands. As a young man Ḥusayn-'Alí often made the sixty-mile trek by horseback from the family's home in Tehran to their mansion in the village of Tákur. The mansion in Tákur stood on the cool mountain slopes north of Tehran in the district of Núr—which means "light"—in the province of Mázindarán. The trails between Tehran and Tákur wound through narrow green valleys and rocky river gorges, then climbed through mountain passes as high as ten thousand feet, where mountain goats and sheep grazed in precarious places. Ḥusayn-'Alí guided His horse expertly and drank in the beauty of the rugged nature that surrounded Him.

Along the way Ḥusayn-'Alí might stop to visit His favorite older sister, Sárih, who was married now. By seventeen Ḥusayn-'Alí, too, had reached marriageable age. In those days it was the custom for people to marry at a young age and for their families to arrange the marriages. Sárih proposed that her own husband's younger sister, Ásíyih Khánum, would make a perfect match for her younger brother. Ásíyih Khánum had always been lively and full of fun, gentle and kind. She was slender and graceful, with dark hair and deep blue eyes, and she had grown into a young woman as goodhearted as she was beautiful. Ḥusayn-'Alí and their parents agreed with Sárih's suggestion. So it came to pass in the autumn of 1835 that Ḥusayn-'Alí, who was nearly eighteen, and Ásíyih Khánum, who was fifteen, were married, and the family of Mírzá Buzurg celebrated another happy marriage feast.

When Ásíyih Khánum left her childhood home to begin married life with Ḥusayn-'Alí, her family sent with her the many things she would need. In the months before the wedding, fine cloth bought from the marketplace had been measured, cut, and sewn, for there were no stores with ready-made clothing. Little by little, trunks were packed with fine dresses, all stitched carefully by hand. Many had buttons of gold set with precious stones.

On the journey to Tákur, forty mules carried on their backs all the trunks that belonged to Ásíyih Khánum. Slowly the surefooted animals made their way. Deer, half-hidden in thickets of leafy shade, might peer at the passing travelers, then bound away, while squirrels chased along the branches above. From time to time a scree of small stones, set loose by hooves, clattered down the steep sides of a mountain pass. A family of fat partridges might skitter across the trail in front of them, or a hare dart for cover to escape the fox, but the sure-footed mules walked steadily on until they arrived, at last, in Tákur.*

People called it a marriage of wealth to wealth, but never before had the poor gained so much from a marriage of the wealthy. The love and tenderness that Ḥusayn-'Alí and Ásíyih Khánum felt for each other spilled over to reach far beyond themselves. They took their greatest pleasure not from attending the parties of the rich, but in caring for the needs of the poor. The doors of their home were always open to those in need, and the hungry were always invited to eat at their table.

According to Persian custom, men visited Ḥusayn-'Alí in the outer rooms of the house called the *bírúní*. Women visitors, wrapped in their long, black veils, came to visit Ásíyih Khánum in the private inner rooms called the *andarún*. In the twilight of evening oil lamps glowed from the niches of the mansion's whitewashed walls, shedding their warm light on the faces of those who had no one else to help them.

Not everyone understood their generosity, however. The grand vizier, closest advisor to the shah, was suspicious.

"What is the purpose of all this feasting and banqueting in which you seem to delight?" the grand vizier complained to Ḥusayn-'Alí. "I, who am the Prime Minister of . . . Persia, never receive the number and variety of guests that crowd around your table every night." Then he added a dangerous accusation. "You surely must be meditating a plot against me."

"Gracious God!" replied Ḥusayn-'Alí. "Is the man who, out of the abundance of his heart, shares his bread with his fellowmen, to be accused of harboring criminal intentions?"[2]

The grand vizier made no reply. He was familiar with the aspiring rich and power-hungry, who were ever greedy to gain more for themselves and plotted to get what they wanted. That this couple wanted nothing for themselves was something he could scarcely imagine. Ḥusayn-'Alí and Ásíyih Khánum, however, did not let the suspicions of the grand vizier stop them. No one who came to them was ever turned away, and they became known as "Father of the Poor" and "Mother of Consolation" for their kind and generous ways.

---

* Ḥusayn-'Alí and Asíyih Khánum would divide their time between the family's homes in Tákur and Tehran.

One day Ḥusayn-'Alí would write God's instructions to the wealthy: "O Children of Dust! Tell the rich of the midnight sighing of the poor . . . To give and to be generous are attributes of Mine . . . O ye Rich Ones on Earth! The poor in your midst are My trust; guard ye My trust, and be not intent only on your own ease."[3]

Ḥusayn-'Alí and Ásíyih Khánum were helpmates to each other in all things.* Ḥusayn-'Alí treated His young wife with loving respect and called her *"Navváb,"* a title meaning "Highness" or "Excellency." The joy of their marriage increased with the birth of two sons, Káẓim and Ṣádiq. Yet they suffered grief, too, when neither child lived beyond infancy—an all too common occurrence among families in that time. Assured as they were that these young souls, the pearls of their love, would live on in the spiritual worlds of God, the young couple still mourned their loss in this world.

Then in 1839, when Ḥusayn-'Alí was twenty-two years old, Mírzá 'Abbás Buzurg—the father who had cherished and nurtured Him with loving care—passed away. At the family home in Tákur Ḥusayn-'Alí could solace His pangs of grief with the balm of remembrance. There He could walk among the fragrant roses that Mírzá Buzurg had tenderly planted with his own hands. He would never forget the noble father who had lived a life of justice and courage, of kindness and generosity. Ḥusayn-'Alí found His greatest solace in knowing that His father's spirit was free now—free to live in those "heavenly places that the pen cannot tell nor the tongue recount," free to mingle with other noble souls in the "exalted rose garden" of the spirit.[4]

After Mírzá Buzurg's passing, the members of his large family looked to Ḥusayn-'Alí for leadership. According to the custom of the time, His father had married more than one wife and had fathered seventeen children in all. Some of Ḥusayn-'Alí's ten brothers and six sisters were still young. To these Ḥusayn-'Alí became like a kind father, guiding them and taking care of their needs as though they were His own children.

Ḥusayn-'Alí was asked to take His father's place in the government, but He did not accept the offer. The grand vizier expressed no surprise.

---

* Bahá'u'lláh would also take two other wives, not in self-indulgence, but because of obligations delineated by Persian culture at that time. However, only Ásíyih Khánum was named by Bahá'u'lláh as His *"consort through all the worlds of God."* See appendix 2 for a more detailed explanation.

"Leave him to himself," he said. "Such a position is unworthy of him. He has some higher aim in view. I cannot understand him," the grand vizier admitted, "but I am convinced that he is destined for some lofty career. His thoughts are not like ours. Let him alone."[5]

In 1843, when Ḥusayn-'Alí was twenty-six years old, a great comet appeared in the sky and astonished people everywhere. The comet had a tail 105 million miles long and was bright enough to be seen at noon. A famous astronomer, James Jeans, wrote that great comets appeared in the heavens when important events were about to occur. The feeling of expectation stirred and deepened in the world.

5
No Time to Lose

Before Bahá'u'lláh was born Shaykh Aḥmad, a Muslim scholar known as "the most learned among the most learned,"[1] had made a profound discovery. In his studies of Islamic scripture, he had determined that the time promised by all the Prophets of God was at hand—a time in which the world would receive not just one, but two new divine Messengers. These two "Promised Ones" would come like two trumpet blasts, said the Koran, one shortly after the other.* According to the Shia branch of Islam,† the first Messenger would herald and prepare His followers to recognize the Messenger yet to come. The title of the first would be the *Qá'im,* meaning in Arabic "He Who Shall Arise." The title of the great Messenger yet to come would be the *Qayyúm,* meaning "The All-Compelling."‡

---

* See Koran 39:68.

† One of the two major branches of Islam. The other branch, to which the majority of Muslims belong, is Sunni Islam. For more details, see appendix 3.

‡ Shia Muslims also referred to the return of the Imám Ḥusayn, while Sunni Muslims referred to the descent of the "Spirit of God" (Jesus Christ). Tradition in both branches also uses the term *Mahdí,* meaning literally "one rightly guided," to refer to the Promised One to come.

Human history had seen the appearance of such divine Messengers before. Their ranks had included Moses, Jesus Christ, Muḥammad, Zoroaster, Krishna, and Buddha. They were the world's great Teachers—each One "a pure and stainless Soul" entrusted by God with a sacred mission.[2] Unlike philosophers and other ordinary teachers, each divine Messenger not only infused the world with new knowledge, but also released a tremendous new spiritual energy that gave rise to the advancement of whole civilizations.

The history of religion had often recorded heavenly signs—stars or comets—which seemed to announce the coming of each divine Messenger. Certain teachers, chosen by God, prepared the way for each Messenger. These spiritually gifted teachers served as guides, helping the people of their time better understand the signs and prophecies that heralded the coming of a new Messenger. Shaykh Aḥmad was one of these chosen teachers.

For twenty-five years Shaykh Aḥmad devoted himself to study until, at last, he was ready to teach others what he had learned. He left his island home of Bahrain in the waters of the Persian Gulf and traveled north to the city of Karbala, Iraq, on the banks of the great Euphrates River. Farther north, Baghdad straddled its sister river, the Tigris. The land around Karbala, which had once been the rich farmland of the ancient Fertile Crescent, was now mostly grassland and parched desert. Still, many people lived in Karbala, and many more traveled to the city. It was a place of pilgrimage for Shia Muslims* and a center of study for Muslim scholars.

There, where sparse palm trees offered little shade from the intense heat, Shaykh Aḥmad began to teach. Many Muslims were eager for the coming of the promised Qá'im, but their expectations were clouded by their own wishful thinking. They wanted the Qá'im to come as a king who would conquer their enemies. Shaykh Aḥmad knew better. The Qá'im would not be king of any earthly dominion, for His was a far greater sovereignty.

Patiently Shaykh Aḥmad tried to teach those who studied with him how to look with spiritual eyes. The truth of the holy scriptures was not always found in their plain, literal meaning, but in the spiritual meaning

* Karbala is the site of the martyrdom and of the shrine of the Imám Ḥusayn, a prominent figure in the history of Shia Islam.

hidden within the language of metaphor. Only sincere seekers, willing to open their minds and purify their hearts—to let go of false ideas and self-centered desires—would grasp the truth and be able to recognize the promised Qá'im.

Shaykh Aḥmad taught his students the signs that would identify the promised Qá'im. Some signs were physical. He would be of medium height and in age a young man. He would also be a descendant of the Prophet Muḥammad. Other signs were not as obvious or easy to understand. Among the most important was that the Messenger's learning would come from God, not from any mortal teacher.

Shaykh Aḥmad did not share with others everything that he knew. When he traveled to Persia he did not say why he was drawn to the cities of Shiraz and Tehran. That these cities would each cradle a Messenger from God—the Qá'im in Shiraz, the Qayyúm in Tehran—was a truth he held close to his heart. To tell all was not the course of wisdom, for with the appearance of every Messenger also came those who wished to harm Him. For these holy ones to grow up as children among others—their true identity unknown—was their best protection.

When he learned of the birth of Ḥusayn-'Alí in Tehran, the shaykh did not tell others how his heart leapt with joy. He only prayed that the people of the land might recognize and cherish "this hidden Treasure of God" amongst them and arise to "proclaim His excellence to all nations and peoples."[3]

Years passed, and the aging Shaykh Aḥmad saw his days in this world growing shorter; yet his work was not complete. In this unique time, when two holy Messengers would walk upon the earth in the same lifetime, two teachers were needed to prepare the way. Shaykh Aḥmad was the first of these, but who would be the second?

One day a young man, the son of a silk merchant, joined the group who studied with Shaykh Aḥmad. His name was Siyyid Káẓim. He had come to Shaykh Aḥmad because of a vision he had received. Like the shaykh himself, the young Siyyid Káẓim was gifted with extraordinary powers of mind and spirit. In only a few weeks' time Shaykh Aḥmad knew his question was answered: This was the one who was destined to continue his work. The shaykh did all that he could in his remaining years to prepare Siyyid Káẓim to teach others.

As he felt his life drawing to a close, Shaykh Aḥmad spoke urgently to Siyyid Káẓim. "You have no time to lose," he warned. "Every fleeting hour should be wisely utilised. You should gird up the loin of endeavour and strive day and night to rend asunder, by the grace of God and by the hand of wisdom and loving-kindness, those veils of heedlessness that have blinded the eyes of men."[4] At the age of eighty-one, Shaykh Aḥmad passed away, content that he had carried out the task that was his to fulfill.

Siyyid Káẓim, like Shaykh Aḥmad before him, made his home in Karbala, where he carried on the work entrusted to him. Some of his students found Siyyid Káẓim so wise that they thought he must be the promised Qá'im, but he grew angry and immediately stifled such talk. "My knowledge is but a drop compared with the immensity of His knowledge," he told them sternly, "my attainments a speck of dust in the face of the wonders of His grace and power."[5]

Patiently Siyyid Káẓim prepared his followers to look for the promised Qá'im—"He Who Shall Arise," who would lead them to the Qayyúm—"the All-Compelling." "When the star of the Former has set," Siyyid Káẓim promised, "the sun of [the Latter] will rise and illuminate the whole world. Then will be unfolded in all its glory the 'mystery' and the 'secret' spoken of by Shaykh Aḥmad."[6]

When Siyyid Káẓim himself knew that his own days were numbered and his life was drawing to a close, he urged his followers to begin their search for the promised Qá'im. By now the Qá'im would be a grown man, ready to begin His mission from God. The time of fulfillment, long promised, was at hand.

"O my beloved companions!" Siyyid Káẓim addressed them, "How great, how very great, is the Cause! How exalted the station to which I summon you! . . . I pray to God graciously to assist you to weather the storms of tests and trials which must needs beset you, to enable you to emerge, unscathed and triumphant . . . and to lead you to your high destiny. It is incumbent upon you to renounce all comfort, all earthly possessions and kindred," he told them, "in your quest of Him who is the Desire of your hearts and of mine. Scatter far and wide . . . and humbly and prayerfully beseech your Lord to sustain and guide you. Never relax in your determination to seek and find Him."[7]

One day, when Siyyid Káẓim was in his sixtieth year, an Arab shepherd approached with a message to deliver—a message given to the shepherd in a dream. "Three days ago I was shepherding my flock in this adjoining pasture," he said, "when sleep suddenly fell upon me." In this dream, he said, the Prophet Muḥammad had spoken to him, telling him where to find Siyyid Káẓim and what to say. The shepherd conveyed the Prophet's words: "Rejoice, for the hour of your departure is at hand. . . . Soon after shall He who is the Truth be made manifest."[8]

Siyyid Káẓim smiled. "Of the truth of the dream which you have dreamt there is no doubt," he told the shepherd. Tenderly he consoled his devoted disciples and, in the days left to him, encouraged them all to go forth to seek the Promised One. His companions were overcome with grief, but Siyyid Káẓim spoke to them calmly, asking, "Would you not wish me to die, that the promised One may be revealed?"[9]

Shortly thereafter, Siyyid Káẓim passed away. Those who had studied with him, devoted as they were, could not agree on what to do next. Where should they begin in their search for the promised Qá'im? Siyyid Káẓim had not mentioned a particular place. There was much discussion, for they were not eager to leave Karbala and strike out for the unknown.

As they talked, they remembered one of their companions—Mullá Ḥusayn. Siyyid Káẓim had often praised him for his spiritual insights and abilities in argument. Before his death, Siyyid Káẓim had sent him on an important mission, and Mullá Ḥusayn had not yet returned from his travels. But the more his companions talked among themselves, the more they became convinced of one thing: Mullá Ḥusayn must be the Promised One. They decided to await his return. It seemed a good solution to their dilemma, and they went about their business in the city.

Around the world, believers of different faiths—Hindus, Buddhists, Zoroastrians, Jews, Christians, American Indians—also expected the coming of a Great World Teacher. Many Christians expected the return of Christ, and these very years—1843–1844—were a time of great expectation. Bible scholars studying independently in different parts of the world had arrived at the same exciting conclusion: This was the time promised for Christ's return.*

* For more background on this topic, see appendix 4. Additional information can be found at the Web site "Prophecy Fulfilled" at http://bci.org/prophecy-fulfilled/; see also Michael Sours, *The Prophecies of Jesus* (Oxford: Oneworld, 1991).

"Now is the hour!" was announced from pulpits in Europe, the Americas, Asia, Africa, and Australia. "Christ may come at any moment," was the message. "Watch, therefore, and pray." The message of Christ's return and the coming of the judgment hour was written in pamphlets and reported in the press. More than a thousand ministers in Great Britain and America alone preached the news. One of these was the eloquent evangelist Harriet Livermore,* who not only preached throughout the United States, but also at the seat of power—the House of Representatives in Washington, D.C.

Livermore, who was the daughter of a former Congressman, had persuaded the Speaker of the House to allow her to address Congress on more than one occasion. Increasingly her attention had become more focused on her belief in the imminent return of Christ. In 1843, from the Speaker's chair in the House of Representatives, she shared her passion with an estimated crowd of a thousand—so many that the doors were left open for spectators, who lined up outside the hall and into the street. Harriet Livermore herself would travel five times to Jerusalem, for it was there, she felt, that Christ would appear.

Even so, the greater number of Christians in all these places did not take the message seriously. Most of those who heard the passionate speeches listened with tolerance, then went about their business. Yet the dedicated and faithful made preparations for the Great Event, each in his own way. Many shopkeepers sold their merchandise at reduced prices or gave it away in acts of charity. People sold their possessions to pay off their debts. There were farmers who decided not to plant crops, for they did not expect to see a harvest time.

Some people confessed to crimes they had committed. A woman confessed to murder and wanted to stand trial. A man sent $120 to an insurance company with the note, "The Lord is at hand. This was unlawfully taken from you and I ask forgiveness, for the Lord has given me much."

---

* Harriet Livermore preached to Congress first in January 1827, again in 1832 and 1838, and finally in 1843. She was one of at least one hundred women who were evangelical preachers in the early antebellum United States, a group largely forgotten in American history. Most of them did not preach the imminent return of Christ, however, as Livermore did.

In the last days before Christ's predicted return, many of the sincere left their jobs and devoted their full energies to spiritual preparation for the time at hand. Some attempted to persuade others to prepare as well, for many were convinced that Christ's return would mean the end of the world.

6

The Quest

When Mullá Ḥusayn returned to Karbala and learned of the passing of his illustrious teacher, he asked his fellow disciples about Siyyid Káẓim's last days and what he had said to them. Siyyid Káẓim had told them to "scatter far and wide" and search for the Promised One, they said. Mullá Ḥusayn expressed surprise to see them all remaining in Karbala. "Why is it that you have not dispersed, and arisen to carry out his earnest plea?" he asked.

They gave a number of weak excuses, then pledged their loyalty to Mullá Ḥusayn as their new leader. "Such is our confidence in you, that if you claim to be the promised One," they vowed, "we shall all readily and unquestionably submit."

Mullá Ḥusayn was shocked to hear them say this. "God forbid!" he exclaimed. "Far be it from His glory that I, who am but dust, should be compared to Him who is the Lord of Lords!" Seeing the way things were with his companions, he left them to themselves. Although like the others he did not know where to begin his search, Mullá Ḥusayn was determined to find the Promised One.

"Nothing short of prayerful endeavour," Siyyid Káẓim had told his followers, "of purity of motive, of singleness of mind," would enable them to find the promised Qá'im.[1]

To prepare himself, Mullá Ḥusayn withdrew from the company of others, retiring to a small room in a mosque. Only his brother and nephew came with him. There Mullá Ḥusayn spent his time fasting and keeping vigil. He wrapped himself in deep prayer, beseeching God to purify his heart. For forty days he stayed at the mosque. At the end of the forty days—in the cool of a starlit night—Mullá Ḥusayn left Karbala and set out on his quest. He would travel on foot, in the company of his brother and nephew, and trust in God to guide him. His heart drew him in the direction of Persia, toward the city of Shiraz.

The journey continued for many weeks, mile after dusty mile. There were no hotels in which to relax at the end of the day, no soft beds to rest a weary traveler. The only bed was a blanket on the bare ground or the hard stone floor of a sheltering caravansary. At long last the road approached a towering gate that opened into the city of Shiraz. Mullá Ḥusayn asked his brother and nephew to go ahead of him and arrange for their stay at a room in a local mosque. God willing, he would join them for evening prayers.

The journey to Shiraz had been long and tiring. As he walked near the city gate, Mullá Ḥusayn wondered where he should go. How would he find the promised Qá'im? As he pondered, Mullá Ḥusayn noticed a young man standing nearby. He wore a green turban, which marked him as one of the descendants of the Prophet Muḥammad. The young man walked over to Mullá Ḥusayn and greeted him warmly, smiling as he spoke and embracing him as though he were a good friend.

Perhaps this was a disciple of Siyyid Káẓim come to welcome him, thought Mullá Ḥusayn. It was a few hours before sunset. The friendly young man, whose name was 'Alí-Muḥammad, invited Mullá Ḥusayn to come to his home and refresh himself after his journey. Politely Mullá Ḥusayn begged to be excused, saying that he had plans to join his traveling companions.

"Commit them to the care of God," replied 'Alí-Muḥammad. "He will surely protect and watch over them." The stranger's loving courtesy and dignified manner impressed Mullá Ḥusayn. He accepted the invitation and followed the young man, arriving in a short time at the gate of a modest house.

As his host stepped across the threshold, he recited a verse from the Koran: "'Enter therein in peace, secure.'"[2] A deep feeling of joy washed over Mullá Ḥusayn as he followed 'Alí-Muḥammad into his house and was seated in an inner room. Perhaps this visit would lead him nearer to finding the Promised One.

At 'Alí-Muḥammad's direction a pitcher of water was brought so that Mullá Ḥusayn might wash the dust of travel from his hands and feet. 'Alí-Muḥammad himself prepared hot, sweet tea for them to drink. When the time for evening prayer arrived, the two men performed their ablutions and, standing side by side, proceeded to say their prayers.

Exhausted from his search, Mullá Ḥusayn prayed humbly and earnestly: "I have striven with all my soul, O my God, and until now have failed to find Thy promised Messenger. I testify that Thy word faileth not, and that Thy promise is sure."

It was an hour after sunset when the the two men began to talk about Mullá Ḥusayn's quest. Had Siyyid Káẓim mentioned any features that would distinguish the Qá'im? asked 'Alí-Muḥammad. "Yes," replied Mullá Ḥusayn, and one by one, he told of the signs that would mark the promised Qá'im. When he finished, quiet settled upon the two men. Then the host spoke in a clear, strong voice, "Behold, all these signs are manifest in Me!" He went on to prove how each and every sign did, indeed, apply to him.

Mullá Ḥusayn was startled. He did not know what to think. Could the one sitting across from him truly be the promised Qá'im, the One Mullá Ḥusayn was yearning with all his soul to find? His pulse quickened. In his heart feelings of hope at the possibility warred with feelings of fear lest he make a mistake. He must be certain. The truth was too important.

"Observe attentively," said 'Alí-Muḥammad. "Might not the Person intended by Siyyid Káẓim be none other than I?"[d]

Mullá Ḥusayn knew that a divine Messenger would possess a knowledge of spiritual matters far surpassing that of ordinary men. At the beginning of his quest, he had decided on two standards by which to test the truth of anyone who claimed to be the promised Qá'im. The first test would be to read and comment on a long paper he had written himself. The paper referred to the deep spiritual teachings of Shaykh Aḥmad and Siyyid Káẓim and contained some mysterious allusions.

To one who understood the mysteries contained in that treatise, Mullá Ḥusayn would make his second request—that he reveal a commentary on the Súrih of Joseph, a certain chapter of the Koran. Like the book of Genesis in the Bible, it told the story of Joseph, who was sold into slavery by his brothers but later became ruler of Egypt. The story also contained spiritual mysteries that had puzzled scholars for hundreds of years—mysteries that a divine Messenger would surely be able to unravel.

Mullá Ḥusayn brought out his own written work. "Will you read this book of mine," he asked his host, "and look at its pages with indulgent eyes? I pray you to overlook my weaknesses and failings."

Within a short time, his host not only explained the truths embedded in that treatise, but also explained other related spiritual truths that were new to Mullá Ḥusayn. Then, taking up a fresh reed pen, 'Alí-Muḥammad smiled at Mullá Ḥusayn and said, "Now is the time to reveal the commentary on the Súrih of Joseph."

Quickly and without hesitation he began to write, intoning the verses as he wrote them. The rich beauty of his voice and the spiritual power that poured forth as he chanted captivated Mullá Ḥusayn. These verses spoke to the deepest questions of his soul—questions, Siyyid Káẓim had assured him, that could only be answered by the promised Qá'im.

As his host continued to write without pause, Mullá Ḥusayn's every doubt dissolved. Excitement and joy, awe and wonder flooded his being, for he knew his quest was complete. "This Revelation, so suddenly and impetuously thrust upon me," Mullá Ḥusayn would later report, "came as a thunderbolt which, for a time, seemed to have benumbed my faculties. I was blinded by its dazzling splendour and overwhelmed by its crushing force." When at last he rose from his seat and politely asked permission to depart, his host smiled and gently replied, "If you leave in such a state, whoever sees you will assuredly say: 'This poor youth has lost his mind.'"

It was two hours and eleven minutes after sunset on the evening of May 23, 1844—the year 1260 A.H. by the Muslim calendar. "This night," his host declared, "this very hour will, in the days to come, be celebrated as one of the greatest and most significant of all festivals. Render thanks to God for having graciously assisted you to attain your heart's desire."

Then his host directed a servant to bring dinner, and a delicious meal was served. Partaking of those choice foods in the presence of the One he had longed to find, Mullá Ḥusayn felt as though he were eating of the fruits of Paradise. Intense happiness seemed to fill every cell, every atom of his being as, heedless of sleep or the passage of time, he listened that night to the prayers and verses revealed by his host. Surely these were the delights, the priceless possessions given by the Almighty to the dwellers of Paradise. Not until the muezzin's call to morning prayer announced the dawn of a new day did Mullá Ḥusayn become aware, once again, of time and place.

"O thou who art the first to believe in Me!" said his host. "Verily I say, I am the Báb, the Gate of God." To Mullá Ḥusayn, the first to find the promised Qá'im, He gave the title "Bábu'l-Báb," meaning "the Gate of the Gate."

The Báb cautioned Mullá Ḥusayn not to tell anyone what he had seen and heard. "Eighteen souls must, in the beginning, spontaneously and of their own accord, accept Me and recognise the truth of My Revelation," said the Báb. "Unwarned and uninvited, each of these must seek independently to find Me." He instructed Mullá Ḥusayn to spend his time at a nearby mosque in prayer and in teaching others to search for the Promised One.

A different Mullá Ḥusayn stepped over the threshold that morning, as he left the house of the Báb, than the man who had first stepped across it the previous evening. How feeble, dejected, and timid he had felt before. What gladness and strength surged through him now! "The knowledge of His Revelation had galvanized my being," Mullá Ḥusayn would recall later. "I felt possessed of such courage and power that were the world, all its peoples and its potentates, to rise against me, I would, alone and undaunted, withstand their onslaught. The universe seemed but a handful of dust in my grasp."[4] In such a state he walked through the streets of Shiraz to join his brother and nephew, with whom he could not yet share his secret.

7

Witnesses of the Dawn

While people in many parts of the world had been preparing for the coming of a new divine Messenger, 'Alí-Muḥammad—the Báb—had been growing up quietly in Shiraz. Born October 20, 1819, to parents who were descendants of the Prophet Muḥammad and were themselves loved and respected, He was, after His father died, raised by a loving uncle. Young 'Alí-Muḥammad, like Ḥusayn-'Alí in Tehran, was blessed with innate knowledge and extraordinary wisdom. After only a little time in school His teacher took Him home, saying to the uncle, "He, verily, stands in no need of teachers such as I."[1]

Even so, obedient to the wishes of His uncle, young 'Alí-Muḥammad continued to attend school for a few short years. Sometimes He was late for school. When His teacher asked why, 'Alí-Muḥammad would answer that He had been in the house of His grandfather—a reference to His ancestor, the Prophet Muḥammad. His meaning was that He had been at prayer.

From His childhood the Báb showed deep attraction and devotion to spiritual pursuits. When other boys played games in the orchards, the gentle-natured 'Alí-Muḥammad might be found in a shady spot beneath a tree, away from the others, deep in prayer and meditation. As a young man He would often withdraw for hours to pray on the flat roof of His house, unmindful even of the intense heat of the noonday sun. And the dawn of each day, when others turned in prayer toward Mecca, found Him gazing north, in the direction of Tehran. With what feelings of love and joy He greeted each day's rising sun—to Him a brilliant symbol of that Daystar of Truth Who was soon to brighten the world.

The Báb worked as a merchant, as did His uncle, from the age of fifteen. Always considerate, courteous, and truthful, fair in His dealings and generous to the poor, He earned a reputation as one whose character was above reproach. In one business matter a man entrusted an item to the Báb with instructions to sell it when its value reached a certain price. Some time later the man received from the Báb a much greater sum of money than the price he had set. When he wrote to ask the reason, the Báb replied, "What I have sent you is entirely your due . . . There was a time when the trust you had delivered to Me had attained this value. Failing to sell it at that price, I now feel it My duty to offer you the whole of that sum."[2] The astonished man wanted to return the excess money, but the Báb insisted that he keep the entire sum.

Later the Báb married the purehearted Khadíjih Bagúm, whom He had known since childhood. Their only child, a boy named Aḥmad, died in infancy. They had been content to live a quiet life, but from the night of His meeting with Mullá Ḥusayn, the quiet life of twenty-five-year-old 'Alí-Muḥammad—now known as the Báb, "the Gate," would be sacrificed for something greater.

Obedient to the wishes of the Báb, Mullá Ḥusayn spent his time at the mosque in Shiraz teaching others about the signs of the Promised One. Often, at day's end, a servant would appear at the mosque, inviting him to come to the Báb's home that evening. With what eagerness did Mullá Ḥusayn look forward to those evening visits! With what rapt attention would he listen to the Báb as He spoke! How quickly the hours passed until, as before, the night sky would turn to dawn. With what regret would Mullá Ḥusayn leave once again the presence of that holy one Who was the promised Qá'im.

One night the Báb told Mullá Ḥusayn, "To-morrow thirteen of your companions will arrive. To each of them extend the utmost loving-kindness . . . Pray to God that He may graciously enable them to walk securely in that path which is finer than a hair and keener than a sword." That morning at sunrise, thirteen men, known by Mullá Ḥusayn as disciples of Siyyid Káẓim, arrived at the mosque, just as the Báb had said.

Following Mullá Ḥusayn's example, they, too, had fasted and prayed and traveled to Shiraz in their quest for the Promised One. How amazed they were to find that Mullá Ḥusayn's former sense of urgency and agitation had been replaced by a calm and serene spirit. They soon realized that nothing could explain such a transformation but that he had found the promised Qá'im. "We have followed you to this place, ready to acknowledge whomsoever you accept," said one. "Tell us. . . . that we too may be delivered from our present state of suspense. . . ."

"Beseech me not," said Mullá Ḥusayn, "to grant you this favor. Let your trust be in Him, for He will surely guide your steps, and appease the tumult of your heart."

And so it happened for each of the thirteen companions. Whether by fasting and prayer, in meditation, visions, or dreams, each in his own way was able to find the Báb and, with Mullá Ḥusayn, attain His presence. A handful of other souls were also guided to declare their belief in the Báb. Among them was one bold and brilliant woman known as Ṭáhirih, meaning "the Pure One," who never met the Báb but saw Him in a dream and, having read something of His writings, pledged her belief by letter. The Báb welcomed these first believers as His chosen disciples and referred to them as the "Letters of the Living."

"Seventeen Letters have thus far enlisted under the standard of the Faith of God," said the Báb to Mullá Ḥusayn one night. "There remains one more to complete the number . . . To-morrow night the remaining Letter will arrive and will complete the number of My chosen disciples."

The last disciple was a young man who recognized the Báb at once. "Why seek you to hide Him from me?" he asked Mullá Ḥusayn, who was walking behind the Báb on the way to His home. "I can recognize Him by His gait," the young man declared as he looked at the figure of the Báb ahead of them. "I confidently testify that none besides Him, whether in the East or in the West, can manifest the power and majesty that radiate from His holy person."

When Mullá Ḥusayn hurried to tell the Báb of his conversation, the Báb replied, "Marvel not at his strange behavior. We have in the world of the spirit been communing with that youth. We know him already. We indeed awaited his coming. Go to him and summon him forthwith to Our presence." The young man was twenty-two-year-old Quddús, whose name meant "the Most Holy"—the last of the Letters of the Living to find the Báb, but first in spiritual rank.[3]

With the number of His chosen disciples complete, the Báb gave them a sacred mission, directing them "to teach the Word of God and to quicken the souls of men." His Cause, He told them, was to proclaim the coming of the Qayyúm, "the All-Compelling," the Promised One of all religions. His own revelation from God, said the Báb, was for this purpose and no other. "'*Lord of the visible and invisible,*'" He called the next divine Messenger, and spoke humbly of Himself in relation to that great one. "I Myself am, verily, but a ring upon the hand of Him Whom God shall make manifest," the Báb wrote. He referred to Himself as "'*a letter*'" of that "'*Most Mighty Book*'" and "'*a dew-drop*'" from that "'*Limitless Ocean.*'"[4]

"O My beloved friends!" said the Báb to the Letters of the Living, "You are the bearers of the name of God in this Day. . . . O My Letters! . . . You are the witnesses of the Dawn of the promised Day of God. . . . Scatter throughout the length and breadth of this land, and, with steadfast feet and sanctified hearts, prepare the way for His coming."

To each disciple the Báb assigned the task of teaching in his own home province in Persia. They were to proclaim to one and all that the gate to the Promised One had been opened. He instructed them to say that whoever believed in Him had believed in all the Prophets of God, and whoever denied Him had denied all of His saints and chosen ones. The Báb Himself planned to make His great announcement in the holy city of Mecca, the birthplace of Muḥammad and the spiritual heart of Islam. Quddús would accompany Him on this important journey.

To Mullá Ḥusayn, the first of His noble disciples, the Báb said with affection, "The days of our companionship are approaching their end. . . . Verily He [God] shall surround you with His loving protection, and shall lead you from victory to victory." He directed Mullá Ḥusayn to travel and teach in the cities of northern Persia. "Even as the cloud that rains its bounty upon the earth, traverse the land from end to end," He said, "and shower upon its people the blessings which the Almighty, in His mercy, has deigned to confer upon you."

Mullá Ḥusayn received an additional bounty from the Báb: a special mission for one of the cities He was to visit—Tehran. "A secret lies hidden in that city," said the Báb, which "shall turn the earth into paradise." He gave to Mullá Ḥusayn a precious scroll of His verses to deliver there, but He did not name the one who should receive the scroll. God would guide him, as He had before, to the right person.

One dawn, in obedience to the Báb, the Letters of the Living left Shiraz. The fragrance of roses wafted after them as they passed through the city gates and journeyed into the hills beyond. They were the first of the "Dawn-Breakers," the ones who would push back the dark night of ignorance to bring the dawning light of God's new Message into the world.

There was no easy means of travel for the Dawn-Breakers. They would go by horse, mule, or on foot. There was no quick communication to broadcast the Báb's good news. Reaching the minds and hearts of their countrymen would require skill and initiative, courage and perseverance, and would draw on all the knowledge and wisdom at their command. They were certain to meet with opposition, but they kept the Báb's words in their hearts.

"Heed not your weaknesses and frailty," the Báb had told them. "Fix your gaze upon the invincible power of the Lord, your God, the Almighty. . . . Arise in His Name, put your trust wholly in Him, and be assured of ultimate victory."[5]

The knowledge of the Day in which they lived filled them with joy. God had kept His promise, and the city of Shiraz—already renowned for its beauty, its philosophers, and its poets—would soon become known to everyone in Persia as the birthplace of the Báb, the Gate to the Promised One.

On the other side of the world, the American inventor Samuel F. B. Morse was testing a new invention—the telegraph. It was, before the invention of the telephone, a modern miracle of science, for it used electrical impulses to send messages from one city to another. Newspapers predicted the telegraph would make the planet smaller and unite the world.

Samuel Morse knew nothing about the Báb or His Letters of the Living, but on May 24, 1844—one day after the Báb had revealed to Mullá

Ḥusayn that He was the Gate, the promised Qá'im—Samuel Morse sent the first official telegram. The message, taken from the Bible, said simply, "What hath God wrought!"

That short verse, traveling from Washington, D.C., to Baltimore, Maryland, reflected the same feelings of wonder and joy and gratitude that had stirred in the heart of Mullá Ḥusayn half a world away when he realized that the young man in the green turban who had served him tea was the first trumpet blast of God—the first new divine Messenger sent to wake a sleeping world.

8

Noble Descendant of a Noble Father

On the same spring evening that Mullá Ḥusayn had first found the Báb in Shiraz—May 23, 1844—a baby was born to Ḥusayn-'Alí and Navváb in Tehran. He was a healthy boy with dark hair and blue eyes, and His parents named him 'Abbas, which means "Lion." When he grew up, he would take the name 'Abdu'l-Bahá.

In the earliest weeks of 'Abdu'l-Bahá's life, Mullá Ḥusayn made the long northward journey from Shiraz to Tehran—over four hundred miles. Obedient to the Báb's instructions, Mullá Ḥusayn had shared news of the Báb along the way in the cities of Isfahan, Ká<u>sh</u>án, and Qom.

Not everyone believed Mullá Ḥusayn's good news. The religious students of Isfahan became angry. Who was this 'Alí-Muḥammad who called himself the Báb? He was not a mujtahid who had studied religion for long years. He was not even a mullá who led the people in prayer. He was only a merchant from Shiraz. How dare he claim to be the promised Qá'im!

A man by the name of Mullá Ja'far, a poor sifter of wheat who could neither read nor write, was the only person in Isfahan who believed Mullá Ḥusayn. In the city of Ká<u>sh</u>án, a prosperous merchant became the first believer. But no one in the city of Qom would listen to Mullá Ḥusayn, so he traveled on. Finally, in the summer heat of August, Mullá Ḥusayn arrived at the capital city of Tehran.

A high wall with six gates and eighteen towers surrounded the city. Mount Damavand, the tallest mountain in Persia, stood at its back. From the eighteen towers the shah's men could observe all who passed through its gates. When the six gates were closed, Tehran was a fortress city, and the shah felt secure inside the city walls.

On most days, though, the gates remained open, and travelers of every kind passed through them as they had for generations. A delicate music of bells jingled from the halters of long-legged camels. Their caravans brought treasures from every part of Persia: turquoise from Mashhad, silverwork from Tabríz, polished brass from Isfahan, finely carved wood from Shiraz, and from every province beautiful, handwoven carpets.

Shouts of *"Kúr s͟hid! Rad s͟hid!"* (Depart! Be blind!)[1] were heard when the women of the shah's household passed by in their carriage. Quickly people would turn their faces away and move aside. Anyone who disobeyed, who dared even to look in their direction, could be killed on the spot.

In all the bustle no one took notice of Mullá Ḥusayn, who looked like just another dusty traveler. No one suspected that Mullá Ḥusayn was himself the courier of a treasure—a scroll inscribed with the verses of the Messenger of God. He found a small room at a local religious school where he could stay the night. There he pondered the mission entrusted to him by the Báb. Now that he had reached Tehran, where would he find the person to whom he should deliver his precious trust?

He began by talking with the chief religious teacher at the school, but when he tried to tell him about the Báb, the teacher was not interested. A student in the next room, however, who overheard their conversation was eager to hear more. At midnight he knocked at Mullá Ḥusayn's door, and Mullá Ḥusayn received him warmly. They had talked for a short time when Mullá Ḥusayn asked, "What is your name, and which city is your home?"

"My name is Mullá Muḥammad," the young man replied. ". . . My home is Núr, in the province of Mázindarán."

When Mullá Ḥusayn heard this he remembered Mírzá Buzurg, the just and generous vizier of the shah. Although Mírzá Buzurg was no longer living, Mullá Ḥusayn knew he had come from Núr and maintained a home there. Was there anyone among the family of Mírzá Buzurg, asked Mullá Ḥusayn, who had the same noble character as he?

"Yea," replied Mullá Muḥammad, "among his sons now living, one has distinguished Himself by the very traits which characterised His father. By His virtuous life, His high attainments, His loving-kindness and liberality, He has proved Himself a noble descendant of a noble father."

"What is His occupation?" asked Mullá Ḥusayn.

"He cheers the disconsolate and feeds the hungry," said the student.

"What of His rank and position?"

"He has none, apart from befriending the poor and the stranger."

"What is His name?" asked Mullá Ḥusayn.

"Ḥusayn-'Alí."

"How does He spend His time?"

"He roams the woods and delights in the beauties of the countryside."[2]

By the end of the conversation Mullá Ḥusayn felt strongly that this son of the noble Mírzá Buzurg was the one for whom the Báb's scroll was intended. When he learned that Mullá Muḥammad often visited Ḥusayn-'Alí, Mullá Ḥusayn brought out the precious scroll, carefully wrapped in a piece of cloth. Would he deliver this scroll to Ḥusayn-'Alí, Mullá Ḥusayn asked, then return and tell him how the message had been received? Mullá Muḥammad agreed.

Dawn of the next day saw Mullá Muḥammad in the northern quarter of the city, near the Shimírán gate, where he approached the mansion of Ḥusayn-'Alí. Finding Mírzá Músá, a brother of Ḥusayn-'Alí, standing at the gate, he told him of his purpose. Mírzá Músá went inside to inform his brother and returned shortly with a message of welcome. Together they entered the house. Ḥusayn-'Alí bade them be seated and received the scroll. He unfolded it and scanned its contents, reading aloud certain passages to them. Mullá Muḥammad sat captivated by the beauty of His voice as its melody filled the room.

Ḥusayn-'Alí read no more than a page when He stopped. He did not need to meet the Báb to know that He was no ordinary teacher. These verses—which the Báb had first written and chanted to Mullá Ḥusayn—made one thing clear. Ḥusayn-'Alí turned to His brother. "Músá, what have you to say?" He asked. "Verily I say, whoso believes in the Qur'án* and recognises its Divine origin, and yet hesitates, though it be for a

---

* Koran.

moment, to admit that these soul-stirring words are endowed with the same regenerating power, has most assuredly erred in his judgment and has strayed far from the path of justice."

Ḥusayn-'Alí accepted at once that the Báb was the promised Qá'im. Mírzá Músá, too, would declare his belief in the Báb. Ḥusayn-'Alí knew that the time for His own mission would come later. For now, the mantle of divine authority rested on the shoulders of the Báb, and every soul was bound to obey Him.

Ḥusayn-'Alí gave a loaf of Russian sugar and a package of tea to the waiting Mullá Muḥammad as a gift for Mullá Ḥusayn. With these tokens—rare and cherished items in Persia at the time—Ḥusayn-'Alí expressed His gratitude to Mullá Ḥusayn for delivering so precious a message.

Hurrying back, Mullá Muḥammad delivered the gift to Mullá Ḥusayn and told him all that had transpired. With great joy Mullá Ḥusayn kissed the gift of tea and sugar. "My dearly beloved friend!" he said, "I pray that even as you have rejoiced my heart, God may grant you eternal felicity and fill your heart with imperishable gladness." Mullá Ḥusayn's happiness at receiving so small a token from Ḥusayn-'Alí was a mystery to Mullá Muḥammad, but Mullá Ḥusayn knew that his mission in Tehran was accomplished.

A few days later, as he prepared to leave, Mullá Ḥusayn cautioned Mullá Muḥammad, "Breathe not to anyone what you have heard and witnessed. . . . Divulge not His name, for they who envy His position will arise to harm Him." Not everyone would believe in the Báb. There were those who would oppose the divine Messenger and rise against His followers with all their strength and power. "Many a soul will, in this city," warned Mullá Ḥusayn, "shed his blood in this path."[3]

Ḥusayn-'Alí, however, did not choose to remain safe and quiet in His home while the promised Qá'im walked among them. Instead, He rode His horse across the mountains to His home district of Núr. Like the Letters of the Living, He was eager to spread the momentous news.

The shah might feel strong and secure behind the walls of his fortress city, but a new spirit was beginning to stir in Persia—a spirit that could not be turned back by the walled city's six gates and eighteen towers, a spirit that could not be kept out by the mountain at its back. A mighty new force was beginning to move in Persia, and nothing—not even the shah—could stop it.

9

The Mujtahid and the Dervish

As soon as the nobles and officials of Núr heard Ḥusayn-'Alí had arrived, they came to visit Him, eager to learn the news from Tehran. They questioned Him about the shah and his court and the political twists and turns of the day, but Ḥusayn-'Alí showed no interest in discussing such matters. "I have come to Núr solely for the purpose of proclaiming the Cause of God," He said. The interests of Persia could best be served, He told them, by taking up the Cause of the Báb.

None of the notables of Núr had heard of the Báb, and they were surprised that Ḥusayn-'Alí would champion the Báb's Cause with such enthusiasm. Yet they were drawn to listen to Ḥusayn-'Alí as He explained that the Báb was the Promised One, Who would prepare the way for the great Messenger to come. So eloquent were the arguments He presented, and so convincing the proofs, that those who heard Him in the province of Núr were soon won over. This was the Day for which many had fervently prayed, and now, at last, their prayers were answered. Those who accepted the Báb and were convinced of the truth of His Cause were called *"Bábís."*

The new Bábís told their friends, neighbors, and others until the whole of Núr was abuzz with the news. On everyone's lips were the questions "Have you heard of the Báb?" and "Who else has become a Bábí?"

Not everyone was pleased by the growing excitement over the Báb. Among Ḥusayn-'Alí's own relatives, an uncle named 'Azíz became alarmed. He knew his nephew was not trained as a religious teacher. What business did He have to spread such teachings? As more and more people became Bábís, the angry uncle called on the mujtahid of Núr, Mullá Muḥammad, for help. Surely, 'Azíz reasoned, the learned Mullá Muḥammad, who had spent many years in religious study, could put a stop to this dangerous nonsense.

'Azíz complained to the mujtahid about Ḥusayn-'Alí's effect on those who listened to Him and urged the mujtahid to take action. "Arise and resist his onslaught!" 'Azíz demanded. "Whoever attains his presence falls immediately under his spell, and is enthralled by the power of his utterance. I know not whether he is a sorcerer, or whether he mixes with his tea some mysterious substance that makes every man who drinks the tea fall a victim to its charm."

"Have you not partaken of his tea," inquired Mullá Muḥammad, who realized the foolishness of 'Azíz's suspicions, "or heard him address his companions?"

"I have," he replied, "but, thanks to your loving protection, I have remained immune from the effect of his mysterious power."

The mujtahid was not eager to confront Ḥusayn-'Alí, Whose powers of persuasion, he knew, were not a matter of sorcery or magic tea. He gave only a vague answer to 'Azíz, hoping to avoid the issue altogether.

Mullá Muḥammad's own disciples would not be put off so easily. It was his duty as mujtahid of Núr, they reminded him, to investigate every cause so that he could protect the Faith of Islam. Finally Mullá Muḥammad chose two of his most distinguished disciples, his sons-in-law, to investigate on his behalf. Whatever they decided about the truth of the Báb and His teachings he pledged to accept without reservation, and the two set out on their mission.

When at last they sat in a room with others and listened to Ḥusayn-'Alí speak, the mujtahid's two disciples were deeply moved. Although they were well seasoned in religious debate and accustomed to discussions among the learned, they found themselves strangely stirred by the words of Ḥusayn-'Alí. Quietly the first disciple got up from his seat and walked to the back of the room as a gesture of humble reverence toward Ḥusayn-'Alí. The tears that filled his eyes betrayed his strong emotions.

"The questions I had planned to ask Him have vanished suddenly from my memory," he confided to his companion. "You are free either to proceed with your enquiry or to return alone to our teacher. . . . Tell him from me that 'Abbás [the disciple's name] can never again return to him." But the second disciple felt just as inspired as his companion. "I have ceased to recognize my teacher," he replied.

News about the conversion of Mullá Muḥammad's two disciples traveled throughout Núr. Now more people than ever came to the home of Ḥusayn-'Alí to investigate the new faith. Religious dignitaries, state officials, merchants, and peasants all came to learn about the Báb, and many became Bábís. The mujtahid of Núr, however, did not accept the new faith, despite what he had pledged to his disciples. Many of those who admired Ḥusayn-'Alí and had, through Him, become enthusiastic believers in the Cause of the Báb, urged Him to talk with Mullá Muḥammad. If the respected mujtahid of Núr were to accept the Báb, others would no doubt follow.

"If I were told that at a distance of a hundred leagues a seeker yearned for the Truth," Ḥusayn-'Alí replied, "and was unable to meet Me, I would, gladly and unhesitatingly, hasten to his abode, and would Myself satisfy his hunger." Then Ḥusayn-'Alí, with a few companions, mounted His steed and rode to the village where Mullá Muḥammad lived.

Mullá Muḥammad received the noble Ḥusayn-'Alí with ceremony, but Ḥusayn-'Alí said courteously, "I have not come to this place to pay you an official or formal visit. My purpose is to enlighten you regarding a new and wondrous Message, divinely inspired and fulfilling the promise given to Islám. Whosoever has inclined his ear to this Message has felt its irresistible power," Ḥusayn-'Alí told the mujtahid, "and has been transformed by the potency of its grace. Tell Me whatsoever perplexes your mind, or hinders you from recognising the Truth."

The proud but nervous mujtahid had hoped to avoid such a meeting with Ḥusayn-'Alí. As a religious leader, he did not care to be addressed as though he were in need of enlightenment. "I undertake no action unless I first consult the Qur'án," he answered curtly.

Ḥusayn-'Alí was agreeable.

Opening the holy book, the mujtahid silently read the first verse upon which his eyes fell, following a customary method of seeking divine guidance. Whatever the guidance revealed in that verse, no one else would find out. Quickly, he closed the book and refused to tell anyone in the room what he had read, although fear showed in his eyes. He said only, "I have consulted the Book of God, and deem it inadvisable to proceed further with this matter."

Ḥusayn-'Alí let the matter drop. That decision was between the mujtahid and God. The truth could not be forced upon anyone. Asking to be excused, Ḥusayn-'Alí bid a friendly and courteous good-bye. There were others who were eager to hear about the Báb.[1]

One day as Ḥusayn-'Alí rode with a few companions through the countryside of Núr, He saw a young man sitting by the side of the road. His bedraggled hair and the clothes he wore identified him as a dervish—one who had given up worldly possessions and responsibilities to pursue spiritual truth. A dervish usually lived a nomadic life, moving about from place to place with little more than a bowl to beg for food. It was considered a good deed to give a little of one's food to those who had chosen this path. Such a simple life, bereft of the many distractions of daily living, was thought to draw a man nearer to God and assist him in developing spiritual qualities.

Ḥusayn-'Alí approached the young man, who had kindled a fire next to a small stream and was cooking and eating his dinner. "Tell Me, dervish," said Ḥusayn-'Alí kindly, "what is it that you are doing?"

The dervish, who had a simple understanding that God lived in everything—including the food that was his dinner—replied matter-of-factly, "I am engaged in eating God. I am cooking God and am burning Him."

Ḥusayn-'Alí smiled. He very much liked this dervish who answered with such straightforward honesty. He began to talk with the dervish, whose name was Muṣṭafá, explaining in a most tender and loving way the true nature of God. The humble Muṣṭafá listened intently. Unlike the mujtahid of Núr, the dervish was not so proud of his own knowledge that he could not learn from someone else. Before long, Muṣṭafá's old ideas—the idle fancies of imagination—were shadows melting in the light of Ḥusayn-'Alí's words. A new and powerful insight took the place of his previously simple understanding. How freed the dervish felt! Like a bird released from its cage, his spirit seemed to sing with joy!

Intuitively Muṣṭafá the dervish recognized the truth that Shaykh Aḥmad had known: Here was no ordinary teacher, but a spiritual treasure from God. When Ḥusayn-'Alí turned at last to leave, Muṣṭafá could not contain himself. Leaving his cooking utensils by the side of the road and following on foot behind Ḥusayn-'Alí's horse, he chanted a spontaneous poem of love and praise for the One Whose words had opened his eyes to the truth: "Thou art the Day-Star of guidance," sang Muṣṭafá in refrain. "Thou art the Light of Truth. Unveil Thyself to men, O Revealer of the Truth."[2]

Ḥusayn-'Alí, in the privacy of His own prayers, expressed His gratitude to God for the gift of His Messenger, the Báb:

> "Praised be Thou, O my God, inasmuch as Thou hast aided us to recognize and love Him. I, therefore, beseech Thee . . . to enable us to serve and obey Him, and to empower us to become the helpers of His Cause and the dispersers of His adversaries. . . ."[3]

As the Cause of the Báb spread, His adversaries would soon appear.

10

Awake, Awake!

The Báb was glad to receive a letter from Mullá Ḥusayn telling of events unfolding in the province of Núr. That people were embracing the Cause of God with enthusiasm cheered His spirit. That Ḥusayn-'Alí was at the center of teaching in that region was especially encouraging to Him. Whatever fate might befall the Báb, He had no doubt now that the Cause of God would not only survive, but flourish in the loving and able hands of Ḥusayn-'Alí. Heartened by this assurance, the Báb prepared to travel to the holy city of Mecca.

It was October 1844 when the Báb set out for Mecca with Quddús. For three months they traveled by land, south from Shiraz to Bushehr on the Persian Gulf, then by ship through the rough seas beyond, rounding the Arabian Peninsula to Jiddah, a port on Arabia's western coast. The last sixty miles to Mecca stretched across the Arabian Desert. The Báb rode on camel, but Quddús would not ride. He preferred to walk humbly alongside, holding onto the camel's bridle and chanting prayers as they made their way. As the voice of Quddús rose and fell, its tones penetrated the rich silence of the desert, lingering until they melted into the heat-soaked sands. Whenever the Báb rested, Quddús stayed awake, standing guard against the threat of attacking thieves.

At last, in one of the treeless valleys scooped from the desert, the sacred city of Mecca—birthplace of the Prophet Muḥammad—emerged before them. At the heart of the city rose the Great Mosque; and at the center of the Great Mosque, in a wide-open courtyard, stood the Kaaba—the holiest shrine of Islam. The Kaaba, a flat-roofed, cube-shaped building, held in its eastern corner the Black Stone. Muslims believed that the Kaaba had been built by Abraham—Prophet and patriarch to Judaism, Christianity, and Islam—and His son Ishmael. Tradition said that the Black Stone had been given to Abraham by the Angel Gabriel. The story of this sacred place reminded Muslims of their connection to God.

Here, too, at the sacred Kaaba, the Prophet Muḥammad had thrown out the lifeless stone and wood idols that men had fallen to worshiping. He taught His followers to worship one God—the All-Powerful Creator, the Lawgiver—and not what they could make with their own hands. It was in this direction, toward the Kaaba in Mecca, that Muslims everywhere turned in prayer five times a day. It was also to Mecca that every faithful Muslim who had the means to do so would journey on *hajj*—pilgrimage—at least once in a lifetime.

When the Báb and Quddús entered Mecca, its streets were crowded with pilgrims. The Báb, with Quddús, carried out the rites of pilgrimage, distributing food among the poor and circumambulating the sacred Kaaba. To circumambulate a holy place was a Muslim custom and one way for a believer to express his love for the Messengers of God and other holy souls. Walking along with the throng of other pilgrims, each reciting verses from the Koran, the Báb and Quddús circled the Kaaba the required number of times. Then at the door leading into the Kaaba, the Báb stopped and took hold of the iron ring by which it opened. There, at the sacred center of the Muslim world, He announced in a loud, clear voice, "I am that Qá'im whose advent you have been awaiting."[1]

Three times He repeated the same words. The crowd of pilgrims grew quiet. When they looked at the Báb they did not see the king they had expected, nor did they recognize Him as a well-known religious teacher. They saw only a pilgrim like themselves—an unknown merchant from Shiraz who looked like an ordinary man. Unprepared for the Báb's great announcement, most resumed their pilgrimage rites and turned their backs on the promised Qá'im.

Undeterred, the Báb wrote a letter, which Quddús delivered to the sharif of Mecca, the city's highest-ranking religious leader. In the letter the Báb set forth clearly Who He was and the divine Mission entrusted to Him, and He called upon the sharif to embrace His Cause. The sharif had never heard of the Báb. He was a busy man and set the letter aside to attend to other important matters. When a few days had passed, Quddús returned to ask if the sharif had read the letter, but he had not.

For the first time in more than a thousand years, Mecca was blessed with the presence of a Messenger of God—not only a Prophet, but the promised Qá'im. Yet the busy sharif of Mecca had not spared the time to meet Him or even to read His letter. As Muslim pilgrims returned to their homes in various places, many brought with them the story of the Báb's announcement at the holy Kaaba, and so the news of it spread. Still, when the Báb and Quddús set out from Mecca, they left a city mostly asleep to the call of God.

The Báb and Quddús returned to Persia in the spring of 1845—a little more than six months after the start of their journey—and stopped at the port city of Bushehr. There the Báb directed Quddús where to go next and gave him some of His writings to share with others. Then the Báb bid a tender good-bye to Quddús. They would not meet again in this life, said the Báb. Each of them, He predicted, would suffer severe trials for the Cause of God.

"The hand of destiny will ere long plunge you into an ocean of tribulation for His sake," said the Báb, but He counseled Quddús to "Rejoice with exceeding gladness." "The hosts of the Unseen will hasten forth to assist you," He assured him, "and will proclaim to all the world your heroism and glory. . . ." "I, too, shall tread the path of sacrifice," the Báb told Quddús, "and will join you in the realm of eternity."

While the Báb and Quddús had been away, Persia had come alive to the Báb's message. Obedient to His direction, the Letters of the Living were teaching in every corner of the land. The Báb had told Mullá Ḥusayn, "Raise the cry, 'Awake, awake, for, lo! the Gate of God is open, and the morning Light is shedding its radiance upon all mankind! The promised One is made manifest'!" "Those whom you find receptive to your call," He had instructed, "share with them the epistles and tablets We have revealed for you. . . ." Now people throughout Persia were learning about the Báb, and many were becoming Bábís.[2]

This growing enthusiasm for the Cause of the Báb was disturbing to many of Persia's religious leaders, the mullás. In the Báb's hometown of

Shiraz the mullás complained to the governor, Ḥusayn Khán. The Báb had grown up in Shiraz, they said, known to all as 'Alí-Muḥammad, the merchant. How dare He claim to be the Qá'im!

Normally Ḥusayn Khán cared little about religious matters, but the complaining mullás were troublesome; and the Báb, it seemed, claimed a certain authority for Himself as Qá'im. On this subject the governor was more concerned; *he* was the authority in Shiraz. Ḥusayn Khán ordered his guards to ride to the port of Bushehr, where the Báb was taking care of business matters. He directed them to arrest the Báb and bring Him in chains to Shiraz. The guards obeyed at once and soon rode out of the city gates, heading south.

As the governor's guards approached Bushehr, they were surprised to see the Báb riding out to meet them. "The governor has sent you to arrest Me," said the Báb. "Here am I; do with Me as you please." His courage impressed the guards, and their captain expressed reluctance to arrest Him.

"O light of the eyes of the Prophet of God!" said the captain, "I beseech you to escape from this place and to flee from before the face of Ḥusayn Khán." But the Báb refused to run away from danger.

"Never will I turn My face away from the decree of God," replied the Báb. ". . . Deliver Me into the hands of your master. Be not afraid," He added, "for no one will blame you."[3]

Although the captain of the guards did as He asked, he refrained from placing the Báb in chains. Instead, the detachment of armed guards rode behind the Báb all the way into Shiraz, much like an honor guard escorting royalty.

This angered Ḥusayn Khán, who had the Báb brought before him. "Do you realise," said the angry governor, "what a great mischief you have kindled?" After further chastisement, he commanded the Báb to remain at home and see no one except His own relatives. With this the governor expected peace and calm would return to Shiraz, but restraining the Báb did not restrain His Cause.[4]

Before long, news about the young man Who called Himself the Báb—"the Gate"—traveled as far as the court of Persia's ruler, Muḥammad Sháh. The fact that so many of his people were drawn to the Cause of the Báb made the shah both curious and concerned. He decided he must find out more about the Báb and His claims. To investigate on his behalf, he called on the one man acknowledged throughout the land as the most brilliant of religious scholars. At whatever gathering he spoke, no matter how learned the participants, all others would choose to sit in respectful silence and listen to him. Knowledgeable and wise beyond all others, he was also a man of integrity, truthful and trustworthy. His name was Siyyid Yaḥyá, but he would become known as Vaḥíd, meaning "the Peerless One."

The shah commanded Vaḥíd to meet with the Báb in Shiraz and there investigate the truth of His claims, then return to Tehran and report his findings. Vaḥíd was pleased to obey. He, too, had heard of the Báb and His Cause and wished to satisfy his own desire for more information. On the journey from Tehran to Shiraz, he thought of the many questions with which he would test the Báb. Vaḥíd did not plan to make the interview easy, but thorough and demanding. The truth deserved no less. Little did the brilliant Vaḥíd know that nothing in his previous experience had prepared him for what lay ahead.

11

The Scholar and the Governors

As it turned out, Vaḥíd did not have one interview with the Báb, but three—each one more remarkable than the one before. At their first meeting Vaḥíd presented each of his questions. He made certain to reveal, as well, something of his own vast range of religious knowledge. The Báb listened patiently to all that he said, then began to address Vaḥíd's questions briefly but persuasively. As Vaḥíd listened to the Báb's answers, each one clear and concise, he felt suddenly embarrassed at his own display of self-importance. Though he had more questions, Vaḥíd asked the Báb if he might continue the interview a little later and resolved to himself to return with a more humble attitude.

Vaḥíd's second interview with the Báb, however, did not go at all as he had intended. As soon as he entered the Báb's presence, Vaḥíd forgot all of the questions he had planned to ask. They were as thoroughly erased from his memory as though written in sand at the water's edge and washed away by the tide. Yet to his surprise, as Vaḥíd conversed with the Báb, the Báb answered every question that Vaḥíd had temporarily forgotten. Still Vaḥíd could not quiet the small, doubting voice that whispered within him, "Might not this, after all, have been an accidental coincidence?"

For his third interview with the Báb, Vaḥíd decided on a different strategy. He would keep his next request a secret and hold it silently in his heart. This request, which Vaḥíd would tell no one, was for the Báb to reveal a commentary on the spiritual truths in the Súrih of Kawthar (Paradise), a chapter of the Koran. If the Báb could, of His own volition, detect Vaḥíd's secret request and reveal a commentary unlike any other, then Vaḥíd would be convinced that the Báb was of God. If not, Vaḥíd decided, he would refuse to acknowledge the Báb.

This time, when Vaḥíd came before the Báb, he was overcome suddenly with feelings of fear and awe and began to tremble so that he could barely stand. Why should he be so affected in the presence of the Báb? He wondered. How many times had he been in the presence of the shah, whose power gave reason to fear, yet had never felt timid or afraid in his presence? Why now should he stand trembling, unable to take a step or to utter a word?

When the Báb saw Vaḥíd's predicament, He got up from His seat and took Vaḥíd gently by the hand, leading the scholar to sit next to Him. "Seek from Me whatever is your heart's desire," the Báb told Vaḥíd. "I will readily reveal it to you." But Vaḥíd could say nothing. "Were I to reveal for you the commentary on the Súrih of Kawthar," said the Báb, "would you acknowledge that My words are born of the Spirit of God? Would you recognise that My utterance can in no wise be associated with sorcery or magic?" Vaḥíd could say nothing except to recite a verse of the Koran: "'O our Lord, with ourselves have we dealt unjustly: if Thou forgive us not and have not pity on us, we shall surely be of those who perish.'"[1]

With that, the Báb asked for His pen-case and paper and began at once to reveal His commentary. It was early afternoon when the Báb began to write. He continued to write for the rest of the day, rapidly and without pause, intoning the verses as He wrote them. Vaḥíd listened, enraptured not only by the beauty of what he heard, but also by the inexpressible majesty of the Báb. Not until sunset did the Báb lay down His pen and ask for tea. The commentary—two thousand verses—was complete.

Also complete was Vaḥíd's transformation. Vanished was every trace of his former sense of superiority. In its place was the humble acknowledgment and deep certitude that the Báb was indeed the promised Qá'im. "If all the powers of the earth were to be leagued against me," declared Vaḥíd, "they would be powerless to shake my confidence in the greatness of His Cause." So did Persia's most learned and respected religious scholar declare himself a Bábí. It was the Báb Himself who gave to Vaḥíd—known until then as Siyyid Yaḥyá—his new name.

When Vaḥíd had opportunity a short time later to speak with Ḥusayn Khán, the governor who had had the Báb arrested, Vaḥíd's belief in the Báb was roundly disparaged by the governor. Vaḥíd was simply another victim of the Báb's magic influence, declared Ḥusayn Khán. Vaḥíd replied unwaveringly, "No one but God, who alone can change the hearts of men, is able to captivate the heart of Siyyid Yaḥyá [Vaḥíd]."

Vaḥíd wrote his report about the Báb and sent it to the shah, telling in detail the truth he had discovered, but he did not return to Tehran. Instead, like Ḥusayn-'Alí and the Letters of the Living, Vaḥíd set out to share the news of his discovery with people in every town. When the shah received Vaḥíd's letter and learned that he had become a Bábí, he commented, "If this be true, it behoves us to cease belittling the Cause of that *siyyid*.*"[2]

Ḥusayn Khán, however, refused to be satisfied. He sent secret agents to spy on the movements of the Báb and those near Him. The spies reported that more people than ever were coming to see the Báb, among them the most noble and learned. Not even the governor received as many visitors at His door, they said. Angry that the Báb continued to teach His Cause so freely, Ḥusayn Khán decided to take more decisive action. He made plans to secretly execute the Báb.

In the middle of the night the governor sent his chief constable, 'Abdu'l-Ḥamíd Khán, to arrest the Báb. His orders were to scale the garden wall, climb to the roof, and enter the house by surprise. The constable obeyed, arresting the Báb, and within a few hours was on his way through the dark streets back to the governor's house with his prisoner. Near the mar-

* The term *siyyid*—meaning "lord," "chief," or "prince"—denotes a descendant of the Prophet Muḥammad.

ketplace a loud weeping and wailing could be heard. The constable was alarmed to see grief-stricken mourners following behind dozens of coffins. Others ran here and there, fleeing the city. Shiraz was in the grip of a deadly outbreak of cholera.

The constable hurried on to the governor's mansion, but when he arrived, Ḥusayn Khán was nowhere to be seen. He, too, had fled the city in fear, hoping to escape death. 'Abdu'l-Ḥamíd Khán decided to go to his own home with the Báb in custody and there await further orders from the governor. When the constable reached home he was met with the chilling sounds of weeping and wailing and found his own son near death—a victim of the city's epidemic.

It was nearly dawn and the Báb was in the midst of ablutions, preparing for His dawn prayer, when the distraught 'Abdu'l-Ḥamíd Khán came to Him. Throwing himself at the Báb's feet and clutching the hem of His garment, he tearfully begged the Báb to save his son's life. "Suffer not that he, in the prime of youth, be taken away from me," he implored. "Punish him not for the guilt which his father has committed. I repent of what I have done, and at this moment resign my post. I solemnly pledge my word that never again will I accept such a position even though I perish of hunger."

The Báb told 'Abdu'l-Ḥamíd to take some of the clear water that He had just used for His ablutions and give it to his son to drink. This, He promised, would cure the boy. 'Abdu'l-Ḥamíd did as the Báb instructed. What feelings of relief and joy surged in his heart when he saw his son begin to recover and retreat from death's door.

'Abdu'l-Ḥamíd wrote at once to the governor, "Have pity on yourself, as well as on those whom Providence has committed to your care. Should the fury of this plague continue its fatal course, no one in this city, I fear, will by the end of this day have survived the horror of its attack."

Ḥusayn Khán's plans to execute the Báb might have been thwarted, but as governor of Shiraz he refused to admit defeat. He replied that the Báb should be released, but commanded that He must leave the city and never return.[3]

Although invested with divine authority, the Báb was obedient to the governor's command. He prepared to leave the city of His birth, the city

He had called home since childhood, the city that would remain home to the friends and family He must leave behind—including His beloved wife, Khadíjih. From the beginning of His mission, Khadíjih had recognized the truth of the Báb's revelation, had felt its intensity and realized its glory. But severe trials lay ahead for the Báb; He could not take Khadíjih with Him. Before He left, the Báb confided to His beloved wife all that would transpire and revealed a prayer especially to comfort her in times of difficulty. "Recite this prayer ere you go to sleep," He told her. "I Myself will appear to you and will banish your anxiety."[4]

In September 1846—after more than a year under house arrest—the Báb passed one last time through the gates of Shiraz. This time He turned north, towards the city of Isfahan, knowing with certainty that there would be no turning back.

Manúchihr Khán, the governor of Isfahan, was as kind to the Báb as Ḥusayn Khán had been cruel. He welcomed the Báb to his city and arranged a comfortable place for Him to stay. Unlike the governor of Shiraz, Manúchihr Khán was deeply interested in religious truth. In particular, he had his own heartfelt questions about the truth of Islam.

One day Manúchihr Khán respectfully presented a challenge to the Báb—the same challenge he had presented to others before Him. Could He demonstrate Muḥammad's divine mission, asked the governor, with proofs and evidences such that none could deny the truth of Islam? Until now, no one had been able to answer this challenge to the governor's satisfaction.

The Báb responded to the challenge at once. In less than two hours He wrote some fifty pages, proving the divine nature of Muḥammad and His teachings in clear language that Manúchihr Khán found deeply moving. He was convinced not only of the truth of Muḥammad, but also of the Báb and His Cause. So it was that Manúchihr Khán, governor of Isfahan, became a Bábí, and was eager to assist in every way.

"The almighty Giver has endowed me with great riches," Manúchihr Khán told the Báb, and resolved to use all of his wealth to advance the Cause of the Báb. He would ride to Tehran, said the governor with enthusiasm, and convince Muḥammad Sháh of the truth of the Báb's Cause. The shah had unshakable confidence in him, said Manúchihr Khán, and he was certain that the shah would embrace the Báb's Cause and arise to promote it far and wide.

The Báb gave gracious praise to Manúchihr Khán for his noble intentions. "So lofty a purpose is to Me even more precious than the act itself," He told the governor, but it was not to be. "Your days and Mine are numbered," He said. "They are too short to enable Me to witness, and allow you to achieve, the realisation of your hopes." Lovingly the Báb told the good governor, "Of the span of your earthly life there remain only three months and nine days, after which you shall, with faith and certitude, hasten to your eternal abode."

God would accomplish His purpose, the Báb assured Manúchihr Khán, not through the rich and powerful but "through the poor and lowly of this land, by the blood which these shall have shed in His path. . . . That same God," said the Báb, "will, in the world to come, place upon your head the crown of immortal glory, and will shower upon you His inestimable blessings."[5]

Manúchihr Khán accepted the Báb's prophetic words with joy and, setting his affairs in order, prepared to leave this world for the next. Six months from the Báb's arrival in Isfahan, in the time predicted by the Báb, the good governor grew sick with a fever and died.

The shah himself now wished to meet the Báb, the young siyyid Whose Cause was attracting people such as Vaḥíd and Manúchihr Khán, the most learned and loyal of his subjects. He sent his trusted chief courier, Muḥammad Big, to bring the Báb to Tehran with an escort of mounted horsemen. The shah instructed him to treat the Báb with the greatest consideration on His journey.

The grand vizier, Ḥájí Mírzá Áqásí, was not pleased by this turn of events. He cared little about a new divine Messenger, especially if it meant his own influence over the shah might be diminished. As the shah's closest advisor, the grand vizier had more power and influence over him than anyone else in the kingdom, and he did not want that to change. Ḥájí Mírzá Áqásí was determined that the shah should never meet the Báb and set about to put his own plan into action.

12

The Open Mountain and the Grievous Mountain

When Muḥammad Big had escorted the Báb to a point that was within a day's journey of Tehran, he received a secret message from the grand vizier. He should not bring the Báb to Tehran, the message said, but take Him instead to the village of Kulayn, west of Tehran. He should stay there until he received further orders. Muḥammad Big obeyed, and the treacherous grand vizier plotted his next step. He must convince Muḥammad Sh̲áh that meeting with the Báb would be a dangerous mistake.

The grand vizier enjoyed the power he wielded with the shah, but he was unschooled in the skills needed to lead a nation. The sharp-featured and shrill-voiced Ḥájí Mírzá Áqásí had tutored the shah in his youth, and the shah had favored his old tutor by appointing him grand vizier. But his influence had been the source of many difficulties and much misery for the people of Persia. Now he was about to interfere with Persia's surest source of hope.

At the village of Kulayn a tent was pitched for the Báb on a gentle hill among orchards and meadows and small streams. Although the beauty of the spot pleased Him, the Báb was heavy of heart. Saddened by thoughts of His wife and the loved ones He would never see again, He was grieved even more by the treachery that surrounded Him and the stubbornness of those who resisted the Cause of God. More than once His companions saw Him weeping.

One day two Bábís from Tehran brought a sealed letter and a few small gifts for the Báb from Ḥusayn-'Alí. As soon as He received these things, the Báb's face brightened. His sorrow lifted, and the light of a new confidence radiated from Him—a confidence that would never leave Him in all the difficult days to come. The Báb's companions were amazed. Why, they wondered, would these few small tokens from Ḥusayn-'Alí have so great an effect on the Báb?

But the Báb knew what the others did not. The precious letter and gifts He had received were not themselves the treasure. It was the One Who had sent them, Ḥusayn-'Alí of Tehran, Who was the hidden treasure of God—the Promised One for Whom the world waited, the very One for Whom He Himself was preparing the way. The Báb knew that when the time was right, Ḥusayn-'Alí would reveal His secret: That Day would be the Day of the second "trumpet-blast" of God.[1]

Weeks passed. When the Báb still was not summoned to Tehran, He wrote a letter requesting the shah's permission to come to the capital and present His Cause. Once again the scheming grand vizier interfered. He persuaded the shah to postpone meeting with the Báb until a later date and suggested the Báb be sent, in the meantime, to the castle fortress of Máh-Kú. Máh-Kú stood high on a mountain in the northwest corner of Persia, near the Russian and Turkish borders—far removed from Tehran. In such a remote place, thought the grand vizier, the troublesome Báb and His Cause would soon be forgotten.

Although it was called a castle, Máh-Kú was a prison—a dark fortress set back in a pocket of the mountain, away from the open sky. Freezing in the winter, sweltering in the summer, it could be reached by neither rain nor snow, nor the light of the stars at night. In the summer of 1847 when the Báb arrived, sunlight baked the brown rocky mountain, but the cool breezes did not reach Máh-Kú. The Báb was forced to live in a mud-walled cell without even a lamp for light. A few guards and their dogs, under the command of the prison warden, 'Alí Khán, were posted to keep watch. The grand vizier had instructed 'Alí Khán to allow the Báb no visitors.

The Báb did not let His circumstances, however, keep Him from His work as a divine Messenger. In the isolation of Máh-Kú He began to reveal the new laws and teachings given to Him by God. Day after day the Báb dictated, while His amanuensis wrote. When finished, He had revealed some eight thousand verses in all. Together these verses made up the Báb's holy book, which He called the Bayán, meaning "Exposition." The Bayán was not simply a book of laws. Woven throughout its eight thousand verses were myriad references and tributes to "Him Whom God will make manifest"—the great Messenger Who was yet to come.

As the Báb dictated the verses of the Bayán, He chanted them in a strong, melodious voice. The sound of His chanting escaped through the prison window and echoed from the mountain to the village below. The words of the Báb could be heard clearly by the Kurdish people who lived there, and they were captivated by what they heard. Surely this is a holy man, they said to one another, and they began to gather each day beneath the fortress walls of Máh-Kú to ask for the Báb's blessing.

Even the prison warden, 'Alí Khán, felt the warming touch of the Báb's loving spirit. He relaxed the grand vizier's strict orders and allowed the Báb to have visitors. As summer turned to autumn, many Bábís braved the rugged journey to be near the Báb in that remote place. The Báb named Máh-Kú "the Open Mountain."

When winter descended the prison grew so cold that water froze in droplets on the Báb's face as He washed. The harsh winter gave way, at last, to spring, and the welcome days of light and thawing warmth brought an especially welcome visitor, Mullá Ḥusayn. Mullá Ḥusayn had traveled nine hundred miles, walking all the way from his home in Mashhad, in northeastern Persia, to see his beloved Báb—the Qá'im, the Messenger of God on earth. Tenderly the Báb embraced him.

For nine days Mullá Ḥusayn stayed with the Báb at Máh-Kú. 'Alí Khán brought choice fruits and sweetmeats for them to eat, for it was the feast of *Naw-Rúz,* the Persian New Year.* Together they celebrated and conversed about many things. The Báb told Mullá Ḥusayn of events that would come to pass, but He cautioned him not to tell others. Great and terrible days were approaching, days that would test the mettle of all who called themselves followers of the Báb.

"You are destined to exhibit such courage, such skill and heroism as shall eclipse the mightiest deeds of the heroes of old," the Báb told Mullá Ḥusayn. All too soon the time came for the Báb—"the Gate"—to bid a tender good-bye to Mullá Ḥusayn, who would be forever remembered as the Bábu'l-Báb, "the Gate of the Gate"—first among the Báb's disciples to find Him on that spring night in Shiraz nearly four years before.

As Mullá Ḥusayn made the long journey back to Mashhad, he stopped in cities along the way to bring the Báb's loving greetings to the Bábís and to assure them of His tender affection for them all. As he walked, Mullá Ḥusayn carried in his heart the lasting echo of the Báb's words to him: "Arise . . . and let nothing detain you from achieving your destiny."[2]

---

* *Naw-Rúz,* meaning literally "New Day," is the Persian New Year, observed on the vernal equinox in March. Persians had celebrated *Naw-Rúz* for centuries, even before the days of Muḥammad.

Although the grand vizier was far from Máh-Kú, he had spies in place to report on the Báb. The spies told him about the Báb's visitors and about the villagers who gathered every day for His blessing. Ḥájí Mírzá Áqásí fumed when he heard their reports. He had expected to shut the Báb away from the world, to stifle His influence and to suffocate His Cause. Furious that his orders to isolate the Báb had not been followed at Máh-Kú, he ordered the Báb to be moved at once.

On April 10, 1848, eleven days after Mullá Ḥusayn had gone, the Báb was taken to a different mountain fortress. This fortress, called Chihríq, was even more difficult to reach than the first. The Báb called it "the Grievous Mountain" because He knew what lay ahead.

In spite of His own suffering, the Báb continued His work. From Chihríq He sent a letter calling all the Bábís to "hasten to the land of Khá," which was the northeast province of Khurasan.[3] As soon as Ḥusayn-'Alí received the Báb's call, He proceeded to plan a gathering in Khurasan, to be held outside the village of Badasht. It would come to be known as the Conference of Badasht.

Before the conference plans were complete, Ḥusayn-'Alí received disturbing news. A murder had been committed in the city of Qazvín, west of Tehran, and three innocent Bábís had been arrested for the crime. Sent to prison in Tehran, they awaited final judgment on their lives. To come to the aid of the Bábís was to risk one's very life. Vengeful relatives were determined to get what they wanted, and they were more interested in blood than in justice. It seemed that no one was willing to risk his life for the three Bábís—no one except Ḥusayn-'Alí.

13

Rage and a Secret Rescue

Ḥusayn-'Alí wasted no time in gathering the facts. Then He took immediate action. He sent a trusted person to explain the case to the grand vizier. He gave money to prison officials to buy food for the Bábís imprisoned in Tehran. The Bábís' accusers were angry when they learned that Ḥusayn-'Alí was helping them, and had cast Him into prison, too. But the charges were proved false and He was released. The three innocent Bábís were also released, and they departed from Tehran to return to their homes in Qazvín.

By this time the real murderer had confessed, but his confession did not interest the vengeful relatives of the murdered Mullá Taqí. They continued to aim an angry barrage of accusations against the Bábís, insisting they were to blame for the murder. Their hate-filled words enraged the people of Qazvín until the whole town became of one mind—the Bábís must pay for the crime. When the three Bábís returned, they were met by a frenzied mob wielding knives and swords, axes and hatchets. Not one person spoke up in defense of the three Bábís, nor were they allowed to speak on their own behalf before they were brutally attacked by the mob and killed.

With this deed done, the vengeful relatives turned their attention toward another Bábí who was passing through Qazvín—Ṭáhirih, the only woman among the Báb's Letters of the Living. She had stopped in Qazvín, where her family lived, as she traveled to the gathering in Khurasan. Ṭáhirih's family had insisted on it. They did not approve of her being a Bábí, and they hoped to persuade her to change her mind, or at least to quiet her.

Ṭáhirih was a woman of rare accomplishment. Most Persian women were not educated, but Ṭáhirih's father had recognized early on that his young daughter was gifted with an especially keen mind. He loved her dearly and educated her the same way he educated his sons. Ṭáhirih had grown into a woman as famous for her intelligence as for her beauty—more than equal to any man in her knowledge of religion and in her ability to present strong, clear arguments. She possessed other talents as well. In a land where people had, for centuries, turned to their poets as often as their prophets for inspiration, Ṭáhirih was known for the exquisite poetry she wrote. Her father, highly regarded among Persia's religious leaders, had taught his daughter well.

Still, she was a woman in a Muslim society. When men gathered in her father's house for religious discussion, Ṭáhirih had to speak from behind a curtain, for women were not permitted to be in the company of men who were not members of their immediate family. She could never expect to be a spiritual leader, no matter how great her knowledge and skill. Some mullás even argued that women did not possess souls and ranked little higher than animals. How could they possibly understand religion?

"Would that she had been a boy," said her father, "for he would have shed illumination upon my household, and would have succeeded me."

Ṭáhirih's marriage had been arranged according to the customs of the day, and she became mother to a daughter and two sons. One day in the library of her cousin's house, she had happened upon the writings of Shaykh Aḥmad, which captured her interest and led her into correspondence with Siyyid Káẓim. Determined to study with him, Ṭáhirih had traveled to Karbala, but ten days before her arrival Siyyid Káẓim died. Ṭáhirih had stayed among his followers in that city, spending her time in prayer and meditation, until one night she was visited with a remarkable dream. In this dream a young man wearing a black robe and a green turban appeared to her in the heavens and, with upraised hands, recited certain verses—the same verses that she later read in a copy of the Báb's commentary on the Súrih of Joseph.

When the fearless Ṭáhirih declared her belief in the Báb, she had indeed become a spiritual leader. Her passionate and persuasive arguments convinced multitudes in city after city of the truth of the Báb and His Cause. Princes, mullás, and government officials were won over by her knowledge, her eloquence, and the indomitable force of her character. Ṭáhirih taught many women as well, among them the respected widow of Siyyid Káẓim.

On her return to Qazvín, Ṭáhirih had caused a furor. She had refused to return to the home of her husband, Mullá Muḥammad, who thought of himself, along with his father and uncle, as the best of the mujtahids of Persia. Ṭáhirih sent her reply with his messenger: "Say to my presumptuous and arrogant kinsman, 'If your desire had really been to be a faithful mate and companion to me, you would have hastened to meet me in Karbilá and would on foot have guided my howdah all the way to Qazvín. I would, while journeying with you, have aroused you from your sleep of heedlessness and would have shown you the way of truth. But this was not to be. Three years have elapsed since our separation. Neither in this world nor in the next can I ever be associated with you. I have cast you out of my life for ever.'"

For a Muslim husband to be addressed with such words by his wife was unheard of and enraged both Mullá Muḥammad and his father, Mullá Taqí. They subsequently branded Ṭáhirih a heretic and bent all their efforts to sully her reputation. It was Mullá Taqí who was later murdered in the mosque—struck down by a man enraged at his cruel condemnation of a man who had done nothing more than praise Shaykh Aḥmad and Siyyid Káẓim.

Yet even after the murderer had confessed, the family and friends of Mullá Taqí were determined to make the bold and independent Ṭáhirih suffer for the crime. "No one else but you is guilty of the murder of our father," they said. "You issued the order for his assassination."

Her accusers questioned her for hours about the crime, but to every question Ṭáhirih replied with calm dignity, "This deed has been perpetrated without our knowledge." Her father tried to protect her by keeping her in his own house, but her accusers were determined to have their way. It was not justice they wanted, but blood. Ṭáhirih's life was in grave danger.

When Ḥusayn-'Alí learned of Ṭáhirih's situation, He at once set in motion a plan to rescue her. Swiftly, in the dark of night, He sent a trusted Bábí and his wife to Qazvín, giving them careful instructions. The woman, disguised as a beggar, was to deliver a letter directly into Ṭáhirih's hands and wait. When Ṭáhirih was ready, the two women were to walk together along the back ways of Qazvín until they came to the city gate. There the Bábí man would meet them with three horses, and they would ride the back roads to Tehran.

"As soon as the gates [of Tehran] are opened, you must enter the city and proceed immediately to My house," Ḥusayn-'Alí instructed them. "You should exercise the utmost caution lest her identity be disclosed. The Almighty will assuredly guide your steps and will surround you with His unfailing protection."

The Bábí husband and wife did just as Ḥusayn-'Alí told them. Ṭáhirih's life depended on their obedience to His instructions. Morning brought the angry relatives of the murdered man of Qazvín to Ṭáhirih's door, but Ṭáhirih was not at home. The surprised and angry relatives searched everywhere in Qazvín, but she was nowhere to be found. Ṭáhirih was safely in Tehran.[1]

Ṭáhirih rested for a few days in the home of her protector, Ḥusayn-'Alí. Because of Ḥusayn-'Alí's social position and the great esteem in which He was held by all, His home was a safe haven in which Bábís could gather. One day the illustrious Vaḥíd—the shah's messenger who had become a Bábí—was a visitor in Ḥusayn-'Alí's home. Vaḥíd sat explaining certain spiritual traditions while others listened. Ṭáhirih herself listened from behind the customary curtain, holding the four-year-old child 'Abdu'l-Bahá on her lap.

Vaḥíd was eloquent as always, but Ṭáhirih was tired of talk. This was a brilliant new Day, the Day of the Qá'im! Suddenly she could contain herself no longer. "Cease idly repeating the traditions of the past," she said from behind the curtain, "for the day of service, of steadfast action, is come. Now is the time to show forth the true signs of God, to rend asunder the veils of idle fancy, to promote the Word of God, and to sacrifice ourselves in His path. Let deeds, not words, be our adorning!"[2]

Because of Ḥusayn-'Alí's swift action, Ṭáhirih would be able to join her fellow believers at Badasht. Though Ḥusayn-'Alí would direct the course of the conference, Ṭáhirih herself would make it a gathering that none would forget.

14

The Blast of the Trumpet

Warm breezes rustled the leaves of trees whose fruits would slowly ripen into peaches and pomegranates, cherries and apples—plump, juicy, and sweet. It was the end of June, 1848. Northeast of Tehran, on the other side of the Elburz Mountains, Ḥusayn-'Alí chose three gardens outside the village of Badasht for the conference of Bábís. There, near the gentle ripple and splash of a stream, with the mountains tall and purple in the distance, tents were pitched for the eighty-one Bábís who attended. The three largest tents, spread with soft carpets to walk upon and large enough for guests to gather, were reserved for Ḥusayn-'Alí, Quddús, and

Ṭáhirih—the only woman present among them. Mullá Ḥusayn was unavoidably absent, detained by authorities in Mashhad.

The conference at Badasht lasted twenty-two days. Its purpose was to make clear the Báb's true mission and to make a decisive break with past traditions. With the Báb in a remote prison, few of His followers had been able to talk to Him or to have access to His holy book, the Bayán. Many still thought of the Báb as a reformer of Islam, unaware that His Cause was much greater. From its first day the conference at Badasht began to open the eyes of the Bábís.

Each day of the conference a newly revealed tablet was chanted to the gathered Bábís; each day a Muslim law or tradition was repealed. Each Bábí received a new name symbolizing their new spiritual reality. It was at Badasht that Ṭáhirih, whose name means "the Pure One," received her name, and Quddús, whose name means "the Most Holy One," received his. Ḥusayn-'Alí took the title *"Bahá,"* meaning "Glory." The message became clear. The Báb's divine revelation, with its new laws and teachings, was a fresh and distinct branch on the sacred tree of religion.

Lively discussions could be heard as the days passed. Most Bábís eagerly accepted that the Cause of the Báb was a new religion, independent of Islam. Others were not ready to hear that the laws of the Koran must give way to the laws of the Bayán. They found it hard to let go of the traditions and guidance they had honored all their lives. For them, the conference at Badasht was a test of their faith in the Báb.

Ṭáhirih grew impatient. The long-awaited Qá'im had come and His followers were quibbling over details, unaware, it seemed, of the power of the Cause which they espoused. She had seen mullás use words to trample religion into a dead thing. She could not bear to see the Cause of the beloved Báb treated so.

Ṭáhirih was a poet who knew the power of symbol, and a woman courageous enough to do what other Muslim women would not. One day she walked quietly into Ḥusayn-'Alí's tent, where the other believers were gathered. When her fellow Bábís looked up, they gasped in horror at what they saw. Ṭáhirih stood before them with her face unveiled—an unthinkable act for any decent Muslim woman of the time. Though she was modestly dressed, it was as if she stood unclothed before them.

The Bábí men, who normally refrained even from looking upon her shadow, were aghast. Some quickly covered their eyes with their hands or hid them in the folds of their clothing to avoid looking upon her face. Others ran out of the tent altogether. One Bábí was so distressed that he cut his own throat with a knife.*

Ṭáhirih remained calm. The removal of her veil expressed her insight into the true spirit of Badas͟ht more powerfully than a thousand well-chosen words. The time had come to cast aside old ideas and outworn ways, to open wide one's arms and receive the bounties of a new revelation. One bounty to come, of which Ṭáhirih was confident, would be the unveiling of the true and equal worth of women.

"I am the blast of the trumpet, I am the call of the bugle," Ṭáhirih proclaimed. "This day is the day of festivity and universal rejoicing, the day on which the fetters of the past are burst asunder. Let those who have shared in this great achievement arise and embrace each other," she said to the assembled Bábís.[1]

But the emotional disturbance caused by her bold act was like the unsettling tremor of an earthquake. Some Bábís were shaken to the very core, their perceptions so shattered that they left the gathering at Badas͟ht and no longer chose to call themselves Bábís. Ḥusayn-'Alí soothed the other agitated Bábís and restored calm to their assembly by calling for a chapter from the Koran to be read aloud. The passage referred to the Day of Judgment, "when the earth shall be shaken with a shock, And the mountains shall be crumbled with a crumbling, And shall become scattered dust."[2]

The words seemed to describe how many of the believers felt that very day at Badas͟ht, but their deeper meaning predicted an upheaval for all humankind—the beginning of a great new cycle in the world. That this passage from the Koran was chosen to be read that day, under the guiding hand of Ḥusayn-'Alí, was not accidental. The great new cycle had begun, and it could not be turned back.

When the followers of the Báb left the gardens of Badas͟ht at the end of the twenty-two days, their new spirit matched their new names. They felt enlightened and energized, strong and eager to teach the Cause of the Báb. Most did not know, however, that their new names had been given to them by Ḥusayn-'Alí, nor did they know that each new tablet at the conference had been revealed by Ḥusayn-'Alí, though some guessed

* This attempt at suicide was unsuccessful.

that it might be so. The Báb alone knew, for between Him and Ḥusayn-'Alí had flowed a constant stream of letters.

Together the Báb and Ḥusayn-'Alí had guided the Bábís a step closer toward their destiny. The tremendous change in store for humankind would require not only new laws and customs, but a new mind and spirit—a transformation that would not take place easily. At Badasht the Bábís had seen the first glimmer of what it would mean for them to be the dawn-breakers for a new Day.

Outside of Persia the year 1848 was a year of revolution in Europe. Uprisings occurred in France, Germany, Austria, Italy, and Great Britain. Ordinary people everywhere were demanding change. Farmers, merchants, and craftsmen were no longer content to see their rulers live in splendid comfort while their own families lived difficult, impoverished lives. They wanted affordable food, the ability under the law to own land, and they wanted a society that treated them justly. In certain places people who spoke the same language wanted their own independent nation. Many people demanded a voice in electing the leaders who governed them. Some read a new pamphlet by Karl Marx titled *The Communist Manifesto*. Marx did not put his trust in religion to change society, but in revolution. If people wanted justice, he wrote, the proletariat—the working class—must revolt against the rulers and the wealthy.

Those in power, long accustomed to doing what they pleased, were slow to respond. When the French National Assembly wrangled in disagreement over reforms, angry citizens broke into its chambers and overran the Assembly. King Louis-Philippe was forced to flee the country. In the ongoing struggle for reform, the French fought bloody street battles. They were not alone.

Newspapers, with the aid of the newly invented telegraph, carried the news of protests and revolts from one country to the next. More people than ever before could read, and the news of one revolt would inspire people in other places to take action themselves. The spirit that blazed in one country soon caught fire in the next—and the fire would not be put out.

Others sought change in more peaceful ways. In 1848 peace itself was the topic at an international conference in Brussels, the second in a series of peace conferences. Slavery roused people to action on both sides of the Atlantic. It had been abolished throughout the British Empire, but America was divided over the issue—its states half slave and half free. Abraham Lincoln, a newly elected congressman from Illinois, could see a short distance from the Capitol building the slave pens crowded with black men and women kept in iron manacles. He voiced the mind of many when he later wrote to a friend, "If slavery is not wrong, nothing is wrong."[3]

By 1840, more than two hundred thousand Americans became abolitionists, organizing as many as two thousand antislavery groups to speak out against slavery and the laws that sanctioned it. Among their members was Frederick Douglass, who had escaped from slavery in Maryland to become a free man in Massachusetts. An eloquent speaker and writer, Douglass also belonged to a daring network known as the Underground Railroad—people who put themselves at risk to help runaway slaves escape to freedom.

Many at the forefront of the abolitionist movement were inspired by their religious beliefs. Among them was the older Lucretia Mott, a Quaker activist who met the younger Elizabeth Cady Stanton in London at the 1840 World Anti-Slavery Convention. When convention organizers would not allow any women to participate, the two were astonished and infuriated. Refused even a seat in the main hall, they were seated behind a curtain in the gallery. It was there in London that Elizabeth Cady Stanton and Lucretia Mott first talked about a convention to address the rights of women.

But it was not until the summer of 1848—the same summer as the Conference of Badas͟ht in Persia—that the two American women convened the first women's rights convention. On July 19, three hundred women and men gathered at the Wesleyan Chapel in Seneca Falls, New York, where for two days they listened, debated, and finally accepted the Declaration of Sentiments drafted by Elizabeth Cady Stanton. The Declaration of Sentiments called for equal rights in education, religion, and law—including the right to vote. Frederick Douglass was present at the convention and became one of their staunchest supporters. "We hold woman to be justly entitled to all we claim for man," he wrote in his newspaper, the *North Star*.[4]

News of the convention and its Declaration of Sentiments traveled by telegraph to newspapers throughout the country. It sparked heated debate, a debate welcomed by Elizabeth Cady Stanton. "It will start women thinking, and men, too," she said, "and when men and women think about a new question, the first step in progress is taken." She was looking for a new mind and a change of heart as much as a change in law.[5]

Neither Elizabeth Cady Stanton nor Lucretia Mott knew of the gathering at Badasht on the other side of the world or of the outspoken Ṭáhirih who boldly removed her veil. But in their determined desire for justice they were not nearly so far apart. A spirit of change was stirring in the world, and the spiritual heart of it, Ṭáhirih knew, beat in Persia. Yet not even the Bábís could imagine how far-reaching was the change set in motion by the Báb.

15

The Sermon of Wrath and a Royal Command

On the other side of Persia, the grand vizier's plan had been thwarted once again. He had expected to isolate the Báb at Chihríq, but the Báb was not so easily shut away. The hardened heart of the fierce prison warden—this time Yaḥyá Khán—grew soft under the warmth of the Báb's loving-kindness. Like the warden at Máh-Kú, he relaxed the grand vizier's orders and allowed the Báb to see visitors. A growing number of Bábís came to visit Him at Chihríq. The villagers who lived near Chihríq, like the villagers near Máh-Kú, were also attracted to the Báb and daily stood near the prison walls to ask His blessing on their work.

The grand vizier was angry and uneasy when he heard these things. Not only had the Báb's influence not been stifled, but it was actually growing. Something must be done and quickly, he decided. From Tehran he called for an assembly of religious leaders and government officials to meet in the city of Tabríz, not far from Chihríq. He directed that the Báb be brought to the assembly for interrogation. They should discredit the Báb and make Him look foolish, ordered the grand vizier, so that the Persian people would cease listening to this merchant from Shiraz.

When the Báb arrived under guard at the appointed place of meeting in Tabríz, He walked with authority to the last empty seat in the assembly. It was the place of honor reserved for the prince, but no one interfered when the Báb took His seat. An officer of the assembly began the interrogation. "Whom do you claim to be?" he asked, "and what is the message which you have brought?"

"I am, I am, I am, the promised One!" answered the Báb in a clear voice. "I am the One whose name you have for a thousand years invoked, at whose mention you have risen, whose advent you have longed to witness, and the hour of whose Revelation you have prayed God to hasten. Verily I say, it is incumbent upon the peoples of both the East and the West to obey My word and to pledge allegiance to My person."

When the Báb finished speaking, a profound silence settled over the room. His majesty and power were unmistakable. At last the silence was broken as the mullás began to ask questions. They were not sincere questions that would lead them to learn more about the Báb and His Cause, but questions intended to find fault and insult the Báb. When He saw that the mullás were not interested in the truth, the Báb got up from His chair and walked out of the assembly. No one tried to stop Him.[1]

The mullás were clearly defeated, having failed to humiliate the Báb in debate. Still they had the power to punish, and they ordered the Báb to be bastinadoed—beaten on the soles of His feet with a thick wooden rod. The governor's guards refused to carry out the order. A religious matter, they said, was none of their concern. But the chief mullá, undeterred, inflicted the punishment himself. Taking the heavy rod in his own hands, he struck the soles of the Báb's feet again and again, leaving them torn and bleeding. When all was finished at Tabríz, the Báb was taken back to His prison cell at <u>Ch</u>ihríq.

The story of the Báb's great announcement and of His noble behavior—such a contrast to the cruel mullás at Tabríz—confounded the grand vizier's plan to discredit the Báb. More Persians were convinced to take the message of the Báb seriously and to investigate His Cause. Many became Bábís. Victory had not gone to the mullás and the grand vizier, but to the prisoner.

The Báb was fully aware that it was Ḥájí Mírzá Áqásí who had stood between Himself and the shah. Because of fear, jealousy, and his own selfish ambition, the grand vizier had betrayed the trust of his sovereign. The shah might have believed in the Báb, had they met, and led all of Persia peaceably to the truth. Now it would never be.

The Prophet Zoroaster, Who had lived in ancient Persia before the time of Cyrus the Great, had taught His followers that evil battles with good in this world. Each person must choose, Zoroaster had said, whether to fight on the side of good or evil. Many people in Persia would soon be faced with that choice, each waging battle in his own soul, for Persia itself would become a battleground of unimaginable choices. The grand vizier, by his own choice, was already drawing the battle lines.

When the Báb returned from Tabríz to the prison at Chihríq, He wrote a strong letter to the grand vizier called the Sermon of Wrath. It began with the words "O thou who hast disbelieved in God and hast turned thy face away from His signs!"[2] The grand vizier's treachery, said the Báb in His letter, would be the cause of his own downfall. Little did the grand vizier know how soon the Báb's predictions would come true.

Until that time came, the grand vizier would continue to stir up trouble—this time for Ḥusayn-'Alí. Together with a few jealous noblemen, He came before the shah with serious charges. Ḥusayn-'Alí must be organizing a rebellion against the shah. Why else would so many Bábís gather at Badasht?

Although the noble Ḥusayn-'Alí had always been a loyal subject, He was not at court to defend Himself. Muḥammad Sháh made his own decision, choosing to believe the evil whisperings of the grand vizier. Then he issued a royal command. Bring Ḥusayn-'Alí to Tehran, he ordered, to be executed for plotting against the shah.

16

Bandar-Gaz and the Black Standard

On the other side of the mountains from Tehran Ḥusayn-'Alí was riding His steed the long way home from Badasht, along the warm, wet lowlands next to the Caspian Sea. Fields of cotton and rice grew green and lush. Forests dense with oak and ash, elm and beech, teemed with game for the hunter, and no matter what the season, the air was sweetened with the scent of flowers.

As Ḥusayn-'Alí drew nearer the sea, a tang of salt sharpened the air. The Caspian Sea—largest lake in the world—was salty. The lake lay mostly in Russia, with only its southern shore in Persia, its waters home to an abundance of fish, as well as seals. Here, in the port city of Bandar-Gaz, Ḥusayn-'Alí stopped to rest and visit with friends.

When He arrived, His friends at Bandar-Gaz planned a banquet in His honor and invited the city's notable people to come. On the day before the banquet the shah's order to return to Tehran was delivered to Ḥusayn-'Alí.

Everyone knew the cruel and fickle nature of the shah. They urged Him not to return to Tehran but to flee from the shah's wrath. Leave the country, they told Him. He could save Himself that very day by boarding the Russian ship docked at Bandar-Gaz. But Ḥusayn-'Alí—known as "Bahá" (Glory)—did not choose to run away.

The day of the banquet arrived, and the festivities were about to begin, when suddenly a courier from Tehran galloped into the city. Breathlessly he delivered the news: Muḥammad Sháh was dead!

The gathered friends could hardly believe Ḥusayn-'Alí's good fortune. With the shah's death, the orders for His execution were empty words, their authority as dead as the sovereign himself. Ḥusayn-'Alí was safe.

The mean-spirited grand vizier, Ḥájí Mírzá Áqásí, was not so fortunate. He who had misused his power now found it taken away. At the death of Muḥammad Sháh, he left Tehran and was not allowed to return. His dishonesty was revealed, and his ill-gotten wealth taken away by the new government. No one in all of Persia called him friend, and Ḥájí Mírzá Áqásí was forced to leave his homeland. Poor and alone, the man who had plotted against the Báb lost everything he cherished. In little more than a year's time, he died.

The religious leader of Tabríz who had bastinadoed the Báb with his own hands also suffered a change of fortune. That same year, he fell ill with a paralyzing disease and died a painful death.

But the Cause of the Báb, which they had hoped to destroy, continued to grow, and Ḥusayn-'Alí—Bahá—remained unharmed.

Since the Conference of Badasht the Bábís were teaching fearlessly in every part of Persia. Their efforts not only attracted more interest in the Cause of the Báb, but also stronger opposition to it. In the town of Sárí, Quddús was under house arrest. When the Báb learned of it, He sent His green turban and a message to Mullá Ḥusayn in the city of Mashhad. "Adorn your head with My green turban, the emblem of My lineage," said the Báb's message, "and, with the Black Standard unfurled before you, hasten . . . and lend your assistance to My beloved Quddús." Mullá Ḥusayn obeyed at once.[1]

The Báb had referred to Quddús as "a hidden treasure," and Ḥusayn-'Alí had given Quddús his name, which meant "Most Holy One." But Mullá Ḥusayn had discovered for himself that his own vast knowledge, acquired from years of study, paled before the God-given spiritual insight and qualities of Quddús. Among all the Letters of the Living it was Quddús, he had found, who most purely reflected the glory of the Báb. Humbly Mullá Ḥusayn had pledged to Quddús his undying loyalty.

They had become close companions. In Mashhad they had worked together to teach the Faith of the Báb, and there Mullá Ḥusayn, at the request of Quddús, had built a house especially for that purpose. They called it the *"Bábíyyih"* (House of the Bábís) and opened wide its doors to welcome a steady flow of visitors. With what energy had Mullá Ḥusayn prepared the seekers to accept the Faith! With what wisdom had Quddús enlightened them even further, until the Bábíyyih became a gathering center for enthusiastic new believers. Because of Mullá Ḥusayn and Quddús, more people became Bábís in that province than anywhere else in Persia. Now Quddús, the treasured companion of Mullá Ḥusayn, needed his help.

On July 21, 1848, Mullá Ḥusayn mounted his horse and set out from Mashhad. A band of 202 Bábís traveled with him. Mullá Ḥusayn wore the Báb's green turban and carried a black standard, a banner that waved above their heads as they rode.

The Prophet Muḥammad, according to Islamic tradition, had told His followers, "Should your eyes behold the Black Standards proceeding from Khurásán, hasten ye towards them, even though ye should have to crawl over the snow, inasmuch as they proclaim the advent of the promised Mihdí, the Vicegerent of God." The black banners were a sign, He told them, that the promised Qá'im had come. The long journey from Mashhad in the east to Sárí took them over rugged mountains and into the central lowlands, near the Caspian Sea. Wherever they stopped to rest, they taught people about the Báb, and all along the way people became Bábís. A few rode with them toward Sárí.

Mullá Ḥusayn remembered all the things the Báb had told him at the prison of Máh-Kú. As they drew closer to Sárí, he spoke to those who rode with him. "I, together with seventy-two of my companions, shall suffer death for the sake of the Well-Beloved.* Whoso is unable to renounce the world, let him now, at this very moment, depart, for later on he will be unable to escape."

Twenty chose to leave. To the courageous souls who remained, Mullá Ḥusayn said, "Leave behind all your belongings, and content yourselves only with your steeds and swords . . ." The Bábís obeyed without protest. One Bábí, a merchant, threw to the ground his rich bag of precious turquoise and never looked back. No one could accuse this band of companions of riding for selfish reasons.

Mullá Ḥusayn and his group had almost reached Sárí when they saw a threatening mob coming towards them. Sunlight glinted off the sharp edges of the swords and knives, guns, and axes they carried in their hands. Their faces were filled with hate. A mullá in the nearby town of Barfurush had enraged the townspeople with lies about the Bábís. Now the angry mob was prepared to attack.

At first, Mullá Ḥusayn did not allow the Bábís to fight. But when the savage mob attacked and killed some of the Bábís, Mullá Ḥusayn unsheathed his sword. He rushed toward one attacker, who tried to hide behind a small tree. With a single fierce stroke, Mullá Ḥusayn cut in two the tree, the musket, and the man.[2]

Their frightened attackers ran away crying, "Peace! Peace!" But the hateful mullá of Barfurush again incited the villagers. They must defend Islam from its enemies, he shouted. Again and yet again, the townspeople attacked the small band of Bábís, but each time they were repulsed.

---

* The Báb.

The Bábís did not want to fight. They wished only to defend themselves. Thirteen miles away from Barfurush, they found refuge in a small, simple building. It was a shrine built to honor the memory of a respected religious teacher, Shaykh Ṭabarsí. The resourceful Bábís built walls of mud strengthened with tree trunks around the shrine and dug a deep ditch, forming a moat all around. The shrine was now a fortress from which the Bábís could defend themselves.

When Ḥusayn-'Alí heard the news in Tehran, He rode at once to Ṭabarsí to offer assistance. Mullá Ḥusayn was glad to see Him and showed Him all they had built. Ḥusayn-'Alí praised their work. All that was needed to make their company "complete and perfect," He said, was Quddús. Ḥusayn-'Alí directed Mullá Ḥusayn to send seven believers to Sárí and demand the release of Quddús.

Mullá Ḥusayn did just as Ḥusayn-'Alí told him and, to the surprise of all, Quddús was set free. The brave band of Bábís had started the fort at Ṭabarsí in October 1848. It was the end of the year when Quddús joined them. Ḥusayn-'Alí had already gone, planning to return with supplies.

Encouraging the Bábís to be patient and resigned to the will of God, Ḥusayn-'Alí had said before leaving, "If it be His will, We shall once again visit you at this same spot and shall lend you Our assistance." His presence at the fort had inspired the Bábís with courage and determination, but who among them could know the will of God?[3]

17

Danger at Amul

The mullá of Barfurush who had first incited the townspeople to attack was furious to learn the Bábís had not been killed. He wrote a letter to the new ruler of Persia, Náṣiri'd-Dín Sháh, accusing the Bábís of revolt. "They have built themselves a fort," wrote the mullá, "and in that massive stronghold they have entrenched themselves, ready to direct a campaign against you." He urged the shah to wage war against the Bábís, calling them "this hateful creed that has dared to conspire against you."

None of it was true, but Náṣiri'd-Dín Sháh was young—only seventeen years old—and eager to prove himself a strong king. The Bábís at Ṭabarsí were only a "handful of untrained and frail-bodied students," one observer told the shah. They could be easily defeated by a small detachment of soldiers, he advised, "within the space of two days."

The shah agreed and gave consent for an officer to recruit whatever forces he might need to fulfill the task. An army of twelve thousand men was called together from the chiefs of the country and the men who served them. The army of twelve thousand camped near a village overlooking Ṭabarsí. They set up barricades in front of the fort, and no one was allowed to enter or leave. Inside the fort were 313 Bábís.

One morning as the shah's army made ready to attack, they heard a mighty shout from inside the fort: "O Lord of the Age!" Suddenly the gates of the fort opened and the small band of Bábís charged into their midst. Confused and frightened, the shah's army scattered like rabbits. In less than an hour's time they had all retreated in disorder. On orders from Quddús, the Bábís did not pursue the soldiers.

"We have repulsed the assailants; we need not carry further the punishment," said Quddús. "Our purpose is to protect ourselves that we may be able to continue our labours for the regeneration of men," he told the other Bábís. "We have no intention whatever of causing unnecessary harm to anyone."

Ashamed of their own disgraceful retreat, the shah's army regrouped for attack. But the large, unwieldy army was repeatedly surprised. Time after time Quddús commanded the Bábís, "Mount your steeds, O heroes of God!" The gates of the fort were thrown open, and the small band of courageous Bábís—none of them trained in battle—charged bravely into the enemy. Time after time, the soldiers sent to defeat the Bábís were themselves routed. Although the army outnumbered the small band in the fort, the Bábís were strong in spirit. There would be no easy triumph for the shah's army at Ṭabarsí. The army of twelve thousand settled in for a long siege against the 313 Bábís.[1]

In December 1848 Ḥusayn-'Alí set out from Tehran once more to keep His promise and return to Ṭabarsí. Eleven Bábís rode with Him—including Mírzá Yaḥyá, a younger half-brother of Ḥusayn-'Alí. The journey by horseback was long and hard, leading them over mountain paths and into the lowlands. They rode with haste, intent on coming to the aid of their fellow Bábís at Ṭabarsí. Ḥusayn-'Alí urged them to ride without stopping in order to reach the fort under cover of night. Guards from the shah's army might intercept them at any time.

Hour after hour they rode, the flanks of their horses glistening with sweat. Only nine miles from Ṭabarsí the bone-weary, bleary-eyed companions begged to rest. Ḥusayn-'Alí agreed to stop and kept watch while the others slept. Suddenly, out of the darkness, a party of guards appeared. "We have received strict orders to arrest every person we chance to meet in this vicinity . . ." the chief guard told Ḥusayn-'Alí.

"The matter has been misrepresented in your eyes," replied Ḥusayn-'Alí calmly. "You have misconstrued our purpose. I would advise you to act in a manner that will cause you eventually no regret."

The dignity with which Ḥusayn-'Alí spoke had its effect. Adopting a tone of courtesy, the chief guard bade the weary travelers to mount their horses and go with him to the nearby town of Amul. Despite the considerate manner of the chief guard, the Bábís could only guess at what awaited them.

A messenger raced ahead to the town with news of the Bábís' arrest. When the mullás of Amul heard the news, they were eager to have the Bábís punished. They called the townspeople to come out of their houses and shops and behold the fate of the enemies of Islam. By the time Ḥusayn-'Alí and His companions arrived in Amul, more than four thousand people had gathered, crowding together in the mosque and on the rooftops. They strained to watch as the prisoners were brought forward.

The governor of Amul was absent—gone to fight the Bábís at Ṭabarsí. The temporary governor left to act in his place did not like this turn of events. When he recognized that one of the prisoners was Ḥusayn-'Alí, a nobleman of good character, he was even more distressed. He knew that he must proceed very carefully. The mob was dangerous and the mullás more so. Both would like to see blood. In an effort to satisfy the mullás, the acting governor condemned the Bábís.

"We are innocent of the guilt they impute to us," replied Ḥusayn-'Alí. "Our blamelessness will eventually be established in your eyes. I would advise you to act in a manner that will cause you eventually no regret." Then the chief mullá questioned Him about the Báb. Ḥusayn-

'Alí answered that He "cherished . . . a great affection for Him" and that the Báb had never acted against the Faith of Islam.

The chief mullá refused to listen and continued to shout his accusations. "You have perverted the faith of Islam and sullied its fame!" he insisted. Like the mullá of Barfurush, he stirred up the people of Amul with his venomous words. Then he demanded death for the Bábís.

The acting governor did not want to punish the Bábís, but the mullás—like bloodthirsty animals hunting their prey—would be satisfied with nothing less. If he did not act, the mullás could easily rouse the mob to riot. He ordered his attendants to prepare to administer the punishment of the bastinado. "We will afterwards keep them in prison pending the return of the governor," he said, hoping that this course of action would satisfy the mullás.

Ḥusayn-'Alí spoke up. "None of these men are guilty of any crime," He objected. "If you insist on inflicting your punishment, I offer Myself as a willing Victim of your chastisement." The reluctant governor, under the watchful eyes of the mullás, agreed.

When a prisoner received the bastinado punishment, he was forced to lie on his back with his legs up and his feet tied to a bar held by two men. The prisoner's bare feet were beaten with strong rods—a painful ordeal. The Báb had been bastinadoed just five months earlier in Tabríz. Now the crowd watched as Ḥusayn-'Alí suffered the same cruel treatment, His feet beaten with the thick rods until they bled. The acting governor knew that the punishment was unjust, but at least it was not the sentence of death for which the mullás had clamored.

When the sentence had been carried out, the Bábí prisoners were taken to a room of the mosque. But the acting governor did not trust the mullás. He had no doubt they would try to kill the Bábís. Secretly he gave orders for an opening to be cut into the prisoners' room. Then he brought them quietly to his own home to await the governor's return.

Late one night the governor of Amul rode back into town. He was returning from the battle at Ṭabarsí with new admiration for the Bábís. He had seen more than skill in Mullá Ḥusayn and the others. They had displayed a fearlessness and nobility that commanded his respect, and he wondered at the power of a Cause that could inspire such heroism in its followers.

When he learned that the mullás had demanded death for Ḥusayn-'Alí and the other Bábís, he was angry. If the mullás wished to defend their faith, "Let them betake themselves to the fort of Shaykh Ṭabarsí," said the governor, where they could face the Bábís in honorable battle.[2]

The governor apologized to Ḥusayn-'Alí for the treatment He and His companions had received in Amul. A few days later he arranged for them to be escorted safely to Tehran. Ḥusayn-'Alí had left Tehran to assist the Bábís at the fort of Ṭabarsí, but that was no longer possible. Their destiny and His lay on different paths.

18

Courage at Ṭabarsí

Fall turned to winter as the siege of Fort Ṭabarsí continued. One day Mullá Ḥusayn stood in an open field and called out to the soldiers of the shah's army, "Why . . . do ye act so cruelly towards us, and strive without cause to shed innocent blood? Be ashamed before the Creator of the universe, and at least give us passage, that we may depart out of this land." His words softened the hearts of the soldiers, who were moved by his courage. But the officers in charge knew they could not return to the shah and report that they had been beaten by this little band of Bábís. They ordered the soldiers to open fire, and the fighting continued.[1]

One day in early February 1849, the soldiers prepared to mount an intense attack against the fort. They set up a series of seven barricades, and when all was completed the soldiers retired to sleep before the morning's battle. Inside the fort, Mullá Ḥusayn also prepared for the battle to come. He bathed and performed his ablutions, then dressed in fresh garments. On his head he placed the Báb's green turban. All the while his face reflected a spirit of deep joy. For a time he talked alone with Quddús, whose spirit most clearly brought to mind for Mullá Ḥusayn the beloved Báb.

A little after midnight, when the morning star first rose, the gates of the fort were opened at Mullá Ḥusayn's command and a mighty shout filled the air: "O Lord of the Age!" The call reverberated from fort to forest to the soldiers' camp as Mullá Ḥusayn, mounted on his charger, led the Bábís in attack. Charging the first barricade, he broke through its defenses in a short time, and with the same fierce courage charged the second barricade and the third. Both the fearful and the brave scattered before him as barricade after barricade fell. Musket fire lit the night, but neither Mullá Ḥusayn nor the Bábís who followed him gave heed to the bullets that flew all around them.

Amid the commotion, one soldier scrambled with his musket up a tree and hid himself in its branches, watching and waiting in the dark. In the glare of the battle's gunfire he spied a horse and rider breaking through the last barricade. When the horse became tangled in a tent rope, the soldier saw his chance. Quickly he took aim and fired, striking the enemy full in the chest. The rider who felt the force of its impact was Mullá Ḥusayn.

Wounded and bleeding, Mullá Ḥusayn got down from his horse, staggered a few steps, and fell to the ground. Two Bábí companions, seeing him fallen, came quickly to his aid and carried him back to the fort.

When Quddús saw Mullá Ḥusayn so gravely wounded and wet with blood, he knew that his friend would not abide long in this world. He asked the others to leave them alone, and when they had gone, Quddús and Mullá Ḥusayn spoke quietly together— the first and last Letters of the Living, beloved disciples of the Báb and companions closer than brothers. No one knew what passed between them in those last hours of Mullá Ḥusayn's life, except for a little that was overheard.

"You have hastened the hour of your departure," a tender Quddús was heard to say, "and have abandoned me to the mercy of my foes. Please God, I will ere long join you and taste the sweetness of heaven's ineffable delights."

"May my life be a ransom for you," replied Mullá Ḥusayn. "Are you well pleased with me?"

How could Quddús be displeased? Mullá Ḥusayn, at the age of thirty-six, had fulfilled all that the Báb had predicted at Máh-Kú. "You are destined to exhibit such courage, such skill and heroism," the Báb had told him, "as shall eclipse the mightiest deeds of the heroes of old."

After a long time Quddús opened the door and permitted the other Bábís to rejoin him. "I have bade my last farewell to him," he said. They knew then that the noble spirit of Mullá Ḥusayn dwelt in this world no longer.

Quddús prepared Mullá Ḥusayn for burial, using his own shirt to clothe the body of his friend. Then he directed a few Bábís as to where the body should be laid to rest. Before they carried out their task, Quddús bent low over Mullá Ḥusayn and in a last farewell gently kissed his closed eyes and forehead. "Well is it with you to have remained to your last hour faithful to the Covenant of God," he said. "I pray God to grant that no division ever be caused between you and me."

Those who stood beside Quddús wept. With his own hands he laid to rest the mortal remains of Mullá Ḥusayn. He cautioned the others to keep the burial place a secret lest their enemies desecrate it.

Then Quddús directed that the other thirty-six Bábís who had died that night be laid to rest together in one grave. "Let the loved ones of God take heed of the example of these martyrs of our Faith," said Quddús. "Let them in life be and remain as united as these are now in death."[2]

The siege of Fort Ṭabarsí continued. Cannons and flaming projectiles were fired against the fort. The Bábís ably defended themselves, but their supplies could not be replenished. Food and water eventually dwindled to nothing, yet the Bábís would not surrender. They ate grass and tree bark, then the leather of their saddles, belts, and shoes. For eighteen days they had nothing but a mouthful of water each morning. Still they refused to be downhearted. Each day Quddús lifted their spirits with words of cheer and hope.

Winter gave way to spring. In May the prince who led the shah's army decided that, one way or another, the siege must end. He sent a messenger to Quddús with a copy of the Koran and his written pledge. The prince swore by the holy book that he would let the Bábís go safely on their way and return to their homes with honor. "Come forth from your stronghold and rest assured that no hand will be stretched forth against you," the prince promised.

Quddús and the others suspected that the prince would betray them, but Quddús decided to accept the prince's promise. "By our response to their invitation," said Quddús, "we shall enable them to demonstrate the sincerity of their intentions."

The Bábís came out of the fort and were taken to the prince, but the faithless prince did not keep his promise. He ordered the Bábís to be seized as prisoners. They received neither justice nor mercy. Many were killed by the very soldiers who could not defeat them in battle, while others were sold as slaves. Their only crime was belief in the truth of the Báb and His Cause.

Quddús was taken to Barfurush, the town of his birth. There the cowardly prince abandoned him to his fate, giving over responsibility for his prisoner to the hate-filled mullá who had first inflamed the townspeople to attack. Barefooted, bareheaded, and in chains, Quddús was paraded through the streets. Finally he was brutally attacked and killed by the mob that followed him.

Those closest to Quddús heard him, in his last moments, whisper a prayer: "Forgive, O my God, the trespasses of this people. Deal with them in Thy mercy, for they know not what we already have discovered and cherish. . . . Show them, O God, the way of Truth, and turn their ignorance into faith."[3]

The siege at Fort Ṭabarsí, which had begun in October 1848, ended in May 1849. More than 170 Bábís had died for their faith. Among the martyrs were nine of the Báb's eighteen Letters of the Living. When the dark news was delivered to the Báb at Chihríq, grief overwhelmed Him.

For nine days He would neither eat nor drink nor admit any visitor. When He thought of the last days of those devoted believers at Ṭabarsí—their agonies, their betrayal, their butchery at the hands of the ignorant—tears rained from His eyes. Night and day He could think of nothing but their suffering. For six months the Báb refrained from revealing any sacred verses, His pen stilled by His grief. Neither the grandeur of His writings nor the beauty of His melodious voice could be heard from His mountain prison. In the corridors beyond the privacy of His cell only the cries of an anguished heart and the sounds of prayer could be heard.

When the Báb finally lifted His pen to write again, it was to the memory of Mullá Ḥusayn that He dedicated His first page. He wrote in praise of Mullá Ḥusayn, Quddús, and all those who had laid down their lives at the Fort of Ṭabarsí. The Báb continued His labor of love for one whole week. Then He instructed a trusted Bábí named Sayyáh to make a pilgrimage on His behalf to Ṭabarsí.

"As you approach the precincts of that hallowed ground," the Báb instructed him, "put off your shoes and, bowing your head in reverence to their memory, invoke their names and prayerfully make the circuit of their shrine. Bring back to Me, as a remembrance of your visit, a handful of that holy earth which covers the remains of My beloved ones, Quddús and Mullá Ḥusayn."

Sayyáh faithfully carried out the mission entrusted to him by the Báb. On his return he stopped at the home of Ḥusayn-'Alí, where Vaḥíd was also visiting. When Vaḥíd learned where Sayyáh had been, he embraced his mud-covered legs and reverently kissed them. They had walked the earth at Ṭabarsí, where the Bábís had chosen to sacrifice their lives for love of the Báb.[4]

Ḥusayn-'Alí would later write about the martyrs who had willingly offered their lives for the Cause of the Báb:

> If these companions be not the true strivers after God, who else could be called by this name? Have these companions been seekers after power or glory? Have they ever yearned for riches? Have they cherished any desire except the good-pleasure of God? If these companions, with all their marvelous testimonies and wondrous works, be false, who then is worthy to claim for himself the truth? I swear by God! Their very deeds are a sufficient testimony, and an irrefutable proof unto all the peoples of the earth. . . .[5]

19

Embattled

The Bábís who had fallen at Fort Ṭabarsí were not forgotten. Their sacrifice inspired Ṭáhirih, Vaḥíd, and the other Bábís to teach the Cause of God with even greater urgency.

Like their spiritual brethren at Fort Ṭabarsí, they did not wish to wage war—only to defeat the enemy of ignorance. The weapons they wielded were the swords of speech and reasoned argument. Their armor was knowledge and truth. Their power lay in the shining splendor of upright character and the fire of their love for the Báb. Armed with these, they won the hearts and minds of people across the land. These were the only victories they desired for the Cause of the Báb.

But the new grand vizier, Mírzá Taqí Khán, had no love in his heart for the Báb and His followers. He fumed with anger whenever he thought of Fort Ṭabarsí and the 313 Bábís who had withstood the shah's army of twelve thousand. More ruthless even than the previous grand vizier, he was determined to rid Persia completely of this new religion. He began with the capital city of Tehran.

Fourteen Bábís in Tehran had been arrested and imprisoned. They would be executed—beheaded in the open square, said the grand vizier. It was possible to save their lives, he told them, simply by saying they did not believe in the Báb. The imprisoned Bábís were tortured, and seven who could not bear the torture denied their faith. Among those who remained steadfast was the Báb's kind uncle, Siyyid 'Alí, who had raised the Báb from childhood.

Just one word of denial, the grand vizier told Siyyid 'Alí, would set him free. But the Báb's uncle refused. To deny that the Báb was a Messenger from God, replied Siyyid 'Alí, would be the same as denying the divine station of Muḥammad, Jesus, and Moses. Never could he do such a thing, even to save his own life.

"I only request of you that you allow me to be the first to lay down my life in the path of my beloved Kinsman," said Siyyid 'Alí.

The grand vizier could find no words to reply. Why should a respected merchant like Siyyid 'Alí—whose friends were willing to pay for his release—choose to give up his life for his young kinsman, the Báb? He would never understand these Bábís. The grand vizier motioned for the Báb's uncle to be taken away for execution.

Outside a crowd gathered to watch the execution of the seven Bábís. Siyyid 'Alí stepped up to the block on which he would lay his head. He turned to face the people of Tehran and spoke: "Hear me, O people. I have offered myself up as a willing sacrifice in the path of the Cause of God. . . . For over a thousand years, you have prayed and prayed again that the promised Qá'im be made manifest. . . . And now that He is come, you have driven Him to a hopeless exile . . . and have risen to exterminate His companions."

He looked around at the friends and neighbors he had known. "With my last breath, I pray that the Almighty may wipe away the stain of your guilt and enable you to awaken from the sleep of heedlessness," said Siyyid 'Alí.

The sword spoke the final word as it fell on the neck of Siyyid 'Alí. It was the last sentence of death in which the executioner would take part.

"When I was appointed to this service," he said, "they undertook to deliver into my hands only those who had been convicted of murder and highway robbery." But now, the executioner lamented, he had been ordered to shed the blood of one who was holy. He walked away and wept for what he had done.

Later he left Tehran and refused anymore to earn his living as an executioner. Another executioner was called to carry out the death sentence for the remaining six Bábís. The seven Bábís were martyred in February 1850.[1]

Ṭáhirih was also arrested in Tehran, where she was taken first before the shah. A woman of her position was not sent to prison, however. Instead, she was taken to the house of the mayor and confined there. But the young shah could not forget the beautiful Ṭáhirih. He wrote a letter, trying to persuade her to forget the Báb. Become a true Muslim again, urged the shah, and he would marry her. She would be honored in his household and would have all that she could desire.

Other women might envy such a royal proposal, but the shah's dazzling promises did not tempt Ṭáhirih. How could she turn her back on the Báb? The shah's wealth and exalted social position were, to Ṭáhirih, merely the fleeting badges of this world. The Báb's teachings removed the veils to life's deeper realities—the treasures of the spirit—which were the only riches that could be carried into the next world.

For Ṭáhirih the choice was clear. She might pay with her life, but she could never deny the Báb. Ṭáhirih rejected the shah's proposal and remained under house arrest.

Abuse of Bábís took place in other parts of Persia, too. In May of 1850, more than seventy Bábís in the town of Nayríz, southeast of Shiraz, were forced to defend themselves against a government army of one thousand men. Led by Vaḥíd, the Bábís of Nayríz gathered in a fort to defend themselves.

Like the Bábís at Ṭabarsí, the courageous Bábís of Nayríz beat back repeated attacks of the army. They did not come out of the fort until four weeks later, when army leaders—like those at Ṭabarsí—made false promises. In the end, all of the Bábís, including Vaḥíd, were killed and their families taken away.

About the same time in May of 1850, the governor of Zanján, a city northwest of Tehran, took action against the Bábís. He ordered the people of that city to divide themselves into two groups—those who believed in the Báb and those who did not. Many families were divided—husband from wife, sister from brother, child from mother. Then the governor ordered all those who believed in the Báb to deny their faith or lose their lives.

The Bábís would not deny their faith. How could they speak against the Báb when they believed that He was, indeed, the promised Qá'im? Led by a noble-hearted Bábí named Ḥujjat, the Bábís of Zanján—three thousand men, women, and children—took refuge in a fort within the city. The governor mustered reinforcements from neighboring villages—more than three thousand men—and, time after time, sent his regiments against the Bábís. Each time they were repulsed.

Ḥujjat wrote an appeal to the shah, but his messenger was intercepted by the governor and killed. Ḥujjat's fair-minded message to the shah was replaced with one of insult and abuse. Upon reading it, the indignant shah at once ordered two regiments with guns and munitions to go to Zanján and commanded that no Bábí there should be left alive. The Bábís took refuge in a fort within the city, where the governor sent his regiments against them.

Once again the courageous Bábís—like those at Ṭabarsí and Nayríz—fought off their attackers. Once again the frustrated army turned the battle into a siege, denying food and water to the Bábís and their families. Days lengthened into weeks. The Bábís, who still refused to deny their faith, remained undefeated.

As the siege at Zanján continued, the grand vizier, who had been thwarted at every turn in his attempts to stifle the new faith, grew angrier than ever. The Báb might be imprisoned in a remote corner of the country, but His Cause continued to spread. Nothing seemed to dampen the enthusiasm of His followers. To crush their spirit, the grand vizier decided, he must eliminate their leader. He ordered that the Báb be brought one last time to Tabríz—this time to be executed.

Forty days before the grand vizier's orders arrived, the Báb gathered together His few belongings—His pen-case, His rings, His precious writings, and the seals with which He stamped the wax that sealed His letters. The Báb sent all of these things with a trusted servant to Ḥusayn-'Alí, along with a special gift—a scroll of fine blue paper embellished with the design of a five-pointed star.

The delicate lines of the star were lines of words written in the Báb's own elegant handwriting—five hundred words all related to the word *"Bahá,"* meaning "Glory." The scroll was a gift of praise from the Báb to Ḥusayn-'Alí, Who had taken the title "Bahá" at Badasht. The Báb had always known what Shaykh Aḥmad had first recognized with the birth of

Ḥusayn-'Alí. This was "the hidden Treasure of God" brought forth into the light of the world. Destined to bring to Persia "incalculable blessings," Ḥusayn-'Alí would fulfill God's greatest promise.

The illustrious teacher Siyyid Káẓim had told his followers that the death of the Qá'im would be like the setting of a star, which was followed by the rising sun. "For when the star of the Former has set," He said, "the sun of the beauty of Ḥusayn will rise and illuminate the whole world."* That sun would be the Promised One of all religions. The Báb had told His followers to look for the Qayyúm (the All-Compelling) to be revealed in the "'*year nine*'"—nine years from 1844, when the Báb had first announced His own mission. He had referred to that Exalted One as "'*Lord of the visible and invisible,*'" and "'*Him Whom God will make manifest.*'"[2] The Báb had even assured certain ones among His followers that they would meet the Promised One.

For Himself, the Báb was satisfied that His work was complete. He was content with the Will of God. Though the grand vizier and others might scheme to extinguish the divine light, the Báb remained untroubled. His trust was in the truth, "they plotted—but God plotted: and of plotters is God the best!"[3]

20

No Peace in the City of Tabríz

The governor of the province refused to execute the Báb. The Báb had committed no crime, and He was a descendant of the Prophet Muḥammad, Who therefore deserved to be treated with honor. "The task I am called upon to perform is a task that only ignoble people would accept," said the governor.

The grand vizier would let no objection stand in his way and turned to his brother, Mírzá Ḥasan Khán, to carry out his command. He must execute the Báb immediately, the grand vizier told his brother, along

* In Shia Islam the Promised One is also considered the return of the Imám Ḥusayn, who was martyred in 680 A.D.

with anyone claiming to be a Bábí. The execution should take place in a public square of Tabríz so that everyone would know of the Báb's death.

Mírzá Ḥasan Khán agreed to do his brother's bidding and prepared to transfer the Báb to a cell in the city barracks to await execution. First he ordered the removal of the Báb's green turban and sash, the emblems of His lineage to the Prophet. Then the Báb and His amanuensis, Siyyid Ḥusayn, were marched to the barracks that housed the soldiers. People crowded and strained to see the prisoner who would be executed. The Báb would receive no honor in Tabríz.

Suddenly a young man broke through the crowd and threw himself on the ground at the Báb's feet. "Send me not from Thee, O Master," he begged. "Wherever Thou goest, suffer me to follow Thee."

"Arise," the Báb answered in a loving voice, "and rest assured that you will be with Me. To-morrow you shall witness what God has decreed." The youth, a Bábí, was arrested and taken to the same prison cell as the Báb. The Báb gave him a new name, "Anís," meaning "Close Companion."

Anís was condemned to die with the Báb, but a sentence of death did not frighten him. For months he had yearned to be with the Báb. His father had locked him in the house to keep him from traveling to Chihríq. He must forget this Bábí foolishness, his father told him, and get on with life's normal activities. But Anís could not forget.

Then, in a dreamlike vision, the Báb had appeared and spoken to Anís. "The hour is approaching when, in this very city, I shall be suspended before the eyes of the multitude and shall fall a victim to the fire of the enemy," said the Báb. "I shall choose no one except you to share with Me the cup of martyrdom. Rest assured that this promise which I give you shall be fulfilled."

The Báb's promise filled Anís with a deep joy that was unreachable by any earthly sorrow. In the days and weeks that followed, the loving voice and tender smile of the Báb, along with His promise, lingered in Anís's memory. Now, at long last, his greatest wish—to be with the Báb—was granted, and Anís was content.[1]

In His barracks cell, the Báb was bound with iron shackles around His wrists and an iron collar around His neck. An attendant tied a long cord to the iron collar and, taking the cord in hand, led the Báb, with a guard of soldiers, through the streets and bazaars of the town. Execution alone would not satisfy the grand vizier. The Báb must be seen helpless and humiliated.

Nearly ten thousand people crowded into the streets and the public square. They had poured into Tabríz from surrounding villages especially to watch the execution. Onlookers jeered and shouted insults at the Báb. If He was from God, let Him save Himself! Let Him perform a miracle! The Báb suffered all in silence until finally He was returned to His cell. The hour of execution was at hand.

When the chief attendant came for the Báb and Anís, the Báb was speaking with Siyyid Ḥusayn, His amanuensis. The attendant would not permit the Báb to complete His conversation. "Not until I have said to him all those things that I wish to say can any earthly power silence Me," warned the Báb. "Though all the world be armed against Me, yet shall they be powerless to deter Me from fulfilling, to the last word, My intention." But the chief attendant paid no heed to the prisoner. The Báb and Anís were taken to the public square.

A firing squad of 750 soldiers prepared for the execution. The officer in charge was Sám Khán, a Christian. Sám Khán was moved by the Báb's noble spirit and greatly disturbed to think that he might execute a holy man. But Sám Khán was also a soldier who must follow orders. What was he to do?

"I profess the Christian Faith and entertain no ill will against you," Sám Khán said to the Báb. "If your Cause be the Cause of Truth, enable me to free myself from the obligation to shed your blood."

"Follow your instructions," the Báb replied, "and if your intention be sincere, the Almighty is surely able to relieve you from your perplexity."

The Báb and Anís were tied together with ropes, Anís with his head resting on the Báb's chest. A nail was pounded into a pillar between the doors of the barracks. With another rope the two prisoners were suspended in front of the firing squad.

The regiment of 750 soldiers lined up in three rows. Each row of soldiers took aim. Then, with a sad heart, Sám Khán gave the final order: "Fire!" One after another, each row fired their weapons. The square filled with smoke, but when the air cleared, the watching crowd saw Anís standing unharmed, his ropes cut by the bullets. The Báb was nowhere to be seen.

The onlookers were astonished. Confusion and fear rippled through the crowd. Was this the miracle for which they had asked? The attendants began a frantic search. They did not have far to go. The Báb was found back in His prison cell, talking to Siyyid Ḥusayn. "I have finished My conversation with Siyyid Ḥusayn," said the Báb calmly when the chief attendant found Him. "Now you may proceed to fulfil your intention."

The chief attendant was deeply shaken. Nothing like this had ever happened to him before. Was this a sign of the power of God? He did not know, but he left the barracks cell and the public square of Tabríz. He gave up his job as chief attendant and never again would have anything to do with the enemies of the Báb.

Sám Khán made his own decision and ordered his regiment to leave. God had spared him from shedding the Báb's blood. He would have nothing more to do with the execution of the Báb, even if it meant his own death for disobeying orders.

Another regiment volunteered to take the place of the first. Once again the Báb and Anís were tied up and suspended against the wall. "Had you believed in Me, O wayward generation," said the Báb to the watching crowd, "every one of you would have followed the example of this youth . . . The day will come when you will have recognised Me; that day I shall have ceased to be with you."

This time, when the rows of soldiers fired their weapons, the Báb and Anís were killed. Their bodies were rendered inseparable by the force of the bullets from 750 rifles. But the faces of the Báb and Anís were left unmarked. A look of calm and peace was upon the face of the Báb. The time was twelve o'clock noon on Sunday, July 9, 1850.[2]

There was no peace in the city of Tabríz that day. From the very hour of the Báb's death, a fierce wind visited the city. With it came a thick, gritty dust that sifted into people's clothes and eyes as the wind whipped through city streets. The dust was so thick that it hid the afternoon sun, and the day grew dark as evening.

The darkness outside was akin to the blindness within of those who had turned their backs on the Messenger of God. They had looked for a king but saw only a merchant from Shiraz. They had closed their eyes to His light and stopped their ears to His truth. They had used their powers to extinguish His life, the life of the promised Qá'im. These lived, indeed, in a dark place.

The Báb had walked upon the earth for the short span of thirty-one years. His mission, from the time He first revealed it to Mullá Ḥusayn that night in 1844, had spanned a brief six years.

"No sooner did He reveal Himself," Ḥusayn-'Alí wrote of the Báb, "than all the people rose up against Him." "How many the edifices which they reared with the hands of idle fancies and vain imaginings, and how numerous the cities which they built! At length those vain imaginings were converted into bullets and aimed at Him Who is the Prince of the world."[3]

The bodies of the Báb and Anís were dragged through the streets of Tabríz. Then they were left, without honor or ceremony, in a moat outside the city gate. No one should move them, on pain of death, warned the authorities, and guards were posted to stand watch.

But Ḥusayn-'Alí, knowing that the Báb was about to be martyred, had already set in motion a plan to recover His sacred remains. In Tehran Ḥusayn-'Alí had summoned the courageous and faithful Ḥájí Sulaymán Khán, who was also highly influential, to carry out the dangerous task. Ḥusayn-'Alí had directed him to travel with all haste to Tabríz.

When Sulaymán Khán arrived in Tabríz, he went to the home of the mayor, who was a personal friend, and told him about his secret plan. The mayor was a man who held no prejudice toward any religious group, and he knew how to help his good friend. He called at once on a fellow known for his daring, Ḥájí Alláh-yár. In the dark of night Ḥájí Alláh-yár, along with a few of his men and two Bábí friends, ventured forth to retrieve the remains of the Báb and Anís. The guards on duty did not dare to interfere, and in the morning told their superiors that wild beasts had devoured the bodies.

Meanwhile, the Bábís wrapped the bodies in an aba and placed them in a wooden chest, which they took to another town. There, in a silk factory owned by a Bábí, the precious remains were wrapped in shrouds and hidden, then placed in a special casket and moved to another safe place. Ḥájí Sulaymán Khán sent a message to Ḥusayn-'Alí, and Ḥusayn-'Alí replied at once with instructions. Bring the casket secretly to Tehran, He directed, and in slow stages. They must not arouse suspicion.

News of the Báb's execution reached the city of Zanján, where those who had taken refuge in the fort continued to hold off their attackers. When the soldiers learned of the Báb's death, they taunted the Bábís. "For what reason will you henceforth be willing to sacrifice yourselves?" they asked. "He in whose path you long to lay down your lives, has himself fallen a victim to the bullets of a triumphant foe. His body is even now lost both to his enemies and to his friends. Why persist in your stubbornness when a word is sufficient to deliver you from your woes?"

Grief-stricken by the news, the Bábís still refused to deny their faith. As the weeks passed, villages near Zanján sent reinforcements for the shah's army. Now there were more than seventeen regiments of soldiers on foot and on horseback and fourteen cannons to be used against the Bábís.

The Bábí women were as strong and active in their defense as the men. Some chose to fight alongside the men, astonishing the enemy with their bravery. Others took care of the sick and carried skins of water on their shoulders to the wounded. They shouted encouragement to those who fought. Several women cut off their long, dark hair and used the thick tresses like rope to wrap around the guns and make them stronger. Even the children helped where they could.

As the siege continued, the summer heat softened into fall, then turned quickly into the bitter cold of winter. Supplies ran low in the fort. The big guns and months of fighting took their toll. Finally, by January 2, 1851, all of the Bábís of Zanján were either killed or captured. It had taken the shah's army seven months and as many as twenty thousand troops well-supplied with munitions and field artillery. Eighteen hundred Bábís had perished, but none had denied their faith.

"The mind is bewildered at their deeds, and the soul marvelleth at their fortitude and bodily endurance. . . ." Ḥusayn-'Alí would later write. "With what love, what devotion . . . they sacrificed their lives. . . . Hath any age witnessed such momentous happenings?"[4]

In the next several months followers of the Báb continued to be beaten, imprisoned, tortured, and killed in the towns and villages of Persia. Through it all they remained steadfast in their faith. The grand vizier wondered how they could keep up their courage, now that the Báb was gone. Did they look to another leader for inspiration? He suspected they did, and he called Ḥusayn-'Alí to come before him at the shah's court.

21

A Promise Kept in Karbala

Although the grand vizier welcomed Him cordially, Ḥusayn-'Alí knew all too well the treacherous spirit that lay behind the welcome. The grand vizier's true intention surfaced soon enough. "I am well aware of the nature and influence of your activities," said Mírzá Taqí Khán. He proceeded to accuse Ḥusayn-'Alí of giving material support and assistance to the Bábís at Ṭabarsí. How else could such a band of frail-bodied men, scholars of religion, have resisted the imperial army for so many months? Wolflike, the predatory grand vizier waited for His reply—and a chance to bring down this influential nobleman.

Ḥusayn-'Alí was wise enough to avoid the trap. He had never made a secret of His belief in the Báb, but He protested strongly the accusations of the grand vizier. That Ḥusayn-'Alí's detention in Amul had prevented Him from assisting the Bábís at Ṭabarsí was a fact of which the grand vizier would remain unaware. Mírzá Taqí Khán would like nothing better than to accuse Ḥusayn-'Alí of plotting a revolution against the shah, but he was unable to ascertain Ḥusayn 'Alí's true position.

Then the grand vizier appeared friendly. He would recommend that the shah appoint Ḥusayn-'Alí to a position as head of the court, said the grand vizier. He must wait, of course, for the shah to return from his trip. Until then, advised the grand vizier, it would be best for Ḥusayn-'Alí to leave the capital city. Mírzá Taqí Khán's suggestion was a thinly veiled order for Ḥusayn-'Alí to leave Tehran.

Ḥusayn-'Alí replied that He had no interest in a government position. He would, however, like to go on pilgrimage to the neighboring country of Iraq. It was agreed. He would leave as soon as possible for the holy cities of Karbala and Najaf,* not far from Baghdad.[1]

* Karbala is the site of the martyrdom and shrine of the Imám Ḥusayn, and Najaf is the site of the shrine of the Imám 'Alí.

As He prepared for the journey, Ḥusayn-'Alí left instructions for His trustworthy brother Mírzá Músá. When the casket with the bodies of the Báb and Anís arrived in Tehran, it was to be hidden, He directed, in a nearby Muslim shrine. This was in accord with the wishes of the Báb Himself, expressed in a tablet in which He addressed the saint buried there: "Well is it with you to have found your resting place in Rayy under the shadow of My Beloved. Would that I might be entombed within the precincts of that holy ground!" The authorities were unlikely to look in the shrine for the sacred remains of the Báb. To guard the location's secrecy, not even the Bábís were to be informed.

Too soon the time came for Ḥusayn-'Alí to leave Tehran. Navváb and the children—seven-year-old 'Abdu'l-Bahá, his younger sister Bahíyyih, and the baby, Mihdí—would stay behind. Pilgrimages were not unusual, and Persian families were accustomed to such separations. Navváb understood that danger simmered in Tehran for her husband. Perhaps calm would return to the capital city in the months He was gone. Perhaps time would quiet the rage of those who waged war against the Bábís. Perhaps. In the meantime Navváb would endure their separation patiently.

Ḥusayn-'Alí tried to convince His younger half-brother, twenty-year-old Mírzá Yaḥyá, to leave Tehran as well. During the Báb's imprisonment in Chihríq, when the Báb and Ḥusayn-'Alí had corresponded, it was agreed to appoint Mírzá Yaḥyá as leader of the Bábís after the Báb's death. This responsibility would last only until the Promised One proclaimed Himself. Mírzá Yaḥyá could be in danger, too, if his position in the Bábí community were discovered by the grand vizier.

From the time of their father's death, when Mírzá Yaḥyá was nine years old, Ḥusayn-'Alí had lovingly looked after His younger half-brother, teaching and guiding him in matters great and small. But this time Mírzá Yaḥyá did not take his brother's advice. When Ḥusayn-'Alí set out on His westward journey to Iraq and the holy city of Karbala, Mírzá Yaḥyá decided to stay behind.

It was June 1851, nearly a year after the martyrdom of the Báb, when Ḥusayn-'Alí left Tehran. Everywhere the followers of the Báb were sad and disheartened. When Ḥusayn-'Alí arrived among the Bábís in Karbala, He found it was no different. The Bábí spirit had ebbed, the life of the community drained along with the lifeblood of their spiritual leaders.

The Bábís' great joy in discovering the promised Qá'im had been cut ruthlessly short by the Báb's untimely martyrdom. Within months they were bereft not only of the Báb, but also of Mullá Ḥusayn, Quddús, and half of the Letters of the Living. The episodes of Ṭabarsí and Zanján had also taught them, if they had ever doubted it, that the followers of this new religion lived in mortal danger. No wonder the Bábís felt dispirited and as directionless as a ship lacking compass or commander.

One Bábí who lived in Karbala was unknown to the others—an old man by the name of Shaykh Ḥasan. Shaykh Ḥasan had served the Báb as a scribe during the months of His imprisonment in Máh-Kú and Chihríq, copying the verses that the Báb had dictated to His amanuensis. When news of the ongoing struggle at Ṭabarsí had reached them in prison, the shaykh had been ready to go and join the others, but the Báb had advised him differently.

"Participation in that struggle is not enjoined upon you," the Báb had said. He told Shaykh Ḥasan to proceed, instead, "to Karbilá and . . . abide in that holy city." There he would behold with his own eyes, the Báb had promised, "the beauteous countenance" of the Promised One.

Shaykh Ḥasan had obeyed the Báb and moved to Karbala, where he married and earned a meager living as a scribe. He never forgot the Báb's promise, but it seemed a promise for the distant future.

One day Shaykh Ḥasan was walking along a market street in Karbala when he saw a man whose extraordinary presence immediately caught his attention. The shaykh stopped and looked more closely, captivated by what he saw—the "exquisite features which no pen or brush dare describe, His penetrating glance, His kindly face, the majesty of His bearing. . . ." The One Who so impressed Shaykh Ḥasan was Ḥusayn-'Alí from Tehran.

Seeing the elderly shaykh bent with age, Ḥusayn-'Alí came to him and took him lovingly by the hand. He spoke to Shaykh Ḥasan and, much to the shaykh's surprise, said, "This very day I have purposed to make you known as a Bábí throughout Karbilá."

They continued to talk and walk together along the market street. At the end Ḥusayn-'Alí said, "Praise be to God that you have remained in Karbilá, and have beheld with your own eyes the countenance of the promised Ḥusayn."

Instantly Shaykh Ḥasan remembered the Báb's promise—a promise that the shaykh had told no one else—and he knew, as deeply and certainly as if the Báb Himself had said it, that His promise was fufilled. Ḥusayn-'Alí, with Whom Shaykh Ḥasan now walked along the market street, was the One foretold by the Báb—the Qayyúm, the Promised One of all religions!

A flood of joy washed over Shaykh Ḥasan. He wanted nothing more than to share with everyone the wonderful news. "Not yet," Ḥusayn-'Alí whispered into the shaykh's ears, "the appointed Hour is approaching. It has not yet struck. Rest assured and be patient."

From that moment, even though he was poor and very often hungry, Shaykh Ḥasan felt rich—so rich that "all the treasures of the earth melted away into nothingness" when compared to the knowledge he held in his heart. The Promised One of God walked among them—the Great One for Whom the Báb had prepared the way This was the Day in which the Prophets of old had yearned to live! Never again would Shaykh Ḥasan find room in his heart for sorrow. It was too filled with gratitude for so great a favor—to live on earth when the earth itself was blessed with the footsteps of these holy ones.[2]

Though the other Bábís remained unaware of what Shaykh Ḥasan knew, they welcomed the presence of Ḥusayn-'Alí in Karbala. With what great love He spoke to them! How He uplifted their spirits! Gently but firmly He strengthened their understanding of the Báb's mission, reminding them of the sacred task with which the Báb had entrusted His followers—to prepare the way for "Him Whom God Will Make Manifest," the Promised One of all religions. Ḥusayn-'Alí's unshakable confidence in the Báb, and His own fearless teaching, rekindled the Bábís' courage and reinvigorated their community.

Not everyone, however, was grateful for Ḥusayn-'Alí's presence in Karbala. Siyyid Muḥammad was one Bábí who chafed with jealousy at every sign of love and respect shown to Ḥusayn-'Alí. He kept his feelings quietly coiled in the hidden recesses of his heart, but even there they did not escape the notice of Ḥusayn-'Alí. During all the months He stayed in Karbala, Ḥusayn-'Alí was patient and said nothing, but Siyyid Muḥammad's malignant feelings only grew stronger. He was happiest when Ḥusayn-'Alí decided, after nine months in Karbala, to return to

Tehran. But their paths were destined to cross again, and then Siyyid Muḥammad would bare the fangs of his true nature.

As He prepared to leave Karbala, Ḥusayn-ʿAlí received an official letter from the grand vizier, inviting Him to return to Tehran. The signature on the letter, however, was not that of the grand vizier who had ordered Him to leave the capital city. That grand vizier had fallen out of favor with Náṣiri'd-Dín <u>Sh</u>áh. He had been dismissed from office and executed.

Persia's latest grand vizier, newly restored to favor, was Mírzá Áqá <u>Kh</u>án. Mírzá Áqá <u>Kh</u>án had not forgotten his days as an outcast, or the kind Bábís of Ká<u>sh</u>án, in whose company he had come to appreciate the Báb's teachings. Nor had he forgotten his promise to those same Bábís while the Báb was still alive. Now that he was grand vizier, with the reins of power in his hands once more, Mírzá Áqá <u>Kh</u>án intended to keep his promise.

22

A Plot against the Shah

The horse's hooves clattered along stony paths as Ḥusayn-ʿAlí rode back across the mountains towards Tehran. Winter snows were melting in the warm sun, and streams of water trickled and splashed down the rocky crevices. New spring grass and wildflowers—purple crocuses, yellow buttercups, red poppies—made a lush carpet on the mountain slopes. The earth smelled fresh and sweet.

It was May 1852 when Ḥusayn-ʿAlí at last entered the gates of Tehran. The new grand vizier, Mírzá Áqá <u>Kh</u>án, sent his own brother, Jaʿfar-Qulí <u>Kh</u>án, to meet Ḥusayn-ʿAlí and invite Him to be the grand vizier's honored guest. The grand vizier had not forgotten his own time of trouble, when no one but Ḥusayn-ʿAlí had helped him.

In those days Mírzá Áqá <u>Kh</u>án had been sent in disgrace from Tehran to the far province of Ká<u>sh</u>án; he had been given neither time nor money to make arrangements for his family. To assist one who was out of favor with the shah could be dangerous, and others in the court kept their distance. Only Ḥusayn-ʿAlí had refused to concern Himself with the politics of the day. As soon as He learned of their plight, Ḥusayn-'Alí had arranged for the family of Mírzá Áqá Khán to join him in Káshán. He had made certain their living expenses were provided, and had asked nothing from Mírzá Áqá Khán for His efforts.

While he was living in Káshán, not knowing what would happen next in his life, Mírzá Áqá Khán had come to know the Bábís and the teachings of the Báb. He was greatly attracted by what he learned and by the warm and intelligent spirit of the Báb's followers. Mírzá Áqá Khán made a promise to the Bábís in Káshán: If ever he regained his lost position in the government, he would do his best to protect the Bábí community.

Now once again Mírzá Áqá Khán was in Tehran, second in power only to the shah, and willing to keep his promise to the Bábís. What better way to repay the kindness of Ḥusayn-'Alí than to use his political power to forge peace between the Bábís and the Persian government?

News of Ḥusayn-'Alí's return from Karbala traveled quickly, as did the news that He was the honored guest of the grand vizier. Everyone wanted to welcome Him home and find out the news from Karbala. Each day so many nobles and officials came to call on Ḥusayn-'Alí that He barely had time to enjoy His own family.

May quickly passed into June, bringing with it the scorching heat of summer. Most people in Tehran lived in flat-roofed homes of sun-dried brick. During the hottest part of the day those who could escaped to their cool, underground cellars. At night they unrolled their bedding on the flat roof and slept under the moon and stars. The wealthy left the city altogether, retreating to their summer homes in the cool mountain villages to the north, known as the Shimírán district. There the harsh sun that baked the city shone a little more kindly.

Ḥusayn-'Alí, too—still an honored guest of the grand vizier—left Tehran for the cool mountainside. It was there that one Bábí watched and waited for a quiet time, when others were not around, to speak privately with Ḥusayn-'Alí. He was known as 'Azím—meaning "the Great One"—a title given to him by the Báb.

When they were alone at last, 'Azím began to tell Ḥusayn-'Alí about a secret plan—a plot to avenge the deaths of the Báb and His martyred followers. Náṣiri'd-Dín Sháh was to blame, claimed 'Azím, for shedding the blood of innocent Bábís. He was to blame for the death of the Báb.

The shah himself must pay for these crimes. 'Azím, with a few other Bábís, planned to assassinate Náṣiri'd-Dín Shāh.

Ḥusayn-'Alí would have nothing to do with 'Azím's reckless plan and warned 'Azím to forget his treachery. Revenge was not among the teachings of the Báb. Nothing would come of such a foolish and dangerous plan but disaster—disaster not only for the conspirators, but for all the Bábís in Persia.

Ḥusayn-'Alí's stern warning rang in 'Azím's ears as he left. It was not the response he had expected, but 'Azím was not ready to give up his plan.

Ḥusayn-'Alí's younger brother, Mírzá Yaḥyá, also knew about 'Azím's plan. Unlike his brother, Mírzá Yaḥyá felt certain the plot to kill the shah would succeed. The Báb, Who had given Mírzá Yaḥyá the title "Ṣubḥ-i-Azal" (Morn of Eternity), had also appointed him temporary head of the Bábí community. This was his opportunity, decided Mírzá Yaḥyá, to show that he was leader of the Bábís. He rode to Tákur, the village where their family home stood, and persuaded Bábís there to put on fighting gear. He planned to be ready, in the chaos that followed the shah's death, to lead the Bábís to a mighty victory.

On the fifteenth day of August, in the foothills of the Shimírán district outside Tehran, Náṣiri'd-Dín Shāh rode leisurely out of the gates of his summer palace with his hunting party. Nobles and officers followed behind, and his usual hunting attendants rode ahead. Some carried lances while others had rifles slung over their shoulders or swords hanging from their saddles. The shah rode some distance from the others, away from the cloud of dust that rose from the horses' hooves and swirled lazily in the air.

Not far from the palace, three men stood by the side of the road, two on the left side of the road and one on the right. They were the three Bábís—Ṣádiq, Fatḥu'lláh, and Qásim—who were to be the deadly instruments of 'Azím's plot. Patiently they waited for the shah to draw nearer. When he was close they bowed low, as any humble man who wished to approach the shah might do, saying, "We are your sacrifice! We make a request!" The shah slowed his pace.

All of a sudden the three men rushed at him. "Rascals, what do you want?" shouted the surprised shah. Ṣádiq ran to the shah's right side and, taking hold of the horse's bridle, fired his gun.

At the same time, Fatḥu'lláh and Qásim fired their guns. The shots cut the collar of pearls around the horse's neck and frightened the animal, causing it to rear and neigh in terror. Ṣádiq grabbed the shah's leg and tried to pull him from his horse. In the confusion, Fatḥu'lláh and Qásim began pulling on the shah's other leg, trying to unseat him from the opposite side. The shah's arm and back burned with pain as he tried to fend off his attackers with his fists.

Hearing the noisy commotion, the royal attendants turned and saw the shah in trouble. Instantly they raced to his defense. Drawing their swords, they killed Ṣádiq on the spot, then pushed Fatḥu'lláh and Qásim to the ground. The two attackers were quickly tied up to prevent their escape. The captives declared themselves to be Bábís, come to avenge the deaths of the Báb and His innocent followers.

In a walled garden near the place of attack the court physician treated the shah's wounds. Among those who gathered outside the walls, no one knew exactly what had happened. In all the excitement and confusion, one rumor took on a life of its own.[1]

"The shah is dead!" whispered people to one another. "Assassins have killed the shah!" Alarmed officials and nobles returned with haste to the capital city. The rumor raced like fire through the marketplace. "The shah has been murdered! Assassins have killed the shah!" In panic, merchants closed their shops and hurried home to their families.

The governor of Tehran ordered his soldiers to prepare for war. The gates of the city were closed, its large guns pointed outward, ready to fire. If the shah had been killed, there might be a plot to overthrow the government of Persia—but who was the enemy?

To everyone's surprise, Náṣiri'd-Dín Sháh rode into Tehran the next morning, alive and well. With great ceremony he visited the mosque and there gave thanks to God for escaping death at the hands of his attackers. The shah had been only mildly injured in the attack, for the three Bábís had not even used the kind of shot that could kill a man. It was a happy ending for the shah but the beginning of a new disaster for the Bábís.

The shaken and angry shah was afraid. His attackers had been Bábís. Other Bábís might still be hiding in the shadows, plotting against him. He wanted their names and ordered that Fatḥu'lláh and Qásim be tortured for the information. Even in the extreme pain of torture, the two would not betray their fellow Bábís. Fatḥu'lláh died when his captors, frustrated because he said nothing at all, finally poured molten lead down his throat. Qásim was also executed.

A tiny handful of conspirators had failed in their attempt to kill Náṣiri'd-Dín Sháh, but their deaths alone did not satisfy the shah. He wanted the Bábís punished—all of them. As Ḥusayn-'Alí predicted, the misguided actions of a few would cost the Bábís of Persia dearly.

Mírzá Áqá Khán, the grand vizier who had wanted peace with the Bábís, could not ignore this terrible crime against the shah. He ordered the immediate arrest of anyone in Tehran who might be a Bábí. The shah's mother, who had no love for the Bábís, urged him on. She turned the full force of her anger toward the one Bábí whom she knew, the one of noble birth who was nearest the court of the shah—Ḥusayn-'Alí.

When the shah's mother raised her voice and called someone an enemy, the people around her paid close attention. She had plotted the death of the previous grand vizier. Now, even Ḥusayn-'Alí might not escape the reach of her wrath.

23

Prisoner

The grand vizier's brother, Ja'far-Qulí Khán, wrote a hasty letter to Ḥusayn-'Alí, warning Him to stay away from the dangers of Tehran: "The Sháh's mother is inflamed with anger," he wrote. "She is denouncing you openly before the court and people as the 'would-be murderer' of her son. She is also trying to involve Mírzá Áqá Khán in this affair, and accuses him of being your accomplice." He urged Ḥusayn-'Alí to stay in hiding on the mountainside until calm returned to the capital city. The letter was sent secretly in the hands of an old and trusted servant, whom he instructed to stay with Ḥusayn-'Alí wherever He might choose to go for safety.

Ḥusayn-'Alí read the letter from Ja'far-Qulí Khán, but He did not choose to go into hiding. Instead, the next morning He mounted His horse and rode calmly toward the headquarters of the shah's army. On His way to the military camp, Ḥusayn-'Alí passed through a village that was home to the Russian ambassador and the seat of the Russian legation. There Ḥusayn-'Alí was met by His younger sister's husband, Majíd, who served as secretary to the Russian legation and whose house adjoined the ambassador's. Majíd welcomed Ḥusayn-'Alí and invited Him into his home. A few officials in the area who recognized Ḥusayn-'Alí sent word at once to the shah. News that Ḥusayn-'Alí had appeared so openly despite the accusations against Him amazed everyone. Náṣiri'd-Dín Sháh himself was impressed with Ḥusayn-'Alí's fearlessness. Nevertheless, he sent an officer to demand that the ambassador surrender Ḥusayn-'Alí.

The Russian ambassador had no desire, however, to deliver the nobleman to so uncertain a fate. He asked, instead, that Ḥusayn-'Alí be allowed to proceed to the nearby home of the grand vizier, Mírzá Áqá Khán. It was agreed, and the Russian ambassador, Prince Dimitri Dolgorukov, acting on behalf of his government, secured the grand vizier's promise to protect Ḥusayn-'Alí as his guest. With assurances from Mírzá Áqá Khán, the ambassador was satisfied that Ḥusayn-'Alí would be safe.[1]

But as the shah's vengeful mother continued to voice her accusations against Ḥusayn-'Alí and the clergy clamored for punishment, Mírzá Áqá Khán grew steadily more uneasy. He had experienced the consequences once before of falling out of favor with the shah. He was not prepared to suffer them again. When the shah's officers arrived at his house, Mírzá Áqá Khán surrendered his guest without protest—despite his promises to the Russian ambassador and to the Bábís in Káshán.

The army officers took Ḥusayn-'Alí roughly in hand and brought Him to their headquarters on the mountainside. "We were in no wise connected with that evil deed," Ḥusayn-'Alí would write about the attack on the shah.[2] But His captors refused to listen and treated their prisoner with neither the respect that He deserved nor with any shred of mercy.

His shoes were removed and the soles of His feet were beaten with bastinado rods. Then Ḥusayn-'Alí was shackled in chains for the walk to Tehran. The hat was snatched from His head. Deprived of shoes, His feet sore and bleeding, Ḥusayn-'Alí was forced to keep pace with the officers on horseback as He made the long, dusty journey bareheaded and barefoot in the blazing heat. Several times He was stripped of His clothes, exposing Him to the scorching August sun.

All along the way, crowds of people jostled to get a look at the prisoner and to jeer their insults at Him, for Ḥusayn-'Alí's enemies had convinced them that He was not only a troublemaker, but also an enemy of the shah. Some in the crowd threw stones at Ḥusayn-'Alí as He passed—that same One Whom they had previously called "Father of the Poor" for His unfailing generosity and kindness to them.

As Ḥusayn-'Alí and His escorts neared their destination in Tehran, an old woman shaking with rage and clutching a stone in her hand stepped from the crowd. "Give me a chance to fling my stone in his face!" she cried out to the guards as they hurried along ahead of her.

Ḥusayn-'Alí turned to his guards when He heard her. "Suffer not this woman to be disappointed," He said. "Deny her not what she regards as a meritorious act in the sight of God."

The journey ended in the heart of Tehran. There Ḥusayn-'Alí was pulled from the glaring sunlight into the thick darkness of the underground prison called *"Síyáh-Chál"*—"the Black Pit." The heavy links of chain clanked and ground together as Ḥusayn-'Alí was led down a dark corridor, then down again—three steep flights of stairs, all wrapped in pitch-black.

The heat stayed on the surface with the daylight. No sunlight ever reached these depths. The air was icy cold and filled with the stench of men deprived, in their confinement, of even the barest necessities. More than a hundred of Persia's worst criminals were imprisoned here—thieves, assassins, and highwaymen—men bereft of hope, for they were not expected to survive the Black Pit.[3]

24

The Black Pit

"""The master, the master, he is arrested—I have seen him!""" A servant rushed into Ḥusayn-'Alí's house in Tehran. The words tumbled out on top of one another as he told Navváb the terrible scene he had witnessed. """He has walked many miles! Oh, they have beaten him! They say he has suffered the torture of the bastinado!""""

Navváb's face turned white as she listened to the news of her husband. """His feet are bleeding! He has no shoes on! His turban is gone! His clothes are torn! There are chains upon his neck!"""[1] Little eight-year-old 'Abdu'l-Bahá and his younger sister and brother started to cry. Why would anyone treat their dear father so cruelly?

When the servant told them about the riotous crowd, incited by the mullás' accusations, it was clear that anything might happen. Fearing the worst, relatives, friends, and servants made haste to leave. Navváb and the children were left at the mercy of whatever trouble might come. The master of the household was protector of family members and servants. With Ḥusayn-'Alí being held prisoner, their protection was gone. Only two servants were loyal and courageous enough to stay with Navváb and the children.

Quickly Navváb gathered up a few of her marriage treasures, then fled from their home with the three children in hand. Mírzá Músá, Ḥusayn-'Alí's loyal brother, helped them escape into hiding. They went to the home of Navváb's kind great-aunt and her husband, Mírzá Yúsif, who was a Russian subject and a friend of the Russian consul in Tehran. Their escape was none too soon.

Before long an uncontrollable mob broke into the mansion of Ḥusayn-'Alí. Like a great beast it moved from room to room, with the people who were part of it pillaging as they went. Whatever they could lay hands on—furniture, carpets, anything of value—was taken away or destroyed. In a few short hours, the house that had always been open to those in need was stripped bare of its treasures.

Navváb cared about only one treasure—her precious Ḥusayn-'Alí. What had they done to Him? And what would happen to Him now in the dreaded Black Pit? Navváb had reason to worry.

For the first three days and nights in that dark prison, Ḥusayn-'Alí was given neither food nor water. The damp prison floor on which He sat was thick with filth and crawling with vermin. The air was rank with the foulest of odors. One of two notoriously heavy chains—called *"Salásil"* (Iron Chains) and *"Qará-Guhar"* (Big and Heavy)—was always fastened around Ḥusayn-'Alí's neck, cutting deep into His skin. The one called "Big and Heavy" weighed 110 pounds. A wooden support, forked at the top, was needed to hold it up.

In the next few days the frenzy increased in the city above Ḥusayn-'Alí's head. From their pulpits in the mosques, mullás passionately denounced the "murderous" Bábís, agitating the people with their words of hate. A servant of one of the Bábís was persuaded by threats of torture to walk through Tehran and point out those who were Bábís and those who would pay a bribe to be set free. As the servant pointed out first this one, then that one, more and more Bábí prisoners joined Ḥusayn-'Alí in the Black Pit—until there were eighty-one altogether.

Navváb, fearing that her presence would endanger the lives of those trying to help her, left the home of her kind aunt. With the help of Mírzá Yúsif, she found two rooms for herself and the children not far from the prison. The delicate jeweled gold buttons, beautifully crafted for the happy day of her marriage, she sold. From that money she was able to pay the jailers to give food to her husband. Mírzá Yúsif, despite the danger to himself, made sure that Ḥusayn-'Alí received the food in prison. By the end of the week, the executions began.

Ṭáhirih, who was among the few remaining Letters of the Living, was also being held captive in Tehran. A delegation of religious leaders, in a series of seven conferences, had questioned her thoroughly about the Báb and His Cause. Ṭáhirih, in her own compelling style, presented clear proofs that the Báb was, indeed, the promised Qá'im. She related verses from the Koran that supported her arguments, but grew steadily more impatient with the mullás' insistence on a literal interpretation of the sacred scriptures. Finally, frustrated with their limited understanding, Ṭáhirih spoke bluntly to her interrogators: "Your reasoning is that of an ignorant and stupid child; how long will you cling to these follies and lies? When will you lift your eyes toward the Sun of Truth?"

The delegation proceeded to formally denounce Ṭáhirih and to recommend she be sentenced to death. Because she was a woman and of renowned family, she remained confined in a room at the house of the mayor of Tehran.

During her time there, the wife of the mayor—though not a Bábí herself—had come to hold Ṭáhirih in great esteem and became her devoted friend. One night Ṭáhirih sent for the mayor's wife, who found her dressed in a gown of snow-white silk as though she were a bride about to be wed. The rich fragrance of the choicest perfume scented the air about her. When the mayor's wife expressed surprise at this, Ṭáhirih replied, "I am preparing to meet my Beloved. . . . the hour when I shall be arrested and condemned to suffer martyrdom is fast approaching."

Her friend wept at the thought of so final a separation, but she listened closely as Ṭáhirih confided her last wishes. She requested that her friend's son accompany her to the scene of her execution and that afterward her body be cast into a pit and covered with earth and stones. Finally Ṭáhirih asked the mayor's wife to lock the door to her room so that she might remain undisturbed in her final devotions.

With great sorrow her friend did as Ṭáhirih bid her. Then the mayor's wife retired to her own room, where she lay upon her bed, sleepless and heartbroken to think of losing so precious a friend. In her room Ṭáhirih awaited her final hour, wrapped in prayer and meditation. Four hours after sunset she was pacing and chanting melodiously a prayer whose words expressed both grief and triumph, when a knock was heard at the door of the house. They had come for Ṭáhirih.

As she bid a final farewell, Ṭáhirih placed in the hand of the mayor's wife a key to a small chest. It contained a few small tokens for her friend as a remembrance of her stay at that house.* "Whenever you open this chest and behold the things it contains," said Ṭáhirih, "you will, I hope, remember me and rejoice in my gladness."

Then the beautiful Ṭáhirih emerged from the safety of the mayor's house into the night, where she mounted the horse brought for her. With what agony of grief did her friend watch as Ṭáhirih rode away, escorted by the mayor's son and the official attendants marching on each side of her, until she was swallowed at last by the dark.

They rode to a garden outside the city gates, where they found the executioner and his lieutenants engaged in drunken behavior. Ṭáhirih gave a piece of fine silken cloth to the mayor's son. "I set aside, long ago, a silken kerchief which I hoped would be used for this purpose," she told

---

* In the chest were found Ṭáhirih's last few earthly possessions. The wife of the mayor recalled finding "a small vial of the choicest perfume, beside which lay a rosary, a coral necklace, and three rings, mounted with turquoise, cornelian [*sic*], and ruby stones" (Maḥmud Khán-i-Kalántar quoted in Nabíl, *Dawn-Breakers,* p. 627).

him. "I deliver it into your hands and wish you to induce that dissolute drunkard to use it as a means whereby he can take my life."

"Interrupt not the gaiety of our festival!" shouted the executioner when the mayor's son approached him. Then he ordered his attendants to strangle Ṭáhirih and throw her body into a pit. The mayor's son gave the kerchief to the attendants.[2]

Before they carried out their orders of execution, Ṭáhirih spoke with the same bold courage she had always shown. "You can kill me as soon as you like," she declared, "but you cannot stop the emancipation of women."[3]

When the deed was done a gardener directed the mayor's son to a freshly dug well left unfinished. With the help of a few others, the mayor's son lowered Ṭáhirih's body into the well and filled it with earth and stones as she had wished. Her noble spirit joined the heroic souls of the Báb and all those who had shed their life's blood in His path.

"O Ṭáhirih! You are worth a thousand Náṣiri'd-Dín Sháhs!" the well-known Turkish poet Sulaymán N'Azím Bey would later lament.[4] But hers would not be the last Bábí life to be sacrificed in Tehran. Many more would follow.

25

Cruel Days

A sound, muffled as if coming from a distance, flowed and ebbed in the night like ocean waves breaking against the shore. Hour after hour it continued until it penetrated the palace of Náṣiri'd-Dín Sháh and reached the shah's own ears. It seemed to be the sound of many voices raised together. That could mean trouble.

"What means this sound?" the shah demanded to know.

"It is the anthem the Bábís are intoning in their prison."

The answer surprised the shah, but it did not change his heart. The Bábís might chant all they wanted in their prison. What did he care? Soon he would be rid of them.

Not far from the shah's palace, in the Black Pit, the Bábís were shackled together in two rows, one row facing the other. Every night, into the early hours of morning, the two rows of Bábís chanted the verses taught to them by Ḥusayn-'Alí. "God is sufficient unto me; He verily is the All-Sufficing!" one row would intone, and the other would answer, "In Him let the trusting trust."

Back and forth they would intone the verse and its response, their voices growing ever stronger and more joyful. In that dark, dismal place their souls were ablaze with the light of the remembrance of God. This was the joyful sound that reached beyond their thick prison walls and into the palace of the shah.

That same spirit greeted the jailer who opened their prison door each morning. Each day the jailer entered the dungeon and called out the name of the Bábí chosen to die that day. When his chains were removed, the chosen man would jump to his feet and embrace with joy each of his companions, then bravely follow the jailer to the place of execution.

One night a little before dawn, when everyone else in the prison was sleeping, a voice awakened Ḥusayn-'Alí. It was the youthful 'Abdu'l-Vahháb, a Bábí who was chained near Ḥusayn-'Alí. He began to relate to Ḥusayn-'Alí a wonderful dream he had just dreamed.

"I have this night been soaring into a space of infinite vastness and beauty," he said with wonder. "I seemed to be uplifted on wings that carried me wherever I desired to go. A feeling of rapturous delight filled my soul. I flew in the midst of that immensity with a swiftness and ease that I cannot describe."

The mystery of 'Abdu'l-Vahháb's dream was clear to Ḥusayn-'Alí. It was a glimpse into the next life—the world a soul enters when it leaves the mortal life of this world. "To-day it will be your turn to sacrifice yourself for this Cause," Ḥusayn-'Alí told him.

'Abdu'l-Vahháb's greatest test, the test of each imprisoned Bábí, was close at hand—to keep his faith even in the face of death. "May you remain firm and steadfast to the end," said Ḥusayn-'Alí. Then 'Abdu'l-Vahháb would find himself in that world of which he had dreamed, Ḥusayn-'Alí assured him, soaring with swiftness and ease, his soul filled with that same delight.

Morning arrived and with it the jailer who entered their cell and called out the name of the one to die that day. The name he called was 'Abdu'l-Vahháb. When the jailer unshackled him 'Abdu'l-Vahháb got up and embraced each of his fellow Bábís, one by one. He was not afraid. The wonder and joy of his dream and Ḥusayn-'Alí's assurances had strengthened his heart.

Finally he embraced Ḥusayn-'Alí. At that moment in their dark dungeon, Ḥusayn-'Alí discovered that 'Abdu'l-Vahháb had no shoes. Ḥusayn-'Alí removed His own shoes and gave them to 'Abdu'l-Vahháb, sharing with him as well a few last words of encouragement. When 'Abdu'l-Vahháb walked forth to his execution, Ḥusayn-'Alí's love went with him each step of the way.

The executioner returned later, praising the courageous spirit of 'Abdu'l-Vahháb—a spirit he had manifested to the very end. Ḥusayn-'Alí was thankful to know that 'Abdu'l-Vahháb's spirit would now be soaring in that vast and beautiful realm of which he had dreamed.[1]

Above the prison, a wild excitement had taken hold of Tehran. Fanatic mullás condemned the Bábís as "infidels," a charge that enraged faithful Muslims. An infidel did not believe in Muḥammad, the Prophet of God; he dishonored Islam. These things were not true of Bábís, but unlike the more fair-minded mullás, those who were fanatics did not care about the truth. They were concerned that the new faith threatened their own power and prestige.

Nor did the mobs try to discover the truth. They were intent on dealing out punishment. Infidels were not simply killed by the shah's executioner. They were handed over to be put to death by ordinary people. As each condemned Bábí—man or woman—was brought forth, a noisy crowd gathered to watch. To the loud, steady beat of a drum the ordeal would begin. Bakers and butchers, shoemakers and blacksmiths—each group used its own cruel inventions to inflict their punishment.

But these days the crowds could not be fully satisfied, for most Bábís did not shrink away in fear or cry out in their suffering. Each endured the barbaric and painful tortures without flinching. Chanting prayers, they praised God and asked forgiveness for their murderers. The angry onlookers only cursed and shouted for more, while through it all, the steady drumbeat continued.

The cruel sounds sifted into the small rooms where the children of Ḥusayn-'Alí clung to their mother. Only in the dark of night or the twilight of early morning could Navváb leave, braving the danger to learn the latest news. Each day she went to the home of her kind aunt, whose husband brought news from the court. Each day she asked the questions that she carried in her heart: Who had been executed? What had they done to her beloved Ḥusayn-'Alí?

Navváb often took her eldest son, 'Abdu'l-Bahá, with her. Six-year-old Bahíyyih stayed behind with her little brother, Mihdí. Bahíyyih would wrap her slender arms around Mihdí as they listened in the dark to the horrible sounds outside. Shivering with terror, they would wait for their mother's return. Even she might not escape the mobs, for women and children were not spared. How they clung to her skirts with relief when she arrived!

Days passed into weeks this way. How the children longed for their father's return—especially 'Abdu'l-Bahá. So strong was his desire to see his beloved father that he was willing to go to the dreadful prison itself. A prison official agreed to allow a visit, and Isfandíyár, the family's faithful manservant, brought 'Abdu'l-Bahá to the Black Pit. They entered the narrow doorway of the prison, 'Abdu'l-Bahá carried on the strong shoulders of Isfandíyár. Halfway down the dark stairs 'Abdu'l-Bahá heard his father's voice say, "'"Do not bring him in here."'"[2]

Isfandíyár obeyed and returned outside with 'Abdu'l-Bahá, but they did not go home. Each day the prisoners were brought out of the dungeon for an hour in the prison yard. If 'Abdu'l-Bahá could not visit, perhaps he could see his father from a distance. At noon the prisoners emerged from the Black Pit into the bright daylight. 'Abdu'l-Bahá spied his father among them, but he hardly recognized the man he saw.

Ḥusayn-'Alí was chained to several other men, His back bent under the chain's heavy weight. His beard and hair were matted, His neck bruised and swollen from the heavy steel collar He wore. He walked with difficulty, for His feet had not healed from the beating with the bastinado rods. 'Abdu'l-Bahá's tender heart was so overwhelmed at seeing his dear father in that terrible state that he fainted and had to be carried home unconscious by Isfandíyár.

Hardships continued, coming in many guises for their family. Often when 'Abdu'l-Bahá ventured out onto the streets, he was harassed by other boys. When they saw him they would crowd around him shouting loudly, "Bábí! Bábí!" 'Abdu'l-Bahá usually ignored their shouts. Quietly he would go about His business and return home.

One day a rougher, more menacing gang of boys chased after 'Abdu'l-Bahá. As they shouted, "Bábí! Bábí!" they picked up stones and threw them at him. To their surprise, young 'Abdu'l-Bahá turned around to face them. Then He ran straight toward the gang of bullies with such a look of determination that they all stopped, turned around, and ran away in fear. 'Abdu'l-Bahá could hear their voices in the distance, "The little Bábí is fast pursuing us! He will surely overtake and slay us all!"

But 'Abdu'l-Bahá had no desire to fight. Once he had chased them away, he turned back and began walking home. One man had seen the whole encounter. "Well done, you brave and fearless child!" he shouted. From that day on, none of the boys on the streets of Tehran bothered 'Abdu'l-Bahá again.[3]

September turned to October, then November. Food, and the money to buy it, grew scarce for Navváb and the children. Their kind aunt and uncle and Ḥusayn-'Alí's brother Mírzá Músá helped when they could. Others were too afraid of danger to themselves to help a Bábí family. One day there was nothing to eat—not even bread—only a handful of plain flour for each child to soothe the pangs of hunger.

Ḥusayn-'Alí's younger brother Mírzá Yaḥyá was no help at all to his brother's family. When Mírzá Yaḥyá thought the shah would be assassinated, he had gone to Tákur to raise an army of Bábís. His actions had raised the suspicion that a Bábí rebellion was stirring, and a regiment of soldiers had been sent to Tákur. They burned the village and killed many who lived there as they hunted for Bábís. The Bábís who survived were imprisoned in Tehran with Ḥusayn-'Alí, where they awaited execution.

All the while Mírzá Yaḥyá was in hiding like a frightened animal, far away from Tehran and Tákur. The Báb had appointed Mírzá Yaḥyá leader of the Bábís during this time before the Promised One was revealed, but Mírzá Yaḥyá was too afraid to think of anyone but himself.

Deep in the Black Pit of Tehran, weighted with one or the other of the notorious chains, Ḥusayn-'Alí thought day and night about the Bábí community. "What could have led a people so high-minded, so noble, and of such intelligence," He wondered, "to perpetrate such an audacious and outrageous act against the person of His Majesty." Ḥusayn-'Alí resolved that He would, upon His release from prison, "arise . . . and undertake, with the utmost vigor, the task of regenerating this people."[4]

Then one night He heard these words on every side: "'Verily, We shall render Thee victorious by Thyself and by Thy Pen. Grieve Thou not for that which hath befallen Thee, neither be Thou afraid, for Thou art in safety. . . .'"[5] And in that Black Pit, blanketed in darkness and surrounded by men not expected to live, Ḥusayn-'Alí experienced something truly wonderful.

26

The Mystery of God and His Treasure

Rest was difficult for Ḥusayn-'Alí in the Black Pit, but when He was able to sleep a little He experienced the first powerful stirrings of something deep within His soul. It felt as if something flowed from the crown of His head over His breast, like "a mighty torrent" plunging to earth from a lofty mountaintop. "Every limb of My body would, as a result, be set afire," He would write later. "At such moments My tongue recited what no man could bear to hear."[1]

In the darkness of that foul prison, He heard "a most wondrous, a most sweet voice" calling above His head. Turning His face, He saw a radiant Maiden suspended in the air before Him. She was, He knew intuitively, "the embodiment of the remembrance of the name of My Lord." Her face shone with joy and the good-pleasure of God.[2]

"Betwixt earth and heaven she was raising a call," He would declare, bringing "tidings which rejoiced My soul, and the souls of God's honoured servants." Pointing her finger at Ḥusayn-'Alí's head, she proclaimed to all in heaven and on earth:

> By God! This is the Best-Beloved of the worlds, and yet ye comprehend not. This is the Beauty of God amongst you, and the power of His sovereignty within you, could ye but understand. This is the

> Mystery of God and His Treasure, the Cause of God and His glory unto all who are in the kingdoms of Revelation and of creation, if ye be of them that perceive.[3]

The Holy Spirit, which had appeared as a Burning Bush to Moses, as a Dove to Jesus, as the angel Gabriel to Muḥammad, and in distinct form to every Prophet—signaling for each the beginning of His mission from God—appeared now as a chaste and radiant Maiden to Ḥusayn-'Alí.

"I lay asleep on the bed of self when lo, Thou didst waken me with the divine accents of Thy voice," Ḥusayn-'Alí declared, "and didst unveil to me Thy beauty, and didst enable me to listen to Thine utterances, and to recognize Thy Self, and to speak forth Thy praise, and to extol Thy virtues, and to be steadfast in Thy love."[4]

From this hour forth He was more than Ḥusayn-'Alí, son of Mírzá Buzurg; more than Bahá (Glory), Whom the Bábís knew at Badasht. The mantle of Prophethood lay upon His shoulders, and Ḥusayn-'Alí was now Bahá'u'lláh—"the Glory of God." But His authority lay in His service to the Divine Will and Purpose. "I find myself to be as a leaf," He wrote, "which lieth at the mercy of the winds of Thy decree, and is carried away whithersoever Thou dost permit or command it. . . . Thy Cause is not in my hands, but in Thy hands . . . the reins of power are held not in my grasp but in Thy grasp, and are subject to Thy sovereign might."[5]

The Báb had told His followers to look for "Him Whom God Will Make Manifest," Who was to come shortly after Him. That Promised One would appear "'in the year nine,'" He had told them.[6] Now it was the ninth year after the Báb had first declared His mission to Mullá Ḥusayn in 1844. The time was complete.

The Bábís were not alone in their expectations of a Promised One. The followers of every great religion expected the coming of a Great Teacher promised to them by God. Jews expected the King of Glory, to Whom all nations would turn. Zoroastrians expected the Sháh-Bahrám to bring peace to the world. Buddhists awaited the Maitreye, the Buddha of universal fellowship. Hindus awaited the Tenth Avatar, a World Educator. Christians awaited the return of Christ, Who had told His followers to look for the Spirit of Truth, "Who will guide you to all truth."[7]

Muslims awaited the Mahdí, or Mihdí, meaning "One Rightly Guided," Who would be, more specifically, the return of the Imám Ḥusayn (also known as the Qá'im) for Shia Muslims and for Sunni Muslims, the descent of the "Spirit of God" (Jesus Christ).

Other peoples, too—among them, the diverse nations of American Indians—expected the imminent coming of a Great Redeemer and Teacher, promised to each in accordance with their own sacred traditions. Bahá'u'lláh, "the Glory of God," was that Holy One destined to fulfill, one and all, those Divine Promises.

This was the call for which all humankind had yearned. How would they now respond to the One Who was sent in answer to their prayers?

"I entreat Thee . . . O my God," wrote Ḥusayn-'Alí—now Bahá'u'lláh, "to open the eyes of Thy people that they may recognize in this Revelation the manifestation of Thy transcendent unity . . . Cleanse them . . . O my God, from all idle fancies and vain imaginations, that they may inhale the fragrances of sanctity from the robe of Thy Revelation and Thy commandment. . . ."[8]

A legend in Persia told of a celestial tree that grew in the northern province of Mázindarán. The branches of this marvelous tree would reach to heaven, the legend predicted, and its fruit would be "for the life of nations."[9] Many had searched for the wondrous tree, but none had discovered it. Little did they guess, as they watched Ḥusayn-'Alí grow to manhood under their eyes, that He was the Heavenly Tree planted in their midst—the divine Messenger sent to fulfill the promises of God. His fruits, yet to come, were for all—justice and peace and the healing of humankind.

At the very time Bahá'u'lláh was cast into the Black Pit in August 1852, astronomers were amazed at what appeared to be a wonder in the heavens. An unusual comet had revisited the sky. It was named Biela's Comet and had first been sighted in 1826, reappearing every 6.6 years thereafter. But when it appeared again in 1846, the comet broke into two, and in 1852 the fragments returned as twin comets that were never seen again. Half of the original comet shone brightly in the night sky. The other half glowed more faintly in the background, with over a million miles between them. The rare twin comets were a cause of much excitement, for astronomers had never before seen such a phenomenon.

The story of the twin comets was like the story of the Báb and Bahá'u'lláh—two divine Messengers Whose missions were linked as one. The Báb, Who prepared the way for Bahá'u'lláh, had shone brightly at first. Later, with His mission complete and His earthly life at an end, the Báb was like the comet-half that glowed faintly in the background. Now was the appointed time for Bahá'u'lláh—like the bright portion of the comet—to shine forth.

"Praised be Thou, O my God! How can I thank Thee for having singled me out and chosen me above all Thy servants to reveal Thee," wrote Bahá'u'lláh. "I testify, O my God, that if I were given a thousand lives by Thee, and offered them up all in Thy path, I would still have failed to repay the least of the gifts which, by Thy grace, Thou hast bestowed upon me."[10]

But the time was not yet right to tell others. Ruthless enemies were all around. They had put the Báb to death and, like ferocious beasts, were determined to kill as many of His followers as possible. If God's promises were to be fulfilled, Bahá'u'lláh's secret must be guarded until the time was right to reveal it.

The shah's mother, who continued to rage against Bahá'u'lláh, was a most dangerous enemy. "Deliver him to the executioner!" she demanded.

A few who wished to gain her favor poisoned the food that Bahá'u'lláh's family sent to Him in prison. Bahá'u'lláh detected the poison as soon as He tasted the food. Though He ate no more, He would not escape the poison's ill effects for a long time to come.

Authorities tried to persuade 'Azím, who had plotted to kill the shah, to name Bahá'u'lláh as a fellow conspirator. They took 'Azím to the Black Pit, hoping to induce him to denounce Bahá'u'lláh. 'Azím refused to ease his own situation by accusing Bahá'u'lláh, though he knew that the truth would surely mean his death.

"The Leader of this community was none other than the Siyyid-i-Báb,* who was slain in Tabríz, and whose martyrdom induced me to arise and avenge His death," declared 'Azím. "I alone conceived this plan and endeavoured to execute it." His only helpmates, 'Azím insisted, were

---

* Refers to the Báb; *siyyid* is an honorific title denoting one's lineage as a descendant of the Prophet Muḥammad.

the three Bábís who had attacked the shah on the road. Bahá'u'lláh had had nothing to do with it.[11]

Convinced finally that 'Azím was speaking the truth, the authorities took him from the prison and turned him over to the mullás, who immediately put him to death. 'Azím's plot to kill the shah had precipitated much bloodshed. Bahá'u'lláh, nevertheless, praised 'Azím for speaking the truth in that dark and difficult hour. "'In truth he was 'Azím, a great one,'" said Bahá'u'lláh.[12]

Even though 'Azím had confessed that he alone was the instigator behind the attempt to kill the shah, some determined mullás were still calling for Bahá'u'lláh's execution. One day in the court that decided these matters, the Russian ambassador unexpectedly stood up. He was the same Russian prince who had protected Bahá'u'lláh for a time before his arrest. Now he spoke fearlessly in defense of Bahá'u'lláh.

"'"Have you not taken enough cruel revenge? Have you not already murdered a large enough number of harmless people . . . ? . . . Has there not been sufficient of this orgy of brutal torture to satisfy you? How is it possible that you can even pretend to think that this august prisoner planned that silly attempt to shoot the Sháh?

"'"It is not unknown to you that the stupid gun, used by that poor youth, could not have killed a bird. . . . You know very well that this charge is not only untrue, but palpably ridiculous.

"'"There must be an end to all this."'"

Then the Russian prince gave a stern warning. "'"I have determined to extend the protection of Russia to this innocent nobleman,"'" said the ambassador to the court, "'"therefore beware! For if one hair of his head be hurt from this moment, rivers of blood shall flow in your town as punishment."'"[13]

That night, when they learned about the speech of the Russian ambassador, Navváb and the children wept for joy. 'Azím's confession and the Russian ambassador's warning worked together in Bahá'u'lláh's favor. Bahá'u'lláh had been proved innocent of any crime. There was no reason to keep Him prisoner. Four months after He was led in chains from the daylight down into the cold Black Pit of Tehran, Bahá'u'lláh was finally released.

Even as He regained His freedom Bahá'u'lláh did not think only of Himself. Determined to help the Bábí community, He did not go directly home, but proceeded first to the place of government. There He requested to speak with Mírzá Áqá Khán, the powerful grand vizier, who had once made a promise to the Bábís.

27
Banished

Bahá'u'lláh stood before the grand vizier dressed in the dirty, ragged clothes of a prisoner. His body was bruised and cut from the heavy chains He had worn, His feet still not healed from the bastinado beating. Yet He stood with a strength and dignity of spirit that even the Black Pit could not diminish.

Bahá'u'lláh's battered condition did not soften the heart of Mírzá Áqá Khán. "Had you chosen to take my advice," said the grand vizier, "and had you dissociated yourself from the faith of the Siyyid-i-Báb, you would never have suffered the pains and indignities that have been heaped upon you."

"Had you, in your turn, followed my counsel," Bahá'u'lláh replied, "the affairs of the government would not have reached so critical a stage."

The grand vizier recalled what he had once told Bahá'u'lláh—that the death of the Báb would be the end of His Cause. But Bahá'u'lláh had replied at the time, "The flame that has been kindled will blaze forth more fiercely than ever." His prediction had proven all too true.

The Cause of the Báb had spread, and so had the violence against the Bábís. Everywhere in Persia the followers of the Báb were suffering. Authorities arrested and imprisoned them. Mullás stirred their countrymen to violence against them, while government officials gave them no protection. Order in the land had given way to daily bloodletting and chaos. Even hardened executioners were amazed at the uncontrolled cruelty of the mobs.

"The warning you uttered has, alas, been fulfilled," admitted the grand vizier. "What is it that you advise me now to do?"

"Command the governors of the realm to cease shedding the blood of the innocent," Bahá'u'lláh replied, "to cease plundering their property, to cease dishonouring their women and injuring their children. Let them cease the persecution of the Faith of the Báb; let them abandon the idle hope of wiping out its followers."

The grand vizier followed Bahá'u'lláh's advice. That same day he sent an order addressed to all the governors of the realm, telling them to stop their cruel acts. "What you have done is enough," the grand vizier wrote. "Cease arresting and punishing the people. Disturb no longer the peace and tranquillity of your countrymen."

At last there was rest from the killing. The bakers and butchers, shoemakers and blacksmiths, put away their shameful instruments of torture. The sound of drumbeats was no longer heard in the market square. The terrible noise of mobs bent on murder gave way to the more usual noises of the marketplace. Things seemed almost as they had always been, but they were not. In the bloodbath of killing, many thousands of Bábís had died—men, women, and children.* Only small numbers of Bábís remained here and there, but their spiritual leaders were gone, and the Cause they loved so dearly seemed in danger of disappearing.

Still the shah and his government were not satisfied. They wanted no trace of the Báb and His Cause left in Persia. As soon as Bahá'u'lláh was released from prison, He was ordered to leave the country. The Russian ambassador invited Him to go north to Russia, but Bahá'u'lláh declined that offer. Instead, He received permission to go west to Iraq, to the city of Baghdad and its surrounding area. Bahá'u'lláh and His family were allowed one month to prepare for the journey.[1]

Even such harsh news could not dampen the joy of Navváb and the children. To see Bahá'u'lláh walk through their door again was a cause for happiness beyond measure! He was alive—and freed from Tehran's terrible prison. Oh, how delicious to embrace their own dear father and husband once more!

Their tears of joy were mingled with tears of sorrow to see Bahá'u'lláh's pitiful condition. His skin bore ugly cuts where the heavy chains had held Him. The untreated wounds on His feet hobbled His steps with pain. He could not eat plain, coarse food. One month was too short a

---

* An estimated ten to thirty thousand Bábís were killed in the early years of the religion (see Nabíl, *Dawn-Breakers*, p. 605 n1).

time to heal the wounds from four months in the Black Pit, but they would do the best they could.

They could not return to the mansion they had called home in Tehran. That house had been plundered in the early days of His imprisonment. Nor could they go to the family home in the village of Tákur. After Mírzá Yaḥyá's attempt to raise an army, that house had been pillaged and burned to the ground.

With Bahá'u'lláh in need of recovery, the family found refuge in the home of his half-brother, Mírzá Riḍá-Qulí, who was a doctor. His wife, Maryam, a cousin of Bahá'u'lláh, was also a devoted Bábí. Slowly, with proper food, medicine, and the loving care of Navváb and Maryam, Bahá'u'lláh began to regain His strength.

During those days of healing, Bahá'u'lláh said little about His own suffering in the Black Pit. Later He would write about the "stainless hearts and sanctified souls" of the Bábís imprisoned with Him. He would praise their fortitude in that dreadful place and their courage in the face of death. "Instead of complaining, they rendered thanks unto God," He wrote, "and amidst the darkness of their anguish they revealed naught but radiant acquiescence to His will."[2]

Bahá'u'lláh said nothing about the Maiden who had spoken to Him in prison, nor about His sacred mission from God. Yet He could not hide the new radiance that enveloped His being. His family wondered at it but could not guess His secret. Only nine-year-old 'Abdu'l-Bahá knew, with a certainty beyond his years, that the One foretold by the Báb—the Promised One—was their own father returned home. But young 'Abdu'l-Bahá also knew the danger that surrounded them and kept His silence.

The days grew busy with preparations for the journey to come. Two of Bahá'u'lláh's brothers, Mírzá Músá and sixteen-year-old Muḥammad-Qulí, helped to find some of the family's scattered belongings. Both Mírzá Músá and Muḥammad-Qulí had been cared for by Bahá'u'lláh after the passing of their illustrious father, and they would serve Bahá'u'lláh faithfully for the rest of their lives.

As the family's possessions were sold, the money was used to buy food and other provisions. Navváb sold her jewels, embroidered garments, and other precious bits she had saved from her marriage treasures. The money they brought was not nearly as much as their true worth. Altogether the family had barely enough to supply them for their journey.

Their loyal servant, Isfandíyár, added his own meager savings to help the family he loved. Navváb had sent Isfandíyár away from Tehran into safety when their troubles began, but the faithful Isfandíyár would not abandon the family he served. Despite the dangers, he had returned. How often did Bahá'u'lláh praise the excellent character of Isfandíyár, who had never failed to live up to Bahá'u'lláh's praise. Alas, Isfandíyár could not accompany them on their journey, although he wished to do so. The governor of Mázindarán desired his service and would not release him.

All too soon came the day for their departure. It was January, and winter had set in. The youngest child, four-year-old Mihdí, was too sickly to make the hard winter trek over the mountains. He would stay behind with his grandmother, the mother of Navváb, until the seasons turned warm and he was strong enough to travel. How Navváb hated to leave her little Mihdí! Navváb herself was in full pregnancy with another child.

On January 12, 1853, Bahá'u'lláh and His family, escorted by a Persian officer and a Russian official, set out on their journey west to Baghdad. Bahá'u'lláh's two brothers who had helped prepare for the journey rode with them. Although the brothers had not been named in the order of banishment, they had chosen to share the family's exile. Navváb and seven-year-old Bahíyyih rode in a howdah, a covered seat for two people that was strapped on the back of a mule or horse. Young 'Abdu'l-Bahá was old enough to ride on horseback in the company of his uncles and the other men.

No one except Navváb's mother came to say good-bye. It was still not wise to be seen in the company of Bábís. Who could know what new terrors might be visited upon them?

The family of exiles passed through the southwest gate of Tehran, leaving behind the city that Bahá'u'lláh would call "the holy and shining city." "Let nothing grieve thee, O Land of Ṭá [Tehran]," Bahá'u'lláh would later write, "for God hath chosen thee to be the source of joy of all mankind. . . . Rejoice with great joy, for God hath made thee 'the Dayspring of His light,' inasmuch as within thee was born the Manifestation of His Glory."[3]

Bahá'u'lláh would praise, as well, the many Bábís of Tehran who had sacrificed their lives for the Cause of God. "How vast the number of those sanctified beings, those symbols of certitude, who, in their great love for thee, have laid down their lives and sacrificed their all for thy sake! . . . Which one of the multitude of thy sincere lovers shall We remember, whose blood hath been shed within thy gates, and whose dust is now concealed beneath thy soil? . . . Our Pen is moved . . . to extol the victims of tyranny, those men and women that sleep beneath thy dust."[4]

The group of exiles would never enter the gates of Tehran again. Once beyond the borders of Persia, they would never again see their homeland. They were banished forever from the life they had known and the people they had loved. One day the name of Bahá'u'lláh, "the Glory of God," would be honored by people in every nation on earth, but His hardships were far from over, and His greatest struggles were only just beginning.

28

Terrible Journey

With every step of the mule, the howdah on its back jostled and swayed like a boat in rough seas. Inside, little Bahíyyih rode with her pregnant mother, Navváb. Another howdah carried the family of Mírzá Músá, Bahá'u'lláh's brother. Bells jingled on the harnesses of the other mules and horses, packed with provisions.

Baghdad lay six hundred miles to the southwest, on the far side of the Zagros Mountains. In the early stages of their journey, they crossed the Persian plains. Then the little caravan began the long days of climbing upward—across the Saveh Pass, across the icy and dangerous Qara Char River. The final stage lay across towering, snow-covered mountains.

The winter was harsh, its cold "'so intense that one cannot even speak,'" wrote Bahá'u'lláh, the "'ice and snow so abundant'" that it was "'impossible to move.'"[1] The travelers suffered continually from the cold. They had had neither the time nor the money in Tehran to make the warm clothing needed for such a journey.

The howdahs provided some protection from the sharp winds, but young 'Abdu'l-Bahá and the men on horseback had none. They rode for hours in the piercing cold. 'Abdu'l-Bahá was stricken with frostbite on his feet and fingers, with painful effects that would last a lifetime.

Mile after mile, the animals plodded across the frozen mud of rocky paths and made their way through the snow. They could travel only fifteen to twenty miles a day. At night they sometimes camped outdoors in the wilderness. Other times they stayed in the simple stone rooms of a caravansary, a basic roadside inn for travelers.

At the caravansary they were allowed only one room for each family and for one night only. There were no beds on which to sleep, and no light was permitted in the rooms at night, but it was a shelter from the winter outside. There they could sip some hot tea, share a few eggs between them, or eat a little cheese and coarse bread—except for Bahá'u'lláh. Still recovering from the effects of prison, He could not eat the rough food.

Navváb was beside herself with worry, for Bahá'u'lláh seemed to grow weaker from lack of food. One day she got a little flour to make something special for Him. That night when they stopped at a caravansary, Navváb set out to make a sweet cake. But when she reached in the dark for sugar, she picked up salt instead. In spite of her loving intentions, the cake could not be eaten.

The exiles traveled on. Whenever they came to a town or city, they spent some time at the public baths. Every Persian town had a building for its public bath, where the local people gathered. On certain days the women came; on other days the men. In the steamy rooms, while they soaped and scrubbed and cleaned, they also talked and joked together.

After days on the road, the baths were a welcome relief to the bone-weary band of exiles. How good the warm water felt on their skin! Navváb also washed their clothes at the baths, but drying them was nearly impossible. Often she had to carry the cold, wet clothes in her arms. Her delicate hands grew chapped and painfully sore.

Even in the midst of her own troubles, Navváb never complained. Large with child and sharing her husband's exile, still she always looked for the heart that needed cheering. Day to day Navváb shared a kind word here, a kind deed there—wherever she saw the need. She remained the "Mother of Consolation," even as she was when she had been counted among the rich and favored of Tehran.

After 350 miles—a little more than halfway to Baghdad—the caravan stopped in the Persian town of Kirmanshah, and here they rested for several days. They stayed at a small, two-story inn built around a large inner courtyard. The animals and baggage were kept on the ground floor of the inn. The travelers took the upper rooms, where mats were spread on the floor for sleeping.

The small band of exiles did not expect to meet anyone they knew in this faraway place. What a surprise for them when Bahá'u'lláh's younger brother Mírzá Yaḥyá came to their door! Mírzá Yaḥyá had been appointed by the Báb as an interim leader of the Bábís until the Promised One revealed Himself. But when their troubles began he had disappeared, and no one knew where he had gone.

Mírzá Yaḥyá had kept himself hidden, moving from place to place. Disguised as a seller of burial shrouds, he had settled for a time in Kirmanshah, but no one there knew his real name. Now, when Mírzá Yaḥyá discovered that Bahá'u'lláh and the others were on their way to Baghdad, Mírzá Yaḥyá said that he, too, would like to go to Baghdad. He wished to live near his brother, he said, but in his own house.

Bahá'u'lláh gave Mírzá Yaḥyá a little money, and Mírzá Yaḥyá bought some bales of cotton. When Bahá'u'lláh and the others left Kirmanshah, Mírzá Yaḥyá did not go with them. He traveled, instead, on his own route to Baghdad, now in the disguise of a cotton merchant. He was still too fearful to let anyone else know his true identity.

The small caravan of exiles set out on the last stage of their journey—the hard crossing of the high Zagros Mountains. Once again they climbed upward through mountain passes blanketed in snow. More icy rivers lay ahead of them. Mile after freezing mile, each weary traveler reached deep into his soul for the strength to persevere. Days passed slowly into weeks.

February turned to March as they finally traveled down the last mountains and out of Persia. Spring flowers showed their colors in the valleys, and trees were covered with the soft green fur of spring buds. At last they reached the frontier of the Ottoman Empire. A group of Turkish soldiers came to escort them to the city of Baghdad. The Persian and Russian officers who had traveled with them returned to Persia.

It was nearly March 21, the date of the spring equinox and of Naw-Rúz—the Persian New Year. Bahá'u'lláh asked His brother Músá to ride ahead of the caravan and rent an orchard. There they would make camp and celebrate the days of Naw-Rúz.*

Naw-Rúz was a joyful and generous time in Persia—a festival celebrated there for centuries. People packed baskets of delicious food for picnics in the country. They wore new clothes and visited friends, and those who could gave out gold coins. In every Persian home a dish of wheat or lentil sprouts grew into tall, green shoots. On the thirteenth day of the new year, the dish of green shoots was thrown into a stream of running water. It was hoped that bad luck—like the green shoots in the swiftly moving stream—would be carried away from their homes in the new year.

Bahá'u'lláh and the other exiles had neither new clothes, gold coins, nor mouthwatering feasts, but they had survived the terrible journey. Ice, snow, and freezing mountain winds were left behind. The campsite chosen by Músá was next to an orange grove, and the scent of orange blossoms wafted over them. Date palms grew all around. The green of winter wheat and barley stretched over the fields beyond. But their Naw-Rúz joy was bittersweet. Perhaps it was the sweet songs of birds that reminded them of Persia, the homeland they had left behind forever. At least they could be grateful to have one another.

They could be grateful for even more. Everything Bahá'u'lláh's enemies had devised, He told them, had come to nothing. Bahá'u'lláh had not died in the Black Pit. The family had not perished in the cruel winter journey of exile. These things were not a matter of Naw-Rúz luck. They were part of the plan of God. Bahá'u'lláh's enemies had plotted to destroy the Cause of the Báb, but it, too, would survive and flourish. Bahá'u'lláh well knew what had been revealed in the Koran: "They plotted—but God plotted: and of plotters is God the best!"[2]

On April 8, 1853—three months from the time the exiles had left Tehran—Bahá'u'lláh and His family entered the eastern gate of Baghdad. The city they entered was a city of sixty thousand people in a province of the fading Ottoman Empire. A thousand years before, Baghdad had been a city of more than a million people—capital of the Islamic world.

---

* *Naw-Rúz* means, literally, "New Day."

Through the centuries the city had survived wars, fires, and floods. Though it was no longer the city of splendors or the center of learning it had once been, Baghdad remained a crossroads of travel and trade.

The little caravan did not draw much attention. Travelers came to Baghdad every day. They came from lands as far away as China, India, and Africa. They came in caravans of camels and mules, or in boats along the river. The great Tigris River flowed through the city, dividing it in two—the eastern half of Baghdad on one side, the western half on the other.

Here in the ancient city once called "the Abode of Peace" by its founder,* Bahá'u'lláh and His family would make their new home.[3] But in their early days in Baghdad they would know more struggle than peace.

---

* Abu-Ja'far al-Manṣúr, one of the Islamic leaders with the title of caliph, founded the city as the capital of his empire in the year 763.

Part 2
The Sun in Its Splendor

29
Baghdad

The exiles moved into a small house in Baghdad. The extreme hardships of their journey lay behind them. Now they set about making their home in a strange city. There was much to be done. The task of organizing the household fell mainly upon Navváb.

Just as in Persia, there was marketing to do and meals to prepare. Rice bought at the market had to be cleaned, usually by spreading it in a flat basket and tossing it into the air where the breeze would blow away the outer chaff. Then it would be picked clean of small bits of stone and straw.

Laundry needed to be washed, often by stirring it with a long stick in a big pot of boiling water, then hanging it out to dry in the sun. Water for every need was drawn by hand from a deep well at the house. The bucket in the well was heavy, and the ropes for pulling it up were thick and rough.

Navváb struggled with the household work. The winter journey, along with her pregnancy, had worn down her strength. At the mansion in Tehran there had been servants to carry out these daily tasks. But Bahá'u'lláh and His family were no longer wealthy. They could not hire servants to help them with the work.

Bahá'u'lláh was saddened to see the hardships Navváb endured. He sometimes helped with the cooking to lighten her load, but He could do little else. He was still recovering from the ills of His days in prison.

It was Bahá'u'lláh's kindhearted brother Mírzá Músá who came to their rescue. He pulled the heavy buckets of water from the well and helped with the never-ending laundry. Mírzá Músá's best talent, though, was in cooking, and before long he had quite willingly taken over that task.

Mírzá Músá's kind help was especially welcome in the following weeks. Navváb gave birth to a baby boy—the sweet burden she had carried in her womb all through their bitter journey. Now their new home was blessed with new life.

Two months after their arrival in Baghdad, the exiles had a guest. Mírzá Músá opened the door to find a dervish standing with his begging box in hand. It was a good disguise. Not even Mírzá Músá recognized that the dervish standing before him was Mírzá Yaḥyá, once again seeking out Bahá'u'lláh. When Mírzá Yaḥyá revealed who he was, the family made him welcome.

Mírzá Yaḥyá stayed with them only a few days. Even now he did not feel safe and insisted they tell no one else of his arrival in Baghdad. Although Mírzá Yaḥyá was the appointed leader of the Bábís, the persecutions in Persia had made him fearful. He wanted no one—especially the Bábís—to know where to find him.

In Baghdad Mírzá Yaḥyá disguised himself anew. He wore a large turban on his head and, assuming the name of Ḥájí Furú<u>sh</u>, took up a new trade as a charcoal dealer. He set up shop on the street of the charcoal dealers in the bazaar and moved into a rundown part of the city. No Persians lived there, and no one there knew his real name. Most important to Mírzá Yaḥyá was that no one there knew he was a Bábí.

Still, Mírzá Yaḥyá took no chances. He stayed inside during the day and came out only at night. Late in the night, he often came to the house where the exiles lived and would visit with Mírzá Músá. But Mírzá Yaḥyá insisted that no Bábís were to visit him and that no one was to reveal his true identity. Any Bábí who disobeyed his wishes, Mírzá Yaḥyá threatened, would be expelled from the Bábí community.

Bahá'u'lláh urged Mírzá Yaḥyá to take courage and return to Persia, where he was needed to serve the Cause of the Báb. The Bábís in Persia were in a dispirited state following the martyrdom of the Báb and the horrible persecutions there. Not only were they fearful of further attacks from without, but they were also plagued by divisions within.

There were no printed books of the Báb's writings—only a few handwritten copies. Some Bábís could not even read. The brilliant teachers of the faith—Quddús, Mullá Ḥusayn, Ṭáhirih, Vaḥíd—all were gone. Educated believers like Mírzá Yaḥyá, who had had opportunity to read and study the Báb's writings, were needed to teach the others and uplift their spirits.

Bahá'u'lláh Himself had vowed to assist the Bábís when He was released from prison, but He could not return to Persia. Mírzá Yaḥyá could. He had not been named in the government's order of banishment, and he was free to travel wherever he wished. But Mírzá Yaḥyá cared more about his own safety than he cared about the Bábís. He refused to return to Persia.

While Navváb, with Mírzá Músá's help, handled the challenges of the household, Bahá'u'lláh gradually regained His strength. At length He was able to turn to the challenge of revitalizing the Bábí community.

Bahá'u'lláh found the Bábís in Iraq as dispirited as those in Persia. The lionhearted Ṭáhirih had inspired countless souls in Baghdad, but now the Bábís in that region had lost all heart and seemed paralyzed by fear. They would not even be seen together in public. "The fire of the Cause of God had been well-nigh quenched in every place," wrote one Bábí, adding that he could detect "no trace of warmth anywhere."[1] Now Bahá'u'lláh's thoughts turned toward reviving those dying embers.

Bahá'u'lláh had shown no fear in Persia when He was hunted by the shah's army. He had been fearless in the Black Pit of Tehran, where even as a prisoner He had lifted the spirits of the Bábís imprisoned with Him. In Baghdad, too, Bahá'u'lláh acted without fear.

As soon as He was able Bahá'u'lláh came out of His house and walked openly on the public streets. He visited the coffeehouses, where it was the custom for men to gather and talk. He visited with the Bábís and let others know that He, too, was a Bábí.

Bahá'u'lláh still did not tell anyone that He was the Promised One and made no claim to be leader of the Bábís. No one in Baghdad knew of the Maiden He had seen in the Black Pit or of His mission from God.

Yet nearly everyone, from the ignorant to the educated, recognized something different in Bahá'u'lláh. The people of Baghdad, like those in Persia, were naturally attracted by the warmth of His loving-kindness and His gentle sense of humor. Though Bahá'u'lláh was an exile stripped of worldly riches, they recognized that He possessed a wealth of knowledge and wisdom and a dignity that hardship had not erased. They could also sense in the presence of Bahá'u'lláh the mantle of majesty that was His and His alone.

Gradually, inspired by His example, the Bábís in the Baghdad region shed their fears and ventured out once more. Because of Bahá'u'lláh, others began to show the Bábís more respect, and a new confidence took root in the Bábí community.

Mírzá Yaḥyá saw it all and grew more jealous by the day. The Báb had appointed Mírzá Yaḥyá to be leader of the Bábís until the Promised One made Himself known. Yet once again it was his brother Who received loving attention and respect from people all around. Still in disguise and hiding, Mírzá Yaḥyá was blind to the fact that his own actions—so different from his brother's—were the true cause of his unhappiness. He only brooded and wished for things to be different.

Very soon Mírzá Yaḥyá would forge a dark friendship with another jealous soul. Together they would scheme to make Mírzá Yaḥyá's wishes come true.

30

Thousands of Oceans of Light

Near the edge of the great Tigris River, gardens flourished under the summer sun. Melons fattened on the vine. Prickly cucumbers ripened to a smooth green. Orange and lemon trees filled with their sweet and sour fruits. The Baghdad air shimmered with heat, even in early morning.

Bahá'u'lláh, well enough to travel now, set out to visit the Bábís in Karbala, to the south of Baghdad. At times the road followed one of the many canals cut into the land. The canals carried slender streams of water from the Tigris to the thirsty fields beyond.

The precious waterways were hubs of village activity. Women talked together as they washed their cooking pots or laundry in the nearest canal. Village farmers led their water buffalo there to drink. When sheep were sheared, the wool was washed in the canal before the work of carding and spinning. Closer to Karbala, weary pilgrims rested and washed their hands and feet in the canal's cool water.

Shia Muslim pilgrims came from far and wide to the city of Karbala. Hundreds of years before, their beloved leader, the Imám Ḥusayn, had been killed in Karbala. His death made the city a holy place to the Shia Muslims. Traders and travelers of all kinds also came to the holy city. But Bahá'u'lláh traveled to Karbala with a different purpose: to rekindle the spirit of the Bábís as He had done in Baghdad itself.

Karbala had already earned a place in Bábí history. There the learned Siyyid Káẓim had prepared his followers to look for the promised Qá'im. After the learned siyyid's death, Mullá Ḥusayn had set out from the holy city on his quest for the Promised One and had been the first to find the Báb, "the Gate."

Bahá'u'lláh Himself had visited Karbala in 1851, after the martyrdom of the Báb. There Shaykh Ḥasan had recognized Him as "Him Whom God Will Make Manifest"—the One promised by the Báb. He was eager to tell others, but Bahá'u'lláh had whispered into his ear, "Not yet. The appointed Hour . . . has not yet struck." Nor had that hour come yet; none but Bahá'u'lláh would know when the time was right to reveal His Cause.

Now, two years later, Bahá'u'lláh once more inspired the Bábís of Karbala with their noble purpose. His own fearless example and the healing balm of His love for them revived their ailing spirits. Again, as in Baghdad, those who were not Bábís were also drawn to the noble and wise Bahá'u'lláh.

Bahá'u'lláh stayed at the home of one of the Bábís in Karbala, where He liked to spend the hot summer nights on the flat roof, as people often did. There He chanted His prayers under a canopy of stars and slept in the fresh night air.

One night Bahá'u'lláh invited a new believer who had just arrived in Karbala to join Him on the roof. Bahá'u'lláh was already sleeping when the sixteen-year-old youth, Mírzá Áqá Ján, spread out his bedding nearby on the carpet and lay down for a brief rest. Later he got up to say prayers, but just as he began, he saw Bahá'u'lláh rise and walk toward him.

""*You, too, are awake,*""said Bahá'u'lláh, Who then began to pace back and forth in the moonlight and to chant in a rich, melodious voice. Mírzá Áqá Ján could not take his eyes away from Bahá'u'lláh as he listened with rapt attention to the verses He intoned. But nothing could have prepared Mírzá Áqá Ján for the mystery that Bahá'u'lláh would reveal to him.

"Methinks, with every step He took," Mírzá Áqá Ján would later recall, "and every word He uttered thousands of oceans of light surged before my face, and thousands of worlds of incomparable splendor were unveiled to my eyes, and thousands of suns blazed their light upon me! . . . Every time He approached me He would pause, and, in a tone so wondrous that no tongue can describe it, would say: *'Hear Me, My son. By God, the True One! This Cause will assuredly be made manifest.'*"[1]

Bahá'u'lláh continued pacing and chanting until the first light of dawn. At that early hour Mírzá Áqá Ján prepared tea for Bahá'u'lláh—so ordinary an act to follow so extraordinary an experience. What in this world could ever compare to that moonlit night on the rooftop in Karbala?

Mírzá Áqá Ján was neither learned nor rich; in Ká<u>sh</u>án he had been a maker of soap. But he was also a seeker of truth who had seen the Báb in his dreams and believed in Him. He had read the writings of Bahá'u'lláh and left his home in Ká<u>sh</u>án to come and learn from Him. Yet he had never expected this. Bahá'u'lláh had allowed him a glimpse of another world—a wondrous realm of the spirit—and Mírzá Áqá Ján could never forget it.

From that night on, Mírzá Áqá Ján knew with certainty that Bahá'u'lláh was the Promised One sent by God. He wanted nothing more than to remain in the presence of Bahá'u'lláh and to serve Him.

Bahá'u'lláh allowed Mírzá Áqá Ján his heart's desire, permitting him to serve as His amanuensis, who would write the tablets Bahá'u'lláh revealed. For the next forty years Mírzá Áqá Ján would serve Bahá'u'lláh, writing down the divine tablets He revealed and the letters He dictated, and sending them to believers near and far.

The other Bábís of Karbala did not see the "thousands of oceans of light" that Mírzá Áqá Ján saw. They saw only that Mírzá Áqá Ján began to treat Bahá'u'lláh with even greater reverence and devotion than before. They were not surprised. People all around loved and admired Bahá'u'lláh. But one Bábí, Siyyid Muḥammad, did not.

Siyyid Muḥammad's jealousy had not abated since Bahá'u'lláh's last visit. Although Bahá'u'lláh had been aware of Siyyid Muḥammad's hostile feelings even then, He had said nothing. Now, once again, Siyyid Muḥammad chafed to see Bahá'u'lláh receive the respect and reverence that he desired for himself.

Never mind that his own faith—tested at the death of the Báb—had proven weak and shallow. When the Bábís desperately needed the guidance and comfort of a leader, Siyyid Muḥammad had provided neither. Although he showed none of the qualities that were so resplendent in Bahá'u'lláh, nevertheless, he was ambitious and cunning.

With Bahá'u'lláh living in nearby Baghdad, Siyyid Muḥammad looked for a way to stir up trouble for Him. He found the perfect tool for his scheme in Bahá'u'lláh's younger half-brother, Mírzá Yaḥyá.

Like Siyyid Muḥammad, Mírzá Yaḥyá was ambitious and jealous of the attention showered on his elder half-brother. Yet Mírzá Yaḥyá paid scant attention to the many Bábís who had tried to meet with him. They had turned with their questions to him—the one appointed by the Báb as temporary leader of the Faith—but Mírzá Yaḥyá continued to keep his distance, disguised as the charcoal dealer Ḥájí Furú<u>sh</u>. The few who did meet with him face-to-face came away disappointed.

One believer pleaded with Mírzá Yaḥyá until he agreed to meet with him—not in town, where people might see them, but on a hilltop outside of Baghdad. There Mírzá Yaḥyá asked the believer to guess the distance between two telegraph poles, which were new to the countryside, and talked about other trivial things. At the end of their meeting the believer—who had longed to hear wise and loving words—left no more enlightened than when he arrived.

Another believer wanted to unravel the mystery of a verse from the Koran and asked Mírzá Yaḥyá to write a commentary. For some time Mírzá Yaḥyá put him off, but finally he could avoid the matter no longer and agreed to write the commentary. Although he had lived in disguise for a number of months, in his writing Mírzá Yaḥyá could not hide himself. The commentary that he wrote was a mirror to his own soul—a mirror that reflected but a shallow understanding of spiritual reality.

The believer, bitterly disappointed, turned to Bahá'u'lláh with the same request. Without delay Bahá'u'lláh revealed a tablet both beautiful in its language and profound in its spiritual insight. When the believer finished reading it, he understood the meaning of the Koranic verse. And he gained another insight that was even more important: Bahá'u'lláh was the real spiritual leader—the One whose announcement they all awaited, that Holy One promised by the Báb. The believer would have told everyone at once, but Bahá'u'lláh cautioned him to wait. The time was not yet right.

Most Bábís who met Mírzá Yaḥyá were disappointed, for they saw in him nothing of the qualities of a spiritual leader. He was leader of the Bábí Faith in title only. Still, Mírzá Yaḥyá dreamed of being honored by the Bábís as Bahá'u'lláh was honored. Timid by nature, Mírzá Yaḥyá did not know how to achieve what he wanted—until he met Siyyid Muḥammad.

Siyyid Muḥammad sought out Mírzá Yaḥyá and became friendly with him. He managed skillfully to gain Mírzá Yaḥyá's trust. When they talked together about Mírzá Yaḥyá's ambitions and his frustrations with Bahá'u'lláh, Siyyid Muḥammad agreed heartily with everything Mírzá Yaḥyá said. It pleased Mírzá Yaḥyá to find such a sympathetic friend—and Siyyid Muḥammad told him just what he wanted to hear.

Even better, Siyyid Muḥammad proposed to help Mírzá Yaḥyá. After all, Baghdad and Karbala, where Siyyid Muḥammad lived, were not so far apart. If they worked together, they could accomplish everything.

The cunning Siyyid Muḥammad knew how to manipulate truth and falsehood. He could bring down Bahá'u'lláh, Siyyid Muḥammad promised, and then the position of honor would belong to Mírzá Yaḥyá. To Mírzá Yaḥyá it sounded like a fine plan, and the two conspirators began their dark campaign.

31

The Dark Campaign

Siyyid Muḥammad did not stand and accuse Bahá'u'lláh face-to-face. He was more cunning, lying in wait with a few words of criticism here, a few more fault-finding words there, and hints spoken slyly into the ears of faithful Bábís. He knew the power of lies unleashed behind one's back—of rumor presented as if it were truth. It was not the first time Siyyid Muḥammad had caused trouble. In Persia, before he became a Bábí, Siyyid Muḥammad had been expelled from a religious school because of his disgraceful behavior. He had not given up his old ways.

Mírzá Yaḥyá himself, though still in hiding, carried out his part in Siyyid Muḥammad's plan. With the help of a Persian merchant who acted on his behalf, Mírzá Yaḥyá disseminated his own misguided instructions to the Bábí community and made accusations against Bahá'u'lláh that he could never say in His presence.

Gradually, with Mírzá Yaḥyá as his partner, Siyyid Muḥammad grew bolder in his accusations. Bahá'u'lláh's activities in Baghdad and Karbala were all part of a scheme, he told the Bábís. Bahá'u'lláh was plotting to take Mírzá Yaḥyá's rightful place as leader of the Bábís.

The campaign of lies caused suspicion to rear its ugly head among the Bábís. Doubt replaced the confidence that Bahá'u'lláh had inspired. Some Bábís joined Mírzá Yaḥyá and Siyyid Muḥammad in their attacks on Bahá'u'lláh. The mischief-makers criticized everything that Bahá'u'lláh did. They twisted the meaning in the letters and commentaries that

Bahá'u'lláh wrote. Other sincere Bábís became confused. They admired Bahá'u'lláh, but now they did not know what to think.

"'*The days of tests are now come,*'" Bahá'u'lláh would write. "'. . . *The Banners of Doubt are, in every nook and corner, occupied in stirring up mischief. . . .*'" Bahá'u'lláh was not fooled. He knew the source of the vicious campaign against Him. The secrets of their hearts—the "odors of jealousy," "malice, envy, and hate"—were not hidden from Him.[1]

"A number of people who have never inhaled the fragrance of justice," wrote Bahá'u'lláh, "have raised the standard of sedition, and have leagued themselves against Us. On every side We witness the menace of their spears, and in all directions We recognize the shafts of their arrows. This, although We have never gloried in any thing, nor did We seek preference over any soul. To everyone We have been a most kindly companion, a most forbearing and affectionate friend."[2]

Bahá'u'lláh was especially saddened that Mírzá Yaḥyá, His own younger half-brother, was one of the mischief-makers. After the death of their father, when Mírzá Yaḥyá was only eight years old, Bahá'u'lláh had showered His younger brother with loving care and protection. When the Báb declared His mission in 1844, Bahá'u'lláh had helped Mírzá Yaḥyá, who was then thirteen, to recognize and accept the Báb as God's Messenger, the promised Qá'im. He had encouraged Mírzá Yaḥyá to read for himself the writings of the Báb.

Later, Mírzá Yaḥyá took pride in the titles given to him by the Báb: *Mir'átu'l-Azalíyyih* (Everlasting Mirror), *Ṣubḥ-i-Azal* (Morning of Eternity), and *Ismu'l-Azal* (Name of Eternity).[3] The Báb gave inspiring titles to many of His followers. But now Mírzá Yaḥyá, who had been nineteen when the Báb was martyred, claimed greater significance for his titles. The Báb had chosen him, said Mírzá Yaḥyá, to take His place as leader of the Bábís.

In truth, the Báb had named Mírzá Yaḥyá as a temporary leader for the brief period before the Promised One made Himself known. Now, encouraged by Siyyid Muḥammad's meddling, Mírzá Yaḥyá imagined grander things for himself. He cared little that the rumors he was spreading about his brother, and the damage they inflicted on the Bábís, pierced Bahá'u'lláh's heart like arrows.

For some time Bahá'u'lláh endured the mischief-makers with patience, but their attacks against Him continued. "I swear by God, the one true

God!" wrote Bahá'u'lláh, "grievous as have been the woes and sufferings which the hand of the enemy and the people of the Book inflicted upon Us, yet all these fade into utter nothingness when compared with that which hath befallen Us at the hand of those who profess to be Our friends."[4]

One early morning before sunrise, Mírzá Áqá Ján saw Bahá'u'lláh suddenly come out of His house, greatly disturbed. "*'These creatures are the same creatures,'*" he heard Bahá'u'lláh say angrily, "*'who for three thousand years have worshipped idols, and bowed down before the Golden Calf. Now, too, they are fit for nothing better.'*"[5]

Mírzá Áqá Ján stood motionless, rooted to the spot by the power of Bahá'u'lláh's utterance. It was clear that His anger was directed at those who put their own selfish ambitions above the Cause of God. Then Mírzá Áqá Ján heard Bahá'u'lláh say, "*"Bid them recite: 'Is there any Remover of difficulties save God? Say: Praised be God! He is God! All are His servants, and all abide by His bidding!' Tell them to repeat it five hundred times, nay, a thousand times, by day and by night, sleeping and waking, that haply the Countenance of Glory may be unveiled to their eyes, and tiers of light descend upon them."*"[6]

Still the situation did not change. Division and difficulties among the Bábís grew worse. When Bahá'u'lláh prayed, "Is there any Remover of difficulties save God," a prayer revealed by the Báb, His face was filled sadness. All of Bahá'u'lláh's efforts to unify the Báb's followers and regenerate the Bábí community were being undone.

"*'Oceans of sadness have surged over Me,'*" wrote Bahá'u'lláh, "*'a drop of which no soul could bear to drink.'*" "*'Give ear . . . to the voice of this lowly, this forsaken ant, that hath hid itself in its hole,'*" He wrote, "*'and whose desire is to depart from your midst, and vanish from your sight, by reason of that which the hands of men have wrought.'*"[7]

At last Bahá'u'lláh did just that. Very early on April 10, 1854, while the household slept, Bahá'u'lláh quietly left His home. He told no one, not even His beloved family, where He was going. One servant, Abu'l-Qásim, came with Him.

"The one object of Our retirement," Bahá'u'lláh later wrote, "was to avoid becoming a subject of discord among the faithful, a source of disturbance unto Our companions, the means of injury to any soul, or the cause of sorrow to any heart."[8]

Bahá'u'lláh took nothing more with Him than one change of clothes and a small wooden bowl for alms. When He and His servant walked out of the gates of Baghdad, they headed north toward the Zagros Mountains. Safety lay behind them, within the city walls. Ahead lay the wilderness of Kurdistan—a wild and lonely country, dangerous with bandits. Unlucky travelers could be robbed and killed. Who could say if the two travelers from Baghdad would ever return?

32

Alone in the Wilderness

Bahá'u'lláh and Abu'l-Qásim traveled the long, dusty road by foot. Day by day they climbed higher and deeper into the mountains. There was no hurry. No loved ones waited to meet them at their journey's end.

Two hundred miles north, near the town of Sulaimaniya, Bahá'u'lláh parted company with Abu'l-Qásim. He gave His servant a sum of money and told him to start a small business and earn his living as a merchant. Then Bahá'u'lláh walked on alone, away from the town, past the fields of grazing sheep and goats.

Bahá'u'lláh did not stop walking until He was near the top of a mountain called Sar-Galú, three days' journey from the nearest human habitation. Only a few peasants from the village of Sar-Galú came this far up the mountain, and then only twice a year—once in the fall to sow their crops of barley or wheat, and again in the spring to harvest the grain. A crude stone shelter built as protection from the weather was all that they left behind.

Here in the wilderness, where His only companions were "'*the birds of the air*'" and "'*the beasts of the field,*'" Bahá'u'lláh made His home.[1] When He slept, His dwelling place was nothing more than a cave, or sometimes a crude shelter left by the peasants. His clothes were the coarse clothes of the poor, and His meals were bare—a little bread and cheese, sometimes a cup of milk or some rice.

Here, in the wilderness of Kurdistan, the thick velvet silence of the mountainside was undisturbed by the gossiping tongues and intrigues of men. All that could be heard were the calls of sparrows and hawks in the sky, the buzz of insects amid the sunbaked rocks, and the melody of the mountain winds.

Bahá'u'lláh had removed Himself from Baghdad for good reason, like a doctor who diagnoses an illness and prescribes the healing remedy. *"'I shunned all else but God,'"* wrote Bahá'u'lláh, *"'and closed Mine eyes to all except Him, that haply the fire of hatred may die down and the heat of jealousy abate.'"* [2]

Here on the mountain Bahá'u'lláh spent His time in prayer and meditation. Here, where the heavens met the earth, He communed with His Creator and sought to ease His suffering soul.

"From Our eyes there rained tears of anguish, and in Our bleeding heart surged an ocean of agonizing pain," said Bahá'u'lláh. "Many a night We had no food for sustenance, and many a day Our body found no rest. . . . Alone, We communed with Our spirit, oblivious of the world and all that is therein."[3]

In His prayers to God at dawn and in the night, Bahá'u'lláh asked for strength to endure His suffering at the hands of both enemies and friends. Separated now even from the comfort of His beloved family, He lamented His loneliness as God's Messenger in this world. He contemplated, too, the grievous troubles and suffering yet to come.

"'Pour out patience upon Me, O My Lord!'" He wrote in one prayer, *"'and render Me victorious over the transgressors.'"*[4]

Yet His solitude on the mountain was suffused with joy as well as anguish. Bahá'u'lláh had not yet proclaimed that He was the Promised One sent by God and foretold by the Báb. Now Bahá'u'lláh praised God and the Maiden who personified the Spirit of God within Him. He praised "the glories and mysteries" of His revelation from God and promised to offer His life for the Cause that God had entrusted to Him. At such times, in spite of His "showers of afflictions," wrote Bahá'u'lláh, His soul was "wrapt in blissful joy."[5]

As a youth He had found comfort, from time to time, among the mountains of Mázindarán, outside of Tehran. This time, when Bahá'u'lláh withdrew to the mountains of Kurdistan, He had no plans as to when He would return home.

In Baghdad Navváb and the children were filled with sorrow. They did not know where Bahá'u'lláh had gone or when He would return, and they longed for His loving presence.

Of everyone in the family, Navváb knew best, perhaps, what Bahá'u'lláh had suffered, and she had learned long ago to trust His wisdom. She knew how He loved the children and her, and she knew that Bahá'u'lláh had left because of the jealous and hateful actions of others. Instead of competing for leadership of the Báb's Faith, He had left behind the joys of their family life to do what was best for the Cause of God.

Even in their sorrow, Navváb and the children would carry on in Baghdad. How many families in Persia—fathers, mothers, and children—had already shed their blood for this Cause? The sacrifice of those lives could not be forgotten or belittled because of the selfish ambitions of a few. The hardships of Navváb and the children would, for now, be their sacrifice for the Cause of God.

In the time before He left Baghdad, Bahá'u'lláh had invited Mírzá Yaḥyá and his family into their home. Bahá'u'lláh had offered them hospitality and told His own family to treat Mírzá Yaḥyá with kindness and to respect and obey his wishes.

Navváb and the children did their best to be faithful to Bahá'u'lláh's instructions, but Mírzá Yaḥyá was a troublesome houseguest. He complained about the food, even though he received the best the family had to offer. He did not help with the work, nor did he allow anyone else to come to the house and help.

Every day little Bahíyyih spent hours drawing water from the deep well in the house. Only eight years old, she struggled with the rough ropes to pull up bucket after bucket of water with her slender arms. Sometimes Navváb helped, but she was not strong either, and there was other work to do. Mírzá Yaḥyá showed no concern for little Bahíyyih's struggles.

Sometimes, when she felt lonely, Bahíyyih would open the front door a little and shyly peek out. She could see two little girls, about the same age as herself, who lived in the house next door. How she longed to meet them and become friends! But Mírzá Yaḥyá would not allow it. Whenever he saw little Bahíyyih standing at the door and looking out, he shouted at her, then roughly closed the door and locked it.

Mírzá Yaḥyá did not allow anyone in the household to go outside—not even to the public baths. No one was allowed to come in. He kept the house locked and raged at anyone who dared open the door. Timid and cowardly, Mírzá Yaḥyá lived in terrible fear, fear that he might be arrested for being the current Bábí leader. He could think of nothing but his own safety.

When the baby became sick, Mírzá Yaḥyá would not allow a doctor to visit, nor even a neighbor. The baby, the sweet little boy born shortly after the family's arrival in Baghdad, grew more and more ill, and at last he died. Navváb was heartbroken.

Even then, Mírzá Yaḥyá permitted no one to come in to the house and prepare the baby's body for burial. Instead, the children watched as the small body of their baby brother was handed over to a man they did not know. He took it away, and Navváb never knew where the body of her dear little child was laid to rest.

It was difficult to treat Mírzá Yaḥyá with respect when he acted with such heartless disregard for them all. Now, more than ever, Navváb and the children missed Bahá'u'lláh and longed for Him to come home. But months passed, and still Bahá'u'lláh did not return.

When the family moved into a larger house, Mírzá Yaḥyá decided not to move in with them. He was too afraid of being seen and chose instead to move to a small house behind theirs. At last they had some relief! They sent him food and provided for his family, but he was no longer part of their daily life. Navváb and the children could now move about their home, free of Mírzá Yaḥyá's watchful eyes and his angry shouting.

If only their beloved Bahá'u'lláh would return! With the help of a family friend, they questioned travelers for news of Bahá'u'lláh. No one had seen Him.

Mírzá Yaḥyá was the only member of the family who rejoiced. Now that Bahá'u'lláh was gone, his own plans could go forward more easily. The Bábís would soon forget about his brother and turn naturally to Mírzá Yaḥyá as their leader.

33
The Nameless One

A year passed, and still Bahá'u'lláh lived in solitude in the wilderness. Sometimes He walked down the mountainside as far as the town of Sulaimaniya. With His alms bowl in hand and dressed in the plain clothes of the poor, He looked like any dervish who wandered the land and lived a simple life.

In town, He could use the public bath and receive a little food from a few generous townspeople. When a dervish passed their way, it was the custom for people to put a share of their own food into his alms bowl. Kindness toward a dervish, who turned his back on the world to deepen in the life of the spirit, was thought to bring divine blessings.

Bahá'u'lláh called Himself Darvísh* Muḥammad. He did not engage in conversation with other people but kept silent and reserved. No one took special notice of Him until one day when Bahá'u'lláh came upon a weeping boy near a mountain village.

"'Little man, why art thou weeping?'" asked Bahá'u'lláh.

"'Oh Sir!'" replied the boy, "'The schoolmaster has punished me for writing so badly. I cannot write, and now I have no copy! I dare not go back to school!'"

"'Weep no longer,'" said Bahá'u'lláh. "'I will set a copy for thee, and show thee how to imitate it.'"

Later, when the student showed his teacher the sample of Bahá'u'lláh's writing, the teacher was greatly surprised. It was the elegant writing style and script taught only to those of noble birth.

"'Who gave this to thee?'" asked the teacher.

"'He wrote it for me, the dervish on the mountain,'" answered the student.

"'He is no dervish, the writer of this,'" replied his teacher, "'but a royal personage.'"[1]

About this same time, a shaykh of Sulaimaniya, directed by his dream of the Prophet Muḥammad, sought out Bahá'u'lláh on the mountainside.

---

* Another spelling of "dervish."

On his return to town, the shaykh spoke to others about the wise dervish on the mountain. In time, another learned shaykh approached Bahá'u'lláh and asked Him to come and live in Sulaimaniya. There He could join the discussions of teachers and students at the town's religious school—a well-respected seat of learning.

At first Bahá'u'lláh said no. But the shaykh would not give up. Repeatedly he begged Bahá'u'lláh to leave His isolation on the mountain until, at last, Bahá'u'lláh agreed to come to Sulaimaniya. There He took a small room at the religious school. He continued to dress as a dervish and eat simple food, and He still did not reveal His real name to anyone.

People were curious about the dervish whose penmanship suggested he was from royalty. Those who attended the religious college were eager to test his knowledge. They sent a group of their finest teachers and best students to meet with him. Bahá'u'lláh agreed to answer whatever questions they wished to ask.

Together the teachers and students decided on a difficult task. Long before, a book had been written by a well-known mystic. The meaning of the text was difficult to comprehend, even for the most accomplished religious scholars. They asked Bahá'u'lláh to prove His knowledge by explaining the mysteries found in this book.

Though Bahá'u'lláh was not familiar with the book and had never even seen it before, He instantly agreed to the request. For many days Bahá'u'lláh and the scholars met and discussed the text. Each day Bahá'u'lláh would ask one person to read aloud a page from the book. Then He would explain the meanings of the spiritual mysteries that puzzled them. His answers to their questions were so clear, and their truth so undeniable, that everyone was satisfied. Yet He often went further, explaining in greater depth the author's thinking and purposes. Sometimes Bahá'u'lláh would go on to give a far better presentation of the matter than the original author. The depth of His wisdom and the breadth of His knowledge deeply impressed His listeners.

As the days passed, a feeling of admiration for Bahá'u'lláh grew among the scholars. Were there any limits to the abilities of this Darvísh Muḥammad? Eager to explore further, they made yet another request.

No one among the mystics, the wise, and the learned, they agreed, had been able to write poetry as wonderful as that written by the mystic

Ibn-i-Fárid. The students and teachers referred to an especially wonderful poem by Ibn-i-Fárid, a poem known for its difficult rhyme and meter. Would Bahá'u'lláh write such a poem? Could He write a poem with the same beauty of thought, with the same beautiful rhythm and rhyme as the poem by Ibn-i-Fárid? Bahá'u'lláh agreed to grant their request.

Without any preparation Bahá'u'lláh began to dictate verse after verse. The gathering of scholars listened with deep attention as the melody of His voice rose and fell. They were not disappointed. Not only were the verses composed in the very rhythm and rhyme they had requested, but the poem itself was rich in the mysteries of spiritual truth. Its power stirred their souls; its beauty took their breath away.

When He finished, Bahá'u'lláh had composed two thousand verses. It was a poem without equal, all the scholars agreed—a poem beyond even the great Ibn-i-Fárid. Bahá'u'lláh, however, allowed them to keep only 127 verses. The rest He threw away, for there was no one, He said, to understand them.

As news of His accomplishments spread throughout the town, other people began to visit Bahá'u'lláh. Mullás, scholars, and shaykhs, holy men, doctors, and princes came to Him seeking advice. They brought to Him their most complex and troubling questions, and His answers opened new realms of understanding.

Not all who came to visit Bahá'u'lláh were scholars. Whether learned or illiterate, young or old, humble or of high rank—all were welcomed by Bahá'u'lláh. Kurds, Arabs, and Persians came to see Him; the love He showered on one and all was a magnet that none could resist.

The people of the region knew that the wise and holy dervish had not told them His real name. In respect and reverence they called Him *"Hazrat,"* meaning "His Highness," and "the Man of God from the mountain," or "the Nameless One." They did not know that He was Bahá'u'lláh—"the Glory of God," the Promised One of all religions. He still dressed and lived as a poor dervish. But when the people of Sulaimaniya looked upon Him, they saw Him attired in the rich robes of majesty.

Just as Sulaimaniya grew brighter with Bahá'u'lláh's presence, Baghdad had grown darker in His absence. After more than a year without Bahá'u'lláh, the Bábí community had fallen into a depressingly sorry state. Mírzá Yaḥyá, the interim head of their faith, had proven himself an incompetent substitute for his older brother.

Still afraid for his own life, Mírzá Yaḥyá remained in hiding. Steadfast Bábís who made the long, difficult journey from Persia to Baghdad to seek guidance and inspiration from the leader of their faith discovered that Mírzá Yaḥyá would see no one. He forbade the Bábís of Baghdad even to speak the name of the street on which he lived.

Yet Mírzá Yaḥyá was anxious for the Bábí community to acknowledge him as their rightful leader. He wrote letters to the few Bábís he trusted and continued the campaign of lies against Bahá'u'lláh. Nevertheless, Mírzá Yaḥyá did not inspire the Bábís with their lofty purpose, nor did he display any measure of Bahá'u'lláh's boundless love and wisdom.

As the months passed, respect for Mírzá Yaḥyá withered. Many disappointed Bábís believed they themselves could be better spiritual leaders than Mírzá Yaḥyá. In their confusion, some even claimed to be the Great Teacher promised by the Báb. No less than twenty-five Bábís put forward a claim to be the Promised One.

Mírzá Yaḥyá felt threatened, afraid that another Bábí would steal the position of leadership from him. With such dark thoughts he ordered the murder of two honorable Bábís, one of them a cousin of the Báb. Then he persuaded Mírzá Áqá Ján to return to Persia to attempt to kill the shah.*

The Bábís in Karbala, where Siyyid Muḥammad lived, had fallen into as sorry a condition as those in Baghdad. Some who called themselves Bábís behaved no better than ordinary thieves. They regularly stole the shoes left by wealthy Muslim pilgrims at the entrance to the shrine of the Imám Ḥusayn. They snatched the turbans from the pilgrims' heads and made off with the drinking cups from public fountains. They even stooped to stealing candles and couches from the shrine of the Imám Ḥusayn. Siyyid Muḥammad did nothing to stop the shameful behavior.

---

*Mírzá Áqá Ján later realized the foolishness of this plan and refused to carry it out.

These acts so badly stained the Bábís' reputation that no Bábí could walk the city streets without ridicule. The Cause of the Báb was mocked by everyone. How different from the days of the noble Mullá Ḥusayn, Quddús, and Ṭáhirih—whose faith had been immovable and whose deeds remained unsullied by any selfish motive. Now, just a decade later, the Cause of God was suffering its worst blows from those who claimed to be its followers.

In Baghdad Bahá'u'lláh's family continued to look for news of Him, but no one had seen Him. Twelve-year-old 'Abdu'l-Bahá was especially unhappy. He spent long hours copying passages from the writings of the Báb and memorizing them, but his heart ached for his father. One night he stayed awake and prayed through the whole night. Over and over he repeated one prayer as one thought consumed him: His father *must* return home.

The next day 'Abdu'l-Bahá and his uncle Mírzá Músá overheard two people talking about a wise dervish who lived in the mountain district of Sulaimaniya. People called him "the Nameless One," and they were magnetized with his love. 'Abdu'l-Bahá could hardly believe what he heard. The dervish could only be his beloved father! Mírzá Músá agreed with him.

About the same time, a sad piece of news also made its way to Baghdad. Abu'l-Qásim, the servant who had left with Bahá'u'lláh, had been attacked by thieves and mortally wounded. Before he died, he had told his rescuers that the money and goods he carried belonged to Darvísh Muḥammad.

Certain now that Darvísh Muḥammad was indeed Bahá'u'lláh, the family acted quickly. Mírzá Músá's father-in-law, Shaykh Sulṭán, and another Bábí agreed to go to Sulaimaniya to find Bahá'u'lláh. The family sold a rug to buy provisions for their journey.

When he left, Shaykh Sulṭán also carried a pouch with letters from family and believers. The letters pleaded for Bahá'u'lláh to return to Baghdad. One letter was written by Mírzá Yaḥyá. By this time, even he could see that Bahá'u'lláh was needed in Baghdad. The Bábí community was falling apart around him, and Mírzá Yaḥyá himself was powerless to stop it. He, too, begged Bahá'u'lláh to return.

34
A Joyful Naw-Rúz

After two months of travel along rocky mountain paths, Shaykh Sulṭán and his companion reached Sulaimaniya. Even before Shaykh Sulṭán found Him, Bahá'u'lláh knew the time had come to return to Baghdad. The people of Sulaimaniya, who loved Bahá'u'lláh, could not bear to see Him go. They begged to know how they would be able to find Him again.

Go to Baghdad, Bahá'u'lláh told them, and ask for the house of Mírzá Músá from Persia. Assuring them that they could find Him in Baghdad, He set off with Shaykh Sulṭán on the long journey back.

Bahá'u'lláh did not hurry along the way. These were His last days of peace, He told the good shaykh—days that would never come to Him again. He was aware that grievous troubles lay ahead of Him as the Messenger of God. Yet because He was God's Messenger, Bahá'u'lláh was willing to do whatever God asked of Him.

"Here am I with my body between Thy hands, and my spirit before Thy face," wrote Bahá'u'lláh in one of His prayers. "Do with them as it may please Thee, for the exaltation of Thy word. . . ."[1]

In Baghdad Navváb sat patiently sewing with careful stitches. Pieces of soft, red cloth spilled over her lap as she sewed. She had saved the precious Persian cloth called *tirmih* from her marriage treasures in Tehran. She had kept it carefully packed away during all their troubles, saving it for a special time. Now she worked diligently, creating something handsome from the pieces of precious cloth. She wanted it ready in time for her husband's return.

One day Navváb and the children heard a knock at the door. When they opened it, they saw a dervish standing before them. He was covered with the dust of the road, but no amount of dust could hide that beloved face. Bahá'u'lláh—their own dear father and husband—had returned! Quickly they surrounded Him, clinging as though to anchor Him where He stood, to keep Him from ever leaving again.

It was March 19, 1856. In two days they would celebrate Naw-Rúz, the Persian New Year. This year they would celebrate with all their hearts. Bahá'u'lláh had been gone nearly two years, but now He was home.

Navváb brought out the gift she had made from her marriage treasure. Instead of using the precious cloth to make a dress for herself, she had fashioned a beautiful red aba* for Bahá'u'lláh. It was a loving gift for her returning husband, and her precious husband, home at last, was all the gift Navváb needed.

For all the joy Bahá'u'lláh felt at seeing His family, He was saddened by news of the Bábís. The followers of the Báb had dwindled to only a handful of fainthearted souls. The Cause of God, for which so many had died, *"'had ceased to be on any one's lips,'"* Bahá'u'lláh observed, *"'nor was any heart receptive to its message.'"* [2] The Bábís' wretched condition made Him so sad that, for a time, He scarcely left His home and received only a few visitors.

Life in Baghdad went on as usual. Travelers and merchants from many places passed through the city gates. Some rode on horseback. Others led donkeys loaded with sacks of grain or carefully wrapped bundles. Still others came with camel caravans, the camels' humped backs piled high with goods to sell, and headed for the Baghdad market. Brightly colored rugs could be seen as well as shiny copper pots swinging from ropes of braided wool and glinting in the sunlight.

To walk across the great Tigris River that divided Baghdad, people used a floating bridge of boats. Forty wooden rowboats were lined up side by side in the water. A flexible walkway stretched over the top of the boats. It was strong enough for all the traffic of Baghdad—for all the people and beasts of burden who traveled through its gates.

In the city, hungry travelers stopped in front of trays of mouthwatering food for sale. Chicken, fish, and skewered chunks of meat—all roasting over charcoal—gave off their fragrant smells. Grass-lined baskets held carefully packed eggs. There were toasted pumpkin seeds and tempting, sweet barley cakes spiced with cardamom. Men gathered at the coffeehouses, where they talked and sipped from cups of thick Turkish coffee or hot, sweet tea.

---

* A loose, sleeveless outer garment traditionally worn by men in the Middle East.

"Alláh-u-Akbar!" (God is Most Great!) The call to prayer was sounded from the minarets of Baghdad five times a day, just as in Tehran. The people of Baghdad, most of whom were Muslim, unrolled their prayer rugs to pray, then carried on with their work.

Before long Bahá'u'lláh, too, entered into the life of Baghdad. He could be seen in the mosque at prayer time, and at other times He could be found walking along the streets and lanes of the city. He might be seen pacing along the banks of the Tigris in His red aba or walking across the bridge of boats to visit a coffeehouse. Shopkeepers came to know Him in the shops where He stopped from time to time.

Bahá'u'lláh also began to visit the Bábís once again and to receive them at His home. They came in the morning for an hour after breakfast and again in the afternoon. In the evenings, too, Bahá'u'lláh often welcomed Bábí visitors. They came from Baghdad and nearby towns or from as far away as Persia. Bahá'u'lláh would sit on His couch as they talked together, or He would pace up and down the room.

Most Bábís did not yet know that Bahá'u'lláh was the Messenger of God. They knew Him only as a follower of the Báb, as they all were. Yet Bahá'u'lláh explained the teachings of the Báb and answered their questions as no one else had done, and He did it all with such love that the Bábís were naturally drawn to Him.

Not since the early days of the Báb's ministry had there been someone to guide the Bábís. For most of His ministry the Báb had been locked away in prison, far away from His followers. In the persecutions that followed, Bahá'u'lláh Himself had been imprisoned and exiled. When Bahá'u'lláh left Baghdad for the wilderness of Kurdistan, Mírzá Yaḥyá had proven an inept and cowardly leader—always in hiding, fearing for his life.

Like wanderers parched with thirst in the desert, the Bábís had longed for the waters of spiritual guidance. Now at last their thirst was satisfied. The wise and loving counsels of Bahá'u'lláh were like a wellspring of fresh, clear water, and the Bábís drank deeply. They had found their oasis.

Bahá'u'lláh's first counsel forbade the Bábís to take part in any kind of conflict or violence, in quarrels or backbiting. Instead, He told them they must practice kindness and faithfulness toward one another—tolerance, patience, and humility. They must be friendly to all people as well as chaste, honest, and just in their dealings. They must obey the laws of the land. Most importantly, Bahá'u'lláh reminded them, they should remember their love for the Báb and fearlessly proclaim His Cause.

The Bábís began to mend their ways at once. Even most of those who had claimed, in Bahá'u'lláh's absence, to be the Promised One came to Him and humbly begged His forgiveness. All were determined to live up to the noble standard set for them.

Some Bábís, though, found it hard to avoid quarrels. One day, when a believer named Báqir was walking with his Bábí friends, a man began to hurl insults at them. Báqir tried to reason with him, but the sharp-tongued man would not stop his abuse. His vile words pricked at Báqir until he could stand it no longer. Báqir unsheathed his scimitar and attacked.

Báqir's friends grabbed him, pulling him away from the fight before he killed the other man. Quickly they left the scene. At the advice of the Persian consul, Báqir fled the city, but two other Bábís were thrown into jail in his place. Later, Báqir met the same man at another place. Once again the sharp-tongued man insulted him, and again Báqir was ready to do violence. This time Báqir was taken to prison.

He was released some time later, but Bahá'u'lláh was not happy when He learned of Báqir's conduct. To act with vengeance, returning one wrong deed with another, was not acceptable. In a strongly worded letter to Báqir Bahá'u'lláh advised, "'when ye are tormented,'" turn to the legal authorities. "'If ye be slain it is better for you,'" wrote Bahá'u'lláh, "'than that ye should slay.'"[3]

Such troublesome conduct by an individual Bábí could cause even greater trouble for the whole Bábí community. To protect the other Bábís, Bahá'u'lláh ordered Báqir to stay out of Baghdad.

Sometimes a Bábí simply showed greater enthusiasm than wisdom. One day a man named Ḥájí Ḥasan came to see Bahá'u'lláh with a dagger strapped to his side. Ḥájí Ḥasan was a quiet man who usually did not say a word. On this day he asked Bahá'u'lláh's permission to go to the bridge of boats. There, with his dagger drawn, he planned to stand and loudly proclaim the Cause of God to everyone who passed.

Kindly but firmly Bahá'u'lláh replied, "'Ḥájí, put aside your dagger. The Faith of God has to be given with amity and love to receptive souls. It does not need daggers and swords.'"[4]

Little by little, Bahá'u'lláh revived the Bábí community. Soon His admirers from Sulaimaniya began to arrive in Baghdad. They came asking for "Darvísh Muḥammad" at the "house of Mírzá Músá the Bábí." So many mullás and men of learning came looking for Darvísh Muḥammad, and praising His accomplishments, that the religious leaders of Baghdad were astonished.

Who was this Darvísh Muḥammad? they asked one another. The curious mullás of Baghdad decided to find out for themselves. They, too, set out to look for the house of Mírzá Músá. If the One called Darvísh Muḥammad was truly wise, they had many questions for Him.

35

Purity within Purity

The first discovery the religious leaders of Baghdad made about the man called "Darvísh Muḥammad" was that He was, in fact, Bahá'u'lláh, a Persian nobleman living in exile and a brother of Mírzá Músá. Their second discovery, which quickly followed the first, was that Bahá'u'lláh was unlike anyone else they had ever met.

Like the learned men of Sulaimaniya, the religious leaders of Baghdad tested Bahá'u'lláh with questions on a variety of subjects. The profound knowledge and wisdom of His answers astonished them, and the majesty of spirit He evinced could not be denied. The religious leaders of Baghdad, like the learned men of Sulaimaniya, soon became true admirers of Bahá'u'lláh.

They praised Him when they spoke to other people. The others became curious and wanted to meet Bahá'u'lláh for themselves. Soon visitors of all kinds came to Bahá'u'lláh's home. Poets, mystics, mullás, and government officials began flocking to Bahá'u'lláh's home. Princes of royal blood came, too. Some lived in Baghdad; others were visitors to the city. Some were sincere seekers after truth, but many were merely curious.

As months passed, the stream of visitors swelled to such a degree that much of Bahá'u'lláh's time was taken up with receiving them. One day twelve-year-old 'Abdu'l-Bahá took action. He told his family that every visitor who wished to see Bahá'u'lláh must first see 'Abdu'l-Bahá. He would talk with each one and find out who were the sincere among them. Only the sincere would be allowed to see his father.

Then young 'Abdu'l-Bahá made two signs. He put one at the door of his own room. It read, "'Those who come for information may apply within. Those who come only because of curiosity had better stay away.'" The second sign He put up at His father's door. It read, "'Let those who are searching for God come, and come, and come.'"[1]

There were some who asked to meet with Bahá'u'lláh in secret. Bahá'u'lláh did not always agree to this, but He did welcome one sincere soul who asked to meet at midnight. The two of them talked together until morning. When the visitor left Bahá'u'lláh, a friend met him and eagerly asked what he thought of his meeting.

"'"I had been told these Bábís were wine-bibbers,"'" replied the visitor, "'"that there was much wine in the room of Bahá'u'lláh, that, moreover, they had no moral principles whatsoever! I went to investigate for myself and found Purity within Purity. I was filled with amazement at the sanctity of that place, and bewildered to find the exact opposite of that which I had heard. I am firmly convinced,"'" he told his friend, "'"that This is the Truth."'"[2]

The home of Bahá'u'lláh would later become known among followers as the "Most Holy Habitation," but the house itself was modest. The room to which visitors came was not grand; it was made of mud and straw. The roof was low, the garden was small, and the couch where Bahá'u'lláh sat was simple, made from the branches of palms. Yet to many who entered that humble room, its low roof seemed to reach to the stars, for Bahá'u'lláh's presence made it a paradise.

"'I know not how to explain it,'" said one prince to his friend. "'Were all the sorrows of the world to be crowded into my heart they would, I feel, all vanish, when in the presence of Bahá'u'lláh.'"[3]

Another prince decided to build an exact copy of the wonderful room in his own home. When Bahá'u'lláh learned of the prince's plan, He reportedly said with a smile, *"'He may well succeed in reproducing outwardly the exact counterpart of this low-roofed room made of mud and straw with its diminutive garden.'"* But He added, *"'What of his ability to open onto it the spiritual doors leading to the hidden worlds of God?'"* Bahá'u'lláh Himself called His home in Baghdad the *"'Most Great House.'"*[4]

Not everyone, even among the Bábís, recognized at once the unique power of Bahá'u'lláh. Sometimes the most educated were the last to see. One such person was a Bábí known as Nabíl-i-Akbar. Nabíl had been a *mujtahid,* or doctor of Muslim law, highly respected for his extensive religious learning. Others frequently turned to him for answers to their spiritual questions. At most gatherings he was accustomed to taking the seat of honor and talking while others listened. When he visited Baghdad as a Bábí, he did the same.

One afternoon several Bábís, including Nabíl, gathered at the home of Bahá'u'lláh. Bahá'u'lláh sat humbly among the guests, serving them tea with His own hands. Nabíl took the seat of honor, as was usual for him. Someone asked a question about a spiritual matter, and Nabíl began to speak. No one else in the room, he was certain, could answer the question as well as he could.

Everyone sat in respectful silence and listened. Only Bahá'u'lláh added something, now and then, to what Nabíl was saying. Gradually Bahá'u'lláh spoke a little more. Soon it was Nabíl who grew quiet, sitting spellbound as he listened to the words of Bahá'u'lláh—words filled with majesty and power.

Suddenly Nabíl was overcome with awe and fear. He felt deeply ashamed to be sitting in the seat of honor and wanted nothing more than to leave the room. Nabíl watched Bahá'u'lláh and waited impatiently. No longer could he hear Bahá'u'lláh's voice; he knew only by the movement of His lips that Bahá'u'lláh was speaking. Finally Nabíl saw that Bahá'u'lláh had finished talking. He excused himself, got up from the seat of honor, and walked outside.

There he hit his head hard against the wall—once, twice, three times. How arrogant he had been! How spiritually blind! How foolish because of a little learning! From that time on, Nabíl was a humble follower of Bahá'u'lláh and devoted his life to the service of the Cause of God.

Bahá'u'lláh answered the questions of many people during His days in Baghdad and advanced the teachings of the Báb. Bahá'u'lláh did more than simply talk to the Bábís; much of His guidance He put into writing. In a constant effort to encourage the Bábís and to answer their questions, He wrote epistles and tablets, prayers, commentaries, odes, and prophecies. Verses streamed from His pen as abundantly as rain from the sky, in writings that became a river of life for the Bábís.

What was written down would not disappear and be forgotten. It could be read and pondered and passed on to others without mistake. And just as Bahá'u'lláh was unique among men, so were His writings distinct from those of ordinary men. In the mysterious process of revelation, whatever Bahá'u'lláh wrote was first revealed to Him by God within His heart.

Bahá'u'lláh had neither attended university nor studied the books of men. He did not need to. "Whenever We desire to quote the sayings of the learned and of the wise," explained Bahá'u'lláh, "presently there will appear before the face of thy Lord in the form of a tablet all that which hath appeared in the world and is revealed in the Holy Books and Scriptures."[5] His extraordinary knowledge and wisdom were innate and divinely bestowed on Him by God.

Revelation would come to Bahá'u'lláh at different times. When He was alone, Bahá'u'lláh would take up His pen and write the revealed verses Himself. But most of the time His amanuensis Mírzá Áqá Ján was by His side. It was the task of Mírzá Áqá Ján to write down the holy verses as Bahá'u'lláh dictated them. Mírzá Áqá Ján never knew when he would be needed. He kept himself always ready with ten or twelve sharp reed pens at hand, a large ink-pot the size of a small bowl, and stacks of paper.

When revelation did come to Bahá'u'lláh, the words came quickly. Struggling to keep pace with Him, Mírzá Áqá Ján would write as rapidly as he could. The shrill sound of his reed pen moving across the paper could be heard twenty paces away. Almost before the ink of the first word was dry, he would reach the end of a page.

At such times Bahá'u'lláh allowed only His amanuensis to stay with Him. On occasion another believer might be allowed to enter His presence briefly. Those who did witnessed the overwhelming glory and radiance that emanated from Him. The physical effects of being the channel through which the Holy Spirit flows to humankind were amazing to behold. At these moments, Bahá'u'lláh appeared so dazzling that no one could look upon His face. The very room seemed to be transformed.

"'Methought the door, the wall, the carpet, the ceiling, the floor and the air were all perfumed and illumined,'" said one believer. "'They all had been transformed, each and every one . . . and were filled with a spirit of joy and ecstasy. Each object had become refreshed and was pulsating with life.'"[6]

When the process of revelation ended, at least for the moment, the pages on which Mírzá Áqá Ján had transcribed the words looked "'as if someone had dipped a lock of hair in the ink'" and tried to write with it.[7] The words written so rapidly were mostly illegible to anyone except Mírzá Áqá Ján himself. Even he sometimes needed help from Bahá'u'lláh to decipher what he had written.

When Mírzá Áqá Ján had rewritten the tablet in his best handwriting, he would send it on to its destination. Sometimes Bahá'u'lláh instructed that several copies be made and given to the Bábís. So it was with a small collection of verses revealed by Bahá'u'lláh, not in a room of His house, but as He walked along the banks of the Tigris River. No one yet knew the power of these verses, but all of Baghdad was about to find out.

36

Unlocking the Doors of Heaven

The Tigris River that divided Baghdad was also a highway for river traffic. Boats laden with cargoes for market mingled with water taxis that carried people to and fro. Some rode in *quffih*—round boats made from woven reeds and waterproofed with tar. Others preferred the cushioned seats of the *balam*—rowboats with canvas roofs to provide shade against the sun.

The busy river had its quiet places, too. Birds made their nests in the tall reeds. Palm trees with thick clusters of dates rustled their long leaves in the breeze. Bahá'u'lláh could escape the bustle of city life, for a time, along the lush banks of the Tigris.

In a garden spot on the riverbank, Bábí carpenters built a small hut for Him. The roof was made of palm leaves and thornbushes. Inside, Bahá'u'lláh could meditate or dictate to His amanuensis in private. But as often as not He could be seen outside, the soft folds of His red aba moving with each step as He paced along the banks of the river.

The great Tigris stretched for more than a thousand miles and reached back through countless eras of human history. It had lapped the shores of some of the earliest civilizations—Sumer, Assyria, Babylonia. The Prophet Abraham—honored by Jews, Christians, and Muslims—was born in the ancient land of Ur, south of Baghdad, where the Tigris meets the Euphrates River and flows to the Persian Gulf.

So many peoples had walked in the fertile black soil left by the Tigris and had journeyed in its fast-flowing waters. But it was the journey of life itself in every age that filled people's hearts with questions: Where did we come from? Is there a God Who created and cares for us? Is there a purpose to this earthly life—something greater than the stuff of the marketplace? What happens at the close of our days in this world? Is there a life beyond this mortal realm?

God had given answers through His Prophets at different times and in different places, said Bahá'u'lláh. Now Bahá'u'lláh revealed anew the heart of these divine teachings. Here, on the banks of the Tigris, He drew together the divine guidance revealed throughout the ages into a handful of short verses "clothed in the garment of brevity" so that everyone could read and understand.[1] These were God's eternal answers to humanity's deepest questions. The voice that spoke in the verses revealed by Bahá'u'lláh was the Voice of God—the One Great Creator Who loved His creation:

> O SON OF MAN!* Veiled in My immemorial being and in the ancient eternity of My essence, I knew My love for thee; therefore I created thee, have engraved on thee Mine image and revealed to thee My beauty.[2]

> O SON OF BEING! Thou art My lamp and My light is in thee. Get thou from it thy radiance and seek none other than Me. For I have created thee rich and have bountifully shed My favor upon thee.[3]

> O SON OF BEING! With the hands of power I made thee and with the fingers of strength I created thee; and within thee have I placed the essence of My light. Be thou content with it and seek naught else, for My work is perfect and My command is binding. Question it not, nor have a doubt thereof.[4]

---

* In the translation of these writings from their original Arabic or Persian into English, words such as "man" and "son" are used in their generic sense and are intended to encompass all humankind.

This was Revelation—the Word of God, and there was nothing more powerful. Bahá'u'lláh called it "the master key for the whole world." With this key, He said, "the doors of the hearts of men, which in reality are the doors of heaven, are unlocked." "True loss," He would write, "is for him whose days have been spent in utter ignorance of his self."[5]

Bahá'u'lláh revealed 153 verses as He walked along the banks of the River Tigris. Nearly half were in Arabic, which He called the "'language of eloquence.'" The rest were in Persian, which He called the "'language of light'" and "'the sweet language.'"[6] Together they would form a volume entitled the Hidden Words.

The verses were copied carefully by hand and passed among the Bábís. In small groups here and there they gathered together to share the new writings. One gathering place was a bakery owned by a Bábí. By day it was filled with the heat of ovens, the noise of the grinding stone, and the fragrance of warm loaves of bread. But in the quiet at the end of the day's work, Bábí friends would draw close around the light of a sesame oil lamp. Those who could read would recite verses to the others.

As they listened to the Hidden Words in the fading light of evening, the Bábís heard the Voice of God calling them to turn to Him, and in doing so, to discover their own true selves. For it was the mystical connection between the soul and its Creator that was at the heart of all religion.

> O SON OF MAN! I loved thy creation, hence I created thee. Wherefore, do thou love Me, that I may name thy name and fill thy soul with the spirit of life.[7]

> O BEFRIENDED STRANGER! The candle of thine heart is lighted by the hand of My power, quench it not with the contrary winds of self and passion. The healer of all thine ills is remembrance of Me, forget it not. Make my love thy treasure and cherish it even as thy very sight and life.[8]

> O SON OF SPIRIT! Noble have I created thee, yet thou hast abased thyself. Rise then unto that for which thou wast created.[9]

> O MY SERVANT! Thou art even as a finely tempered sword concealed in the darkness of its sheath and its value hidden from the artificer's

> knowledge. Wherefore come forth from the sheath of self and desire that thy worth may be made resplendent and manifest unto all the world.[10]

The true purpose of religion was to nourish the connection between the soul and its God—an eternal connection that could not be severed when earthly life ended:

> O SON OF MAN! Thou art My dominion and My dominion perisheth not, wherefore fearest thou thy perishing? Thou art My light and My light shall never be extinguished; why dost thou dread extinction? Thou art My glory and My glory fadeth not; thou art My robe and My robe shall never be outworn. Abide then in thy love for Me, that thou mayest find Me in the realm of glory.[11]

The Hidden Words also made it clear that in the eyes of God the human race was one race, and every soul was worthy of just and loving treatment:

> O CHILDREN OF MEN! Know ye not why We created you all from the same dust? That no one should exalt himself over the other. Ponder at all times in your hearts how ye were created. Since We have created you all from one same substance it is incumbent on you to be even as one soul, to walk with the same feet, eat with the same mouth and dwell in the same land, that from your inmost being, by your deeds and actions, the signs of oneness and the essence of detachment may be made manifest. Such is My counsel to you, O concourse of light! Heed ye this counsel that ye may obtain the fruit of holiness from the tree of wondrous glory.[12]

Bahá'u'lláh revealed the Hidden Words in 1858—two years after His return from Sulaimaniya. What a change of spirit had taken hold of the Bábí community in those two years! Fortified by Bahá'u'lláh's loving support and guided by His clear counsels, the followers of the Báb no longer felt dejected and confused. The troubles and mischiefs of the past had dissolved, replaced by a new vision and a fresh determination.

Now they were spiritual warriors, one and all engaged in daily battle with the ignoble side of their own human nature. Day by day, hour by hour, they struggled to subdue every unworthy aspect of their conduct.

With fasts and vigils the Bábís tested and strengthened their resolve as they strove with enthusiasm to live the teachings of the Hidden Words. For in that slender volume of verses the command of God was clear: "Everyone must show forth deeds that are pure and holy, for words are the property of all alike, whereas such deeds as these belong only to Our loved ones. Strive then with heart and soul to distinguish yourselves by your deeds. . . ."[13] Even their sleep brought dreams and visions, which they shared with one another.

At night the Bábís gathered in joyful feasts. With prayers and poetry and song they praised the Báb and celebrated the heroes of their faith. On occasion Bahá'u'lláh, too, came to their feasts and would often sprinkle a little rosewater on each person who was present. He was always pleased to see the believers so happy. Later He would write, "We love . . . to inhale from your acts the fragrance of friendliness and unity, of loving-kindness and fellowship. . . . If We inhale the perfume of your fellowship, Our heart will assuredly rejoice, for naught else can satisfy Us."[14]

Their feasts were not costly, for the Bábís in Baghdad had little money. Many nights no less than ten people shared a penny's worth of dates for food. They shared the shoes and cloaks that they wore, not caring to whom they belonged. Yet the Bábís were content, for they did not measure their happiness in the wealth of the world. The palace of a king meant no more to them than the web of a spider.

One day when Bahá'u'lláh visited a few of the Bábís, however, they were embarrassed. They owned no chair for Him to sit upon, no table at which to serve Him tea—not one piece of furniture. But as Bahá'u'lláh looked about the room He said, """Its emptiness pleases Me. In My estimation it is preferable to many a spacious palace, inasmuch as the beloved of God are occupied in it with the remembrance of the Incomparable Friend. . . ."""[15]

Bahá'u'lláh Himself lived simply, keeping very few material possessions. For a time in Baghdad He owned only one shirt, which was washed and dried daily. The money not spent on Himself or His family Bahá'u'lláh used for others—for the poor, the orphans, and the disabled. He gave little gifts of coins to the children. No one was forgotten.

In Baghdad the Bábís were transformed by the presence of Bahá'u'lláh. Where once they had been scorned for their ignoble ways, now they were known in the marketplace as the most honest and trustworthy merchants. Not only in Baghdad, but also in Karbala and as far away as Persia, they became famous for their noble and excellent character, for their pure and praiseworthy deeds. People no longer made fun of the Bábís or scoffed at their beliefs.

For the Bábís themselves every action became a reflection of their deep love for the One Who inspired them—Bahá'u'lláh. He had truly opened for them the doors of heaven, the doors of their own hearts.

One of the believers, a learned man called Dhabíḥ, showed his devotion to Bahá'u'lláh in a quiet way. At the dawn of each day Dhabíḥ swept the approaches to Bahá'u'lláh's house. With humility and reverence he would unwind his green turban, the proud symbol of his link to the Prophet Muḥammad, and use it to gather the dust and rubble on which Bahá'u'lláh had walked. He would carry the sweepings in the folds of his cloak all the way to the Tigris River. There the purehearted Dhabíḥ cast the dust into the water, for he could not bear that others should tread upon the dust on which Bahá'u'lláh had walked.

But there were jealous hearts in Baghdad, too, who were vexed at every sign of esteem shown to Bahá'u'lláh and who bristled at every word of respect spoken about the Bábís. Among these was Shaykh 'Abdu'l-Ḥusayn, who came to Baghdad from Tehran. The jealous shaykh was also crafty and willing to do whatever was required to rid Baghdad of Bahá'u'lláh.

37

The Shaykh and the Assassin

Even in Tehran Shaykh 'Abdu'l-Ḥusayn had caused trouble. His mischief-making in royal circles irritated the shah and his grand vizier. To remove him from the capital the shah devised a special assignment for the shaykh. He was put in charge of a project to repair the Muslim holy sites in Karbala near Baghdad. Shaykh 'Abdu'l-Ḥusayn was pleased to receive so important an assignment, and the shah and his grand vizier were pleased to remove the troublesome shaykh from Tehran.

In Baghdad and Karbala Shaykh 'Abdu'l-Ḥusayn heard a growing number of people praising Bahá'u'lláh and the other Bábís. He became aware of the increasing influence and rising prestige not only of the Bábís, but of Bahá'u'lláh. The Bábís' devotion to Bahá'u'lláh and the high esteem with which the people of Baghdad regarded Him fanned the flames of jealousy and hatred within the shaykh.

Bahá'u'lláh invited Shaykh 'Abdu'l-Ḥusayn to meet Him face-to-face and learn the truth about His Cause. Although he agreed to the meeting at first, Shaykh 'Abdu'l-Ḥusayn never came to it. Instead, the shaykh determined to do everything in his power to remove Bahá'u'lláh from Baghdad.

The scheming shaykh looked for someone who could help him with his plan and found such a man in the new consul-general from Persia. It was 1860 and the newly appointed Mírzá Buzurg Khán had just come to Baghdad. He was a proud and hateful man, given to drink and to following his passions, and he became a willing accomplice in the malicious schemes of the shaykh.

Shaykh 'Abdu'l-Ḥusayn began by spreading rumors about Bahá'u'lláh. Then he proceeded to the authorities with his false accusations and demanded that they order Bahá'u'lláh to leave Baghdad. But the governor of Baghdad, who knew and respected Bahá'u'lláh, was not inclined to pay attention to the lies and demands of the shaykh.

When those in positions of power would not help, the shaykh's partner, Mírzá Buzurg Khán, turned elsewhere. There were always roughnecks who would rather cause trouble than do an honest day's work. He urged some of these people to harass Bahá'u'lláh in public places. Let them insult Bahá'u'lláh and His religion, he instructed them, and do whatever it might take to provoke Him or the Bábís into striking back. Then the governor would have reason to order Bahá'u'lláh out of Baghdad.

But Bahá'u'lláh could be neither fooled nor provoked. As He walked through the city streets to the coffeehouse or the market, He did not avoid the troublemakers. Boldly He walked to where they stood and joked with them about why they were there. It was clear to the embarrassed troublemakers that Bahá'u'lláh knew exactly what they were doing. By the time He left them they wanted nothing more to do with the consul-general's schemes.

These failures only strengthened Mírzá Buzurg Khán's determination, and he decided on a more deadly plan: He would hire an assassin. For the sum of one hundred túmáns a Turk named Riḍá agreed to seek out and kill Bahá'u'lláh. Mírzá Buzurg Khán provided Riḍá with a horse and two pistols and promised to protect him from any punishment.

Riḍá waited for his opportunity. One day when Bahá'u'lláh went to the public bath, Riḍá followed. Hiding a pistol beneath his cloak, he walked past the other Bábís who were present. No one noticed him. Quietly he made his way to the inner chamber of the steamy bath, but when he stood with Bahá'u'lláh before him, Riḍá began to tremble. Overcome with confusion, he turned and quickly left the bath. Bahá'u'lláh was out of danger—at least for a time.

Still Riḍá was not yet ready to give up. One night, with pistol in hand, he lay in wait for Bahá'u'lláh. He watched as Bahá'u'lláh and His brother Mírzá Músá walked in his direction, but as Bahá'u'lláh drew closer and still closer, a great fear suddenly gripped Riḍá's heart. The pistol dropped from his hand, and the fear that clutched him was so strong that Riḍá could not move to bend down and retrieve it.

When Bahá'u'lláh and Mírzá Músá drew near Riḍá they stopped. Turning to His brother Bahá'u'lláh said, "'Pick up his pistol and give it to him, and show him the way to his house; he seems to have lost his way.'"[1] It was the last time Riḍá tried to take Bahá'u'lláh's life.

Still Shaykh 'Abdu'l-Ḥusayn would not admit defeat. He began to write long letters to the shah's closest attendants—letters filled with alarming allegations about Bahá'u'lláh. All the nomadic tribes of Iraq, he claimed, now gave allegiance to Bahá'u'lláh. In one day, he claimed, Bahá'u'lláh could muster at least one hundred thousand men who were ready to take up arms at His command. With these extravagant claims the shaykh portrayed Bahá'u'lláh as a conspirator, plotting with others to rebel against the shah.

Day after day the shaykh's alarming reports came to the court of the shah. Nothing in the reports was true, but how was the shah to know? A rebellion was a serious matter—even if the report came from a troublesome shaykh.

At last the shaykh's campaign had its intended effect. He persuaded the shah to give him full authority to act against Bahá'u'lláh and the

Bábís. He was authorized to get whatever help he needed from the Persian officials and religious leaders living in Iraq.

This was exactly what Shaykh 'Abdu'l-Ḥusayn wanted. Immediately he invited all ranks of Muslim clergy in Najaf and Karbala—mullás, mujtahids, and shaykhs—to an urgent conference in his home. When the members of the clergy had gathered, the shaykh spoke to the assembly. In the strongest language he condemned Bahá'u'lláh and His Cause, claiming that Bahá'u'lláh intended to destroy the Faith of Islam. For the honor of Islam, he declared, they must proclaim a holy war against the Bábís of Iraq and destroy the Bábí Faith at its heart! The mullás enthusiastically agreed—except for one.

The highest-ranking mujtahid—who was known and respected for his wisdom, tolerance, and justice—did not agree. He had not seen the Bábís do anything that contradicted the laws of the Koran, he said, nor did he know enough of the Bábís' beliefs to judge them fairly. He refused to pronounce sentence against the Bábís. With that, the mujtahid got up and walked out of the meeting.

The rest of the mullás were frustrated. Without the approval of the leading mujtahid they could not wage holy war. But they were not yet ready to abandon the matter. Instead, the mullás decided, they would test Bahá'u'lláh, and they drew up a list of difficult spiritual questions. If He could answer these questions to their satisfaction, the mullás agreed, they might believe in the truth of His Cause. The mullás chose one individual, Ḥájí Mullá Ḥasan, to present the questions to Bahá'u'lláh on their behalf.

It was arranged for Ḥájí Mullá Ḥasan to meet with Bahá'u'lláh in His home, and that was where he presented the mullás' questions. To each question Bahá'u'lláh gave a clear and satisfactory answer. Ḥájí Mullá Ḥasan, a sincere and high-minded man, was deeply impressed with Bahá'u'lláh's wisdom.

When Bahá'u'lláh had answered all of the mullás' questions, Ḥájí Mullá Ḥasan made one more request. Could Bahá'u'lláh perform a miracle? A miracle, the mullás had agreed, would be a true and final proof of Bahá'u'lláh's mission.

"'Although you have no right to ask this,'" replied Bahá'u'lláh, "'for God should test His creatures, and they should not test God, still I allow and accept this request.'"[2]

But Bahá'u'lláh required that certain conditions must first be met. All of the gathered mullás must agree on one miracle for Bahá'u'lláh to perform. Then they must put into writing a promise that, after Bahá'u'lláh performed the requested miracle, they would confess the truth of His Cause.

"'Let them seal this paper, and bring it to Me,'" said Bahá'u'lláh. "'This must be the accepted criterion: if the miracle is performed, no doubt will remain for them; and if not, We shall be convicted of imposture.'"[3]

Ḥájí Mullá Ḥasan was pleased with this arrangement. Bahá'u'lláh had given a fair answer to the mullás' challenge. Ḥájí Mullá Ḥasan got up and as a sign of reverence kissed Bahá'u'lláh's robe. His task was completed. He promised to tell the assembly of mullás all that Bahá'u'lláh had said.

Now only one question remained: How would the troublesome shaykh and the other mullás respond?

38

The Eldest Uncle's Questions

The mullás were not pleased. Although Bahá'u'lláh had answered their questions and had even agreed to perform a miracle, His terms made the mullás uneasy.

The mullás discussed the matter at length. After three days of deliberation, they agreed at last on one thing—they would not pursue the matter of the miracle. They had been ready to wage holy war, but now they were defeated by Bahá'u'lláh's challenge. There was nothing left for them to do. The assembly of mullás dispersed, each returning to his separate home.

The news was delivered to Bahá'u'lláh. His challenge had revealed and vindicated the miracles, said Bahá'u'lláh, of all the Prophets of the past. He had removed all reason for doubt, since He was willing to perform any miracle the mullás chose.

Shaykh 'Abdu'l-Ḥusayn had failed once again in his schemes to rid Baghdad of Bahá'u'lláh. But the shaykh was a stubborn man. He continued to send letters to Persia filled with falsehoods and exaggerated claims about Bahá'u'lláh and urging the government to take action and remove Him from Iraq.

Others who admired Bahá'u'lláh were becoming concerned about His safety. The British consul-general in Baghdad offered his protection. He could arrange for Bahá'u'lláh to become a British citizen, which would enable Bahá'u'lláh to leave Baghdad for nearby India or any other land that He wished. Bahá'u'lláh could even ask for help from Queen Victoria.

Bahá'u'lláh knew that great danger lay ahead. His enemies would continue to pursue Him relentlessly, for they were ready to launch a fierce attack. Many of His friends thought He should flee to a place of safety. But Bahá'u'lláh did not choose to run away or retire to a safe place. He politely refused all offers of protection. The Chosen Ones of God, Bahá'u'lláh asserted, are not afraid of suffering and ordeals—not even the most severe.

"I have offered Myself up in the way of God," Bahá'u'lláh wrote, "and I yearn after tribulations in My love for Him, and for the sake of His good pleasure."[1] In another Tablet revealed by Bahá'u'lláh He made it clear that His trust was in God and He would brave any danger in the path of God. Like all of the Prophets of God, He would suffer at the hands of the ungodly, wrote Bahá'u'lláh, but His enemies were powerless to destroy the Cause of God.

Yet not all was darkness and difficulty. The days of Bahá'u'lláh's family were brightened in 1860 with the arrival of His twelve-year-old son, Mírzá Mihdí. When Bahá'u'lláh was banished from His homeland, Mírzá Mihdí had been too small and frail for the winter journey to Baghdad. Navváb had reluctantly left him in the loving care of his grandmother in Tehran. Now, at long last, the gentle Mírzá Mihdí joined his family.

Mírzá Mihdí's sister, Bahíyyih, to whom he had clung for comfort during those frightful nights in Tehran, turned fourteen that year. His brother 'Abdu'l-Bahá was sixteen and every day taking on more responsibility. Now it was 'Abdu'l-Bahá who took charge of the day-to-day work of the household, who made sure that supplies of food and other provisions were enough. More and more he assisted his father and shielded Him from the idle attentions of the curious. Bahá'u'lláh called His eldest son *"Áqá,"* meaning "the Master."

Even ordinary days were sweeter with the family together once more. And despite the scheming Shaykh 'Abdu'l-Ḥusayn, Bahá'u'lláh went about life as usual in Baghdad. He revealed verses and received visitors daily. He visited and encouraged the Bábís at their shops in the nearby market, where they put into daily practice one of the counsels from the Hidden Words: "O MY SERVANTS! Ye are the trees of My garden; ye must give forth goodly and wondrous fruits. . . . Thus it is incumbent on every one to engage in crafts and professions. . . . Trees that yield no fruit have been and will ever be for the fire."[2]

Every day Bahá'u'lláh walked to the coffeehouses near the bridge of boats. Each day an elderly woman stood alongside the road and waited for Him to pass. She was poor and lived in a broken-down house. Bahá'u'lláh stopped each day and spoke kindly to the woman. He would inquire after her health, then give her a little money.

Each day the elderly woman would kiss Bahá'u'lláh's hands to show her thanks, but sometimes she wanted to kiss His face. She was rather short and could not quite reach, so Bahá'u'lláh would bend down to let her kiss Him on the cheek. "'She knows that I like her,'" Bahá'u'lláh would tell His companions, "'that is why she likes Me.'"[3]

Nearer the coffeehouses the air was filled with the fragrance of coffee beans roasting over charcoal. The men of Baghdad came to the coffeehouses daily to learn the latest news and conduct business over small cups of bitter coffee and sweet tea. Some coffeehouses were known for their storytellers, who told heroic tales of adventure. Most were places to talk about poetry and politics, philosophy and religion.

Bahá'u'lláh particularly liked to visit two different coffeehouses—one on the east bank of the Tigris at the entrance to the bridge of boats and one on the west bank at the bridge's other entrance. Wherever Bahá'u'lláh went, men from every walk of life gathered around Him. Merchants and mullás, mujtahids and government leaders crowded the coffeehouses. They loved to debate, to put questions to Bahá'u'lláh, and to listen as He eloquently spoke about the Báb and His Cause.

It was good business, too, for the coffeehouse owners—so many people buying cups of coffee and tea. But it was not business that made coffee house owner Siyyid Ḥabíb look for Bahá'u'lláh. Bahá'u'lláh's very presence brought something extraordinary to the ordinary setting of the coffeehouse. Bahá'u'lláh always asked for the white-bearded Siyyid Ḥabíb and gave him tea when He came. For Siyyid Ḥabíb, a day without Bahá'u'lláh was a day wasted.

At home Bahá'u'lláh continued to reveal verses—far too many for only one person to write down. Other Bábís, including the teenage 'Abdu'l-Bahá, helped Mírzá Áqá Ján with the enormous task of transcribing the verses as they were revealed. But hundreds of thousands of verses, most of them written by Bahá'u'lláh Himself, were cast into the river at Bahá'u'lláh's request.

Mírzá Áqá Ján could not obey at first. To see the ink of that precious writing dissolve into the river currents, forever lost, was beyond thinking. Bahá'u'lláh understood, but He was firm, saying, """None is to be found at this time worthy to hear these melodies.""" [4]

Visitors in astonishing variety continued to come to Bahá'u'lláh's home. Kurds, Persians, Arabs, and Turks came to see Bahá'u'lláh. Christians, Jews, and Muslims came in addition to Bábís. They came regardless of social rank, from princes and nobles to peasants and dervishes. Some came to Bahá'u'lláh for help—the victims of injustice, the poor, the sick, and the aged. The jealous Shaykh 'Abdu'l-Ḥusayn watched it all and continued to write his inflammatory letters to Tehran.

In 1862 the eldest uncle of the Báb came to Baghdad. This uncle, Ḥájí Mírzá Siyyid Muḥammad, had not accepted the Báb as a Divine Messenger. He found it difficult to believe that his own nephew could be the Qá'im. Was it not promised that the Qá'im would have sovereignty and rule over the people? His nephew, the Báb, had been imprisoned and executed. How did He fulfill the promises of Islam? He had many other questions as well. A number of Bábís tried to answer his questions and dispel his doubts, but their answers did not satisfy Ḥájí Mírzá Siyyid Muḥammad.

Now that the uncle was in Baghdad Bahá'u'lláh invited him to visit. As they talked together the uncle confided in Bahá'u'lláh that he thought very highly of his nephew and wanted to believe His claim, but he could not ignore the questions that puzzled him. The uncle begged Bahá'u'lláh to lift the veil of doubt from his heart.

Bahá'u'lláh understood that the Báb's uncle was not making demands like the mullás, nor was he seeking to test Bahá'u'lláh's knowledge. Ḥe had a deep desire to know the truth. Because the uncle was sincere, Bahá'u'lláh promised to help him.

He told Ḥájí Mírzá Siyyid Muḥammad to go home and consider all the questions that were troubling him. These he should write down and bring back to Bahá'u'lláh. The Báb's eldest uncle did as Bahá'u'lláh instructed, and the next day he returned with his list of questions.

Bahá'u'lláh kept His promise. In the space of two days and two nights He revealed a book-length composition of more than two hundred pages in answer to the uncle's questions. Bahá'u'lláh would call this work the *Kitáb-i-Íqán*, the Book of Certitude, a book that would broaden the vision not only of the uncle but of all humankind.

It was 1862 when Bahá'u'lláh revealed His response to Ḥájí Mírzá Siyyid Muḥammad's questions. On the other side of the world Abraham Lincoln had been elected president of the United States of America. The nation was being torn apart by civil war. At the heart of the conflict burned the issue of slavery, a shameful practice that Bahá'u'lláh would, in future writings, clearly forbid: "It is forbidden you to trade in slaves, be they men or women," He would write. "It is not for him who is himself a servant to buy another of God's servants, and this hath been prohibited in His Holy Tablet . . . Let no man exalt himself above another."

In America many people were already working in different ways to end the practice of slavery. Harriet Tubman, who had escaped from slavery, returned to the South time and again to rescue others from its clutches. Nineteen times she braved the dangerous journey, and with the aid of the Underground Railroad, rescued three hundred people in all, including her own aged parents. As the Civil War raged she answered the Union's call for nurses and tended to the suffering of black and white alike.

Sojourner Truth,* the first black woman to speak out publicly against slavery, not only captivated audiences with her abolitionist speeches but also worked to find jobs and homes for escaped slaves and to improve living conditions for blacks. Herself a former slave in Ulster County,

* Isabella Baumfree was her given name; she took the name Sojourner Truth in 1843 after a deep spiritual experience, which she felt was a call from God to preach.

New York, she had been freed by a state law banning slavery. Her efforts in the path of justice would bring her as far as the White House to talk with the president.

President Lincoln also met several times with abolitionist Frederick Douglass to discuss slavery and its harsh effects. In the early days of the war, abolitionists such as Douglass had been impatient with Lincoln, who declared that his objective was to save the Union, not to destroy slavery. But as the war continued Lincoln changed his mind, seeing slavery as a moral sin in a nation that had declared "all men are created equal."

As a result Douglass, too, changed his mind and came to admire Lincoln. He would say of his meetings with the president, "In all my interviews with Mr. Lincoln I was impressed with his entire freedom from popular prejudice against the colored race. He was the first great man that I talked with in the United States freely, who in no single instance reminded me of the difference between himself and myself, of the difference of color, and I thought that all the more remarkable because he came from a state where there were black laws."[5]

But perhaps the most powerful voice against slavery came from the New England writer Harriet Beecher Stowe, whose novel *Uncle Tom's Cabin* was called "'a verbal earthquake, an ink-and-paper tidal wave'" that "sparked a wave of hatred" for the institution of slavery.[6] The novel, published in 1852, portrayed slaves as feeling and thinking individuals whose loves and pains, family ties and spiritual beliefs were every bit as real as their owners' and who suffered terrible abuse as slaves. The book's memorable characters, who seemed so alive to the reader, were drawn from Harriet's own experience in Ohio with runaway slaves from neighboring Kentucky.

The moving portrayal of slavery as written in *Uncle Tom's Cabin* traveled further and faster than the speeches of the most accomplished orators. Within a year, sales of the book reached three hundred thousand and inspired theatrical productions on stages across the country. *Uncle Tom's Cabin* became a best seller in Great Britain, Europe, and Asia as well. It was translated into more than sixty languages, and its author was welcomed enthusiastically at home and abroad.

It was another book, though, that would come to shed new light on the entire reach of human history. As the Kitáb-i-Íqán, the Book of Certitude revealed by Bahá'u'lláh, was read ever more widely, it would break the shackles of ignorance that weighed men down and free people everywhere. It would begin by lifting the veil of doubt from the heart of the Báb's eldest uncle.

39

A Paradox Resolved

Bahá'u'lláh did not begin the Kitáb-i-Íqán (Book of Certitude) with the story of the Báb. He began, instead, with a story that reached through time beyond the furthest recollections of historical memory. It was an epic story of inspiring deeds and unspeakable cruelty—a true story, but one that had never before been fully told. It was the one great story of all the Prophets of God and of those in every age who opposed Them.

A human being is "the noblest and most perfect of all created things," wrote Bahá'u'lláh in the Book of Certitude, and "the most distinguished and the most excellent" of all men are the Prophets, Who are the Messengers of God. They are the "Birds of Eternity," He wrote, sent by God to educate the souls of humankind.[1]

He told the stories of Abraham, Whom He called the "Friend of God," and of Moses, "He Who held converse with God." He told about the light of Jesus and the beauty of Muḥammad. There were other Prophets of God, too, in the far reaches of time and human history. One and all, Bahá'u'lláh wrote, They were "Treasuries of divine knowledge."[2]

Like clearly polished mirrors reflecting the light of the sun, They reflected "the light of unfading glory"—the spiritual light of God Himself. Their lives and teachings revealed "the names and attributes of God," Bahá'u'lláh explained, "such as knowledge and power, sovereignty and dominion, mercy and wisdom, glory, bounty and grace." Through Them "the sun of knowledge, . . . the moon of wisdom, and . . . the stars of understanding and utterance" shone brightly. "Human tongue can never befittingly sing their praise," wrote Bahá'u'lláh in the Book of Certitude, "and human speech can never unfold their mystery."[3]

The birth of each Prophet of God was heralded by various signs in the heavens and on earth. A new star appeared in the sky, and a special teacher prepared the way, instructing others how to recognize the new

Messenger of God. Each Prophet, "a pure and stainless Soul," appeared with God's guidance at a different time and place in human history. It was part of God's Covenant with humanity—His promise that He would never leave them without guidance. "Not for a moment," wrote Bahá'u'lláh, "hath His grace been withheld, nor have the showers of His loving-kindness ceased to rain upon mankind."[4]

Yet in every age the Messengers of God suffered at the hands of men, the very men who prayed for their appearance. With what cruelty they attacked those "Gems of divine virtue," wrote Bahá'u'lláh in the Book of Certitude, with attacks "more fierce than tongue or pen can describe." Every nation "'plotted darkly'" against its Messenger, He wrote, for the Prophets of God did not appear in the manner that men expected.[5]

People in Palestine knew Jesus as a poor, fatherless carpenter and gossiped about His mother, although she was pure and chaste. They were ignorant of the fact that He came from God, and knew only that He was not the king for whom they wished.

In the same way, Bahá'u'lláh wrote, the people of Arabia in Muḥammad's time knew Him as a merchant who could neither read nor write. The religious leaders of His time called Him an impostor, a lunatic, and they "provoked the people to arise and torment Him."[6]

The sovereignty of Jesus and Muḥammad, Bahá'u'lláh explained, "is not the sovereignty which the minds of men have falsely imagined." One and all, He declared, the Messengers of God wielded spiritual power "over all that is in heaven and on earth"—a power that always, in due time, revealed itself to the world.[7]

"Consider how great is the change today!" wrote Bahá'u'lláh in reference to Muḥammad. "Behold, how many are the Sovereigns who bow the knee before His name! How numerous the nations and kingdoms who have sought the shelter of His shadow, who bear allegiance to His Faith, and pride themselves therein! From the pulpit-top there ascendeth today the words of praise which, in utter lowliness, glorify His blessed name. . . ."[8]

So it was with Jesus, Moses, and the other divine Messengers, explained Bahá'u'lláh. They kindled love in the hearts of Their enemies; They brought strangers together under one tent—all through the power of the Word of God. These were the true miracles of the Prophets of God, the real proofs of Their power.

A Prophet demonstrated the truth of His message, wrote Bahá'u'lláh, through His own life, through His revelation of the Word of God, and through the wondrous effects of His revelation on the hearts of His followers. He was steadfast in proclaiming the Cause of God, no matter how bitter the opposition. Each Prophet—the Messenger of God—accepted the Prophets before Him and predicted the One Who would follow Him after a certain period of time.

All of these things were true of the Báb, Bahá'u'lláh explained in the Book of Certitude. Astronomers had found a new star in the heavens.* Shaykh Aḥmad and Siyyid Káẓim, "those twin resplendent lights," had prepared the way among men. The Báb Himself "was afraid of no one" in proclaiming the Cause of God. "All have known and heard this," wrote Bahá'u'lláh. "He was regardless of consequences." The more severe the persecution they inflicted on Him, "the more His fervor increased, and the brighter burned the flame of His love."[9] Already, people who had been strangers had been brought together as believers in the Báb. Could such a thing take place except through the power of God?

The Báb's uncle read the Book of Certitude carefully, page by page. By the end, the doubts and questions that had troubled him were all resolved. The words of Bahá'u'lláh had illumined his thoughts and changed his heart, and he realized that his nephew 'Alí Muḥammad—the Báb—had indeed been a Prophet of God. The mullás had asked Bahá'u'lláh for a miracle and were disappointed. The Báb's uncle desired only the truth, and he was satisfied.

The Book of Certitude would be copied and shared with the other Bábís, too. Through the revelation of this single volume, Bahá'u'lláh had done much more than merely answer the questions of one man. When He revealed the Book of Certitude, Bahá'u'lláh resolved a paradox that had troubled thoughtful people for centuries. How could there be one God and so many religions?

For the first time in the history of religion, believers could see clearly that all the Prophets of God were linked together—each One entrusted with a mission from God. No longer did the followers of different Prophets have reason to look at one another with suspicion or hatred. The story of

---

* Biela's Comet.

the Prophets was the story of one God—the one compassionate Creator Who gave His loving guidance to people in every age and in every part of the world.

Back in Tehran, Shaykh ‘Abdu'l-Ḥusayn's reports were having their intended effect on the shah. Week after week the letters came, filled with lies and accusations, with claims that Bahá'u'lláh was plotting a rebellion against the shah. Why else, they suggested, would so many people, including Persian nobles, come to visit Bahá'u'lláh's home? More and more the shah worried about what might be brewing in Baghdad, so dangerously close to Persia's borders and to Muslim holy places.

Baghdad was part of the Ottoman Empire, which was ruled by Sulṭán ‘Abdu'l-‘Azíz. The shah, through his foreign minister, pressed the sultan to take action. Bahá'u'lláh was a "‘source of mischief,’" the sultan was told—dangerous in a city such as Baghdad, where so many different peoples met and where He was so close to Karbala, the center of pilgrimage for Shia Muslims.[10] He recommended that Bahá'u'lláh be removed at once and sent to live in a city far away from Persian territory.

In January 1863 the governor of Baghdad, Námiq Páshá, received a command from the Ottoman court. Bahá'u'lláh was invited to come and live in Constantinople,* the capital city of the Ottoman Empire. The invitation, though politely worded, was in reality an order that could not be refused. Nevertheless, Námiq Páshá did not pass the order on to Bahá'u'lláh. Instead he waited.

Námiq Páshá referred to Bahá'u'lláh as one of "the Lights of the Age" and had deep respect for Him.[11] Perhaps if he waited the matter would be forgotten. But that was not to be. Again the order came, and again the governor ignored it. Not until the command was repeated three more times did Námiq Páshá finally act. The last command came to him in March near the time of Naw-Rúz, the Persian New Year.

Bahá'u'lláh and several Bábís had left the noise and bustle of Baghdad to celebrate the first days of Naw-Rúz in the green and peaceful countryside. There they pitched their tents and gathered together to share food and tea, prayers and good wishes.

* Present-day Istanbul.

After five days Bahá'u'lláh revealed a new tablet, one that cast a cloud of sorrow over the joy of Naw-Rúz. As Mírzá Áqá Ján chanted the tablet its poetic language seemed to say that Bahá'u'lláh would soon be leaving them. No one among the Bábís wanted such a day to come.

As soon as Mírzá Áqá Ján finished chanting the tablet, Bahá'u'lláh announced that it was time to return to the city. As the believers, with heavy hearts, folded their tents, a messenger rode his horse into their midst. He came from the governor, Námiq Páshá, who asked to meet with Bahá'u'lláh the next day. The believers were gripped with apprehension. Did the governor's message have something to do with Bahá'u'lláh's sorrowful tablet? Could His leaving come so soon? They could hardly bear to think of it.

Bahá'u'lláh Himself knew difficult times lay ahead. He had been visited with a foreboding dream.

> *"I saw the Prophets and the Messengers gather and seat themselves around Me, mourning, weeping and loudly lamenting. Amazed, I inquired of them the reason, whereupon their lamentation and weeping waxed greater, and they said unto Me: 'We weep for Thee, O Most Great Mystery, O Tabernacle of Immortality!' They wept with such a weeping that I too wept with them. Thereupon the Concourse on high addressed Me saying: '. . . Erelong shalt Thou behold with Thine own eyes what no Prophet hath beheld. . . . Be patient, be patient.' . . . They continued addressing Me the whole night until the approach of dawn."*[12]

One person was quite pleased with the turn of events—the troublesome Shaykh 'Abdu'l-Ḥusayn. Finally, he felt, he had achieved victory over Bahá'u'lláh. But it would not be quite the victory the crafty shaykh had imagined.

40

The Garden of Paradise

By evening of the next day the Bábís' fears were confirmed. In a month's time Bahá'u'lláh would leave Baghdad and go to Constantinople, over a thousand miles away. The sorrowful news so disturbed the believers that they could neither eat nor sleep. Bahá'u'lláh had transformed their lives forever, and now their time with Him was short and every hour precious. How could they close their eyes in sleep knowing He must leave them?

The governor, too ashamed to deliver the letter in person, had sent it with his deputy governor. A sum of money for the expenses of the journey was included with the invitation to Constantinople. Bahá'u'lláh accepted the government's invitation, but He did not accept the allowance.

The surprised deputy governor insisted that Bahá'u'lláh must take the money. To refuse would insult the authorities who had offered it. At length Bahá'u'lláh accepted the allowance, but He would not keep it. Instead, on that same day He gave the whole sum away, distributing it all among the poor of Baghdad.

As His final weeks in Baghdad approached, Bahá'u'lláh did everything He could to comfort the Bábís and lift their spirits. Every day He showered them with His love. In the days to come, every Bábí who lived in Baghdad—whether man or woman, child or adult—received a separate tablet from Bahá'u'lláh. The tablets, each written in His own hand, encouraged and inspired one and all to show forth in their lives their faith and their lofty purpose. In each tablet He urged them to be strong and warned them that days of tests and trials lay ahead.

News of Bahá'u'lláh's impending departure traveled quickly through Baghdad and nearby towns. Everyone wanted to say good-bye. So many people came to see Bahá'u'lláh that His house could not accommodate them all, nor with so many visitors could the family make their necessary preparations for the journey to come.

A solution to the problem was suggested by a wealthy man, Najíb Páshá, who greatly admired Bahá'u'lláh. Najíb Páshá owned a large, park-like garden just across the river from Bahá'u'lláh's house. He offered Bahá'u'lláh the use of the garden during His last days in Baghdad. There Bahá'u'lláh would be able to pitch His tent and receive all the visitors who wished to bid Him farewell, while the rest of the family would be free to prepare for the journey ahead. Bahá'u'lláh accepted the generous offer.

On Wednesday afternoon, April 22, 1863, Bahá'u'lláh left His home in Baghdad for the last time and traveled the short distance to Najíb

Pá<u>sh</u>á's garden. For the first time Bahá'u'lláh wore a stately *táj*, a tall felt hat, in place of His usual turban. The finely embroidered táj rested like a crown on His head. Between His house and the river the way was packed with people who had come to see Bahá'u'lláh one last time. Men, women, and children—friend and stranger alike—crowded together to catch a glimpse of Him.

There were Arabs, Kurds, and Persians gathered as well as Muslims, Christians, and Jews. There were merchants, officials, and clergy, as well as those with no rank or learning. Some had come from curiosity, but most came out of respect. Bahá'u'lláh had touched the lives of so many who lived in Baghdad, and their encounters with the Messenger of God had left none of them the same. In the hundreds of years since its founding the city had rarely witnessed such a diversity of peoples come together with one heart.

Some climbed to the rooftops to more easily see Bahá'u'lláh, Who even now gave out coins to the poor and spoke words of comfort as He passed. Many wept openly. Who now would comfort the orphaned, the outcast, and the poor He had befriended? Who would speak on their behalf for justice?

As He stood on the shore of the Tigris River, Bahá'u'lláh spoke to the Bábís who stood with Him. "'*O my companions,*'" He said, "'*I entrust to your keeping this city of Ba<u>gh</u>dád, in the state ye now behold it, when from the eyes of friends and strangers alike, crowding its housetops, its streets and markets, tears like the rain of spring are flowing down, and I depart. With you it now rests to watch lest your deeds and conduct dim the flame of love that gloweth within the breasts of its inhabitants.*'"[1]

Then Bahá'u'lláh turned and stepped into a waiting river taxi. The boatman ferried Him to the garden on the other side of the river. His sons and His amanuensis, Mírzá Áqá Ján, went with Him. Other Bábís would soon follow.

"Alláh-u-Akbar!" (God is Most Great!) The afternoon call to prayer sounded from a nearby muezzin as Bahá'u'lláh entered the garden. Shapely trees and flowering plants grew abundantly along the garden's wide pathways, and the air was rich with the scent of roses. For some time, as the new year approached, Bahá'u'lláh had been hinting at something wonderful to come. A new joy had pervaded His poems, tablets, and conver-

sations with the believers. Day by day He had prepared the Bábís, and now at last the time was at hand. Now, in the garden of Najíb Pá<u>sh</u>á, Bahá'u'lláh announced to a handful of Bábís what so many longed to hear.

He, Bahá'u'lláh, was the Promised One, "He Whom God will make manifest," the Holy Messenger from God promised by the Báb. Bahá'u'lláh, "the Glory of God," was the One for Whom the world had long been waiting. "The Divine Springtime is come," wrote Bahá'u'lláh in a tablet referring to this time. "He that was hidden from the eyes of men is revealed, girded with sovereignty and power!"[2]

For ten years Bahá'u'lláh had told no one of His experience in the Black Pit. No one knew about the Maiden Who had appeared to Him in that black dungeon of Tehran. Mírzá Áqá Ján had had a glimpse, in Karbala, of the "'oceans of light,'" and a few others had guessed that Bahá'u'lláh was the One promised by the Báb.[3] But only Bahá'u'lláh knew the time to openly reveal His secret.

Now, nineteen years after Mullá Ḥusayn had first discovered the Báb, the time was right. Never before had humanity been blessed with two divine Messengers in one lifetime. Not for at least a thousand years, Bahá'u'lláh later wrote, would the world see another Messenger from God. This was a time unlike any that had come before it.

"In this Day a great festival is taking place in the Realm above," wrote Bahá'u'lláh, "for whatsoever was promised in the sacred Scriptures hath been fulfilled." With great joy Bahá'u'lláh declared this very day to be the first day of the Festival of *Riḍván* (Paradise). From this time on, people would celebrate Riḍván, which was the *"'Most Great Festival,'"* He said, the *"'King of Festivals,'"* the *"'Festival of God.'"*[4]

When the Bábís began to grasp what Bahá'u'lláh was telling them, their sorrow turned into blissful joy. They renamed the garden of Najíb Pá<u>sh</u>á the Garden of Riḍván. Surely there could be no happier place on earth! Who among them could imagine anything more wonderful than to stand in this spot, on this Day, with the Promised One from God?

This new Day brought with it new ways. The use of the sword in teaching the Word of God was forbidden, Bahá'u'lláh told them. The mightiest sword belonging to a believer is the tongue, He said, for speech can remove the veils of ignorance from the human heart.

Bahá'u'lláh stayed in the Garden of Riḍván for twelve days. A few Bábís also stayed with Him, pitching their tents near His. At night the small, plain nightingales perched among the roses and sang their beautiful songs in the moonlight. How sweet was their music to Bahá'u'lláh as He walked in the moonlit garden!

Before dawn each day, gardeners picked the roses from the garden pathways and brought them to Bahá'u'lláh. Early each day the Bábís gathered in Bahá'u'lláh's tent for tea. There, in the center, the freshly picked roses were heaped so high that those who were present could not see one another over the mound. The fragrance sweetened their morning tea.

Each day when the Bábís left Bahá'u'lláh, they carried away armfuls of roses to deliver in Baghdad. The velvet-petaled flowers were gifts of remembrance from Bahá'u'lláh to His friends in the city.

Each day a steady stream of distinguished officials, friends, and admirers came to the Riḍván Garden to say farewell. From morning to evening Bahá'u'lláh was busy with the visitors from Baghdad. Food was prepared in the homes of Bahá'u'lláh and another Bábí and was sent to the garden each day.

The governor of Baghdad, Námiq Pá<u>sh</u>á, came to see Bahá'u'lláh. He was greatly sorry to see Bahá'u'lláh leave, and he offered to help in any way he could. "'Whatever you require, you have but to command,'" he said. "'We are ready to carry it out.'" In reply Bahá'u'lláh asked nothing for Himself, only for those He would leave behind. *"'Extend thy consideration to Our loved ones,'"* He said, *"'and deal with them with kindness.'"*[5]

On the ninth day Bahá'u'lláh's family came to the Riḍván Garden. Packing for the journey was nearly complete. In just a few days they would leave the Garden of Riḍván and the city of Baghdad, which Bahá'u'lláh called "'the City of God.'"[6]

Bahá'u'lláh did not forget the old woman who had waited for Him each day as He made His way to the coffeehouse. He had always treated her kindly. Now, before His departure, He arranged to provide for her needs for the rest of her days.

Siyyid Ḥabíb, who owned the coffeehouse near the western entrance to the bridge of boats, closed down his business. The light had gone out of it. He could not bring himself to open the coffeehouse doors, for Bahá'u'lláh would never walk through them again.

41

One Hundred and Ten Days

Twelve days after entering the Garden of Riḍván, Bahá'u'lláh left to begin the journey to Constantinople. Instead of bringing Him the humble donkey He usually rode, the Bábís brought the finest horse they could buy—a magnificent, sleek red roan stallion. Mounted on this regal steed and wearing His crown-like táj, Bahá'u'lláh made His way through Baghdad.

All of Baghdad, it seemed, turned out to bid Him good-bye. The day was filled with the sounds of weeping and lamenting. Many bowed their heads to the dust in respect as He rode by. On every side people crowded close to embrace His stirrups or kiss the hooves of His horse in their last grief-stricken farewells.

Even Bahá'u'lláh's enemies, in the face of such devotion by the people of Baghdad, were sorry to see Him leave. They had expected Bahá'u'lláh to go in disgrace. What a bitter surprise to see Baghdad pour out its love for Him! Bahá'u'lláh had transformed an occasion of disgrace into a procession of triumph, and His enemies regretted their actions.

"'Formerly they insisted upon your departure,'" the governor had told Bahá'u'lláh on the day he called on Him. "'Now, however, they are even more insistent that you should remain.'"[1] But it was not to be. On this day, May 3, 1863, Bahá'u'lláh, His family, and the Bábís who had received permission to travel with them left Baghdad behind.

A few miles north of Baghdad they stopped for seven days. Here they made final preparations for the journey ahead. Nearly seventy-two people would be part of their caravan. Lanterns and cooking supplies, bedding and belongings—all must be readied for a journey of many weeks. Even as Bahá'u'lláh's brother Mírzá Músá took charge of these last details, more visitors came from Baghdad to see Bahá'u'lláh.

By the end of the week all was ready, and the caravan set out. Fifty mules carried burdens of goods or riders. Seven pairs of howdahs—seats strapped on the backs of mules—carried mostly women and children. Four parasols opened over each pair of howdahs to shield the passengers from the sun. Ten soldiers and their officer, mounted on horseback, rode as guards to protect the travelers from attack.

The caravan started out on a route that lay east of the Tigris River, then crossed to the west side of the river and continued slowly north. Námiq Pás̲h̲á, the governor of Baghdad, had written to Ottoman officials along the route, ordering them to treat Bahá'u'lláh and His companions with consideration and to give them whatever they needed. Because of Námiq Pás̲h̲á, Bahá'u'lláh and the band of exiles were welcomed warmly all along their journey.

When the caravan drew near a village or town, a delegation of officials from that place would ride out to greet them. Some towns sent out soldiers, too, carrying banners and beating their drums in welcome. Some villagers cooked food for them and held festivities to honor Bahá'u'lláh. When the caravan left a place, a delegation of officials would ride along for a distance as a courtesy to Bahá'u'lláh.

Still, the journey was not easy. The caravan with its women and children traveled barely thirty miles a day. The hot season with its scorching sun beat down upon them, and traveling in the cool hours of night was often their best escape. When no town or village was nearby, they made camp wherever they could.

At the end of a day's travel, people and animals alike were hungry and thirsty and weary to the bone. Food could be hard to find, for there was famine in the countryside. 'Abdu'l-Bahá, who was now nineteen, took charge of this difficult task. Bahá'u'lláh always dealt fairly with people; on His orders, nothing was taken without paying for it.

Bahá'u'lláh's younger half-brother Mírzá Yaḥyá, who had caused so much trouble in Baghdad, was not among the caravan travelers. While they were still in Baghdad Mírzá Yaḥyá had become unnerved at the news of Bahá'u'lláh's impending departure and anxious about what to do. Bahá'u'lláh encouraged him to come with them to Constantinople, saying to Mírzá Yaḥyá, "'If you wish to come [to Constantinople] I will inform Námiq Pás̲h̲á accordingly; but come in the open.'"[2]

Mírzá Yaḥyá refused. He feared that as soon as Bahá'u'lláh and His companions left the safety of Baghdad they would be handed over to Persian officials or killed. He decided instead to run away to India or Abyssinia (Ethiopia), where no one would know that he was a Bábí. Then he reconsidered. Perhaps it would be safer to stay near Baghdad.

One of the Bábís owned a large garden just outside the city. Mírzá Yaḥyá asked Bahá'u'lláh to instruct the Bábí to build a cottage of reeds for him in the garden. There Mírzá Yaḥyá would live, safely hidden away. Bahá'u'lláh consented, and the Bábí began building the small house for Mírzá Yaḥyá. When the cottage was only half-built Mírzá Yaḥyá changed his mind once more. The cottage was not a suitable hiding place, he said.

At one point Bahá'u'lláh advised Mírzá Yaḥyá to return to Persia. He asked him to take copies of the Báb's writings and share them with the believers there. These copies were the patient result of many hours spent transcribing by hand. Mírzá Yaḥyá himself had helped in the work, and he agreed to take the writings to Persia. But once again Mírzá Yaḥyá, caught in the grip of his own fears, changed his mind and did not go. Instead of following Bahá'u'lláh's guidance, he found a traveling companion and set out from Baghdad before Bahá'u'lláh and His party. When he had traveled about two hundred miles north—as far as the city of Mosul—Mírzá Yaḥyá stopped and waited for Bahá'u'lláh. He had left behind the priceless writings of the Báb. Although the writings would eventually be sent to a safe location, it was clear that Mírzá Yaḥyá placed his own interests above all other considerations.

Bahá'u'lláh and the caravan stopped in Mosul for a few days' rest. There the weary exiles scrubbed themselves clean at the city baths. Each day important people from the city came to welcome Bahá'u'lláh. One night at midnight a message was delivered from Mírzá Yaḥyá, who asked to meet with someone from the caravan.

Bahá'u'lláh's faithful brother Mírzá Músá went that very night to the inn where Mírzá Yaḥyá was staying and invited him to join the caravan. Mírzá Yaḥyá's own family was traveling with them, said Mírzá Músá. Mírzá Yaḥyá agreed to come with the caravan, but only in disguise.

When he reached the caravan, Mírzá Yaḥyá introduced himself to the others as Ḥájí 'Alí, a Muslim pilgrim returning home from Mecca. In front of strangers he pretended not to know Bahá'u'lláh or the other Bábís. At night he might visit his family in their tent, but he slept in a tent by himself.

Many of the Bábís had never met Mírzá Yaḥyá. He had kept himself well hidden in Baghdad. But there was one who knew him very well indeed—his mischief-making friend Siyyid Muḥammad. For the rest of the journey Mírzá Yaḥyá could be found in the company of Siyyid Muḥammad.

In time Bahá'u'lláh and the caravan climbed from the hot, flat plains into the cool uplands. They made their way through lush forests and green mountain passes. Eventually, they came down the other side of the mountains to the shores of the Black Sea. The last four hundred miles of their journey would be by ship.

After a week of waiting in the port city of Samsun, Bahá'u'lláh and the others boarded a steamship and headed west. In a few days' time they arrived at the city of Constantinople. It was August 16, 1863. The journey from Baghdad had taken 110 days—nearly four months.

At the landing station a horse-drawn carriage was brought for Bahá'u'lláh and His family. Mírzá Yaḥyá chose to walk behind the carriage, next to his friend Siyyid Muḥammad. As they walked with a hurried step Mírzá Yaḥyá brooded. With a jealous heart he remembered the honor shown to Bahá'u'lláh all along their journey.

Mírzá Yaḥyá turned to Siyyid Muḥammad. "'Had I not chosen to hide myself, had I revealed my identity," he was heard to say, "the honor accorded Him (Bahá'u'lláh) on this day would have been mine too.'"[3]

Siyyid Muḥammad listened with a sympathetic ear. The troublemaking days of the two conspirators were not done yet.

42

The Sultan's Command

The great seaport of Constantinople bustled with ships and traders. It was the only city in the world that straddled two continents—one part in Asia, the other in Europe. In between, the waters of the Bosporus Strait flowed south from the Black Sea to the warm Mediterranean. Bridges, as well as ferries that carried people back and forth, connected the city's two halves.

For thousands of years Constantinople had been the capital city of empires. When Bahá'u'lláh walked along the city's winding cobblestone lanes it was the capital of the Ottoman Empire. From the mosques on top of its seven hills came the call to prayer each day. On its shores stood the palace of Sulṭán 'Abdu'l-'Azíz, by whose command Bahá'u'lláh had, in effect, been banished from Baghdad.

At first Bahá'u'lláh, along with His family and Bábí companions, lived in a small, cramped place. After some weeks they were allowed to move into a larger, three-story house with enough room for everyone. Before long there were visitors. Officials and other important people came to welcome Bahá'u'lláh, expecting that He, in turn, would call on them. He would, no doubt, beg more money for living expenses and seek to curry favor with them. They knew how to deal with such matters. Certainly He would want to gain their support for His Cause. These things were common among Persian princes and other government guests who came to their city.

But Bahá'u'lláh did not return the officials' visits. He found their welcome heartless, and the officials themselves "cold as ice and lifeless as dead trees." Their interests were shallow. He could find no one ready to learn the spiritual truths that God had taught Him, nor anyone ripe for His words of wisdom. "Our inner eye," wrote Bahá'u'lláh, "wept sore over them."[1]

"'I have no wish to ask favour from them,'" He said. "'I have come here at the Sulṭán's command. Whatsoever additional commands he may issue, I am ready to obey. My work is not of their world; it is of another realm, far removed from their province. Why, therefore, should I seek these people?'"[2]

Except for going to the mosque or to the public bath, Bahá'u'lláh stayed at home. This surprised and puzzled most government officials. Never before had they met a man who showed so little interest in money and political favors. The Persian ambassador to Constantinople, Mírzá Ḥusayn Khán, did not like it at all. Bahá'u'lláh's independent attitude grated against him, and the resentful ambassador began to spread lies about Bahá'u'lláh.

Bahá'u'lláh was a proud and arrogant man, the ambassador alleged. That was why He did not come to visit the officials, clergy, and others. Bahá'u'lláh put Himself above the laws of the land, the ambassador told others, and harbored secret designs against those in authority. No wonder the government had banished Him! Bahá'u'lláh Himself was to blame. Others also vilified Bahá'u'lláh and the exiled Bábís.

Weeks passed as the hot, thick air of summer cooled and thinned into crisp autumn days. The ambassador's lies spread everywhere, like leaves scattered by the wind. When the sharp-tongued gossip reached the ears of the sultan he found it unsettling. Without ever bothering to find out the truth, Sulṭán 'Abdu'l-'Azíz took action.

One cold day a messenger came to Bahá'u'lláh's home with an order from the sultan that commanded Bahá'u'lláh to leave Constantinople at once. He must go without delay to the city of Adrianople* in the far northwest corner of the empire. After less than four months in the capital, Bahá'u'lláh was being banished once again.

But Bahá'u'lláh refused to go. Angry at the sultan's unjust order, He encouraged all those with Him to stand firm. Neither He nor any of the Bábís had done anything wrong. "‘"Our innocence is manifestly evident,"’" Bahá'u'lláh told the Bábís, "‘"and they [the authorities] have no alternative but to declare their injustice."’"[3]

Most of the Bábís were more than willing to stand their ground with Bahá'u'lláh. They were ready to follow in the footsteps of the Dawn-Breakers—to offer everything in the path of God, even their lives. But Mírzá Yaḥyá, alarmed and afraid, pleaded with Bahá'u'lláh to obey the sultan's orders. Though Bahá'u'lláh tried to calm his fears, Mírzá Yaḥyá, as always, cared most dearly about preserving his own life. When he saw that Bahá'u'lláh would not change His mind, he began to conspire secretly with Siyyid Muḥammad and a few others who also thought only of saving their own lives. Their sly meetings made Bahá'u'lláh sad at heart.

He knew that their selfish actions could shatter the unity of the Bábís. The mighty Cause of God, for which the Báb and the Dawn-Breakers had sacrificed their lives, would look weak in the eyes of others. To protect the Cause of God, Bahá'u'lláh decided to accept the sultan's order of banishment. A golden opportunity, He said, had been lost. "‘They called us here as their guests, and innocent as we are, they turned on us with vengeance,’" said Bahá'u'lláh. "‘If we, few as we are, had stood our ground to fall martyrs in the midmost heart of the world, the effect of that martyrdom would have been felt in all the worlds of God. And possibly nothing would have happened to us.’"[4]

Before He left Constantinople Bahá'u'lláh revealed a long tablet to the unjust sultan. He sealed it in an envelope and gave it the following morning to a trustworthy messenger. Deliver this to the grand vizier of the sultan, Bahá'u'lláh instructed, and tell him it was sent down from God. The messenger obeyed.

---

* Present-day Edirne, Turkey.

When the sultan's grand vizier read the strongly worded tablet from Bahá'u'lláh, he turned pale as a corpse. He could not believe that anyone would dare to address the sultan so boldly. “““It is as if the King of Kings,””” said the grand vizier, “““were issuing his behest to his humblest vassal king and regulating his conduct.”””[5]

To the Persian ambassador who had lied and plotted against Him, Bahá'u'lláh also sent a message: *“‘His* [God's] *Cause transcends any and every plan ye devise,'”* Bahá'u'lláh wrote. *“‘Know this much,'”* He continued, *“‘Were all the governments on earth to unite and take My life and the lives of all who bear this Name, this Divine Fire would never be quenched. His Cause will rather encompass all the kings of the earth, nay all that hath been created from water and clay.'”*[6]

Only a small group of Bábís would journey with Bahá'u'lláh to Adrianople. Bahá'u'lláh told the rest to return to their homelands and teach the Bábí Faith to others. Two believers would return to Persia to share the news of Bahá'u'lláh's declaration in the Garden of Riḍvan. Only one Bábí would stay in Constantinople. His task would be to pass letters between Bahá'u'lláh and the believers in Persia.

The next morning, December 1, 1863, in the bitter cold and snow of winter, Bahá'u'lláh left Constantinople. He turned His back on the city that stood on two continents—the capital city of the fading Ottoman Empire—and headed west. The friends who stayed behind wept as they watched Him leave.

Traveling with Bahá'u'lláh and the other exiles were Siyyid Muḥammad, who came against the advice of Bahá'u'lláh, and Mírzá Yaḥyá. Before long, they would be guilty of more than simple disobedience or selfishness. In Adrianople Mírzá Yaḥyá would grow bolder than he had ever been, and Bahá'u'lláh's very life would hang by a thread.

43

The Poisoned Cup

Snow swirled around the departing exiles—men, women, and children—huddled together in rough wagons or mounted on pack animals and hunched against the cold. It fell on the slow-moving oxcarts that carried their meager belongings. During many of the torturous days that followed, the exiles were whipped by sleet-filled winds or pelted with icy rain. Bahá'u'lláh and the others were not prepared for the journey. They had not been given time.

None of them had adequate clothing to protect them from winter's freezing cold—especially this winter. The oldest inhabitants of the region could not remember a harsher winter. Along the road the travelers saw the bodies of people who had perished in the severe cold. Great rivers froze over for weeks. To get water for drinking, the exiles would build a large fire near a frozen spring and keep it burning for two hours or more to thaw the ice.

Bahá'u'lláh and the weary exiles, in the company of their Turkish guards, pushed on. They journeyed through bitter cold and storms, traveling by day and, at times, in the pale moonlight of frigid nights. "Even the eyes of Our enemies have wept over Us," wrote Bahá'u'lláh of that agonizing trip.[1] After twelve days they reached the end of their journey and entered the city of Adrianople.

Bahá'u'lláh had never lived so far away from His Persian homeland. Adrianople, home to over one hundred thousand people, stood on European soil near the borders of Greece and Bulgaria at the junction of three rivers. From ancient times its strategic position on the route between Europe and Asia had made it an important city and the site of many battles. Bahá'u'lláh referred to Adrianople as the "remote prison."[2]

He was not kept behind prison walls or even charged with a crime, but He was no longer a guest of the Ottoman government. Only rebels against the sultan were sent this far away. Bahá'u'lláh had done nothing wrong, yet He was being treated disgracefully, as though He were indeed guilty of some transgression.

The exiles were relieved to have completed their journey, but there was little relief from the cold, which was all the more intense for those accustomed to Baghdad's warmer climate. After several days in a comfortless caravansary, the exiles were moved into a house fit only for summer living. Bahá'u'lláh's room was so cold and drafty that a jug of water would freeze overnight. Snowfalls and the unusually cold weather continued well into spring.

Finally after six months Bahá'u'lláh and His family were able to move into a larger, more comfortable house. It stood in the center of the city and was called the house of *Amru'lláh* (God's command). The other Bábís were able to move into nearby houses.

There was not much money and, as a result, most meals were plain. With the family's meager resources, they bought two cows and a goat. Now they could have a steady supply of milk and yogurt. Bahá'u'lláh accepted a government allowance, mostly to help the fellow exiles who had come with Him. Though He did not have very much Himself, Bahá'u'lláh did not forget the poor. He always shared something with those in need.

In Adrianople Bahá'u'lláh did not appear in public as much as He had in Baghdad. Although He visited the public bath, He did not go to the coffeehouses as before. He went to the mosques from time to time and took part in discussions there. Little by little the people of Adrianople came to know and admire Bahá'u'lláh. They had never met anyone like Him.

As in Baghdad, people of every sort were drawn to Him. Men of learning and city leaders were amazed at His vast knowledge. They were attracted by His resplendent character, untainted by any hint of selfishness. Simple working people were warmed by His genuine loving-kindness. The governor, too, admired this exile in his city.

Soon, when the people of Adrianople spoke to Bahá'u'lláh, they called Him *"Shaykh Effendi,"* a title denoting high honor and prestige. When He walked along their streets, they stood and bowed before Him with reverence. The sultan had sent Him to their city to be forgotten, but nothing could dim the splendor of Bahá'u'lláh's greatness.

At these signs of respect for his older brother, Mírzá Yaḥyá breathed easier. In Adrianople they were far away from Persia, and the authorities here were friendly. For the first time since the cruel days of killing in Tehran, Mírzá Yaḥyá was no longer afraid, and, at Siyyid Muḥammad's urging, he came out of hiding.

Bahá'u'lláh encouraged the Bábís to practice useful trades as they had done in Baghdad. One began work as a tailor, another as a weaver of silk. Other Bábís opened shops of one sort or another in the marketplace. In the daytime they worked at their trades, and in the evenings they gathered at Bahá'u'lláh's house to enjoy one another's company. They were happy to live as exiles in a foreign land as long as they were near Bahá'u'lláh.

But Mírzá Yaḥyá was haunted by darker, turbulent feelings of frustration and envy. No longer afraid for his life, he became more ambitious and jealous than ever. How desperately he wanted to be in Bahá'u'lláh's place—to have the Bábís' adulation and to be their leader! More and more, Mírzá Yaḥyá was willing to do whatever it might take to get what he wanted. The malevolent Siyyid Muḥammad, who hated Bahá'u'lláh, pressed Mírzá Yaḥyá to take action.

Mírzá Yaḥyá began to show a curiosity in the skills of his half-brother Mírzá Músá. Mírzá Músá knew the healing uses of herbs and plants, and Mírzá Yaḥyá asked him many questions. Which part of this plant did he use, and what effect did that plant have? Most important, which ones were poisonous? Mírzá Músá was happy to answer the questions of his curious younger half-brother. He had no suspicion of Mírzá Yaḥyá's real purpose.

Mírzá Yaḥyá soon put to use what he had learned. He invited Bahá'u'lláh to come to his house—an unusual thing for Mírzá Yaḥyá to do. At his home he served Bahá'u'lláh tea. Then he watched as Bahá'u'lláh drank from the thin teacup smeared with deadly poison. Mírzá Yaḥyá was not surprised when news came, shortly after, that Bahá'u'lláh was gravely ill. Mírzá Yaḥyá's plan was working just as he expected.

In His room at the house of Amru'lláh, Bahá'u'lláh looked ashen. The poison was causing high fever and terrible pains. His distraught family called in a doctor, but even he could do nothing to help. Bahá'u'lláh—Who had lovingly guided and protected Mírzá Yaḥyá since his youth, when their father had died—now lay close to death at the hands of His younger half-brother.

The doctor, a Christian, was deeply disturbed that so wise and good a man as Bahá'u'lláh should die. He prayed for God to take him, instead. A few days later the doctor became sick, and Bahá'u'lláh, ill as He was, sent Mírzá Áqá Ján to visit him. God had answered his prayers, the doctor told Mírzá Áqá Ján. In a few days the doctor died.

A week passed, and then another. Still Bahá'u'lláh was too sick to leave His bed. No one knew whether He would live or die. Another week passed. Then one day Bahá'u'lláh was finally able to sit up in bed and later, with help, to walk. The believers were overjoyed. Bahá'u'lláh was still weak, but He would live. Their prayers, and the prayers of the good doctor, had been answered.

Bahá'u'lláh recovered, but the poison left its mark. For the rest of His life, one of His hands would tremble. Even now, Bahá'u'lláh did not wish to punish Mírzá Yaḥyá, and He asked the believers to say nothing about the poisoning. It was Mírzá Yaḥyá who boldly began to say that Bahá'u'lláh had poisoned *him*. Only then did Bahá'u'lláh permit the real story to be told, and soon many Bábís and others close to them knew the shameful truth.

Time passed, and a measure of calm returned to the shaken Bábí community. But Mírzá Yaḥyá was not ready to give up. He had another plan, a plan that would not dirty his own hands at all.

44

The Most Great Separation

"'How fine a thing it is for a man to be brave,'" said Mírzá Yaḥyá.[1] He was talking to Ustád Muḥammad-'Alí, the barber and bath attendant who served in the household of Bahá'u'lláh. He was, at that moment, attending Mírzá Yaḥyá at the public bath. Ustád rubbed henna into Mírzá Yaḥyá's hair. The room was warm and steamy.

Mírzá Yaḥyá had begun to tell a story. It was a bloody tale of a young boy who had killed his enemy at the public bath. The barber wondered why Mírzá Yaḥyá would tell such a story to him. Again, at the end of the story, Mírzá Yaḥyá spoke of the merits of bravery, courage, and boldness. Then he began to talk about the Cause of God and about himself, as though he had been wronged. "'Now see what they are doing to the Cause of God!'" he complained. "'Every one harming the Faith. Every one risen up against me! Even my own brother! And I, never allowed a moment's peace! Never a tranquil breath!'"[2]

Suddenly the barber understood what Mírzá Yaḥyá wanted. The story—and his talk of bravery—was Mírzá Yaḥyá's indirect way of asking Ustád to do something heinous. Mírzá Yaḥyá wanted the barber, while he attended Bahá'u'lláh at the bath, to kill Him. The very thought sickened Ustád. It was unspeakable! His heart pounded. The bathhouse walls seemed to come closer, ready to crash down around him. Ustád hurried out of the room, away from Mírzá Yaḥyá.

Outside he wept until fear gave way to rage. His blood boiled at what Mírzá Yaḥyá wanted him to do. Ustád struggled with himself. More than anything, he wanted to walk back inside and kill Mírzá Yaḥyá on the spot. He would chop his head off, and that would be the end of it. Only one thought stopped him. What would he say to Bahá'u'lláh?

Controlling his fury, Ustád went back inside and shouted angrily, "'Get up and get out. God send you to hell!'"[3] The rage in Ustád's voice and the look on his face frightened Mírzá Yaḥyá, who began to whimper and tremble. Quickly he threw on the rest of his clothes and ran out.

That night Ustád the barber went to Bahá'u'lláh's house. In his hands he carried pages of Mírzá Yaḥyá's writings. There, in the tearoom where the other believers had gathered, he stuffed the papers into the charcoal brazier and burned them. "'Until today I have always worshiped the house of this Azal [Mírzá Yaḥyá],'" he told the others. "'Today, so far as I am concerned, he is less than a dog!'"[4]

Ustád let Bahá'u'lláh know what had happened at the bath. Bahá'u'lláh directed him to tell no one else about it, but the barber could not keep so vile a secret to himself. When it came out into the open, Mírzá Yaḥyá lied again. He accused the barber himself of wanting to kill Bahá'u'lláh.

The news of another attempt on Bahá'u'lláh's life shattered the peace of the Bábí community. This time Bahá'u'lláh took action. Mírzá Yaḥyá might wish to replace Bahá'u'lláh, but the Cause of God could not be held hostage by one man's selfish wishes. The Báb had named Mírzá Yaḥyá leader only as a temporary measure until the Promised One announced Himself.

Bahá'u'lláh revealed a special tablet for Mírzá Yaḥyá that stated clearly what Mírzá Yaḥyá already knew. Bahá'u'lláh was the One promised by the Báb—"He Whom God will make Manifest." He had made His announcement in the Garden of Riḍván. In this tablet Bahá'u'lláh announced His supreme station to Mírzá Yaḥyá in unequivocal language. Bahá'u'lláh—and no one else—was the Messenger of God.

Bahá'u'lláh gave the tablet to Mírzá Áqá Ján to deliver. He must read the tablet aloud to Mírzá Yaḥyá, Bahá'u'lláh told him, and demand an unequivocal, conclusive reply. Mírzá Áqá Ján carried out Bahá'u'lláh's instructions, but Mírzá Yaḥyá did not reply at once. Instead, he asked for one day to ponder his answer. Bahá'u'lláh granted his request.

When the reply came, however, it was yet another lie, this one more outrageous than all the others. Mírzá Yaḥyá claimed that he himself had received a revelation from God. All the world's peoples in both the East and the West, he asserted, must submit to him.

For the protection of the Cause of God the time had come for Bahá'u'lláh to part ways with Mírzá Yaḥyá and his henchmen. At Bahá'u'lláh's instruction, Mírzá Músá divided all the furniture, clothing, and utensils in Bahá'u'lláh's house. Half of everything was sent to the house of Mírzá Yaḥyá. Certain precious items of the Báb's—rings, seals, and manuscripts—that Mírzá Yaḥyá had always coveted, were sent to him. He would also receive his full share of the government allowance given to the exiles.

Then on March 10, 1866, Bahá'u'lláh moved out of the house of Amru'lláh and into another, known as the house of Riḍá Big. Only His own family and one servant accompanied Him. Bahá'u'lláh refused to see anyone else, whether friend or stranger.

Bahá'u'lláh's withdrawal had a purpose—to let the faithful believers sort themselves out from the false. Bahá'u'lláh was a Messenger of God, and no other Messenger would be sent by God for at least a thousand years. Now each of the exiles must choose between Bahá'u'lláh and Mírzá Yaḥyá. Each must decide for himself where he stood.

The exiles were stunned. They had not expected to be cut off from Bahá'u'lláh so abruptly and completely. Bahá'u'lláh was the sun in their midst, the center of their days. What would they do without Him? No one knew how long this separation would last. When Bahá'u'lláh left Baghdad, He had stayed in the wilderness for two years. Even to contemplate being so long without Him again was almost more than they could bear.

Not everyone, however, felt this way. There were a few Bábís whose faith lived more on their lips than in their hearts. With Bahá'u'lláh behind closed doors, they felt bold enough to join Mírzá Yaḥyá. They did not sit idle. Mírzá Yaḥyá, together with Siyyid Muḥammad and the few who joined them, began to write letters. The letters were packets of lies, black lies that muddied the name of Bahá'u'lláh.

Mírzá Yaḥyá sent them far and wide to believers in Persia and Iraq. When they read the disturbing letters, many Bábís became confused. They lived far away from Bahá'u'lláh and knew nothing of Mírzá Yaḥyá's talk with Ustád the barber or of the attempt to poison Bahá'u'lláh. The letters in their hands accused Bahá'u'lláh of the very crimes Mírzá Yaḥyá had committed.

Some Bábís believed what Mírzá Yaḥyá wrote, and a few weak souls lost their faith completely. Others wrote to Bahá'u'lláh with questions. Bahá'u'lláh wrote back, telling them the truth. But most Bábís who knew Bahá'u'lláh did not believe Mírzá Yaḥyá's lies, and they did not remain quiet. Instead, they spoke up to defend the true Promised One of God and traveled to towns and villages in every part of Persia to teach the Faith of Bahá'u'lláh.

The Bábís were not the only targets of Mírzá Yaḥyá's shabby campaign of lies. The governor of Adrianople received a letter, too. In it Mírzá Yaḥyá accused Bahá'u'lláh of cheating him out of his living allowance. "'We come to you in destitution,'" he wrote, "'grant us some corn.'"[5] Mírzá Yaḥyá sent his wife to the government house to beg for food, complaining that her children would starve because of Bahá'u'lláh. None of it was true.

The governor, who knew and admired Bahá'u'lláh, did not believe the shameful accusations. Still, rumors traveled as far as Constantinople, dishonoring Bahá'u'lláh's name even among those who had admired Him. Siyyid Muḥammad himself traveled boldly to the capital. There he planted more lies in the ears of the Persian ambassador. Not only was Bahá'u'lláh a dangerous man, Siyyid Muḥammad told him, but He had even sent an agent to assassinate the shah.

It was clear that Mírzá Yaḥyá and Siyyid Muḥammad, if left unchecked, would gravely hurt the Cause of God. Bahá'u'lláh would not let that happen. After only two months Bahá'u'lláh ended His seclusion and opened His doors once again to believers and other visitors. But things had changed.

Those two months had served to separate the faithful Bábís from those who were not—the good wheat from the useless chaff. Bahá'u'lláh called it the "*'most great separation.'*"[6] Mírzá Yaḥyá, Siyyid Muḥammad, and those who sided with them had broken the Báb's Covenant. They had disobeyed the Báb's teachings by turning against Bahá'u'lláh, the Promised One foretold by the Báb. The inner truth of their hearts could be read plainly in the open book of their actions.

The division they had caused could not easily be repaired. To protect the faithful Bábís, Bahá'u'lláh expelled the treacherous Siyyid Muḥammad from their community. No longer welcome among them, he continued to live in the Muslim part of town. Mírzá Yaḥyá dared not show his face. He and his family lived in a separate house, far removed from Bahá'u'lláh.

Neither Mírzá Yaḥyá nor Siyyid Muḥammad was remorseful. Their hearts were hardened to the pain they had caused Bahá'u'lláh and His followers, and both continued their troublemaking ways. They had forgotten the verse from Islam, "They plotted—but God plotted: and of plotters is God the best!"[7] Though they did not know it, their own downfall was drawing nearer day by day. It would begin with a simple Bábí from Shiraz—a caravan-driver who was, even then, on his way to Adrianople.

45

He Who Feareth No One

Siyyid Muḥammad was an expert rumormonger who knew just how to twist the truth to set tongues wagging. In fact, when Siyyid Muḥammad finished with it, truth was turned inside out. Plying his skills, Siyyid Muḥammad started a new rumor buzzing through Adrianople.

Mírzá Yaḥyá wished to challenge Bahá'u'lláh, said Siyyid Muḥammad. He was ready to meet face-to-face in a public debate. Alas, Siyyid Muḥammad told his friends, only one thing stood in the way. Bahá'u'lláh would not face His younger brother.

Mírzá Yaḥyá remained inside his house. In truth, he had no intention of meeting openly with Bahá'u'lláh, and Siyyid Muḥammad knew this. He knew also that Bahá'u'lláh had never confronted Mírzá Yaḥyá in public. Every sharp barb from His younger brother was met with patience and forbearance from Bahá'u'lláh. The scheming siyyid was certain the rumor would do its work. To those who did not know the truth, Bahá'u'lláh would seem a coward.

After some time the rumor fell into the ears of a Bábí caravan-driver from Shiraz who had just come to town. He was Mír Muḥammad, a lover of truth and a man of action. Mír Muḥammad had little patience with the stuff of rumors. He wanted to know the truth, and he wanted the truth to be known by everyone.

Let there be a public debate, he insisted to Siyyid Muḥammad. Tell Mírzá Yaḥyá to choose the place; he himself would go to Bahá'u'lláh and beseech Him to meet with Mírzá Yaḥyá. The scheming siyyid agreed. After a time

Mírzá Yaḥyá named the mosque of Sulṭán Salím as the meeting place. The two conspirators felt safe. They both agreed nothing would come of it.

But Bahá'u'lláh surprised them. When Mír Muḥammad told Him of the challenge and the meeting place, Bahá'u'lláh agreed to go at once. He did not call for a carriage, although the mosque was far from His home, nor did He wait for a horse to be saddled. Bahá'u'lláh set out from His house on foot, along with Mír Muḥammad.

The midday sun beat down upon them as they walked through the city streets, but Bahá'u'lláh seemed not to notice. *"'O Muḥammad!'"* He said as He walked,

> *"He Who is the Spirit hath, verily, issued from His habitation, and with Him have come forth the souls of God's chosen ones and the realities of His Messengers. Behold, then, the dwellers of the realms on high above Mine head, and all the testimonies of the Prophets in My grasp. Say: Were all the divines, all the wise men, all the kings and rulers on earth to gather together, I, in very truth, would confront them, and would proclaim the verses of God, the Sovereign, the Almighty, the All-Wise. I am He Who feareth no one, though all who are in heaven and all who are on earth rise up against Me. . . ."*[1]

Bahá'u'lláh's voice vibrated with power and majesty. Those who heard Him were startled and stirred with wonder and admiration.

News of the confrontation had drawn crowds of townspeople. Muslims, Christians, and Jews lined the way to the mosque. They greeted Bahá'u'lláh with deep respect, bowing and making way for Him as He passed. Many fell to the ground and kissed His feet, overwhelmed with feelings of reverence in His presence.

Bahá'u'lláh answered the crowd's greetings, raising His hands in the customary way and showering His good wishes upon them. Mír Muḥammad was sent ahead to carry the news to Mírzá Yaḥyá that Bahá'u'lláh would soon arrive at the mosque of Sulṭán Salím.

It was Friday, the day when Muslims gathered in the mosques to pray and to listen to the mullás' sermons. At the mosque of Sulṭán Salím, the mullá who stood at the pulpit was in the middle of his talk when he saw Bahá'u'lláh enter. All at once the mosque fell quiet. The mullá seemed to have forgotten his words. Only after Bahá'u'lláh walked to the front, sat down, and bid him continue did the mullá begin to speak again.

When the sermon came to an end, Mírzá Yaḥyá had not yet appeared. Hours passed. Prayers were finished, but still Mírzá Yaḥyá was nowhere to be seen. At last Mír Muḥammad returned to Bahá'u'lláh with a message. Mírzá Yaḥyá could not meet today, he said. Something unforeseen had prevented his coming, but he would be able to come in a day or two.

Bahá'u'lláh got up and walked out of the mosque of Sulṭán Salím, as there was no more reason to stay. The governor of Adrianople and other dignitaries and mullás walked with Him. In their eyes Bahá'u'lláh had proven Himself once again. Mírzá Yaḥyá, not Bahá'u'lláh, had shamefully hidden himself from the test of truth.

The governor and the others trailed a few steps behind Bahá'u'lláh as a deliberate act of courtesy and a sign of their humility next to the One they so greatly admired. From time to time Bahá'u'lláh stopped and beckoned them to walk in front, but they would not. Though they were men of position and power, none felt free to walk as an equal beside Him.

When Bahá'u'lláh returned to His house, He revealed a new tablet for Mírzá Yaḥyá. In it He told exactly what had happened that day. He also named a new date and time for the meeting between Mírzá Yaḥyá and Himself. Then Bahá'u'lláh sealed the tablet and gave it to a trusted believer to deliver. Mírzá Yaḥyá must agree to one condition, Bahá'u'lláh instructed, before he received this tablet.

If he missed the next meeting, Mírzá Yaḥyá must admit the truth—that he was not a divine Messenger, that all his claims were false. Mírzá Yaḥyá should write this on a paper and seal it, said Bahá'u'lláh. If he did not appear at the meeting, the note would be unsealed and read. But Mírzá Yaḥyá would agree to no such thing. There would be no public debate.

The break was complete. Mírzá Yaḥyá, who had at one time received the title *Mir'átu'l-Azalíyyih* (Everlasting Mirror) from the Báb, was cast out of the company of believers. Mírzá Yaḥyá had often used this title to impress others, but the Báb Himself, Who had given the title "Mirror" to several Bábís, had also issued a warning.

"'O Sun-like Mirrors!'" wrote the Báb, "'Look ye upon the Sun of Truth. Ye, verily, depend upon it, were ye to perceive it.'" A mirror has no light of its own, the Báb had stated, but must be turned toward the source of light if it is to reflect the light's radiance. In this Day, the Báb had declared, the source of light for all souls—the "Sun of Truth"—was the Promised One of God.[2]

Mírzá Yaḥyá's mirror had become bereft of light, for he had turned away from the Promised One, Bahá'u'lláh. Even worse, he had tried to put himself in the seat of God's Chosen One. Mírzá Yaḥyá had made himself into an idol—the *"'Most Great Idol'"*[3] Bahá'u'lláh called him.

Like idols made from stone and worshipped by the foolish, Mírzá Yaḥyá was only a pretense of the real thing. His accomplishments were all lies and deceit, said Bahá'u'lláh; his writings were filled with ignorance, his letters with hate and slander. Where was the wisdom and loving guidance? Where was the purity and majesty that marked a Messenger of God?

Regardless of the suffering and sorrow heaped on Him by Mírzá Yaḥyá, Bahá'u'lláh had never treated His brother harshly. He had not judged him but had patiently looked on his treachery with a sin-covering eye. Not until Mírzá Yaḥyá boldly made his claims in public, setting himself against the Cause of God for all to see, did Bahá'u'lláh expel him from His presence and from the community of faithful Bábís.

The news of Mírzá Yaḥyá traveled to the believers far and wide. With his refusal to meet Bahá'u'lláh, and his subsequent departure from the Bábí community, Mírzá Yaḥyá lost even the pretense of honor. He and Siyyid Muḥammad, as well as the few misguided souls who joined them, became known as *"Azalís."** Like a branch broken from a great tree, they had severed themselves from the life-giving spirit of Bahá'u'lláh. Their efforts to destroy the Cause of God were bound to wither and fail.

The faithful Bábís took on a new name. They were more than followers of the Báb, for they had accepted the Promised One foretold by the Báb. Now they were followers of Bahá (the Glory)—they were *Bahá'ís*. In this new Day they greeted one another with a new greeting, *"Alláh-u-Abhá"* (God is All-Glorious).†

Now Bahá'u'lláh—"the Glory of God"—would use His pen to proclaim the new Day to the kings and rulers of the world.

---

* Meaning "followers of Azal." *Azal* comes from another title bestowed by the Báb on Mírzá Yaḥyá: *Ṣubḥ-i-Azal* (Morning of Eternity).

† Another translation is "God is Most Glorious."

46

O Kings of the Earth!

During the time of crisis when Bahá'u'lláh was filled with sorrow over Mírzá Yaḥyá, still He did not withhold Himself from revealing the verses of God. Day and night His amanuensis Mírzá Áqá Ján was kept busy. When Bahá'u'lláh spoke, Mírzá Áqá Ján wrote as fast as he could to keep up. In just one hour Bahá'u'lláh would reveal the equivalent of a thousand verses.

The verses Mírzá Áqá Ján transcribed were given to scribes to copy more neatly. Mírzá Báqir, who was one of these scribes, copied two thousand verses each day—not for one week or one month, but every day for more than six months.

Pots of ink were refilled time and again. Reed pens were sharpened and worn to nothing. Sheaf after sheaf of paper was covered with the verses of God. And still Bahá'u'lláh revealed more, like sweet rain for a parched world—so many verses that not even Mírzá Áqá Ján could write them all down.

When the troubles with Mírzá Yaḥyá were finally resolved, Bahá'u'lláh revealed a momentous and powerful new tablet. It was called the *Súriy-i-Mulúk* (Tablet to the Kings), and it was addressed to "the concourse of the kings of the earth." Although the sultan still considered Him a prisoner, Bahá'u'lláh was a divine Messenger—the "King of Kings"—and the time had come to proclaim to the kings of the East and the West His unique station and to summon them to God.[1]

"O kings of the earth!" wrote Bahá'u'lláh, "Give ear unto the Voice of God. . . . Fear God, O concourse of kings, and suffer not yourselves to be deprived of this most sublime grace."[2]

Among the proud kings and rulers, few acknowledged that they were answerable to God for their actions. "Set your hearts towards the Face of God," Bahá'u'lláh summoned them, ". . . For your glory consisteth not in your sovereignty, but rather in your nearness unto God and your observance of His command. . . . Should any one of you rule over the whole earth, and over all that lieth within it and upon it, its seas, its lands, its mountains, and its plains, and yet be not remembered by God, all these would profit him not, could ye but know it."[3]

The kings and rulers of nations were the most powerful people on the planet. Their subjects obeyed them as they would obey God, and the lives of millions were entrusted to their care. "God hath committed into your hands the reins of the government of the people," wrote Bahá'u'lláh, "that ye may rule with justice over them, safeguard the rights of the down-trodden, and punish the wrongdoers. . . . Cast away the things ye possess, and cling to that which God hath bidden you observe."[4]

He was well aware that the power and authority so highly prized by the world's rulers was often abused. "Be vigilant, that ye may not do injustice to anyone, be it to the extent of a grain of mustard seed," Bahá'u'lláh warned them. "Tread ye the path of justice, for this, verily, is the straight path."[5]

"Compose your differences," He further instructed them, "and reduce your armaments. . . . Heal the dissensions that divide you, and ye will no longer be in need of any armaments except what the protection of your cities and territories demandeth. . . ." ". . . Rest not on your power, your armies, and treasures," He advised. "Put your whole trust and confidence in God, Who hath created you, and seek ye His help in all your affairs. Succour cometh from Him alone. . . ."[6]

Most sovereigns were eager to satisfy their own hunger for pomp and glory, while those they governed were too often left begging for their basic needs, including the need for justice. "Know ye that the poor are the trust of God in your midst," Bahá'u'lláh informed them. "Watch that ye betray not His trust, that ye deal not unjustly with them and that ye walk not in the ways of the treacherous. Ye will most certainly be called upon to answer for His trust. . . ."[7]

Bahá'u'lláh distinguished clearly between those things that were a ruler's true source of glory and those that men vainly imagined:

> If ye stay not the hand of the oppressor . . . what right have ye then to vaunt yourselves among men? What is it of which ye can rightly boast? Is it on your food and your drink that ye pride yourselves, on the riches ye lay up in your treasuries, on the diversity and the cost of the ornaments with which ye deck yourselves? If true glory were to consist in the possession of such perishable things, then the earth on which ye walk must needs vaunt itself over you, because it supplieth you, and

> bestoweth upon you, these very things, by the decree of the Almighty. In its bowels are contained, according to what God hath ordained, all that ye possess. From it, as a sign of His mercy, ye derive your riches. Behold then your state, the thing in which ye glory! . . .
>
> . . . Nowhere doth your true and abiding glory reside except in your firm adherence unto the precepts of God. . . .[8]

In that same tablet Bahá'u'lláh addressed the divines and people in Constantinople who had, without investigation or provocation, acted so unjustly toward Him: "Methinks ye have clung to outward things, and forgotten the inner things, and say that which ye do not," He wrote in part. "Ye are lovers of names, and appear to have given yourselves up to them."[9]

He addressed certain rulers by name. To the Ambassador of Persia, where the Bahá'ís were still being persecuted and martyred for their beliefs, Bahá'u'lláh wrote an angry and sorrowful rebuke: "How many those who, every year, and every month, have because of you been put to death! How manifold the injustices ye have perpetrated—injustices the like of which the eye of creation hath not seen, which no chronicler hath ever recorded! How numerous the babes and sucklings who were made orphans, and the fathers who lost their sons, because of your cruelty, O ye unjust doers! How oft hath a sister pined away and mourned over her brother, and how oft hath a wife lamented after her husband. . . . !"[10]

For the world's kings and rulers to be addressed in the language of authority used by Bahá'u'lláh in this tablet was unprecedented. Those who ruled did not expect to be questioned about their doings. They expected to give commands, not receive them. Yet the kings and rulers held the destiny of nations in their hands, Bahá'u'lláh reminded them. If they refused to humble themselves before God and mend their ways, their arrogance would be the cause of much suffering: "If ye pay no heed unto the counsels which, in peerless and unequivocal language, We have revealed in this Tablet, Divine chastisement shall assail you from every direction, and the sentence of His justice shall be pronounced against you. On that day ye shall have no power to resist Him, and shall recognize your own impotence. Have mercy on yourselves and on those beneath you. . . ."[11]

To Náṣiri'd-Dín Sh̲áh, the king of Persia, Bahá'u'lláh wrote a separate tablet. Although more than one Bahá'í volunteered to deliver it, Bahá'u'lláh did not entrust the tablet to any of them. He was waiting for the right time and the right messenger, whose name He already knew.

While Bahá'u'lláh revealed tablets that summoned the kings and rulers of the world to the Cause of God, Mírzá Yaḥyá and Siyyid Muḥammad were writing letters of their own. They wrote to the sultan in Constantinople, alleging that Bahá'u'lláh was plotting to conquer that city. They claimed that He had enlisted the help of neighboring leaders.

As usual, their letters were full of lies, but the sultan was nonetheless alarmed. He had received reports indicating that many Bahá'ís traveled in and out of Adrianople. Could they be part of a plot? He wondered. The governor of Adrianople and the people of the city honored Bahá'u'lláh. Would they take part in the plot, too? Bahá'u'lláh's tablet to the kings bespoke no fear of the sultan, even though Bahá'u'lláh was a prisoner. What did this mean?

The sultan did not know what to think, but he was determined to take charge. He decided that Bahá'u'lláh must be isolated, cut off from His followers and from those who admired Him. His religion must be destroyed.

Bahá'u'lláh knew that trouble was brewing. One warm summer evening He told three visiting Bahá'ís to return to Persia at once. The believers did not understand why they should leave, but they obeyed. The next day officials came hunting for one of those who had left. When they were told he was not in the city, the officials went away, but they were not finished.

Early the following morning soldiers surrounded Bahá'u'lláh's house. No one was allowed to enter or leave. In the marketplace, Bahá'ís were abruptly forced to close their shops. They were led away to the government headquarters and questioned. They were Bahá'ís, were they not? The believers did not try to hide the truth.

An order had come from the sultan, said the officials. Bahá'u'lláh and the others must prepare to leave the city in two days' time. The Bahá'ís were told nothing more. They heard only cruel rumors that Bahá'u'lláh and His followers would be separated and sent to different places. Exactly where they were all going, no one knew.

47
Destination Unknown

Two days were not enough time for Bahá'u'lláh and His family to prepare to leave. He refused to leave Adrianople without settling His affairs and paying His debts in the marketplace. The authorities agreed to allow one week—no more—to make ready for the journey.

For eight days and nights soldiers stood guard outside of Bahá'u'lláh's house. What little furniture the Bahá'ís owned and many of their goods were taken away and sold at half their true value.

The governor of Adrianople, powerless to change the sultan's order, could not bear to face Bahá'u'lláh. Embarrassed by the shameful treatment of One he so admired and respected, the governor retreated from the city for a time, leaving the distasteful task of evicting Bahá'u'lláh and His followers to a lesser official.

The consuls of foreign governments that had offices in Adrianople visited Bahá'u'lláh to offer their help. They offered to put a stop to the sultan's unjust actions. They were willing to use the power of all their governments to protect Bahá'u'lláh. He had only to ask.

Bahá'u'lláh listened graciously but declined their offers of help. "'You wish me to give you the word to bring Me relief, but My relief lies in the hands of God,'" said Bahá'u'lláh. "'My focus is God, and to Him alone do I turn.'"[1]

The busy week of preparation passed quickly, and all too soon the day of departure dawned. Luggage was packed into carts and carriages, and townspeople gathered to say good-bye. Sadly they watched as men, women, and children—seventy Bahá'ís in all—crowded into their carriage seats or made ready to walk alongside.

What had this small band of Bahá'ís done to deserve such treatment? the townspeople wondered. They were not criminals. The Bahá'ís were honest and kind—good workers and good neighbors. Bahá'u'lláh and His followers had done nothing to deserve such shameful treatment.

When Bahá'u'lláh emerged from His house, the people wept openly, grieved to see Him go. No one had cared for them as Bahá'u'lláh had. He had lived in Adrianople for only five short years, yet now they could not imagine the city without Him. How drab it would feel without the luster of His loving presence!

With heartfelt sorrow they came forward—Muslims, Christians, Jews—to bid Him good-bye. One by one they bowed and reverently kissed His hands or the hem of His garment. To each one of them, Bahá'u'lláh spoke words of comfort, then to all He bid a loving farewell.

At last everything was ready. It was August 12, 1868, when Bahá'u'lláh, His family, and His followers left Adrianople. The caravan of horse-drawn carriages, with soldiers on horseback riding guard, set out on the first stage of their journey. They were headed for the port city of Gallipoli, four days away, but their final destination was still unknown.

Not until they reached Gallipoli was the sultan's order revealed. Bahá'u'lláh, two of His brothers, and one servant would be taken to prison in Acre. The rest of Bahá'u'lláh's family and all of the Bahá'ís would be returned to Constantinople.

The cruel order threw everyone into distress. Prison they could endure, but separation from Bahá'u'lláh was unthinkable. An uproar of protest ensued, and Bahá'u'lláh insisted the order be changed.

With help from the officer in charge, a new order was issued. Bahá'u'lláh was condemned to lifelong imprisonment in Acre, Palestine. His family would go with Him and nearly all of the exiles, including Siyyid Muḥammad and another conspirator. Mírzá Yaḥyá and four others would be sent to a different place—to the city of Famagusta on the island of Cyprus.

Bahá'u'lláh accepted the new order, but it was still unjust. The sultan had no good reason to imprison them; his actions, however, would not go unpunished. Bahá'u'lláh gave a message to the officer in charge. "'*Tell the king that this territory will pass out of his hands, and his affairs will be thrown into confusion,*'" said Bahá'u'lláh. "'"Not I speak these words, but God speaketh them."'"[2]

Some Bahá'ís were not condemned as exiles and so were not obliged to go, but they gladly bought tickets for the steamships that would carry them all to Acre. The amazed authorities could not understand why anyone would want to pay his own way to prison in an unknown land. To the Bahá'ís, however, it was a simple choice. Separation from Bahá'u'lláh was a far worse punishment than any prison could ever be.

Bahá'u'lláh knew that grave difficulties lay ahead. This journey would not be like the others, He told the Bahá'ís before they left Gallipoli. They would be tested by troubles they could not imagine. Whoever did not wish to face the future in Acre should leave now, He warned, because later on, it would be impossible to leave. But no one chose to leave.

On August 21 Bahá'u'lláh and the others boarded a steamship and left Gallipoli. The ship took them south through the Aegean Sea, then further south across the expanse of the Mediterranean. On the other side—the north coast of Africa—they stopped at Alexandria, Egypt. There the exiles boarded a different ship and traveled east, toward Palestine, and ever closer to prison.

On August 31 the ship finally stopped at the port of Haifa, Palestine. In the early morning light the exiles could see across the Bay of Haifa to the prison-city of Acre. They would board a smaller vessel to complete their journey. Mírzá Yaḥyá and the other four would continue north to the island of Cyprus.

A boat came alongside the ship to take them to the dock. No sooner had Bahá'u'lláh stepped into the boat when a loud shout of *"Yá Bahá'u'l-Abhá!"* (O Thou Glory of Glories!) was followed by a splash and a great commotion. One of the exiles had thrown himself into the sea. Quickly men jumped into action. With great difficulty they recovered the struggling prisoner and dragged him, half-drowned, from the water. But the man, 'Abdu'l-Ghaffár, was a reluctant survivor.

A devoted believer in Bahá'u'lláh, 'Abdu'l-Ghaffár was one of the four condemned to go with Mírzá Yaḥyá to Cyprus. The unhappy 'Abdu'l-Ghaffár was beside himself with grief. Let him remain with Bahá'u'lláh, he begged, or let him die. His pleas had no effect, and in the end he was forced to go on to Cyprus with Mírzá Yaḥyá.*

In Haifa it did not take long to count the prisoners and deliver them into the hands of officials. Then the exiles were packed aboard the small sailing vessel that would carry them across the bay. It should have been a

* Although 'Abdu'l-Ghaffár was imprisoned in Famagusta, he eventually escaped and made his way to Acre, where once again he was able to remain in the presence of Bahá'u'lláh.

short crossing, but there was no friendly wind at their back. The relentless August sun beat down, and the sailing vessel barely moved.

Hour after hour the sun beat down on the miserable band of exiles. The short crossing stretched into eight long and stifling hours. Weary from travel and sick from the heat, they came at last to the sea gate of Acre—and one more problem. There was no dock to allow people to walk from the boat to shore. They were forced to wade through the water.

The men were ordered to carry the women on their backs, but 'Abdu'l-Bahá would not hear of it. Such an arrangement would have offended the women's modesty. Prisoners or not, the women were to be treated with respect. 'Abdu'l-Bahá found a chair that could be used to carry the women ashore, one at a time, and insisted on his plan until the officials agreed.

When the exhausted Bahá'ís reached shore, they were greeted with shouts and jeers. The citizens of Acre had gathered to see for themselves the "'God of the Persians," as they mockingly called Bahá'u'lláh.[3] He was evil, they had been told, and His followers the worst kind of criminals, deserving the cruelest treatment.

Their curses and taunts followed the exiles as they were led through the twisting streets of Acre. Did only prison await them, the Bahá'ís wondered, or a sentence of death? They did not know that the world of the spirit greeted them much differently.

Long before they set foot in Acre, Bahá'u'lláh had seen what the others could not, and heard what no one else could hear. *"'Upon Our arrival,'"* said Bahá'u'lláh, *"'We were welcomed with banners of light, whereupon the Voice of the Spirit cried out saying: 'Soon will all that dwell on earth be enlisted under these banners.'"'"*[4]

In the eyes of the people of Acre, however, Bahá'u'lláh was a despised prisoner. One among them—a white-bearded man who wore a long, black aba—thought Bahá'u'lláh deserved worse than prison. He had dishonored Islam, the charges said. Surely He deserved death.

The white-bearded man was a respected Muslim leader in Acre whose name was Shaykh Maḥmúd. Shaykh Maḥmúd began to think of a secret plan. He would kill Bahá'u'lláh himself, he decided—not at once, perhaps, but in due time. The honor of Islam demanded it.

48
The Most Great Prison

For four thousand years the city now called Acre stood on the eastern shores of the rich blue Mediterranean. The city had been conquered in turn by the Persians, the Greeks, the Romans, the Byzantines, and the Arabs. The Crusaders made it their capital in the thirteenth century. French merchants used it as a port in the sixteenth century. It had fallen to ruin and been rebuilt.

Now the city was protected by stone and earth walls. So thick were the walls that not even Napoleon's cannons had been able to break through them. But Acre's glory days were gone. Under Ottoman rule the city had fallen to use as a penal colony to which the empire's most dangerous criminals—murderers, highway robbers, and political enemies—were sent as punishment.

To be sent to live in Acre was often a sentence of death. The city was filthy and flea-infested, its streets damp and gloomy. Water had to be carried in from a well located in the outskirts, for there was no clean water inside the city gates. Disease spread easily in such conditions. The city's foul air carried the stench of decay. It was said that a bird flying over Acre would drop dead from its putrid air.

Long before the sultan's order, Bahá'u'lláh predicted that Acre would be His next place of exile. Bahá'u'lláh called it "'*the most desolate of the cities of the world, the most unsightly of them in appearance, the most detestable in climate, and the foulest in water.*'" Yet even worse than the city was the prison itself, to which He referred as the "Most Great Prison."[1] The exiles would soon find out why.

At the end of their walk through narrow city streets—past the busy marketplace, past the police station and the mosque—loomed the stone walls of the prison barracks. Wearily the exiles climbed the stairs and passed through the prison gates.

A thick layer of mud covered the floor. The air was heavy with the prison's rank odor. The exiles were led into bare, dirty cells where plaster was peeling and dropping from the ceiling. Overcome by the heat and the foul smell of the place, Bahá'u'lláh's daughter Bahíyyih fainted.

The exhausted prisoners were hungry, but they were given no food that first night. Their throats were parched with thirst, but they were given nothing to drink. The children cried pitifully, and nursing mothers could not feed their infants. "They even begged for water," wrote Bahá'u'lláh, "and were refused."[2] A brackish pool in the prison courtyard was the only source of water, and it was far too dirty to use for drinking.

'Abdu'l-Bahá approached the guards. At least show mercy to the children, he said to them, but his words did not soften their hearts. He sent a message to the governor of Acre requesting food and water, but nothing came of it. The believers suffered until the next morning, when at last they were given water. With it, each prisoner received a ration of three loaves of black bread, but the bread was bitter and too salty to eat.

When officials came to check on the prisoners, they allowed the salty bread to be returned. Each prisoner received, instead, two loaves of better bread, more fit to eat. Later on, they received a sum of money in place of the bread. The sum was small—only enough for the barest amount of food. Each day one or two of the believers would go to the market, under guard, and buy what food they could for everyone.

Three days after the exiles had entered Acre, the sultan's order was read aloud in the mosque. The people of Acre must shun the prisoners, the order warned. Bahá'u'lláh and His followers were enemies of God. They had led true believers astray, and for this they were condemned to live the rest of their lives in prison. There they must die, and their Cause die with them.

Crowded together in the dirty prison with little clean water or good food, the believers soon fell ill. One after another they grew hot with terrible fevers. Their bodies were attacked by deadly diseases—malaria and dysentery. The guards refused to call for a doctor. 'Abdu'l-Bahá, who had not yet fallen sick, took care of those who had.

Some among the exiles were not strong enough to withstand the dreadful attack of illness. Three believers died. Two were brothers who died on the same night, held fast in each other's arms. Bahá'u'lláh expressed particular grief over their untimely deaths. Never before, He said, had two brothers passed away from this dark world and entered the realms of glory in such unity.

Even in death the prisoners received no respect. The guards refused to bury the dead unless they received payment. Because the exiles had no money, Bahá'u'lláh gave His only possession—a small carpet on which He slept—to be sold so that the money could be used for a proper burial.

The sale of the carpet brought more money than was needed to pay for the burial, but the guards pocketed the money. The bodies were never washed or wrapped in shrouds as was the custom. They were left in the clothes that they wore and buried in the ground without coffin or ceremony.

After these three deaths, Bahá'u'lláh revealed a special healing prayer for the believers in the prison. He told them to chant it often and with all their hearts as a protection. 'Abdu'l-Bahá and another healthy believer kept busy tending the sick. With their meager supply of food, 'Abdu'l-Bahá made broth and plain rice. At night he dished out the food to each one, according to his needs.

One week blended into the next as the days blurred with suffering. Then, little by little, their bodies began to mend. As the others regained their strength, 'Abdu'l-Bahá fell gravely ill himself. Slowly, with nursing and prayers from the others, he, too, recovered. The crisis eventually passed. There were no more deaths, and the believers were grateful to be well again.

The prisoners soon learned they were not the only Bahá'ís in Acre. In the marketplace the exiles found someone they knew. His name was 'Abdu'l-Aḥad. He had opened a small shop, and no one suspected that he was a Bahá'í. When the prisoners, under guard, bought food from his shop, they pretended not to know him. They did not want 'Abdu'l-Aḥad to be thrown into prison, too.

'Abdu'l-Aḥad had come to Acre before the sultan's order. He had been sent there by 'Abdu'l-Bahá and had told no one he was a Bahá'í. When Bahá'u'lláh and the others arrived at the prison barracks, 'Abdu'l-Aḥad did not try to contact them, for it was too dangerous.

Meanwhile, the Bahá'ís in Persia did not know what had happened to Bahá'u'lláh. He was imprisoned in Acre, said one rumor; He was drowned at sea, said another, and the worried Bahá'ís did not know what to believe. One day 'Abdu'l-Aḥad was surprised to see two Bahá'í friends newly arrived in Acre. The man and his wife had traveled all the way from Persia with one purpose: to find Bahá'u'lláh.

But danger was all around. As quickly as he could, 'Abdu'l-Aḥad brought the couple to his shop and hid them in the back, behind stacks of boxes. With great care and difficulty he sent a message to Bahá'u'lláh, but for anyone to visit Bahá'u'lláh was out of the question. Bahá'u'lláh instructed that the two believers should return to Persia.

After only three days the couple left Acre. Their happiness lay in the news that they carried with them to Persia. Bahá'u'lláh was alive! He was imprisoned in Acre, as were the other believers with Him, but at least He was alive.

When the couple reached Persia, their news brought relief and joy to the Bahá'ís there. Several believers decided to go to Acre themselves. Even the faintest hope of seeing Bahá'u'lláh was worth the journey.

In Acre Shaykh Maḥmúd was making his own plans to see Bahá'u'lláh. The guards could be persuaded, no doubt, to let him in. He was a respected religious leader. Shaykh Maḥmúd hid the dagger inside his long, black aba, expecting no difficulty.

49

Seeking a Glimpse of the Lord

The Bahá'í pilgrims who set out for Acre did not travel by sea. They traveled west across the high mountains of Persia and across the vast, lonely deserts of Iraq and Syria. The journey was long and dangerous. Some believers, their spirits fired with hope, walked the entire way. Their determination to see Bahá'u'lláh infused their tired bodies with strength.

But mountains and deserts were not the only obstacles that stood between the pilgrims and Bahá'u'lláh. At the end of their journey, spies were watching for any Bahá'ís who might be entering the city. Among the prisoners, Siyyid Muḥammad and another conspirator had made a deal with officials. Now, in a prison room that overlooked the land gate of the city, they watched with a keen eye.

Everyone who traveled overland entered Acre through that gate, and Siyyid Muḥammad and his friend knew most of the Bahá'ís. Whenever they saw a Bahá'í walk through the gate, they reported it to city officials. Quickly the officials would find the Bahá'í and force him to leave the city.

After enduring the hardships of their journey, most Bahá'ís could not get past the land gate of Acre. They could only stand beyond the moat outside the wall. From there they kept their own watch, patiently looking toward the prison and the barred upper window of Bahá'u'lláh's prison room. Hour upon hour they waited, longing for a glimpse of that holy figure.

Even a wave of His hand from afar was enough to quicken their souls. Grateful pilgrims carried the precious memory with them all the way back to Persia. They drew strength from it in the days ahead, for the Persian Bahá'ís were still being persecuted. In the face of enemies eager to destroy them, the Bahá'ís cherished every memory of Bahá'u'lláh, no matter how seemingly insignificant. Though He was imprisoned, He was still alive, and this knowledge strengthened the Bahá'ís' resolve to remain steadfast in their faith.

Isolating Bahá'u'lláh from everyone, including His own followers, was exactly what the sultan intended. During the first months in Acre the sultan's orders were strictly followed. Bahá'u'lláh was put in a separate prison room and was allowed no visitors. He could not even go to the public bath. The barber who came to attend Bahá'u'lláh's hair could not talk to Bahá'u'lláh while he worked, and a guard always stood watch.

Bahá'u'lláh had been called a criminal of the worst sort. But as time passed, Acre's prison authorities began to see Him in a different light. The authorities had experience with criminals, and Bahá'u'lláh behaved nothing like them. He was neither selfish nor mean-spirited, but noble, wise, and kind. In all ways Bahá'u'lláh acted with a majesty that could not be hidden, despite His confinement behind prison walls.

Among His family and followers, officials were especially impressed with Bahá'u'lláh's eldest son, 'Abdu'l-Bahá. Now a young man of twenty-four, he reflected the loving and patient nature of his father like a clearly polished mirror. Gradually, as the eyes of officials were opened, they eased the harsh terms of the sultan's order. After all, the sultan lived far away. Surely he had greater concerns than a prison and penal colony at the edge of his empire.

Conditions in the prison gradually improved for the Bahá'ís. Instead of a small, cramped space, they were given more rooms in the prison barracks. The believers themselves worked together to change their bleak prison life into something more bearable. With 'Abdu'l-Bahá's help, the work of cooking, cleaning, and bringing in water and food was divided among them.

As restrictions relaxed, 'Abdu'l-Bahá was able to bring an Egyptian craftsman into the prison. He was a weaver of rush mats and taught the Bahá'ís his craft. It lifted their spirits to fill the empty prison hours with useful work. The relaxed restrictions also meant that a few fortunate pilgrims were able to visit Bahá'u'lláh.

Unlike the pilgrims, Shaykh Maḥmúd—one of Acre's Muslim leaders—had no trouble getting into the prison. On two separate occasions he climbed the stone stairs of the prison without interference and spoke with authority to the guards. "Tell the prisoner that I wish to see Him," he said. He intended to kill Bahá'u'lláh, Whom he regarded as a heretic, but in this he failed.

"Tell him to cast away the weapon, and then he may come in," had been Bahá'u'lláh's first reply to the guards. On the second occasion He had replied, "Tell him to purify his heart first and then he may come in."

Only when Shaykh Maḥmúd had a dream that awakened long-forgotten memories did he return to the prison on a third occasion, this time as a genuine seeker of truth. When Bahá'u'lláh permitted the shaykh to enter His presence, Shaykh Maḥmúd was able to see Him for what He was—not a prisoner of men, but a Messenger of God. From that time forward the shaykh became a sincere and devoted follower of Bahá'u'lláh and turned all his energy to serving Him.

Shaykh Maḥmúd decided he could serve Bahá'u'lláh best by serving His loved ones, the pilgrims who longed to see Him. The shaykh, who never gave up easily, made plans to thwart the spies who watched the land gate. Sometimes he had ropes lowered over the city walls, out of sight of the gate. Bahá'ís were pulled up and over the walls so they could enter the city without being seen by the spies.

Another of Shaykh Maḥmúd's plans was to leave the city during the day and return at night. On his return, he would enter Acre with a servant who carried a lantern. It was the usual practice of a man traveling at night. There were no streetlights, and a lantern was needed to see the way. No one suspected the truth. The "servant" who carried the lantern for Shaykh Maḥmúd would really be a pilgrim who had traveled to see Bahá'u'lláh.

Once inside Acre, the pilgrim would be safely hidden away by Shaykh Maḥmúd or 'Abdu'l-Aḥad until he could see Bahá'u'lláh. When a pilgrim was ready to leave the city, Shaykh Maḥmúd helped once again. The pilgrim was able to leave Acre in the same secret way he had entered.

But one pilgrim entered Acre easily by himself. He wore a long cloak of coarse cotton, the kind Arabs wore. He carried the leather-skin container of a water-bearer—a common sight in Acre. It was early in the year 1869, and he was a youth of seventeen. His name was Áqá Buzurg.

Áqá Buzurg had walked all the way from Mosul, Iraq—some five hundred miles—to see Bahá'u'lláh. He told no one of his coming, but Bahá'u'lláh knew the heart of Áqá Buzurg and was waiting for him. He had a mission for this Persian youth. When the time came for Áqá Buzurg to leave Acre, he would carry an important message meant for a king, and he would bear a new name.

50

For the Healing of All the World

In 1868 the sultan had condemned Bahá'u'lláh to the wretched prison-city of Acre, certain that He would soon die and His Cause would be forgotten. But even as a prisoner in the "Most Great Prison," Bahá'u'lláh did not interrupt His work as the Messenger of God. He continued to write to the kings and rulers of the world, as He had begun to do in Adrianople.

Never before had a Messenger of God proclaimed His message to so many world leaders—the czar of Russia, the emperor of France, the queen of England, the Pope, the shah of Persia, and others. To one and all He spoke with the voice of divine authority. Bahá'u'lláh wrote first to 'Álí Páshá, grand vizier to the sultan of the Ottoman Empire.

It was 'Álí Páshá who had urged the sultan to send Bahá'u'lláh and His followers from Adrianople to Acre. Because of him, wrote Bahá'u'lláh, innocent women and children were suffering the hardships of prison life. God would punish 'Álí Páshá for his cruelty, Bahá'u'lláh warned, and the whole Ottoman Empire would suffer.

Bahá'u'lláh had not forgotten that the ambassador from Russia spoke up on His behalf when He was in the Black Pit of Tehran. To the ruler of that nation He wrote, "O Czar of Russia! Incline thine ear unto the voice of God, the King, the Holy, and turn thou unto Paradise. . . . Whilst I lay chained and fettered in the prison, one of thy ministers extended Me his aid. Wherefore hath God ordained for thee a station which the knowledge of none can comprehend except His knowledge. Beware lest thou barter away this sublime station. . . . Beware lest thy sovereignty withhold thee from Him Who is the Supreme Sovereign."[1]

Bahá'u'lláh had already written once to Napoleon III, the proud and powerful emperor of France. The tablet had been sent from Adrianople, but the arrogant emperor had reportedly flung it down and said, "'If this man is God, I am two gods!'"[2] He did not bother to reply.

In 1869 Bahá'u'lláh sent Napoleon a second, more strongly worded tablet from Acre. Addressing the emperor's behavior, He wrote, "O King! . . . For what thou hast done, thy kingdom shall be thrown into confusion, and thine empire shall pass from thine hands, as a punishment for that which thou hast wrought. Then wilt thou know how thou hast plainly erred. Commotions shall seize all the people in that land, unless thou arisest to help this Cause, and followest Him Who is the Spirit of God in this, the Straight Path. Hath thy pomp made thee proud? By My Life! It shall not endure. . . ."[3]

To the Pope, spiritual leader to many of the world's Christians, Bahá'u'lláh wrote,

> O Pope! Rend the veils asunder. He Who is the Lord of Lords is come overshadowed with clouds, and the decree hath been fulfilled by God, the Almighty, the Unrestrained. . . . He, verily, hath again come down from Heaven even as He came down from it the first time. Beware that thou dispute not with Him even as the Pharisees disputed with Him (Jesus) without a clear token or proof. On His right hand flow the living waters of grace, and on His left the choice Wine of justice. . . .
>
> O Supreme Pontiff! . . . Sell all the embellished ornaments thou dost possess, and expend them in the path of God, Who causeth the night to return upon the day, and the day to return upon the night. Abandon thy kingdom unto the kings, and emerge from thy habitation, with thy face set towards the Kingdom, and, detached from the

> world, then speak forth the praises of thy Lord betwixt earth and heaven. Thus hath bidden thee He Who is the Possessor of Names, on the part of thy Lord, the Almighty, the All-Knowing.[4]

Bahá'u'lláh's tablet addressed to Queen Victoria of England included words of praise: "O Queen in London! . . . We have been informed that thou hast forbidden the trading in slaves, both men and women. This, verily, is what God hath enjoined in this wondrous Revelation. God hath, truly, destined a reward for thee, because of this."[5]

Bahá'u'lláh also commended the queen for allowing a parliament of representatives elected by the people to be part of her government. "Thou, indeed, hast done well," He wrote, "for thereby the foundations of the edifice of thine affairs will be strengthened, and the hearts of all that are beneath thy shadow, whether high or low, will be tranquillized."[6]

On her part, Queen Victoria did not reject Bahá'u'lláh's claims outright. "'If this is of God, it will endure; if not, it can do no harm,'" she is reported to have said.[7] Unlike Napoleon III, Queen Victoria and the nation she ruled endured and prospered.

In His tablet to Queen Victoria Bahá'u'lláh also addressed the parliaments of the world:

> O ye the elected representatives of the people in every land! Take ye counsel together, and let your concern be only for that which profiteth mankind and bettereth the condition thereof, if ye be of them that scan heedfully. Regard the world as the human body which, though at its creation whole and perfect, hath been afflicted, through various causes, with grave disorders and maladies. Not for one day did it gain ease, nay its sickness waxed more severe, as it fell under the treatment of ignorant physicians, who gave full rein to their personal desires and have erred grievously. And if, at one time, through the care of an able physician, a member of that body was healed, the rest remained afflicted as before. Thus informeth you the All-Knowing, the All-Wise.[8]

The world languished in the hands of inept rulers. "We behold it, in this day," wrote Bahá'u'lláh, "at the mercy of rulers so drunk with pride that they cannot discern clearly their own best advantage, much less recognize a Revelation so bewildering and challenging as this. And whenever any one of them hath striven to improve its condition, his motive hath been his own gain, whether confessedly so or not; and the unworthiness of this motive hath limited his power to heal or cure."[9]

The healing of the world could only be achieved, wrote Bahá'u'lláh, through the guidance of God. "That which the Lord hath ordained as the sovereign remedy and mightiest instrument for the healing of all the world is the union of all its peoples in one universal Cause, one common Faith. This can in no wise be achieved except through the power of a skilled, an all-powerful and inspired Physician."[10] That Physician was the Messenger of God, Bahá'u'lláh.

As each tablet was completed, it was dispatched to the leader whom it addressed—all except one. The tablet addressed to Náṣiri'd-Dín Sh͟áh, king of Persia, which Bahá'u'lláh had revealed in Adrianople, still lay undelivered. But that was soon to change. The messenger for whom Bahá'u'lláh waited had arrived in Acre.

Áqá Buzurg and his water-carrying skins were a familiar sight to Bahá'u'lláh. He was the faithful young Bábí who had carried water for Bahá'u'lláh's household in Baghdad, making trips to the river for water again and again, even though he was attacked by enemies of the faith and several times slashed with daggers.

In his earlier days he had been the disobedient son of a disappointed father. That had changed one night when a Bábí named Nabíl visited Áqá Buzurg in his home. Nabíl had told story after story of courageous Bábís and the faith they championed. The youthful Áqá Buzurg had been so deeply moved by the heroic spirit of those stories that he had wept. By morning Áqá Buzurg declared that he, like his father, was a believer.

What a miraculous change the father saw in his son—like the change from winter to spring. But neither father nor son could know that another change—an even greater miracle—was about to occur in Acre.

Áqá Buzurg had not been able to accompany Bahá'u'lláh to Acre. But early in 1869, upon learning of His imprisonment there, he had made the entire journey on foot to find Him. Looking like an ordinary Arab water bearer, Áqá Buzurg had entered Acre easily. But where should he go now? Alone and uncertain, the seventeen year old wandered about the strange city, then entered a mosque to pray. A heartwarming sight met his eyes: 'Abdu'l-Bahá, whom he recognized from his days in Baghdad.

Áqá Buzurg scribbled a hasty note, and when prayers were finished, quietly handed it to 'Abdu'l-Bahá. 'Abdu'l-Bahá welcomed Áqá Buzurg warmly. He took the travel-weary pilgrim with him back to the prison barracks. No one questioned the young man wearing the usual long cotton cloak and bearing the leather water-carrying skins.

At the prison barracks Bahá'u'lláh summoned Áqá Buzurg to His room. No one else was allowed to enter, and no one knew what passed between them in their time alone together. But the Áqá Buzurg who later left Bahá'u'lláh's room was not the same youth who had entered it.

No words could describe the wonder of what Áqá Buzurg saw there. The drab prison walls could not contain it. Suddenly the limits of this day-to-day world fell away from the eyes of young Áqá Buzurg. His whole being trembled before the splendor of what he saw. Then came a rush of joy—pure joy that filled every cell of his being. His soul was so flooded with intense joy that every trace of fear was washed away. Áqá Buzurg smiled. Nothing in this life could make him fearful again, for he had been given a glimpse of the glory that lay beyond this mortal realm.

Bahá'u'lláh would later say that He had unveiled the "'Kingdom of Revelation'" to the eyes of Áqá Buzurg.[11] In the prison where He was meant to be shut away from the world of men, Bahá'u'lláh had opened the doors onto a vast world of the spirit. He had breathed into Áqá Buzurg, Bahá'u'lláh said, "'the spirit of might and power.'"[12] With the power that only God can give, Bahá'u'lláh had recreated him.

To His new creation Bahá'u'lláh gave a new name, *"Badí'"* (Wonderful). So strongly steadfast of spirit was Badí', said Bahá'u'lláh, that it gladdened the souls of the Prophets and holy ones in the next world.

Badí' visited Bahá'u'lláh one more time alone. When he learned about the tablet to the shah that lay undelivered, he begged Bahá'u'lláh for the privilege of delivering it. Bahá'u'lláh agreed. Many had asked for the honor of this service, but the honor belonged to Badí'.

Bahá'u'lláh knew that He was sending Badí' straight into the mouth of a serpent. And Badí' knew very well that this mission, important as it was, would require him to lay down his life. Yet he was not afraid.

51

Into the Mouth of the Serpent

When Badí‘ left the prison-city of Acre he did not yet carry the tablet for Náṣiri'd-Dín Sháh, but he followed the instructions Bahá'u'lláh had given him. First he made his way to the town of Haifa, across the bay from Acre. There Badí‘ met another Bahá'í, as Bahá'u'lláh had told him to do. Together they walked out of the busy town, away from watchful eyes, and up the rocky slope of Mount Carmel.

When they were quite alone, the other Bahá'í gave Badí‘ a small case and a sealed envelope. Badí‘ took the case reverently in his hands and kissed it. Then he knelt, touching his forehead to the ground. The Bahá'í who brought the case did not know what lay inside. Only Badí‘ knew that it held the precious tablet to the shah.

Inside the sealed envelope was a tablet addressed to Badí‘ himself. As the other believer looked on, Badí‘ walked twenty or thirty paces away and sat down with his face turned toward Acre. Then he opened the envelope and began to read the tablet.

Bahá'u'lláh had written loving and inspiring words to Badí‘. He told him to put on the new and wonderful robe of the remembrance of God and to adorn himself with the crown of His love. Bahá'u'lláh also told Badí‘ how to approach the shah. The Bahá'í who stood nearby had no idea what the message said, but he could see the glow of joy on Badí‘'s face.

When Badí‘ finished reading, he knelt once more and reverently bowed toward Acre, his forehead touching the ground. Then the other Bahá'í spoke. Badí‘ should go back to town with him, he said, and receive a sum of money for his travel. Bahá'u'lláh had arranged for it.

“““‘You go,’””” said Badí‘, “““‘and bring it here.’”””[1] But when the believer returned, Badí‘ was nowhere to be found. He had already started on his journey.

The journey to Persia and the city of Tehran, where the shah lived, was long and difficult. Like the pilgrims who came to Acre, Badí‘ had to cross the same desert and mountain passes. He traveled on foot and mostly alone. Bahá'u'lláh had told him not to mingle with other Bahá'ís, as they, too, could be pulled into danger.

At times he joined other travelers, and they found him a likable youth. Badí‘ never complained. He was quick to laugh, patient with others, and gentle in his manner. He showed a spirit both thankful and humble—a welcome travel companion. No one guessed that he was on a secret and dangerous mission.

Badí‘ often walked by himself, about a hundred feet from the side of the road. He would sometimes stop, turn toward Acre, and humbly prostrate himself face down on the ground to pray. “““‘O God! do not take back through Thy justice what thou hast vouchsafed unto me through Thy bounty,’””” he would pray, “““‘and grant me strength for its protection.’”””[2]

In July 1869, after four months of travel, Badí‘ entered the gates of Tehran. Obedient to Bahá’u’lláh’s instructions, he did not visit any of the Bahá’ís who lived there, not even his own beloved father. None of them knew that Badí‘ was in Tehran.

He did not stay long in the city. The shah, he discovered, was on a hunting trip and was camped in the countryside. Badí‘ left Tehran and walked until he found the place where the royal tent was pitched. Clustered nearby were the other tents of the shah’s escort.

He stopped some distance from the camp. An ordinary person did not come close to the shah without permission. Badí‘ climbed to the top of a large rock some distance from the royal tent and sat all day in the heat. When the sun went down, he stayed throughout the long night. A second day and a second night came and went, but Badí‘ remained where he was.

All this time Badí‘ fasted and prayed that he might complete his mission. A third day passed, then a third night. On the fourth day the shah, looking through his binoculars, was surprised at what he saw. There on a large rock was a man dressed in white and sitting motionless in a respectful attitude. No doubt he wished to beg for help or make some demand for justice. The shah sent his men to find out.

When they questioned him, Badí‘ said that he carried a letter for the shah. It came from a very important person, he told them, and he was charged to deliver it to the shah himself. They searched Badí‘ and, finding no weapon, brought him back to the royal camp.

At last Badí‘ stood face to face with Náṣiri’d-Dín Sháh. Badí‘ stood tall and straight as he recited words that called to mind a well-known verse from the Koran: "O King, I have come to thee from Sheba with a weighty message."[3] With calm and courage he handed the tablet to the shah.

Badí''s fearlessness impressed the shah, and for good reason. Authority at all levels was maintained with a tyrannical and ruthless hand. Officials were more concerned with wielding power than administering justice, and most Persians were justifiably afraid of meeting any government official, let alone the shah. Badí''s fearlessness as he stood before the shah was nothing less than astonishing.

When the shah learned that the message came from Bahá'u'lláh, he ordered for the tablet to be sent to the mujtahids of Tehran to be examined and answered. As for Badí', the shah ordered his arrest. He wanted only one thing from Badí'—the names of other Bahá'ís, particularly those in Tehran. Náṣiri'd-Dín Sháh had not forgotten the two Bábís who had tried some years earlier to take his life.

The shah instructed his chief officer to be gentle with Badí' at first and use promises to persuade him to give the information they wanted. But the shah made clear that should Badí' not cooperate, he expected the officer to use whatever means were necessary to extract the information.

Badí' was taken to another tent. The officer in charge spoke kindly at first. """Give me a full account of all this. Who gave you this letter?""" he asked. """From where have you brought it? Who are your comrades?"""

"""This letter was given to me in 'Akká (Acre) by *Ḥaḍrat-i-Bahá'u'lláh,**""" Badí' answered. After explaining the mission Bahá'u'lláh had given him, he said, """If you want Bahá'ís, they are numerous in Írán, and if you want my comrades, I was all alone and have none."""

The officer was not satisfied. He needed names of individual Bahá'ís to give to the shah. """If you tell me these names I will obtain your release from the Sháh and save you from death,""" promised the officer.

"""I am longing to be put to death. Do you think that you frighten me?""" said Badí'.

The officer ordered Badí' to be tied and beaten with the bastinado. Six men beat the soles of Badí''s feet with the bastinado rods. Not once during the painful ordeal did Badí' cry out in pain.

---

* Literally, "His Holiness Bahá'u'lláh."

"""Give me the names of your comrades,""" said the officer, but Badí' did not answer and began to laugh. The officer had had plenty of experience in forcing a prisoner to talk. He ordered his men to bring a branding iron and a charcoal brazier. A fire was lighted in the brazier and soon the coals were red-hot. The officer turned to Badí'. """Come and speak the truth,""" he said, """or I will have you branded.""" Badí' only laughed more.

The officer grew angry and ordered that Badí' be beaten again, until even his torturers grew tired from the exertion. Still Badí' remained calm and seemed oblivious to the torture. The branding iron was thrust into the fire until it, too, was red-hot. Then the men who had beaten Badí' put the branding iron to his back and his chest—not once, but many times. Though his flesh was burned again and again, Badí' did not cry out or express any agony at his torture, but remained steadfastly calm.

At sunset the shah returned from the day's hunt and called for his chief officer. The shah was displeased to hear the officer's report. Badí' should be made to talk, the shah commanded, and afterwards be put to death.

For three days Badí' was tortured, but he would say nothing. His strength of spirit astonished his torturers. They had never seen anyone like this youth who remained calm, even joyous, during the ordeal. Finally, when it was clear he would tell them nothing, Badí' was brutally put to death. His body was dumped into a pit without ceremony and covered with earth and stones.[4]

In Acre Bahá'u'lláh grieved for the suffering of Badí'. He praised Badí''s heroic spirit and called him the "Pride of Martyrs."* To Badí''s father Bahá'u'lláh wrote that Badí' had reached spiritual heights that no pen could describe. Through Badí' the pillars of tyranny were shaken, declared Bahá'u'lláh, and the face of victory unveiled.

Not only had Badí' heroically laid down his life, but he had also accomplished an important mission. The Cause of the Báb had already reached every corner of Persia. Now the tablet delivered to the shah explained the teachings of Bahá'u'lláh, Whom the Báb had foretold. For

---

* Badí' would later be named an Apostle of Bahá'u'lláh, a designation given to only nineteen Bahá'ís who demonstrated extraordinary service to Bahá'u'lláh and His Faith.

the first time, Bahá'u'lláh set forth clear proofs of His Cause for Persia and its leaders. There could be no more excuse for Persia to set itself against Him.

The story of Badí''s courage made his father proud. Some years later, when he was able to visit Bahá'u'lláh in person and hear from His lips the story of Badí', his beard would grow wet with tears. But the father, who had survived the battle at Fort Ṭabarsí, would follow in the footsteps of his son. One day the beard soaked with tears for Badí' would be stained red with his own blood. Like his son, he would die with honor—a martyr for the Cause of God.

The officer in charge of Badí''s torture met with a less honorable fate. Little more than a year after Badí''s death, he suffered a complete mental collapse and was placed in chains at the order of the shah. He died a miserable death. The whole land of Persia suffered from a terrible famine—God's punishment, affirmed Bahá'u'lláh, for the martyrdom of Badí', the Wonderful.

52

The Greatest Gift

Summer sun shimmered over the blue Mediterranean Sea. Waves rolled in to break in a steady rhythm against the walls of Acre, then ebbed to sea again. It was June 1870, nearly two years since Bahá'u'lláh and His family had first set foot in Acre. How grateful they were to leave those harsh, early days behind them. Life in prison had improved in the past two years, but still the family lived in close quarters with armed guards watching over them.

For the children of Bahá'u'lláh and Navváb, their youthful days in Tehran and Tákur seemed long ago and far away. They had enjoyed only a short span of years in that world of privilege and comfort and carefree days until, overnight, their world had turned upside down.

But that was a bygone time. They were no longer children, frightened at the sounds of the bloodthirsty mobs in Tehran. In Acre they were young adults—two brothers and a sister who gave no time to complaints or jealousies. They had suffered much together, enduring hardships and cruelties too many to tell. But suffering—like a flame in the hands of a metalworker—had fired their souls and shaped each of them into something strong and beautiful.

Bahíyyih Khánum was a graceful, kindhearted young woman of twenty-four. She had golden-brown hair and large, gray-blue eyes that sparkled with intelligence and good humor. No matter what the sorrow, nothing could dim her cheerful spirit. She possessed a calm, heroic courage in the face of trouble, very much like the courage of the Báb, which she had clearly demonstrated during the difficult times in Baghdad and Adrianople—and she deeply loved her brothers.

'Abdu'l-Bahá, the oldest of the three siblings, was twenty-six, with blue-gray eyes and black hair. He moved with the graceful strength and energy of a young lion, his every action and word bespeaking an inner grace as well. People thought he was tall when they looked at him, though he was only of medium height, for they could not help but see something of his greatness of spirit—a strength of will, a power of mind, a deep love and compassion for others that reached far beyond the ordinary.

Their youngest brother, Mírzá Mihdí, was twenty-two. He was slightly taller than 'Abdu'l-Bahá and looked very much like him. Mírzá Mihdí was gentle and patient, a kind and humble youth. Nothing pleased him more than serving his beloved father. Mírzá Mihdí often served as amanuensis for Bahá'u'lláh, writing down the tablets that He revealed.

Bahá'u'lláh loved His children deeply, and they loved Him. But they knew that He was more than their own beloved father. 'Abdu'l-Bahá had been the first to see it that day in Tehran when his father returned from the Black Pit. Bahá'u'lláh was not just the father who loved and cared for them. He was the Glory of God, His holy Messenger and their Lord.

For His part Bahá'u'lláh saw better than anyone else the real qualities of His faithful children. They were noble leaves and branches upon the family tree. To all of them Bahá'u'lláh gave a title of honor to suit their noble spirits. Bahíyyih Khánum He named "the Greatest Holy Leaf." 'Abdu'l-Bahá was "the Most Great Branch," and young Mírzá Mihdí was "the Purest Branch."[1]

As they had shared each stage of their father's exile, they now willingly shared His imprisonment in Acre. No matter the hardships, they were grateful to be at their father's side, grateful for the chance to serve their Lord. They were thankful, too, that the family was together. But in one fateful night, the family they cherished would be forever changed.

It was early evening. Mírzá Mihdí usually spent the last hours of the day with his father, transcribing what Bahá'u'lláh revealed. But today his services had not been needed. Mírzá Mihdí was free, instead, to climb the stairs to the flat prison roof, a favorite place for the prisoners to go. How good it felt at the end of a hot summer's day to stand on the roof in the fresh evening air.

Mírzá Mihdí loved to walk on the roof, chanting his prayers or quietly meditating. The vast evening sky sprinkled with a few early stars made the prison seem farther away and God that much closer. Mírzá Mihdí always walked carefully around the unguarded skylight—a large hole in the roof that opened above the kitchen.

This evening, like so many others, Mírzá Mihdí paced back and forth on the roof's familiar space. Feelings of joy filled his soul as he wrapped himself deeply in prayer, and as his thoughts centered on the world within, his eyes closed to the world outside.

Suddenly the Bahá'ís heard a horrible crashing sound. Quickly they ran to find out what had happened. An alarming sight met their eyes: Mírzá Mihdí lay bleeding on the prison floor directly beneath the skylight. He had fallen through the opening and landed on a wooden crate, which had pierced his ribs.

Bahá'u'lláh gently asked what had caused his fall. Mírzá Mihdí answered that he had been so carried away in prayer that he had forgotten about the hole in the roof as he walked and had accidentally stepped through the skylight.

Mírzá Mihdí was carefully lifted and carried to his room. A doctor was called, but he could do nothing to help. Mírzá Mihdí was too badly injured. No one wanted to believe the terrible news: young Mírzá Mihdí had only hours to live.

With sorrowful hearts, the family and other Bahá'ís gathered at his bedside. Mírzá Mihdí was in terrible pain and was weak from loss of blood. Yet he spoke kindly to those around him and, humble as always, told them he was sorry to be lying down while they were all sitting.

'Abdu'l-Bahá could not bear to see his younger brother die before his face. He realized that one hope remained. The power to heal belonged to the Messenger of God. In a private moment 'Abdu'l-Bahá cast himself down at his father's feet and, with tears in his eyes, begged Bahá'u'lláh to heal Mírzá Mihdí.

As much as Bahá'u'lláh loved both of His sons, He could not make such a promise, for that decision belonged to Mírzá Mihdí. "'O my Greatest Branch,'" Bahá'u'lláh answered 'Abdu'l-Bahá, "'leave him in the hands of his God.'"[2]

At Mírzá Mihdí's bedside, Bahá'u'lláh said that He wished to be alone with His son and dismissed everyone else from His presence. When the others had gone, father and son talked together for some time. No one else knew what was said, except for one thing. Bahá'u'lláh promised Mírzá Mihdí that God could heal him completely. He had only to ask.

"'"What do you wish?"'" Bahá'u'lláh said gently to His son. "'"Tell Me."'"

Despite his own pain, Mírzá Mihdí thought of all the Bahá'ís who longed to see their Lord. As he looked into his father's loving face, the pure-hearted Mírzá Mihdí did not ask for his own healing.

"'"I wish the people of Bahá* to be able to attain Your presence,"'" replied Mírzá Mihdí.

Bahá'u'lláh accepted His beloved son's final request. "'"And so it shall be,"'" He said. "'"God will grant your wish."'"[3]

On June 23, 1870, twenty-two hours after his fall, Mírzá Mihdí, the Purest Branch, drew his last breath. The earthly life of one *"'that was created of the light of Bahá'"* had come to an end. "'"Mihdí! O Mihdí!"'"[4] Bahá'u'lláh lamented.

The sad news was made known. Shaykh Maḥmúd requested the honor of preparing the body for burial. A tent was pitched in the prison barracks and the body placed upon a table in the tent. Clean water was carried in. With loving care Shaykh Maḥmúd began to wash the blessed body of Mírzá Mihdí.

---

* The Bahá'ís.

Outside the tent 'Abdu'l-Bahá paced back and forth. The sorrow etched upon his face told the story of his aching heart. The sound of heartfelt weeping and wailing filled the prison as the believers unburdened their grief. All the while Bahá'u'lláh sat inside next to the body of Mírzá Mihdí, quietly mourning the passing of His son.

When the body was ready, it was wrapped in clean burial cloth and placed in a casket. A few chosen men lifted the casket onto their shoulders. Guards escorted them as they walked out of the prison with measured steps and out of the city of Acre. Outside the city walls they carried their precious burden as far as a local shrine. There, in a nearby spot, the body of Mírzá Mihdí was laid to rest in the earth.

With their work completed, the men were walking back toward Acre when suddenly the earth began to rumble and shake beneath their feet. For three long minutes the tremor continued. People in the region were frightened. To the Bahá'ís it seemed the very earth was grieving at the passing of Mírzá Mihdí.

"'Blessed art thou and blessed he that turneth unto thee, and visiteth thy grave, and draweth nigh, through thee, unto God, the Lord of all that was and shall be. . . . Thou art, verily, the trust of God and His treasure in this land,'" Bahá'u'lláh wrote of the Purest Branch. "'When thou wast laid to rest in the earth, the earth itself trembled in its longing to meet thee.'"[5]

Navváb's face was wet with bitter tears for her son. She wept almost incessantly, and no one but Bahá'u'lláh could comfort her. He spoke to her tenderly. The Purest Branch had chosen to give his life, and God had accepted his gift, Bahá'u'lláh assured her. The power of his sacrifice would open the way for Bahá'ís to be with their Lord. In time, it would bring together all humanity.

Bahá'u'lláh's loving assurances eased the pain in Navváb's heart, and in time she was able to dry her tears. Of the sacrifice of His beloved son Bahá'u'lláh wrote: *"I have, O my Lord, offered up that which Thou hast given Me* [Mírzá Mihdí], *that Thy servants may be quickened, and all that dwell on earth be united.'"* In another prayer He wrote, "I beseech Thee, O my Lord, by him and by his exile and his imprisonment, to send down upon such as loved him what will quiet their hearts and bless their works."[6]

53
The Whisperings of Satan

A seed is planted in the earth. One day, seasons later, the seed is gone, and in its place a mighty tree reaches its great, leafy branches into the sky. How could so great a thing be hidden in that small seed? The mystery of the seed was like the mystery of Mírzá Mihdí's sacrifice, the greatness of which would unfold in its own time. But its first effects were felt in Acre, in the autumn after his death.

The barracks of Acre, where the Bahá'ís were imprisoned, had been built to function as housing for soldiers. In the autumn of 1870 the barracks were needed once more to house the troops of the Ottoman Empire. Bahá'u'lláh objected. Crowding the Bahá'ís, including the women and children, into such close quarters with soldiers was unacceptable.

By this time it was clear that Bahá'u'lláh and His followers were not dangerous criminals. The governor agreed to let them move out of the barracks and into housing in the city. They must remain under guard, but their bleak prison confinement would be greatly eased.

In the autumn of 1870, about four months after the death of the Purest Branch, the exiled Bahá'ís left the prison barracks. For two years, two months, and five days they had lived behind its walls. How grateful they were, at last, to turn their backs on it; how happy to take their first steps toward a freer life—the first step in fulfilling Mírzá Mihdí's wish. Houses were found for Bahá'u'lláh and His family and a few others. Everyone else was moved into a caravansary called the Inn of the Pillars.

Life in Acre still was not easy. The Bahá'ís contented themselves with very little, just as they had in the prison barracks. The ration of food for each person was meager, and the housing was far from comfortable.

The Inn of the Pillars, with its large, graceful arches, had been built for short overnight stays by caravan travelers. Its rooms were not meant to be used as a home. They were damp, dirty, and in poor repair. 'Abdu'l-Bahá stayed at the caravansary and took charge of improving the rooms where the Bahá'ís stayed. To raise money for the task, he sold a gift that had been given to him when he lived in Baghdad.

As usual, 'Abdu'l-Bahá took care of everyone else first. Before his own room could be repaired, the money had run out. 'Abdu'l-Bahá was left with a leaky roof, damp walls, and dusty floors infested with fleas. The fleas were especially troublesome since 'Abdu'l-Bahá had to sleep on a mat on the floor with a sheepskin for covering. Every night as he slept, the fleas would gather on the sheepskin and find their way to him. As they began to bite, 'Abdu'l-Bahá would wake up and turn the sheepskin over, with the fleas away from his body. Then he slept awhile before the fleas found their way to him again. Eight or ten times a night 'Abdu'l-Bahá would turn the sheepskin over to escape the biting fleas.

During that first year outside the prison, Bahá'u'lláh and His household were moved from house to house—three months here, four months there. At last they were moved to a small house owned by 'Údí Khammár, a Christian. Here they would live for the next two years.

Despite their continuing hardships, the Bahá'ís were happy. They were able to visit Bahá'u'lláh and draw strength from His loving support and guidance. Little by little, Bahá'í pilgrims would also be able to visit Bahá'u'lláh. The people of Acre were beginning to relax their suspicions of the Bahá'í exiles among them. But just as life in Acre seemed to be getting better, something terrible took place.

It began with Siyyid Muḥammad, who was up to his usual treachery. In Baghdad and Adrianople Siyyid Muḥammad had masterminded a campaign of lies against Bahá'u'lláh with the aid of Mírzá Yaḥyá. Now, just as the Bahá'ís were getting settled in the city of Acre, Siyyid Muḥammad initiated a new campaign designed to turn the people of Acre against them.

This time there was no Mírzá Yaḥyá to help; he was still imprisoned on the island of Cyprus. But Siyyid Muḥammad had other friends to carry out his malicious schemes, and he himself was a practiced hand at stirring up trouble. Soon his venomous lies began to circulate among the unsuspecting people of Acre.

A few of Bahá'u'lláh's writings were in the hands of the troublemakers. One of them made changes to the writing, corrupting the text with words that were not Bahá'u'lláh's and completely perverting the meaning. They were certain to provoke a strong reaction. These forgeries were attributed to Bahá'u'lláh and passed around town. The troublemakers were not disappointed.

The people of Acre did not yet know Bahá'u'lláh. All they knew of Him were the lies and forged writings created by His enemies. Their budding goodwill was quickly cut short, and their earlier disdain for the prisoners returned with even greater vehemence.

Bahá'u'lláh's faithful followers became angry. It pained them to see Bahá'u'lláh abused by Siyyid Muḥammad's slander. Some believers were prepared to gain peace by any measure. Give us permission, they begged Bahá'u'lláh, to get rid of Siyyid Muḥammad and his devious friends. Let us put an end to this evil mischief once and for all.

But Bahá'u'lláh would hear nothing of it. To lash out in violence, to return evil for evil, was against Bahá'u'lláh's teachings. """Go hence and do not perpetrate that wherefrom mischief will result!""" Bahá'u'lláh wrote to one believer who was determined to kill Siyyid Muḥammad.[1] Time and again He counseled His followers to be patient and tolerant and to shun every form of violence and retaliation.

The task was not easy. Day to day, week to week, fresh attacks poured forth. In a tablet revealed at this time, Bahá'u'lláh wrote about the burdens He was encountering. His face, He wrote, was "hidden in the dust of slander." His "robe of sanctity" was "sullied by the people of deceit." Bahá'u'lláh called Siyyid Muḥammad's war of words the "barking of dogs." It was "the whisperings of Satan"—the Satan that was man's lower self, unsubdued by his higher, spiritual nature. "The lamps of truth and purity, of loyalty and honor, have been put out," wrote Bahá'u'lláh.[2] He alluded in that tablet to the treacherous deeds of Siyyid Muḥammad and his cohorts. Their slanderous campaign kept the people of Acre fired with hostility toward the Bahá'ís, while it kept the community of faithful believers unsettled and upset.

The air of Acre was charged with turmoil. As He had done once before in Adrianople, Bahá'u'lláh withdrew from the company of everyone. He closed the doors of His house and saw no one—neither friend nor enemy. Only 'Abdu'l-Bahá and a small staff were allowed to stay with Him at the house of 'Údí Khammár.

The Bahá'ís were distressed at their separation from Bahá'u'lláh and tormented by the never-ending campaign of lies against Him. Seven of the believers decided that something more than patience was needed, and they began to plot a way to rid Acre and Bahá'u'lláh of the malevolent Siyyid Muḥammad.

In the privacy of His house Bahá'u'lláh continued to reveal tablets. In one of them He prophesied that something was about to occur that would cause an "ocean of tribulation" to surge and cast "billowing waves" against the "Ark of the Cause of God." In only one day the truth of His words would become all too clear.

Not far from where the government had its headquarters, the late afternoon air was split by the sound of pistol shots. Shouts and yelling followed, and the governor quickly came out of his house. The disturbance came from the direction of Siyyid Muḥammad's house, and the news was not good. Siyyid Muḥammad and two of his companions had been killed. The seven Bahá'ís had carried out their terrible plan of action.

The people of Acre were furious. Their angry shouts filled the streets as a crowd gathered. Young and old, proud and humble, they armed themselves with stones and sticks, with swords and rifles. Then the threatening mob set out with the governor, the chief of police, and their troops towards the house of Bahá'u'lláh. Along the way officials arrested any Bahá'ís they met.

The sun was fast sinking below the horizon as they approached their destination. When the governor reached Bahá'u'lláh's house, he commanded his troops to surround it. The shouts of the mob filled the darkening sky as the troops, with swords drawn, obeyed.

Inside, Bahá'u'lláh was dictating tablets to His amanuensis. An officer entered the house and spoke to 'Abdu'l-Bahá. Bahá'u'lláh must come to the government headquarters, he told 'Abdu'l-Bahá, along with the other men in the household. He must answer to the governor for the murders committed by His followers. When the message was given to Bahá'u'lláh, He obeyed the governor's summons.

The long-suffering Navváb was left to wonder what would happen to her beloved husband as the guards led Him away to the government headquarters. Her son, too, was taken with them. How it grieved Navváb to see Bahá'u'lláh threatened with harm from without yet again, even as He agonized over the actions of the believers.

The people of Acre watched as Bahá'u'lláh was escorted through the city streets. It was an hour after sunset. Bahá'u'lláh's path to the headquarters was lit by a man who walked ahead of Him with a lantern. Even in that dim light, the power of Bahá'u'lláh was evident to all. This was no meek or cowardly prisoner, afraid of authorities. Bahá'u'lláh walked with calm majesty to the government center and entered.

54

The Keys of My Mercy

When the officials of Acre reached the government headquarters, they gathered in a room and prepared to call Bahá'u'lláh before them for interrogation. He had been accused of ordering the deaths of Siyyid Muḥammad and his companions, and He must answer for these murders, they all agreed.

But when Bahá'u'lláh walked into the room, it was the officials who stood up in respect. No one spoke as Bahá'u'lláh walked with power and authority to the end of the room and seated Himself in a place of honor. Minutes passed, and silence filled the room.

At last the commander of the garrison addressed Bahá'u'lláh. "'Is it proper that some of your followers should act in such a manner?'"

"'*If one of your soldiers were to commit a reprehensible act,*'" Bahá'u'lláh answered, "'*would you be held responsible, and be punished in his place?*'"

No one answered.

Then officials asked Bahá'u'lláh to give His name and the name of the country from which He came.

"'*It is more manifest than the sun,*'" Bahá'u'lláh answered.

They repeated their question.

"'*I deem it not proper to mention it,*'" replied Bahá'u'lláh. "'*Refer to the farmán* [decree] *of the government which is in your possession.*'"

Once more, most respectfully, the officials put their questions to Him.

With majesty and power Bahá'u'lláh answered, "'*My name is Bahá'u'lláh* (Light of God),* *and My country is Núr* (Light). *Be ye apprized of it.*'"[1] He spoke a few more stern words to those who were gathered. Then Bahá'u'lláh got up from His seat and walked out of the assembly of officials.

That night Bahá'u'lláh was kept under guard at a nearby caravansary. 'Abdu'l-Bahá and twenty-five other Bahá'ís were imprisoned and shack-

* The name Bahá'u'lláh is a compound formed from the Arabic roots *bahá* and *Alláh*. *Bahá* is variously translated as "glory," "splendor," or "light"; *Alláh* means "God."

led in chains. The next night Bahá'u'lláh was moved to better quarters, and 'Abdu'l-Bahá was allowed to join Him. But the people of Acre remained upset, and their city remained in a state of commotion.

Meanwhile, the governor had sent a telegram to his superior, the governor-general of the province, telling him all that had taken place. To his surprise the governor-general was not at all pleased and chastised him for his actions.

On the third day of His captivity Bahá'u'lláh was called into the governor's office. The governor apologized to Bahá'u'lláh for His shameful treatment. He was free to return home, the governor told Him, along with 'Abdu'l-Bahá and the other men from His household.

The seven guilty Bahá'ís were kept in prison. The other believers who were being held were moved out of the prison and into a caravansary. There they were kept under guard, as their fate was not yet decided.

The people of Acre, already suspicious of the Bahá'ís, were not ready to forgive. The actions of these seven Bahá'ís had confirmed their worst suspicions. Not only did Bahá'ís dishonor the teachings of Muḥammad, but if they were willing to commit murder, surely they must not believe in God at all.

In the streets they shouted epithets of contempt at the Bahá'ís, accusing them of heresy, atheism, terrorism, and worse. Even the children of Bahá'ís were chased by the other children, who threw stones at them and called them names.

Only a thin wall separated the house of 'Údí Khammár, where Bahá'u'lláh lived, from the house of His closest neighbor, Ilyás 'Abbúd. After the murders, Ilyás 'Abbúd strengthened the wall between the two houses. He did not want to be the Bahá'ís' next victim.

Although the taunts of the people of Acre saddened Bahá'u'lláh, they were not what grieved Him most. "*'My captivity cannot harm Me,'*" He wrote. "*'That which can harm Me is the conduct of those who love Me, who claim to be related to Me, and yet perpetrate what causeth My heart and My pen to groan.'*" In another passage He wrote, "*'My captivity can bring on Me no shame. Nay, by My life, it conferreth on Me glory. That which can make Me ashamed is the conduct of such of My followers as profess to love Me, yet in fact follow the Evil One.'*"[2]

The Evil One was not an outside enemy, according to Bahá'u'lláh, but the lower nature within. "The actions of man himself breed a profusion of satanic power," Bahá'u'lláh would later write. "The prevalence of sedition, contention, conflict and the like . . . provoke the appearance of the satanic spirit. Yet the Holy Spirit hath ever shunned such matters."[3]

In spite of the turbulence surrounding Him, Bahá'u'lláh had continued His generous outpouring of divine guidance, and His followers were grateful. Yet they thirsted for more. In the numerous letters that came to Bahá'u'lláh from Bahá'ís in different places were not only questions to be answered, but also appeals for the new laws of God.

During His years in Adrianople, Bahá'u'lláh had already revealed many laws that He had not yet shared with the Bahá'ís. "'For a number of years,'" He wrote to one believer, "'petitions reached the Most Holy Presence from various lands begging for the laws of God, but We held back the Pen ere the appointed time had come.'"[4]

In 1873 the appointed time was at hand. It had been twenty years since Bahá'u'lláh had first been summoned in the Black Pit of Tehran to take up His mission, and ten years since He had announced that mission to His closest companions in the Garden of Riḍvan outside Baghdad. Seven years had passed since Mírzá Yaḥyá had been defeated in Adrianople in his final attempt to challenge Bahá'u'lláh.

Now in a quiet corner of the prison city of Acre, in a simple room of His small house, Bahá'u'lláh revealed the book of divine laws that would be central to His revelation from God. He called it the *Kitáb-i-Aqdas* (Most Holy Book) and described it as "'a heaven which We have adorned with the stars of Our commandments and prohibitions.'" The laws laid down by God, wrote Bahá'u'lláh in the Kitáb-i-Aqdas, "constitute the highest means for the maintenance of order in the world and the security of its peoples." He called these ordinances of His Most Holy Book "the lamps of My loving providence among My servants, and the keys of My mercy for My creatures."[5]

The laws revealed by Bahá'u'lláh addressed the needs of the whole human family and the profound need for justice in every compass of life—from the families in which the children of humankind were first nurtured to the great family of cultures and nations in which they all lived.

The new laws balanced rights and freedoms with a clear outline of responsibilities and obligations in every category of relationship: that of individuals to one another and to the society in which they lived; that of society to the individual; and the one relationship that was fundamental to all others—the mystical tie that connects each soul to God. It was the deepening of this most intimate relationship, and the fulfillment of the soul's spiritual destiny, that was the underlying purpose and final goal of the laws of religion. "Think not that We have revealed unto you a mere code of laws," wrote Bahá'u'lláh. "Nay, rather, We have unsealed the choice Wine with the fingers of might and power."[6]

The two duties prescribed by God to every human being, wrote Bahá'u'lláh in the opening lines of the Kitáb-i-Aqdas, were first to recognize the Messenger of God and second to observe all the laws and ordinances revealed by Him. "These twin duties are inseparable," Bahá'u'lláh stated clearly. "Neither is acceptable without the other."[7]

The boundaries set by divine law were not an obstacle to freedom, but the pathway leading to freedom. "Were men to observe that which We have sent down unto them from the Heaven of Revelation," wrote Bahá'u'lláh, "they would, of a certainty, attain unto perfect liberty." Divine law strengthened and developed the loftier side of human nature and restrained its baser aspect. It protected human beings from their own ignorance, Bahá'u'lláh stated, and guarded them "against the harm of the mischief maker."[8]

In every age the laws revealed by the Messenger of God were not a dry, lifeless thing, but an energizing force for change. Obedience to divine law elevated human behavior and possessed the power to release both individual and society from the tyranny of the lower nature—that ever-present element in every soul which was the source of evil. "For were men to abide by and observe the divine teachings," Bahá'u'lláh would write in another tablet, "every trace of evil would be banished from the face of the earth."[9]

The laws revealed by Bahá'u'lláh would meet the needs of a new stage in the development of the human race, but the full range of laws and ordinances in the Kitáb-i-Aqdas would not be applied all at once. They were intended, in their entirety, for a society that had not yet come into being. As the new civilization gradually emerged, the laws, too, would be applied in gradual stages.

"'Indeed, the laws of God are like unto the ocean and the children of men as fish, did they but know it,'" wrote Bahá'u'lláh. Even so, He observed, "'Since most people are . . . far-removed from the purpose of God. . . . One must guide mankind to the ocean of true understanding in a spirit of love and tolerance. The Kitáb-i-Aqdas itself beareth eloquent testimony to the loving providence of God.'"[10]

Not only did Bahá'u'lláh reveal the divine laws for a new age, but for the first time in the history of religion the Messenger of God Himself, in His Most Holy Book, provided for the institutions that would uphold the law and preserve the unity of the new religion. Leading these institutions would be the Universal House of Justice, which Bahá'u'lláh invested with the power both to enact and repeal laws not explicitly laid down by Him in the holy text. The Universal House of Justice would be inspired by God and protected from error.

In that simple house in the prison city of Acre were unveiled the laws of a revelation that would guide humankind, declared Bahá'u'lláh, for no less than "a full thousand years." They were the tools given by God to the human race to forge its future, to thrive and flourish and "build anew the whole world."[11] The Bahá'ís, who had begged for the bounty of His laws, would be the first to take hold of them.

55

The Governor and the Master of Acre

Not long after the murders in Acre, the governor of the city was dismissed and a new man took his place. The new governor, Aḥmad Big Tawfíq, was just getting settled in Acre when an angry woman came to see him. She was the sister of one of the murdered men. Like her brother before her, she was determined to stir up trouble for Bahá'u'lláh.

Bahá'u'lláh was ambitious, she told the new governor. He wanted to rule over men and the kings of men. Nothing less would satisfy Him. To prove her claims, she gave the governor a copy of Bahá'u'lláh's Tablet to the Kings,* along with some other writings. Then she left, confident that Bahá'u'lláh would find no favor with the new governor.

---

* The Súriy-i-Mulúk (Súrih to the Kings), in which Bahá'u'lláh collectively addresses all of the monarchs of East and West. This momentous tablet makes clear the nature of His mission and sets forth the standard of justice that must govern the exercise of their rule in this Day of God. (See chapter 46.)

But the writings of Bahá'u'lláh did not have the effect the woman had intended. The governor was deeply moved by the profound wisdom of what he read. When he saw 'Abdu'l-Bahá at the mosque, he begged to learn more and expressed his desire to meet with the One Who was the author of so wonderful a tablet.

At this point in His life Bahá'u'lláh did not usually meet with officials or others in Acre as He had done in Baghdad. These days He divided His time between revealing tablets and meeting with the Bahá'ís, whom He guided with unfailing love. This was His most important work, and the Bahá'ís flourished in His presence. The task of meeting the public, He left in the able hands of 'Abdu'l-Bahá.

While Bahá'u'lláh attended to the needs of His followers, 'Abdu'l-Bahá went out among the people of Acre. He took care of the needs of the poor, as his father had always done. He listened to the troubles of each and all, and he gave wise counsel when it was sought. He had discussions at the mosque with men of learning, who were deeply impressed with his knowledge and understanding of both spiritual and worldly matters.

In every way 'Abdu'l-Bahá reflected the spirit of his father's teachings. Kind and compassionate, noble and wise, 'Abdu'l-Bahá gradually changed the hearts of the people of Acre. As weeks lengthened into months, their hatred turned to respect and affection. They called him "Father of the Poor," as the people of Tehran had called Bahá'u'lláh, and "Master of Acre."

At the very mosque where the sultan's order of punishment had first been read, 'Abdu'l-Bahá became a welcomed and respected visitor. He was given one of the small, quiet rooms for study and prayer that stood at the edge of the mosque and its court. As the people of Acre became familiar with the noble character of 'Abdu'l-Bahá, they looked with new eyes upon all the Bahá'ís in their city and grew more comfortable in their company.

Even Ilyás 'Abbúd, the Christian merchant who had barricaded his house against Bahá'u'lláh, had a change of heart. He saw the qualities of Christ in the loving spirit and righteous actions of 'Abdu'l-Bahá, and his fears dissolved. In time he also came to know Bahá'u'lláh, in Whom he recognized that same nobility of spirit.

'Abbúd decided that he had sorely misjudged his neighbors. These good people were not his enemies. He tore down the barricade between

Bahá'u'lláh's house and his own, and from that time on, he became a true and devoted friend to Bahá'u'lláh and His noble son. It was because of Ilyás 'Abbúd, who made repeated requests, that Bahá'u'lláh agreed, at last, to meet with the new governor of Acre.

At the appointed hour, Aḥmad Big Tawfíq humbly entered the room where Bahá'u'lláh received guests. The prisoner and the governor spoke for a time. Then the governor, who was even more deeply impressed with Bahá'u'lláh in person, begged Him to accept a gift or a service that would please Him.

Bahá'u'lláh wanted nothing for Himself. Instead He suggested that the governor repair the broken city aqueduct, which had lain useless for thirty years. The aqueduct would bring fresh water into the city—a welcome gift that everyone in Acre could enjoy. Aḥmad Big Tawfíq happily agreed to carry out the project.

Bahá'u'lláh did make one request. Because of the crimes committed by a few, several innocent Bahá'ís were still locked in prison. Bahá'u'lláh asked the governor to review their cases, and the governor agreed.

Aḥmad Big Tawfíq was a just man. Unlike the authorities before him, he did not ask for money to release the prisoners. After looking at the facts, he released all the Bahá'ís who were blameless. Only the seven who were guilty of the murders were kept in prison.

For the two years that he was governor, Aḥmad Big Tawfíq treated all the Bahá'ís with respect. He so admired both Bahá'u'lláh and 'Abdu'l-Bahá that he often asked their advice when he made decisions as governor. He sent his own son to 'Abdu'l-Bahá for instruction.

The days were brighter now for the exiles. Over time, the people of Acre realized that Bahá'u'lláh could have had no connection to the crimes of a few of His disobedient followers. With the clouds of hostility dissipated, the Bahá'ís opened their shops again in the marketplace and were able to earn their living.

Even happier days were in store for 'Abdu'l-Bahá. Someone new had come to Acre—a young woman named Fáṭimih Khánum. She had traveled all the way from Persia in the company of her brother and another Bahá'í, arriving in early 1872. The travelers had entered Acre quietly, with the help of 'Abbúd, in the months after the murders, when there was still open hostility toward the Bahá'ís.

The journey had been difficult and dangerous, but these things were insignificant to Fáṭimih, for she had been summoned to Acre by Bahá-'u'lláh. She could remember when the first heartbreaking news had reached her home in the city of Isfahan—the news that Bahá'u'lláh was imprisoned behind the walls of Acre. How distressed she had been to learn that He, Who had loved the outdoors—the seas, the hills, and the plains, gardens, flowers, and the open air—was a prisoner in so dreadful a place. She had shut herself in her room and wept for His suffering.

But the season of sorrow was now past. Fáṭimih had been called to Acre by Bahá'u'lláh to begin a new life as the wife of 'Abdu'l-Bahá. What joy filled her spirit! It made her remember a dream she once had, a dream she would never forget.

56

Two Birds of the Nest of Thy Love

In her dream Fáṭimih grew more and more weary until she could hardly walk. She carried many things in her arms as she walked across an endless expanse of desert sand, and the burden weighed her down. All her strength seemed to leave her. Suddenly she came upon two rivers with a bridge connecting them, and there she saw an old siyyid.

"What dost thou want? Where dost thou wish to go?" the old siyyid asked her.

"I desire greatly to go to the blessed cities of Jerusalem—Love—and Bahá," replied Fáṭimih.

Carrying the things that burdened her, she would not be able to journey to those cities, the siyyid told her. She would have to cast away her burden, then she would have the strength and power to achieve her desire.

Fáṭimih obediently cast away her belongings. Then the old siyyid, taking Fáṭimih by the arm, plunged her into one river and the other. When she emerged from the water, Fáṭimih found herself flying. How easy it was! How beautiful the land was beneath her, like paradise.

Soon she came to a splendid, gleaming city. On its walls were Arabic letters written in brilliant light. "Love. Bahá. Jerusalem," they read. Inside the city, Fáṭimih came to a great temple. There she stood in the presence of all the Holy Ones—the Lord Christ, Moses, Isaiah, and every other Prophet of Whom she knew.

The Prophet Muḥammad gave Fáṭimih a necklace of brilliant diamonds, which she handed to her mother. Then, trying again to fly, she woke from her dream.[1]

Now in Acre Fáṭimih felt the same wonderful joy she had felt in her dream. Her unburdened heart was light with happiness. Many parents had offered their beautiful daughters for the honor of marriage to 'Abdu'l-Bahá, but 'Abdu'l-Bahá had considered no one until Fáṭimih arrived. From her first meeting with him, Fáṭimih thanked God for bringing them together.

In Isfahan Fáṭimih had loved to chant poetry and prayers alone on the roof of her house in the evenings, while the sky above her deepened from sunset to star-spangled night. Fáṭimih herself reflected the heritage of an illustrious family that was regarded as one of the most distinguished in Isfahan.

Fáṭimih's father, Mírzá Muḥammad-'Alí—a descendant of the Prophet Muḥammad—had added fresh luster to the family's spiritual legacy.* After studying with Siyyid Káẓim, he became a devoted follower of the Báb and then Bahá'u'lláh. He had learned about the Báb's declaration of His mission from Mullá Ḥusayn himself. Mírzá Muḥammad-'Alí had contributed funds to Ṭáhirih for her teaching travels and had himself been an ardent teacher of the new religion. He had met the Báb in Isfahan and later, before he died, traveled as a pilgrim to see Bahá'u'lláh in Baghdad and in Adrianople.

Fáṭimih had been born around the time of the conference at Badasht, in which her father had taken part. Nearly twenty-five years later, on her journey to Acre, Fáṭimih herself enjoyed the privilege of meeting, in Shiraz, Khadíjih Bagum, wife of the Báb. In their conversations together Fáṭimih heard Khadíjih Bagum's own stories.

* One of her father's brothers was also an outstanding Bábí who died from injuries he sustained in an attack on Bábís near Niyala. Two outstanding nephews of Mírzá Muḥammad-'Alí, who accompanied him to see Bahá'u'lláh in Baghdad, would later lay down their lives for their faith. Bahá'u'lláh would refer to them as the "King of the Martyrs" and the "Beloved of the Martyrs."

The wife of the Báb told of lying awake on that memorable night of the Báb's declaration and listening to His voice all through the night as He read the verses of God and presented proofs to Mullá Ḥusayn. She told of that sorrowful night, too, when the chief constable with his men entered their house through the roof and took away her beloved husband, Whom she would never see again. The wife of the Báb told Fáṭimih many stories of those days, but some things were better left untold.

"If I attempt to describe the sufferings and persecutions of those days," Khadíjih Bagum had said to Fáṭimih, "I will not be able to endure talking about them, neither will you have the fortitude to listen to them. . . ."[2] All these things Fáṭimih kept treasured in her heart.

The marriage to 'Abdu'l-Bahá did not take place at once. While she waited, Fáṭimih stayed in the home of Mírzá Músá, Bahá'u'lláh's kindly brother. Sometimes Fáṭimih watched from the window as 'Abdu'l-Bahá swam, strong and graceful, in the sea. Often, late in the afternoon, Fáṭimih would go with the wife of Mírzá Músá to visit Bahá'u'lláh.

As a girl, Fáṭimih had longed to live in the days when a Messenger of God walked the earth. Now her heart's dearest wish had come true. Words alone were too feeble to describe her feelings of joy. When she visited Bahá'u'lláh, her soul seemed to soar in a heaven of peace and loving-kindness.

Mírzá Músá would also visit Bahá'u'lláh. Each time, on his return, he brought from Bahá'u'lláh a marriage gift for Fáṭimih. One day when Mírzá Músá returned from such a visit, a look of great happiness shone in his face.

"'I have brought a most wonderful gift for you,'" he told Fáṭimih. "'It is this—a new name has been given you and that name is Munírih (Illumined).'"

Before Bahá'u'lláh had summoned Fáṭimih to Acre, He had dreamed a dream in which she had appeared as a young woman "'whose countenance was luminous and whose heart was enlightened.'"[3] It was she who would marry 'Abdu'l-Bahá, He had said. From that day forward she was no longer called Fáṭimih. The bride of 'Abdu'l-Bahá would be known as Munírih, the beautiful new name with which Bahá'u'lláh had honored her.

Weeks passed into months, and still the wedding did not take place. One day 'Abbúd asked Bahá'u'lláh, "'Wherefore the delay in the marriage?'"[4] But Bahá'u'lláh did not answer directly. At last the problem became clear to 'Abbúd. The new couple needed a room in which to live as husband and wife.

This was a problem 'Abbúd could solve, and gladly. Since his house and Bahá'u'lláh's stood together, wall to wall, 'Abbúd opened a doorway from Bahá'u'lláh's house into a room in his own house. He had the room furnished simply but comfortably. When all was ready, 'Abbúd presented it to Bahá'u'lláh.

"'I have had this room prepared for the Master,*'" said 'Abbúd.[5] Bahá'u'lláh accepted 'Abbúd's generous gift. Now there was nothing to stand in the way of the marriage. It was March 1873, and after nearly six months, it was time for the wedding day.

On the evening of March 8, Bahá'u'lláh, 'Abdu'l-Bahá, and the wedding guests were gathered together. The guests were few—Navváb and Bahíyyih Khánum, 'Abbúd's wife and three daughters, and the wife of Mírzá Músá.

Munírih Khánum walked into the gathering in a simple white dress. It had been stitched with loving hands by 'Abdu'l-Bahá's mother, Navváb, and his sister, Bahíyyih Khánum. To Munírih it was "more precious than the silks and velvets of Paradise."[6] Munírih's rich black hair, plaited in two braids, was adorned with a fresh white headdress.

The wedding was simple. They had no musicians or fine decorations, but they had Bahá'u'lláh, Who chanted prayers. Munírih, too, chanted in a melodious voice a tablet revealed for the couple by Bahá'u'lláh.

They had no cake in celebration, only cups of hot, sweet tea. Most importantly they had the blessing of Bahá'u'lláh. What love and happiness of spirit enfolded them! "'The glory and beauty of love and happiness," Munírih Khánum related, "were beyond and above all luxury and ceremony and circumstance.'"[7]

"'Many maidens, in Baghdád, in Adirnih,† in this Most Great Prison, hoped for this bounty,'" Bahá'u'lláh told Munírih Khánum, "'but it was not given to them. You must render thanks unto God for this great bounty, and this exalted bestowal given unto you. May God be with you.'"[8]

---

* A reference to 'Abdu'l-Bahá, who by this time was known to many by the title "Master."

† Edirne, or Adrianople.

When the chanting was done and the guests were gone, Munírih Khánum was the wife of her beloved 'Abdu'l-Bahá. She was twenty-five years old and he was twenty-eight. In the years to come, she would cherish his cheerfulness and his sense of humor, his kindness and his unfailing love. How considerate he was to each and every person, she would say. Surely, in all the earth, there was none to equal him.

In her later years she would write, "If I were to write the details of the fifty years of my association with the Beloved of the world, of His love, His mercy and bounty, I would need fifty years more of time and opportunity in order to write it; yet, if the seas of the world were turned into ink and the leaves of the forest into paper, I would not render adequate justice to the subject."[9]

'Abdu'l-Bahá was happy with Munírih Khánum and would later write that in true marriage, husband and wife are "two helpmates, two intimate friends," like "two doves in the nest" of love.[10]

In one of His tablets Bahá'u'lláh referred to marriage as "a fortress for well-being." The marriage of 'Abdu'l-Bahá and Munírih Khánum in Acre took place during the same year that Bahá'u'lláh revealed the Kitáb-i-Aqdas. Among His newly revealed marriage laws in the Kitáb-i-Aqdas was a new wedding vow—a simple verse to be recited by both man and woman: "We will all, verily, abide by the Will of God." The marriage laws revealed by Bahá'u'lláh upheld the principle of the equality of women and men, which He addressed in His writings. Bahá'u'lláh declared, "Women and men have been and will always be equal in the sight of God."[11]

Less than a year after the wedding of Munírih Khánum and 'Abdu'l-Bahá, 'Abbúd moved out of Acre. Before he left, he arranged for his neighbor, Bahá'u'lláh, to have the use of his house. The wall that separated the two houses was removed. Now they stood together as one larger house. Bahá'u'lláh and the members of His family who lived with Him would have a little more of the living space they sorely needed.

Bahá'u'lláh moved into an upper room in the house of 'Abbúd. The room was large and opened onto a veranda that faced the sea. Bahá'u'lláh loved to walk in the open air on the veranda, to feel the fresh breeze and to gaze far out over the sea. Soldiers stood guard on the street below, for He was still a prisoner, but the air stirred with change.

Little more than a year later the governor, Aḥmad Big Tawfíq, left Acre. He had been assigned to another government post. Acre's new governor, 'Abdu'r-Raḥmán Pá<u>sh</u>á, feigned friendliness toward the Bahá'ís, but he was nothing like his predecessor. He thought Bahá'u'lláh and His followers belonged in prison, and secretly he schemed to put them there.

57

The Hand of God

The new governor of Acre, 'Abdu'r-Raḥmán Pá<u>sh</u>á, was angry to find that the Bahá'ís owned shops in the marketplace and enjoyed the freedom of living and working in the city. He wrote a letter to the authorities in Constantinople, complaining about Bahá'u'lláh and His followers. The Bahá'ís belonged in prison, he asserted. Was that not the sultan's order? The authorities replied as the governor had hoped. Bahá'u'lláh and His followers were indeed prisoners and had no right to work. 'Abdu'r-Raḥmán Pá<u>sh</u>á lost no time in devising a plan of action for returning the Bahá'ís to prison.

One evening, when all was ready, he visited a well-known <u>sh</u>ay<u>kh</u>—the most important religious leader of Acre. The governor told the <u>sh</u>ay<u>kh</u> his plan. In the morning, said the governor, when the Bahá'ís came to open their shops in the market, they would be arrested and taken to prison. The governor was pleased with his plan, for it would disgrace the Bahá'ís publicly, and the <u>sh</u>ay<u>kh</u> made no objection.

But when the governor had gone, the <u>sh</u>ay<u>kh</u> hurried out. Through the dark streets of Acre he made his way to the house of 'Abbúd. There he met with 'Abdu'l-Bahá, whom he much admired, and told him of the governor's plan. The <u>sh</u>ay<u>kh</u> suggested that the governor should be bribed. Given enough money, the <u>sh</u>ay<u>kh</u> suggested, the governor would surely forget his plan. If not, in the morning every Bahá'í in Acre would be arrested.

‘Abdu’l-Bahá did not agree. Bribery was not an acceptable way for Bahá’ís to solve a problem. He told the shaykh to leave this matter in the hands of God and return home. He assured him that God would take care of the matter.

The hour was late. Bahá’u’lláh had just retired for the night when ‘Abdu’l-Bahá brought the news. Bahá’u’lláh listened, then answered that the believers must not go to their shops in the morning. ‘Abdu’l-Bahá made sure all of the Bahá’ís were told.

Early the next morning, instead of going to work, all of the believers gathered at the house of ‘Abbúd and waited. When the governor, accompanied by a handful of soldiers, boldly strode through the marketplace to arrest the Bahá’ís, he was greatly surprised. Not one Bahá’í shop was open. Thinking that perhaps the Bahá’ís were simply late, he went to the police station to await their arrival. He waited for some time, but no Bahá’ís came to open their shops.

At last ‘Abdu’r-Raḥmán Páshá saw the shaykh he had visited the night before. The shaykh had come to the marketplace looking for him; he was carrying a telegram addressed to the governor. The message in the telegram was an order of dismissal. ‘Abdu’r-Raḥmán Páshá was no longer governor of Acre. The shaykh was amazed at this sudden turn of events, but Bahá’u’lláh was not. “““No one,””” said Bahá’u’lláh, “““can frustrate God in His purpose.”””[1]

Not only governors, but those in the highest positions, too, could not escape the Hand of God. The sultan’s orders of banishment had caused Bahá’u’lláh and His followers to suffer. His closest advisors, the foreign minister and the grand vizier, had provoked the sultan’s fear and suspicions of Bahá’u’lláh. Their cruel and unjust actions, Bahá’u’lláh had warned, would bring the wrath of God down upon them.

Already the sultan’s advisors had reaped the awful rewards for their actions. The power they had used against Bahá’u’lláh was abruptly taken away. Only one year after Bahá’u’lláh was sent to Acre, the foreign minister died far from home. A few short years later ‘Alí Páshá lost his high position as grand vizier.

It was ‘Alí Páshá who had urged the sultan to banish Bahá’u’lláh to the terrible prison of Acre. Bahá’í women and children had been sent there too. The cruelty of ‘Alí Páshá, said Bahá’u’lláh, caused the Spirit of

God to lament. Now the one who had been nearest the sultan in power would never wield power again. In all the land, the name of 'Alí Pá<u>sh</u>á was forgotten.

Sulṭán 'Abdu'l-'Azíz was about to meet his own fate. Three times the sultan had ordered Bahá'u'lláh to be exiled—first from Baghdad to Constantinople, then from Constantinople to Adrianople in the bitter cold of winter, and finally from Adrianople to the Most Great Prison of Acre. In 1876, a revolution at the palace toppled the sultan from power. Four days later Sulṭán 'Abdu'l-'Azíz was dead, killed by an assassin.

The palace revolution was followed by war a year later. In that war, eleven million people were freed from Ottoman rule, and Russian forces took the city of Adrianople. Forty years later, in another war, the empire would dissolve completely, and there would never be another sultan.

Other kings and leaders, too, lost the power they misused. Some had turned their power against Bahá'u'lláh. Others ignored or treated with disdain His summons in the tablets He sent to them.

Napoleon III, who had contemptuously ignored both of the tablets Bahá'u'lláh had addressed to him, was warned by Bahá'u'lláh that he would suffer divine retribution. In 1870, while Bahá'u'lláh was imprisoned in Acre, Napoleon was defeated in battle. His kingdom was lost, his only son was killed in battle, and the proud emperor was forced to live in exile. In time, his once great empire collapsed altogether, and his homeland fell into fierce civil war. Other rulers—German, Austrian, Russian, and more—lost their empires because they, too, had turned a deaf ear to Bahá'u'lláh's call.

Yet Bahá'u'lláh exalted the station of those kings who would one day heed His summons. "How great is the blessedness that awaiteth the king who will arise to aid My Cause," wrote Bahá'u'lláh. "Such a king is the very eye of mankind . . . the fountainhead of blessings unto the whole world." He made it clear that He harbored no desire for that which the kings of the earth possessed. "It is not Our wish to lay hands on your kingdoms," Bahá'u'lláh stated in His Most Holy Book. "Our mission is to seize and possess the hearts of men."[2]

In Acre 'Abdu'r-Raḥmán Pás͟há was followed by a series of other governors who were friendlier toward the Bahá'ís. Time passed peaceably for the Bahá'ís there. Each day, late in the afternoon, they gathered in front of the house of 'Abbúd. Standing or sitting in small groups, they waited. Each day Bahá'u'lláh invited a few believers to come inside. Those who were called to visit would run eagerly into the house. The very door through which they entered and the walls of the house itself seemed to vibrate with their joy and excitement.

For each, his experience within that house in the presence of Bahá'u'lláh was beyond words. Who else except Bahá'u'lláh knew, without the need to tell, each soul's deeds and aspirations? Yet despite every weakness and shortcoming, in His presence no one was made to feel unworthy or unhappy. Nor did any leave without knowing that, however humble in the eyes of the world, he was a noble and cherished soul.

On any day, no matter who might see Bahá'u'lláh, none was disappointed. The Bahá'ís' love for one another was so great that for one of them to gain his heart's desire created happiness for all.

Day to day, walking on the veranda, Bahá'u'lláh would look down at the ground below and smile. The area surrounding the house was kept beautiful and clean, and Bahá'u'lláh recognized the work of Muḥammad-Hádí. Though short of height, Muḥammad-Hádí was lofty of mind and pure of heart—well-loved among the Bahá'ís and devoted to Bahá'u'lláh.

Muḥammad-Hádí's trade was bookbinder and artist. With loving care and skill he illuminated the writings of Bahá'u'lláh, adding color in delicate designs. Then he bound the writings into books. He was a lover of beauty who wanted Bahá'u'lláh to gaze upon beauty wherever He looked. So, with the same loving hands, Muḥammad-Hádí swept the area outside Bahá'u'lláh's house each day and sprinkled it with water.

"'Muḥammad-Hádí has turned the square in front of this prison into the bridal bower of a palace,'" Bahá'u'lláh would say. "'He has brought pleasure to all the neighbors and earned their thanks.'"[3]

Still, when He looked across the water that stretched as far as the eye could see, Bahá'u'lláh could remember Tehran and Tákur. How He longed for the cool mountains and green forests of His family home. "'I have not gazed on verdure for nine years,'" said Bahá'u'lláh one day. "'The country is the world of the soul, the city is the world of bodies.'"[4]

When 'Abdu'l-Bahá heard this, his heart was moved. Bahá'u'lláh had been a prisoner in Acre for nine long years. But the sultan who had sent Him there was no longer living, and 'Abdu'l-Bahá felt sure that a time for change had come. In the spring of 1877 he decided to test the strength of the sultan's order.

58
Oasis

About four miles north of Acre stood a large, empty house named *Mazra'ih,* meaning "Farm" in Arabic. Gardens grew on every side, and a stream of clear, running water flowed nearby. It was just the place, decided 'Abdu'l-Bahá, to satisfy his father's longing for the beauty of the countryside.

The man who owned Mazra'ih lived in another house inside the city walls of Acre. "I am an invalid and cannot leave the city," he explained when 'Abdu'l-Bahá met with him. "If I go there [to Mazra'ih] it is lonely and I am cut off from my friends."

"While you are not living there and the place is empty, let it to us," said 'Abdu'l-Bahá. The man was surprised at the proposal but soon agreed. A small yearly rent was fixed, and 'Abdu'l-Bahá took charge of the house in the country. He hired laborers to make repairs to the house, to put its gardens in order, and to build a bath. Everything was made ready for Bahá'u'lláh.

More than once during this time 'Abdu'l-Bahá walked openly through the city gates and out of Acre. Guards stood on both sides of the gates. The sultan's orders had forbidden Bahá'ís to pass beyond the city walls. The orders had not changed with the new sultan, but no one stopped 'Abdu'l-Bahá from leaving the prison-city.

'Abdu'l-Bahá made one last test of the sultan's orders. He decided to hold a banquet in the country. He invited the town's officials and other important people. 'Abdu'l-Bahá was well admired and respected in Acre, and those whom he invited accepted his invitation.

The banquet table was spread in the cool shade of pine trees near a great mansion. All afternoon the guests enjoyed the company of one another and the hospitality of 'Abdu'l-Bahá. In the evening all returned to Acre together. Their actions made one thing clear: The sultan's orders confining the Bahá'ís would no longer be enforced in Acre.

At last 'Abdu'l-Bahá was satisfied. The repairs to Mazra'ih were complete, and the gates of Acre were open for them. He went to Bahá'u'lláh and said, “““Mazra‘ih is ready for you, and a carriage to drive you there.”””

But Bahá'u'lláh would not go. “““I am a prisoner,””” He said. Bahá'u'lláh had always obeyed the orders of exile and imprisonment, but 'Abdu'l-Bahá persisted. Again he asked his father to come to the mansion of Mazra'ih, but again Bahá'u'lláh said no. When Bahá'u'lláh refused yet a third time, 'Abdu'l-Bahá knew better than to ask again. Still he did not give up.

Instead of approaching Bahá'u'lláh himself, 'Abdu'l-Bahá turned to a well-known friend and leader in Acre. When the governor had planned to arrest the Bahá'ís in the marketplace, it was this friend, a shaykh, who had come to warn them. He loved and revered Bahá'u'lláh, and Bahá'u'lláh favored him. If anyone could persuade Bahá'u'lláh, it was this good friend.

“““You are daring,””” said 'Abdu'l-Bahá when he spoke to the friend. “““Go tonight to His Holy Presence, fall on your knees before Him, take hold of His hands and do not let go until He promises to leave the city!”””

The friend went at once to see Bahá'u'lláh. Sitting close, he took hold of Bahá'u'lláh's hands. “““Why do you not leave the city?””” he asked.

“““I am a prisoner,””” Bahá'u'lláh answered.

“““God forbid!””” replied the friend. “““Who has the power to make you a prisoner? You have kept yourself in prison. It was your own will to be imprisoned, and now I beg you to come out and go to the palace. It is beautiful and verdant. The trees are lovely, and the oranges like balls of fire!”””

“““I am a prisoner, it cannot be,””” said Bahá'u'lláh.

Still the friend would not let go of Bahá'u'lláh's hands. For a whole hour he pleaded with Bahá'u'lláh to leave the prison-city behind.

At last Bahá'u'lláh agreed. *“““Khaylí khub”””* (Very good).

The friend returned to 'Abdu'l-Bahá with the glad news. The very next day 'Abdu'l-Bahá brought the carriage and took Bahá'u'lláh to Mazra'ih. It was June 1877 when Bahá'u'lláh passed through the city gates and out of Acre.[1]

On its ground floor Mazra'ih held two large rooms. Bahá'u'lláh used one of these rooms as a place to receive guests and to dictate His tablets. For private use He chose a sunny upper room with a balcony. From this room Bahá'u'lláh could look east as far as the hills of Galilee, where Jesus once walked. He could look over to the Mediterranean Sea, which lay half a mile away and stretched to the west.

During His nine years in the Most Great Prison Bahá'u'lláh's only exercise had been to pace back and forth in His cell in Acre. Now, at long last, He was free to walk through the fragrant gardens of Mazra'ih. But they were not the only gardens Bahá'u'lláh enjoyed. 'Abdu'l-Bahá had been able to rent another place of beauty to gladden his father's heart.

Just north of Acre, a little river divided into two streams on its way to the sea. Between the two streams rose a bit of land, a small island called the Garden of Na'mayn. At its edges grew weeping willows. Orange blossoms and jasmine scented its air, and silver-scaled fish swam in its streams. Eventually 'Abdu'l-Bahá purchased the garden for Bahá'u'lláh.

For the Bahá'ís in Persia the news from Acre was a long-awaited joy. Bahá'u'lláh was finally freed from the prison-city! The Bahá'ís felt liberated, too. At Mazra'ih there would be room for all the Bahá'ís in Acre as well as for the pilgrims who journeyed from Persia to come together with Bahá'u'lláh. Every one could see his Lord.

The Bahá'í pilgrims did not come empty-handed to Mazra'ih. Every Persian household, however modest, enjoyed the beauty of a garden. To show their love for Bahá'u'lláh, the believers brought their most beautiful plants to add to the gardens.

In the months it took to cross mountain and desert from Persia to Mazra'ih, the pilgrims took tender care of their gifts for Bahá'u'lláh. Each plant was kept alive from day to day with a little of the traveler's own precious water. When they finally reached Mazra'ih, the treasured plants were fresh and healthy. Many were taken, at 'Abdu'l-Bahá's direction, for planting in Bahá'u'lláh's island-garden.

How Bahá'u'lláh enjoyed visiting that small island, where He would sit on a shady bench beneath two large mulberry trees. Nearby a fountain splashed softly. Gentle breezes carried the rich perfume of flowers—jasmine, geraniums, roses—and the spicy scents of fresh growing herbs—

mint, thyme, and lemon verbena. Pomegranate trees with bright red flowers grew in the garden as well as Bahá'u'lláh's favorite flower, a creamy white rose with a golden center.

What a different world from the dull walls and wretched odors of the prison-city! The fragrant garden, made from the loving efforts of so many, was an oasis of beauty. Bahá'u'lláh so loved it that He named the garden *"Riḍvan,"* meaning "Paradise." For His followers it called to mind another garden named "Riḍvan"—the garden just outside of Baghdad where Bahá'u'lláh had first told them that He was God's promised Messenger.

Now, on some days, Bahá'u'lláh invited Bahá'ís to come to the new Riḍvan Garden with Him. At other times He went alone. From time to time He stayed in a little house that stood at the end of the garden. There, in a room set aside for Him, He could have privacy to rest, take a meal, or reveal tablets.

It warmed the heart of 'Abdu'l-Bahá to see his father sitting on the bench beneath the mulberry trees, refreshed and happy. For all his efforts, 'Abdu'l-Bahá needed no more reward than this.

Among the happiest days were those when a feast was held at Mazra'ih. A tent for the gathering would be pitched on the grounds outside the mansion. Prayers and perhaps a tablet newly revealed by Bahá'u'lláh would be chanted. Food was brought from the mansion. The believers took pleasure in the company of one another and in the wonderful presence of Bahá'u'lláh.

One day Bahá'u'lláh called a feast to celebrate the release of Bahá'í prisoners in Tehran. Other news from Persia was more troubling these days. Many Bahá'ís were treated brutally, and many in Persia were killed by government and religious leaders.

Then Bahá'u'lláh received news that caused Him great sorrow. Two blameless Bahá'í brothers, whom Bahá'u'lláh called "twin shining lights," had been executed in the city of Isfahan, Persia. Two religious leaders had schemed together against the brothers and cruelly ordered their deaths. For their heartless deeds, Bahá'u'lláh named the leaders *"Raqshá"* (the She-Serpent) and *"Dhi'b"* (the Wolf).[2]

Their cruel deeds would not be allowed to pass unnoticed.

59

The King of Martyrs and the Beloved of Martyrs

No one expected the two Bahá'í brothers in Isfahan to be treated so savagely. Mírzá Ḥusayn and his younger brother Mírzá Ḥasan were siyyids—respected descendants of the Prophet Muḥammad—and they were extremely successful merchants who were as generous as they were prosperous. Every day they helped the poor and distressed of Isfahan. When famine came to the city, many would have starved to death had it not been for the merchant brothers. They had sent funds to Bahá'u'lláh as well to ease the hardships of the exiles as they moved from city to city.

The kindly brothers were known as the most honest and trustworthy among merchants. That is why Mír Muḥammad-Ḥusayn, the *imám-jum'ih,* or chief Muslim leader in Isfahan, had asked them to take charge of his financial affairs. In time, through their business dealings on his behalf, he, too, became prosperous. The imám-jum'ih was quite satisfied until the time came to pay the brothers for their services.

Mír Muḥammad-Ḥusayn did not want to pay the debt he owed. Instead, he decided on a way to get rid of the brothers and to gain even more wealth for himself. His plan was simple but deadly. He would make it known that the two brothers were Bahá'ís, then call for their deaths as enemies of Islam. Like a serpent, he made ready to strike.

Mír Muḥammad-Ḥusayn got help to carry out his scheme from another Muslim leader in Isfahan, the mujtahid Shaykh Báqir. Shaykh Báqir was a stubborn enemy of the Faith who hated the Bahá'ís. Together the two religious leaders went to the eldest son of the shah, who was governor of Isfahan. They promised the prince a share of the brothers' wealth if he would help them carry out their plot.

Mírzá Ḥusayn and Mírzá Ḥasan were soon arrested and taken to the government headquarters. They were brought before the prince, who tried to reason with them at first. If only they would say they were not Bahá'ís, the prince told them—and curse Bahá'u'lláh—he could set them free. But the brothers would not denounce Bahá'u'lláh. Although the prince tried to persuade them, the brothers remained firm.

"'If only you knew what I know,'" replied the younger Mírzá Ḥasan, "'you would never demand this of me.'"[1]

This answer angered the prince, who struck Mírzá Ḥusayn across the face repeatedly with his walking stick, then ordered the brothers' return to prison. Still, the prince was not eager to have them executed. But the bloodthirsty Shaykh Báqir and the treacherous Mír Muḥammad-Ḥusayn—the two whom Bahá'u'lláh would stigmatize as "the Wolf" and "the She Serpent"—did not relent. Shaykh Báqir signed a death warrant for the two brothers and convinced the city's other Muslim clergy to sign it as well.

Then they turned their attention to the people of Isfahan, fomenting a frenzy of anger against the Bahá'í Faith. Before long an outraged crowd swarmed into the streets. Headed by the clergy, the mob surged toward the government house and surrounded it. Inside, the prince could not mistake their ferocious shouts. The people of Isfahan were demanding death for the merchant brothers. Succumbing to the pressure of the clergy and the crowd, the prince issued orders for the brothers' execution.

Six days after their arrest, on March 17, 1879, Mírzá Ḥusayn and Mírzá Ḥasan were brought to the place of execution. They stood tall, with their arms around each other, their faces calm and strong. Among the crowd that looked on were many whom the brothers had helped. Many owed their lives to the brothers' compassion and generosity.

The executioner himself was ashamed to look into the faces of the brothers who had once helped him. His hands now wielded the axe that would end their lives. Yet even now the good brothers spoke kindly to him. He must do his duty as executioner, they told him, but he could be sure of their forgiveness.

Each brother begged the other to let him be executed first that day. In the end, it was the younger Mírzá Ḥasan who was beheaded first, followed quickly by Mírzá Ḥusayn.

Their deaths alone did not completely satisfy the She-Serpent and the Wolf. They ordered that the bodies be dragged by ropes through the city streets for all to see. Left at last in a ruined building, the bodies of the martyred brothers were secretly taken for burial by their youngest brother.

Even before the brothers were executed, Mír Muḥammad-Ḥusayn had sent his men to plunder their house. Money, goods, fine furniture, and even fruit trees from the garden were all taken away. Their families were left with nothing but their grief.

Bahá'u'lláh's heart ached with sorrow when He heard the news from Isfahan. Because of Shaykh Báqir's cruelty, Bahá'u'lláh would write, "the inmates of Paradise wept" and the Prophet Muḥammad lamented.[2]

Bahá'u'lláh praised the virtuous brothers, who had lived their lives as nobly as they had met their deaths. He spoke of their high station in the eyes of God, saying it was greater than anyone knew. To Mírzá Ḥasan He gave the title "King of Martyrs" and to Mírzá Ḥusayn the title "Beloved of Martyrs."

The great truth that their fellow Bahá'ís did not realize, wrote Bahá'u'lláh in one tablet, was that these two holy souls had achieved martyrdom even before death. When they had attained His presence in Baghdad,* they had been transformed. From that time they had become so detached from the things of this world, and so firmly connected by the cord of servitude to their Lord, He affirmed, that they had sacrificed every lesser desire for the Cause of God. So glorious was this, their first martyrdom, wrote Bahá'u'lláh, that the Messengers of God and His Chosen Ones desired to attain that exalted station.†

For years to come, in nearly a hundred tablets, Bahá'u'lláh would write of these two "'luminous stars,'" the noble brothers of Isfahan.[3]

Soon after the brothers' deaths, Bahá'u'lláh wrote to those whose greed had started it all. "Woe betide thee, O thou who hast joined partners with God," He wrote to the She-Serpent, Mír Muḥammad-Ḥusayn, "and woe betide them that have taken thee as their leader, without a clear token or a perspicuous Book. . . . Thou hast clung to tyranny and cast away justice." In the same tablet He warned, "By God! The things thou possessest shall profit thee not, nor what thou hast laid up through thy cruelty. Unto this beareth witness Thy Lord, the All-Knowing. Thou hast arisen to put out the light of this Cause; ere long will thine own fire be quenched, at His behest. He, verily, is the Lord of strength and of might."[4]

* They had traveled to Baghdad with their uncle, Mírzá Muḥammad-'Alí, father of Munírih Khánum, who became the wife of 'Abdu'l-Bahá.

† Bahá'u'lláh has given the station of martyr to those who teach His Cause with wisdom.

In a tablet addressed to Shaykh Báqir, the Wolf, He wrote, "Thine act hath consumed the hearts of the Concourse on high, and those of such as have circled round the Cause of God, the Lord of the worlds." He advised the shaykh to remember the fate of Sulṭán 'Abdu'l-'Azíz and of Napoleon III. They, too, had turned their backs on the Messenger of God. Now where were they and their glory? "O Báqir! Rely not on thy glory, and thy power," Bahá'u'lláh wrote. "Thou art even as the last trace of sunlight upon the mountaintop. Soon will it fade away, as decreed by God, the All-Possessing, the Most High."[5]

Bahá'u'lláh urged the shaykh to change his ways so that God might forgive him, for God is merciful to those who turn to Him. "There is no hatred in Mine heart for Thee nor for anyone," wrote Bahá'u'lláh.[6] He advised the shaykh to study the Kitáb-i-Íqán (Book of Certitude) and open his eyes to the truth.

But neither Shaykh Báqir nor Mír Muḥammad-Ḥusayn changed their ways. Soon after the execution, Mír Muḥammad-Ḥusayn began to quarrel with the prince over how to divide their stolen wealth. Once again, in a show of his own power, Mír Muḥammad-Ḥusayn led his followers to surround the government house. Day by day the crowd grew louder and more riotous. News of the disorder reached Tehran, and it was not long before soldiers from the shah arrived in Isfahan.

Mír Muḥammad-Ḥusayn was arrested. His home was plundered, just as he had plundered the homes of the martyred brothers, and all his possessions were taken from him. He was cast out of Isfahan and sent into exile. Later he was struck down with a horrible disease that produced a foul-smelling odor. His own family could not bear to come near him. Poor and alone, the miserable Mír Muḥammad-Ḥusayn died within two years. No one came to his funeral.

Shaykh Báqir, too, was sent far away from Isfahan in disgrace. Cut off from his home and the wealth he had hoped to enjoy, the unhappy shaykh died in a few short years. Even the prince, in later years, was stripped of power and sent to live in exile.

But the faith that the Wolf and the She-Serpent had expected to crush continued to grow. From Persia, Iraq, and Egypt, it spread eastward to India, Burma (Myanmar), and Ceylon (Sri Lanka). It spread largely through the efforts of one wise and energetic Bahá'í: Jamál Effendi, who traveled through those countries at the direction of Bahá'u'lláh. As Jamál Effendi traveled he carried Bahá'u'lláh's message to Buddhists, Jews, Christians, and Zoroastrians. Among the people of each faith were those who embraced the new Cause and became Bahá'ís. Whatever suffering, even death, was inflicted by the enemies of the fledgling faith on its followers in Persia, nothing could stop the advancement of the Cause of God.

60

Blessed Is the Place

In Acre the summer of 1879 saw a fearful enemy breach the city walls and attack its people. The enemy was a deadly epidemic of disease that spread throughout the region, killing many in its path. Among those who died was 'Údí Khammár, the man who had owned the house in Acre where Bahá'u'lláh first lived after His release from the prison barracks.

In later years 'Údí Khammár had built a mansion in the country outside of Acre. He named it *"Bahjí"* (Delight), but now the mansion stood empty. When 'Abdu'l-Bahá learned of it, He arranged to acquire Bahjí for his father, as the house at Mazra'ih was no longer big enough to meet the family's needs and accommodate the many pilgrims who came to see Bahá'u'lláh.

One evening in September 1879, when all was arranged, Bahá'u'lláh mounted His white donkey to go to Bahjí. He began the ride from Acre, where He had been visiting. Behind Him rode His amanuensis, Mírzá Áqá Ján. As their donkeys clip-clopped through the city streets, they passed the house where two Bahá'í friends were staying.

Looking down from their window, the two friends saw Bahá'u'lláh ride by, headed for Bahjí. The two friends came to a sudden decision: They would go to Bahjí, too. They longed to perform a simple act of devotion—to circumambulate the mansion where the Messenger of God would dwell. Quickly they ran down the stairs and outside. As they walked in the gathering twilight along the dusty road to Bahjí, they never dreamed of what they were about to see at their journey's end.

A large oil lamp burned brightly at the mansion, its warm light spilling into the evening. Bahá'u'lláh and Mírzá Áqá Ján had already gone inside. The two Bahá'í friends who followed made their way toward a footpath that encircled Bahjí. They would use the small path to circumambulate the mansion. But as they drew closer, they saw that the footpath was already crowded.

The two friends could hear a murmur of voices all around. On every side of the mansion, people were standing on the path, packed close together. Who were they? The friends wondered. And from where had they come? No one from Acre had followed them to Bahjí.

In a moment of insight the two friends realized that the people gathered around Bahjí that night were not of this world. These were the holy souls of the life hereafter—the Prophets and Messengers of God as well as other noble souls. Once they had walked the earth. Now they were the angels of the Concourse on high who had gathered to circumambulate Bahjí, the dwelling-place of their Lord, Bahá'u'lláh.

The two friends moved farther out from the mansion, away from the crowded footpath, to make their circumambulation. When they had finished and returned to Acre, their hearts were so full they could not sleep. They stayed up all night keeping vigil.

One friend made cup after cup of steaming tea. The other, a skilled poet, wrote stirring poems that told the stories of Bahá'u'lláh's life. They told of His banishments from city to city, of His imprisonments and sufferings, and of their own extraordinary experience that evening.

Bahá'u'lláh Himself wrote, "'Round about whatever dwelling the friends of God may enter, and from which their cry shall rise as they praise and glorify the Lord, shall circle the souls of true believers and all the favored angels.'" In another tablet Bahá'u'lláh wrote, "'Blessed is the spot, and the house, and the place, and the city, and the heart, and the mountain, and the refuge, and the cave, and the valley, and the land, and the sea, and the island, and the meadow where mention of God hath been made, and His praise glorified.'"[1]

'Údí Khammár had built Bahjí while Bahá'u'lláh was still a prisoner in the barracks of Acre. He had spent his wealth freely on the mansion, giving loving attention to its detail. But after 'Údí Khammár died in the epidemic, his family had been afraid to stay where disease might kill again and had fled to another place.

What 'Údí Khammár had not known, said Bahá'u'lláh, was that even as he built the mansion, he was building it to serve the Messenger of God. For such a gift in this world, promised Bahá'u'lláh, 'Údí Khammár would receive the bounties of God in the next.

Bahá'u'lláh called Bahjí the "*'lofty mansion.'*" It was a large and spacious place that stood on the open plain north of Acre. A garden had been planted all around, and tall pine trees cast their shade nearby. 'Údí Khammár had not known that Bahá'u'lláh, "the Glory of God," would make His home at Bahjí, but the inscription he had placed above the doorway to the mansion was truer than he had imagined: "'Greetings and salutations rest upon this mansion which increaseth in splendour through the passage of time. Manifold wonders and marvels are found therein, and pens are baffled in attempting to describe them.'"[2]

Bahá'u'lláh's own room was on the upper floor in the southeastern corner of Bahjí. From it He could see the tall, slender minarets of Acre, where the call to prayer was raised, and beyond the city, the brilliant blue of the sea. In the distance, across the bay where the city of Haifa stood, rose Mount Carmel, to which the Prophet Isaiah had referred as the "mountain of the Lord."[3]

Bahá'u'lláh was sixty-one years old when He moved to Bahjí. Twenty-seven years had passed since His days in the Black Pit of Tehran—years of exile, hardship, and turmoil. At Bahjí Bahá'u'lláh was blessed, at last, with years of peace and with the freedom so long denied Him. Now, whenever He wished, Bahá'u'lláh could visit the places and people that He loved.

He might go to the Riḍvan Garden, to Mazra'ih, or to visit the believers and His two faithful brothers in Acre. Bahá'u'lláh spent time in nearby villages, too, and in other gardens besides the Riḍvan Garden. Wherever He went, He rode His white, quick-footed donkey named *"Barq"* (Lightning). The people there grew familiar with the sight of Bahá'u'lláh on His white donkey, riding out from Bahjí and back again.

In a few special places Bahá'u'lláh would pitch His tent and stay for a time. One of His favorite sites was a hill overlooking Bahjí. With spring came bright red flowers—large-petaled poppies, slender anemones, and more. They bloomed in wide swaths all up and down the grassy hill. The air was sweet and fresh. It was this that Bahá'u'lláh loved—not the wealthy palaces of men, but the rich creation of God. "'Verily, verily, the most wretched prison has been converted into a Paradise of Eden,'" said Bahá'u'lláh.[4]

How fortunes had changed! Bahá'u'lláh had first entered the gates of Acre as a prisoner, hated and jeered. Now governors, generals, and leaders of every kind requested the honor of meeting Him. When Bahá'u'lláh entered a village or passed along a street in Acre, even those who did not know Him felt His majesty. Whatever their rank, they bowed with reverence before Him.

Who could have guessed that the prisoner of Acre would end His days in a kingly mansion, as splendid as the sun in His majesty? Or that the sultan who had tried to destroy Him would have his own days cut short?

Bahá'u'lláh's majesty had nothing to do with displays of wealth and luxury. Even at Bahjí He continued to live simply. In the heat of summer He wore plain cotton garments. In winter's cold His clothing and cloak were of warm wool. The household, too, was kept modest.

From time to time believers sent gifts to Bahá'u'lláh—carpets, clothing, or other valuables. Most often Bahá'u'lláh did not keep them for Himself. Generous as always, He gave the gifts away to others.

When Bahá'ís gave money to the Cause, Bahá'u'lláh never used it for Himself or His own family. Even when the family was in need, Bahá'u'lláh would not touch the funds for the Cause. At His direction, that money was used only to help the teachers of the Faith or to care for the poor. Whether in poverty or in wealth, Bahá'u'lláh lived a life of spotless honor.

The years at Bahjí were also years of intense work. Night and day Bahá'u'lláh busied Himself with uplifting the souls and uniting the hearts of the Bahá'ís. He met with them and answered their many questions. He revealed tablet after tablet to instruct and encourage them. "This is the day to make mention of God, to celebrate His praise, and to serve Him," wrote Bahá'u'lláh, "deprive not yourselves thereof. Ye are the letters of the words, and the words of the Book. Ye are the saplings which the hand of Loving-kindness hath planted in the soil of mercy, and which the showers of bounty have made to flourish. . . . Now is the time for you to put forth your leaves, and yield your fruit. The fruits of the tree of man have ever been and are goodly deeds and a praiseworthy character."[5]

Those who best understood the new religion and whose hearts were aflame with the love of God, Bahá'u'lláh sent to teach others. Some of these teachers He sent to strengthen the faith of the Bahá'ís themselves. Now, more than ever, as Bahá'u'lláh's years on earth grew shorter, He labored to prepare the Bahá'ís for the future.

61

To Conquer the Cities of the Hearts

Ever since the early days of Bahá'u'lláh's exile from Persia, one Bahá'í had been making the journey from Persia to Bahá'u'lláh's threshold, not once, but faithfully every year. Each year he braved mountain and desert—not for himself alone—but in service to all the Bahá'ís of Persia. His name was Shaykh Salmán. His service was that of courier—the carrier of letters and precious tablets between Bahá'u'lláh and the believers.

No matter where Bahá'u'lláh lived—Baghdad, Adrianople, the prison in Acre, or the mansion at Bahjí—Shaykh Salmán would come to visit, 'Abdu'l-Bahá wrote, "with the greatest eagerness and love."[1] Each year, when he arrived at Bahá'u'lláh's doorstep, he carried in hand a bundle of letters from the Bahá'ís. Later, when Bahá'u'lláh had read every letter and replied with loving counsels, Shaykh Salmán would return to Persia, this time with tablets for the Bahá'ís.

He traveled simply, making each trip to and from Persia on foot. His meals were nothing but bread and onions. Once inside Persia, Shaykh Salmán walked to villages and cities all around the land—Tehran, Shiraz, Isfahan, and more. What joy he spread as he carried the tablets of Bahá'u'lláh to each place! What happiness, as he delivered each tablet to the Bahá'í who was meant to receive it!

In all his journeys, despite severe difficulties, Shaykh Salmán remained unharmed by the thieves and highwaymen that threatened travelers. He never lost a letter or a tablet, and even those who were not Bahá'ís spoke of him respectfully as "the Bábís' Angel Gabriel." No wonder that Bahá'u'lláh kept Shaykh Salmán close to His heart. "From the dawn of history until the present day," wrote 'Abdu'l-Bahá, "there has never been a messenger so worthy of trust; there has never been a courier to compare with Salmán."[2]

The services of Shaykh Salmán and others like him helped sustain the believers in Persia. To be a Bahá'í in Bahá'u'lláh's homeland was still dangerous, for Bahá'ís continued to be oppressed and persecuted by those who were hostile to the new faith.

But Bahá'u'lláh's counsel to His followers was clear. Well-reasoned proofs and a life well lived—these were the gentle tools of persuasion used by the Bahá'ís. To wage war in the name of religion, even in their own defense, was forbidden. "'If any one revile you, or trouble touch you, in the path of God, be patient,'" wrote Bahá'u'lláh, "'and put your trust in Him Who heareth, who seeth. . . . He, verily, is the Lord of strength and of might.'"[3]

"'Beware lest ye shed the blood of any one,'" warned Bahá'u'lláh. "'We have abolished the law to wage holy war against each other. God's mercy hath, verily, encompassed all created things, if ye do but understand.'" In another passage He wrote, "'O people of Bahá! Subdue the citadels of men's hearts with the swords of wisdom and of utterance. They that dispute, as prompted by their desires, are indeed wrapped in a palpable veil. Say: The sword of wisdom is hotter than summer heat, and sharper than blades of steel, if ye do but understand.'"[4]

The Bahá'ís refused to be discouraged by the dangers they faced. Nourished by Bahá'u'lláh's loving guidance, by the tablets He wrote to them, and by the teachers He sent, the Bahá'ís worked together to teach the Cause of God to others.

Not every Bahá'í found it easy to talk about religion. Some offered their homes for meetings or served in other ways to facilitate the meetings. Others searched for those people who were seeking spiritual truth. With prayer and perseverance, the Bahá'ís found many such souls among their countrymen. These seekers were invited, a few at a time, to small meetings in the homes of believers.

Great care was taken to make sure that a person claiming to be a seeker was sincere. There were enemies, too, who would pretend to show interest. They had a darker, secret purpose—to find out the names of Bahá'ís and cause them harm.

Once a seeker was known to be sincere in his desire to meet with the Bahá'ís, he was received with warm hospitality. As he sipped tea or coffee by the light of an oil lamp, he would begin to learn about the Bahá'í Faith, step by step, from a Bahá'í teacher.

Bahá'u'lláh had directed that such teachers be appointed in every locality of Persia. Most of them were learned men, but not all. Some had little or no formal study. Even so, each of these teachers knew well the writings of Bahá'u'lláh, and each was familiar with the holy books of the past. Most importantly, each of these teachers had a deep understanding of spiritual truth.

A few of the most exceptional teachers were instructed by Bahá'u'lláh to travel throughout Persia and some to neighboring countries. From town to town and village to village they traveled, teaching those who thirsted for the spiritual message of Bahá'u'lláh. In each place, they taught in meetings arranged by local believers. Because of these teachers, many seekers became Bahá'ís.

Among the Bahá'í teachers were four of outstanding ability, wisdom, and unshakable faith. So enkindled were they with love for the Cause, so knowledgeable about its teachings, and of such praiseworthy character that no believer could remain in their presence without catching a spark of their spirit. Their very presence cast light upon a gathering.

To these illumined souls Bahá'u'lláh gave a special title: Hands of the Cause of God. He called on them to assist the believers to learn His laws and teachings and to put them into practice. It was a vital role, and a role with which these teachers were already familiar. They were not clergy invested with power, but "'the pure in spirit,'" wrote Bahá'u'lláh. They were detached from all earthly things and would serve as lamps of guidance to the Bahá'í community.[5]

Thus did the Bahá'ís in Persia persevere in teaching their faith, no matter what difficulties and obstacles they encountered in their path. All the while the source of their strength, Bahá'u'lláh, guided them onward from Bahjí.

As the years passed, it became Bahá'u'lláh's custom to stay at Bahjí in the spring, summer, and part of the autumn. During the other months He lived in the city of Acre. There His dear wife Navváb and their daughter, Bahíyyih Khánum, lived in the household of 'Abdu'l-Bahá. Whenever they could, they all came to Bahjí.

There were grandchildren now, too—born to 'Abdu'l-Bahá and Munírih Khánum—who brought joy to all. The grandchildren were enamored of their grandfather, Bahá'u'lláh, Who clearly enjoyed their company. When 'Abdu'l-Bahá was busy, Bahá'u'lláh was like another loving father to them. To Him the children told all their difficulties, and to each He gave His kind attention. No trouble was too large or too small to bring to Him.

Bahá'u'lláh liked to give the children treats. He did not give away all the boxes of sweets that He received as gifts; some He set aside for the children. “““Let the dear children come in, and have some dessert,””” He would say later in the evening, even though it might be bedtime.[6]

The children's clothes did not come ready-made. Every year Bahá'u'lláh sent a servant to buy cloth in the big city of Beirut. When the servant returned with bright bundles of new cloth, Bahá'u'lláh would call the children to come and look. Each one chose the colors and patterns he or she liked best. Then their mother, Munírih Khánum, and their aunt, Bahíyyih Khánum, would cut and sew the new cloth into lovely new clothes.

“““Why not put on your prettiest frocks?””” Bahá'u'lláh would say. He always loved to see the children looking clean and neatly dressed. Best of all were the times when Bahá'u'lláh said to them, “““Now children, tomorrow you shall come with Me for a picnic to the Riḍván.”””[7] Their hearts would fairly burst with happiness, and they could scarcely sleep.

Such outings were a wonderful change from their usual days in school. There they sat long hours to learn a little reading and writing. Mostly their teacher read to them long passages from the Koran, which were hard to understand. At school there was no time for fun and play. It made their days in the Garden of Riḍván all the more sweet, for Bahá'u'lláh loved to see the children enjoy themselves.

'Abdu'l-Bahá could not often join his family in their picnics at the Riḍván Garden. His days were busy. The poor of Acre and those who sought justice still came to him for help. Shaykhs, judges, and other officials came daily to ask his advice. 'Abdu'l-Bahá continued to make his home in Acre in the house of 'Abbúd, where those who wanted his help could easily find him.

Everyone looked upon 'Abdu'l-Bahá as wise, compassionate, learned, and practical. But no one among them, not even the Bahá'ís, could see him as Bahá'u'lláh did.

62

The Master

Sunlight and shadow moved in dappled patterns across the gathering of Bahá'ís in the garden. Bahá'u'lláh often invited the Bahá'ís to come with Him to the Garden of Riḍván for lunch. How they savored these times! The beauty of the garden was a welcome change from the narrow streets and crowded marketplace of Acre.

Many believers who kept humble shops in Acre had left their wealth and social rank behind in Persia. Now they labored at simple trades for their daily bread. Yet they were neither sad nor sorry. To be near Bahá'u'lláh was their greatest joy. What privilege could be greater than this: that their span of days on earth should be these days, blessed by the presence of the Promised One of God? That they should walk upon the same ground, be refreshed by the same breezes, and warmed by the same sun. All else faded to insignificance.

On this day, Bahá'u'lláh looked with delight to see 'Abdu'l-Bahá approaching. """The Master is coming,""" He told the others, """hasten to attend Him."""[1] At once the believers went off to welcome 'Abdu'l-Bahá.

Bahá'u'lláh had called 'Abdu'l-Bahá "Áqá" (the Master) since their days in Baghdad. In Persian society "Áqá" was a title of respect meaning "master" or "sir," but Bahá'u'lláh used it to mean something greater when referring to 'Abdu'l-Bahá. If a Bahá'í referred to someone else as "Áqá," the commanding voice of Bahá'u'lláh would be heard.

"""Who is the Áqá?""" He would say. """There is only one Áqá, and He is the Most Great Branch ['Abdu'l-Bahá]."""[2]

'Abdu'l-Bahá was more than a loving son. His every action reflected with absolute purity the spiritual light of Bahá'u'lláh like a stainless mirror. Unlike the Báb or Bahá'u'lláh, he was not a Messenger of God. Yet so perfectly did 'Abdu'l-Bahá blend human and divine qualities that he was unique among men—the perfect example of every Bahá'í virtue and ideal. Bahá'u'lláh called him "'the Mystery of God.'"[3]

Today, as 'Abdu'l-Bahá arrived, Bahá'u'lláh remarked that the garden had not been so pleasant in the morning. """But now with the presence of the Master,""" He said, """it has become truly most delightful.""" Turning to 'Abdu'l-Bahá He added gently, """You should have come in the morning."""

Though Bahá'u'lláh treated him with honor, 'Abdu'l-Bahá was humble in his father's presence. """The Governor of 'Akká and some residents had requested to meet with Me,""" answered 'Abdu'l-Bahá respectfully. """Therefore I had to receive and entertain them."""

Bahá'u'lláh smiled. """Association with the outside people such as these is very, very difficult. It is the Master who stands up to everything, and prepares the means of comfort for all the friends. May God protect Him from the evil of the envious and the hostile."""[4]

"""He [the Master] is a mighty shield facing the world and its peoples,""" Bahá'u'lláh said at one point, """and so He has relieved Us [from every care]. . . . We are engaged in meeting with the believers and revealing the verses of God, while He labours hard and faces every ordeal and suffering. Because to deal and associate with these people is the most arduous task of all."""[5]

For 'Abdu'l-Bahá, a day in Acre began at early morning tea with the family. The children loved this time with their father. He would chant prayers and tell them stories about the holy ones—about Christ and His mother, about Muḥammad, Moses, and the other Prophets. When he was ready, 'Abdu'l-Bahá would take his leave and walk across the street to the *bírúní*—a large room he had rented for receiving visitors. There he began the day's work.

Looking out their windows, the children would soon see a crowd begin to gather. People were coming to request help from the Master. Some brought matters of injustice: A man might be falsely accused of wrongdoing, a woman beaten by her husband, or a child mistreated. With each one, 'Abdu'l-Bahá would send a person to the courthouse to speak to the judge and appeal for justice on behalf of the ones in need.

The sick of Acre, too, received 'Abdu'l-Bahá's loving attention. The city had no hospital, and it was 'Abdu'l-Bahá who paid a doctor to care for the very poor. Each day 'Abdu'l-Bahá sent a servant to look in on those who were ill and inquire about their needs.

Just as often it was 'Abdu'l-Bahá himself who took the time to visit. In one month he made twenty visits to a poor, elderly couple who were too ill to get out of their bed. 'Abdu'l-Bahá attended to all their needs.

Among those who came to see 'Abdu'l-Bahá was a woman named Na'úm, who was poor and handicapped. Every week she came to visit, and every week 'Abdu'l-Bahá gave her a small gift of money. One day a man ran to 'Abdu'l-Bahá with news of her. """Oh! Master, that poor Na'úm has measles!""" he said. """She is lying by the hot room of the *Hammám;** everybody is keeping away from her. What can be done about her?"""[6]

'Abdu'l-Bahá quickly took action. He found a room for the sick woman and gave his own bedding to make her comfortable. He sent a doctor to see her and found a woman to take care of her. He sent food and made sure Na'úm had everything she needed, but she did not recover. Because of 'Abdu'l-Bahá's kindness, however, her last days were peaceful. When she died, 'Abdu'l-Bahá arranged and paid for her simple funeral.

It was not merely the poor and unfortunate who came looking for the Master. The leaders of Acre gathered, too, at the *bírúní* of 'Abdu'l-Bahá. Shaykhs and officials of the court brought their most challenging problems to him, certain that the Master could help sort through their complexities and arrive at the best answers.

The governor brought newspapers with reports of current affairs in nations near and far. Sitting in the *bírúní* and sipping cups of strong coffee, the governor and other guests would talk over the news of the day. On every topic they valued the comments of 'Abdu'l-Bahá, whose explanations and insights added much to the content of their discussions.

Admirers sent gifts of sweets, cakes, and fruits to 'Abdu'l-Bahá. These he took to the *bírúní* to share with all who came. Arabs in the region called 'Abdu'l-Bahá the "Lord of Generosity," and he became the standard by which others were praised. When someone was hospitable and

* Public bath.

generous, people would say of that person, "'"His house is like the *Bírúní*, the home of 'Abbás Effendi.'"'[7]

So passed the days of the Master. From early morning to late in the evening, 'Abdu'l-Bahá served the people of Acre. In Tehran and Baghdad the poor had called Bahá'u'lláh "Father" for His tender care, and many had come to seek His counsel. Now in Acre it was 'Abdu'l-Bahá who walked in the footsteps of his father. He neglected nothing except his own rest and food.

Each week 'Abdu'l-Bahá rode from Acre to Bahjí to visit Bahá'u'lláh. As he neared the fields that stretched before the mansion, a group of Bahá'ís would come to escort him the rest of the way. Bahá'u'lláh always sent such an escort to honor His son. He would stand and watch from the balcony at Bahjí as 'Abdu'l-Bahá approached. Nothing cheered Bahá'u'lláh more than to see His beloved son.

"Blessed, doubly blessed, is the ground which His footsteps have trodden," wrote Bahá'u'lláh, "the eye that hath been cheered by the beauty of His countenance, the ear that hath been honoured by hearkening to His call, the heart that hath tasted the sweetness of His love, the breast that hath dilated through His remembrance, the pen that hath voiced His praise, the scroll that hath borne the testimony of His writings."[8]

As soon as 'Abdu'l-Bahá neared the mansion, he would dismount from his steed and walk the remaining distance. It was not the act of an honored son visiting his father, but that of a lowly servant approaching the threshold of his Lord. Bahá'u'lláh was "the Glory of God"—the Messenger of God on earth—and no other Bahá'í showed as deep a spirit of reverence in His presence as did 'Abdu'l-Bahá.

Even the name that 'Abdu'l-Bahá chose for himself was a mark of humble respect. His given name was 'Abbás, and the people of Acre called him "'Abbás Effendi."* But among Bahá'ís he became known by the title he chose for himself: 'Abdu'l-Bahá, meaning "Servant of the Glory."

When 'Abdu'l-Bahá arrived at Bahjí, he would share the news of the week with Bahá'u'lláh—news from Acre and of world happenings reported in the newspapers. He told Bahá'u'lláh about the people who had requested his advice for their problems and of those who had come with

---

* Effendi is a Turkish honorific for a man of property, authority, or education.

other kinds of questions. Some were Muslims puzzled by passages in the Koran. Others were Christians confused by difficult verses in the Bible. They would ask 'Abdu'l-Bahá for help in understanding the meaning of their holy texts.

What answers had the Master given? Bahá'u'lláh asked about each case, and 'Abdu'l-Bahá would tell Him. *Khaylí Khúb, Áqá* (Very good, Master), Bahá'u'lláh would say.[9]

'Abdu'l-Bahá was peerless, without equal among men, and his role in the world was unique. *"'We have made Thee a shelter for all mankind,'"* wrote Bahá'u'lláh to His eldest son, *"'a shield unto all who are in heaven and on earth, a stronghold for whosoever hath believed in God, the Incomparable, the All-Knowing.'"*[10]

"'Render thanks unto God, O people, for His appearance,'" Bahá'u'lláh instructed His followers, *"'for verily He is the most great Favor unto you, the most perfect bounty upon you."*[11]

Little by little, Bahá'u'lláh prepared the Bahá'ís to look to 'Abdu'l-Bahá for guidance and to follow his example. *"Whoso turneth towards Him hath turned towards God, and whoso turneth away from Him hath turned away from My Beauty, hath repudiated My Proof, and transgressed against Me. He is the Trust of God amongst you, His charge within you, His manifestation unto you and His appearance among His favored servants. . . .'"*[12]

Only the future could unfold the deepest meaning of Bahá'u'lláh's words and the importance of obeying His instructions.

63

O Most Exalted Leaf!

How often had Bahá'u'lláh passed through the city gates astride His faithful white donkey and ridden along the narrow streets of Acre as He did today, on His way to the house of 'Abbúd. How wonderful were those days of visiting His family, especially His beloved wife Navváb.

With the household of 'Abdu'l-Bahá centered at the house of 'Abbúd, it was natural for Navváb to stay there, too. The women in the family worked together to help one another with rearing the children and managing the tasks of the home—a pleasure Navváb had missed for many years. She had been only a young mother when Bahá'u'lláh was exiled from Tehran and she had left behind the cherished company of the women in her life. Now Navváb and her daughter Bahíyyih Khánum stayed with Munírih Khánum, the children, and 'Abdu'l-Bahá, who attended to matters at the *bírúní*. The family of Munírih Khánum, who had moved to the Holy Land after her marriage, also enlarged Navváb's circle of friends. What a welcome change were these peaceful days!

The familiar sight of Navváb—tall, slender, attired in her simple blue dress and fresh white headdress, her small feet in their black slippers—was a welcome one at the house of 'Abbúd. Her sense of humor and unfailing loving-kindness, her gentle courtesy and unselfish consideration of all those around her, endeared her to children and adults alike.

Navváb would visit Bahjí when she could, but transportation was primitive and made traveling difficult for the women in the family. Navváb found it particularly difficult, for she suffered from poor health in these later years of her life. Still she accepted Bahá'u'lláh's move to Bahjí, where so many Bahá'ís could have the opportunity to attain His presence. For the Cause of God, to which she was deeply devoted, she was always willing to sacrifice. Between their visits back and forth, Navváb was reminded of the cherished place she held in her husband's heart through the many loving letters she received from Bahá'u'lláh.

But this visit in 1886 was not a joyous one. The frail Navváb, now in her sixties and weakened by the years of harsh exile and imprisonment, had reached the end of her physical endurance. At the house of 'Abbúd, Bahá'u'lláh joined a sorrowful 'Abdu'l-Bahá and Bahíyyih Khánum in the small, simple room that was Navváb's. They gathered around the narrow, white bed on which she lay, the same bed that had also served as her divan. Her pen case and leaflets of writing paper lay on the small table next to the bed, along with her prayer book and prayer beads.

These were her last hours, yet they could not imagine their days without her beautiful presence among them. How many were the memories they shared—from their earliest joys before the cruelty had begun in Tehran, to their later joys whose sweetness had been savored all the more against the afflictions that had beset them.

Bahá'u'lláh could remember Navváb as a young wife—intelligent and graceful, her dark blue eyes sparkling with fun. She had been born to a noble family and given the name Ásíyih Khánum. Her marriage trousseau had been packed on the backs of forty mules; now a painted box held the one change of garments that belonged to her. Yet she had always been content, whether counted among the rich nobility of Tehran or as an exile at her husband's side. And over the years Bahá'u'lláh had watched Navváb's inner beauty unfold like the petals of an exquisite flower.

How He treasured her pure-hearted and compassionate nature, her eager willingness to forgo the pleasures of the rich as she helped Him to serve the needs of the poor. While He had been called "Father of the Poor" in Tehran, Navváb had been esteemed as the "Mother of Consolation." Even as an exile, when their own comfort was minimal and their challenges were many, she had not complained but had assisted those around her, still the Mother of Consolation despite her own beleaguered circumstances.

Navváb's slight frame and gentle ways belied her formidable strength of spirit. Though she had agonized over every ordeal that beset Bahá'u'lláh, whether it resulted from the schemes of enemies or from the treachery of those who claimed to be friends, she had endured at His side every trial and difficulty with patience and steadfastness.

As a mother she had suffered the heartrending loss of five of their seven children. She had lost three infants in Tehran and later, one in Baghdad under especially grievous conditions.* Finally, in Acre she had lost Mírzá Mihdí, the Purest Branch, in the prime of his youth—a loss that had been almost too much to bear. Nevertheless, Navváb's faith in Bahá'u'lláh and His Cause was resolute and unshakable, and she remained grateful to God for all that she endured in His path. Like a pearl of rare quality, her spirit was only burnished to greater luster by her sufferings.

* The three children born in Tehran who did not survive infancy included the two sons Káẓim and Ṣádiq (mentioned in chapter 4) and another son, not previously mentioned, who was born before Mírzá Mihdí and named 'Alí-Muḥammad. The son who was born in Baghdad and who died under such grievous circumstances was also named 'Alí-Muḥammad.

Her children who remained—'Abdu'l-Bahá and his sister Bahíyyih Khánum*—had so imbibed those noble qualities evinced by both father and mother that they had already, in the face of extraordinary challenges, shown their own nobility of character. Both were destined to cast an even greater light as they dealt with the challenges to come, reflecting befittingly on the mother who had nurtured them.

But now, with her husband and children at her bedside, it was not long before the dearly loved Navváb breathed her last, and her lustrous spirit abandoned the worn-out vessel of this life for the greater worlds beyond. What sorrow filled the room! No more could they embrace the wife and mother who, day to day and year to year, had been their stalwart support and loving refuge.

The funeral procession of Ásíyih Khánum, entitled Navváb, was joined by a large number of mourners who held the family in high regard—prominent people and officials of Acre, Muslim and Christian divines, muezzins and reciters of the Koran, and school children who chanted verses and poems of sorrow at her passing. It was an occasion befitting the one whom Bahá'u'lláh designated as His companion and "perpetual consort in all the worlds of God."[1]

"O Navváb! O Leaf that hath sprung from My Tree, and been My companion!" wrote Bahá'u'lláh. "My glory be upon thee, and My loving-kindness, and My mercy that hath surpassed all beings. We announce unto thee that which will gladden thine eye, and assure thy soul, and rejoice thine heart. Verily, thy Lord is the Compassionate, the All-Bountiful. God hath been and will be pleased with thee. . . ."[2]

Though others honored Navváb at her passing, only Bahá'u'lláh could gauge her exalted station. Addressing His beloved Navváb, He wrote,

---

* Bahíyyih Khánum was titled by Bahá'u'lláh "the Greatest Holy Leaf" and designated the outstanding heroine of the Bahá'í Dispensation. As a young woman she expressed to Bahá'u'lláh her desire to remain unmarried so that she might freely dedicate herself to the service of His Cause. Bahá'u'lláh granted her request. From a youthful age she demonstrated herself "capable of sharing the burden and willing to make the sacrifice which her high birth demanded" and earned, in Bahá'u'lláh's words, "a station such as none other woman hath surpassed."

> "The first Spirit through which all spirits were revealed, and the first Light by which all lights shone forth, rest upon thee, O Most Exalted Leaf, thou who hast been mentioned in the Crimson Book! Thou art the one whom God created to arise and serve His own Self, and the Manifestation of His Cause, and the Dayspring of His Revelation, and the Dawning-Place of His signs, and the Source of His commandments; and Who so aided thee that thou didst turn with thy whole being unto Him, at a time when His servants and handmaidens had turned away from His Face. . . . Happy art thou, O My handmaiden, and My leaf, and the one mentioned in My Book, and inscribed by My Pen of Glory in My Scrolls and Tablets. . . . Rejoice thou, at this moment, in the most exalted Station and the All-highest Paradise, and the Abhá Horizon, inasmuch as He Who is the Lord of Names hath remembered thee. We bear witness that thou didst attain unto all good, and that God hath so exalted thee, that all honor and glory circled around thee."[3]

'Abdu'l-Bahá would store in his heart a lifetime of treasured moments with the mother who had lovingly addressed him as *"Áqá Jan"* (beloved Master), and whom he had addressed with deep love and respect as *"Ḥaḍrat-i-Válidih"* (her eminence, the Mother).

Bahíyyih Khánum would call to mind the mother with whom she had cooked meals for fellow prisoners in Acre or sewed the wedding dress for 'Abdu'l-Bahá's bride. She could close her eyes and see her mother's sweet, smiling face and rapt expression as she chanted prayers. She would remember her mother always as wise and gentle and queenly in her dignity and loveliness.

Bahá'u'lláh in one of His tablets addressed the believers who would come to honor her memory:

> "O faithful ones! Should ye visit the resting-place of the Most Exalted Leaf,* who hath ascended unto the Glorious Companion, stand ye and say: 'Salutation and blessing and glory upon thee, O Holy Leaf

---

* The sacred remains of Navváb and those of Mírzá Mihdí, the Purest Branch, are interred on Mount Carmel.

that hath sprung from the Divine Lote-Tree! I bear witness that thou hast believed in God and in His signs, and answered His Call, and turned unto Him, and held fast unto His cord, and clung to the hem of His grace, and fled thy home in His path, and chosen to live as a stranger, out of love for His presence and in thy longing to serve Him. May God have mercy upon him that draweth nigh unto thee, and remembereth thee. . . ."[4]

64

These Fruitless Strifes, These Ruinous Wars

Bahjí was about to receive another visitor, one willing to leave the comforts of home in England and face the difficulties of a long journey to speak with Bahá'u'lláh. During all the years of Bahá'u'lláh's imprisonment and exile, while authorities attempted to stifle the spread of the new Faith, news of the unfolding events in Persia, and stories of the Báb in particular, made their way to Europe. The Báb's noble life, cut short by a firing squad in 1850, had touched the hearts of many.

Sarah Bernhardt, a famous French actress, begged the playwright Catulle Mendès for a play about the courageous Báb. Another woman—a Russian poet—wrote such a play in 1903. Her drama, "The Báb," was performed in Russia's great city of St. Petersburg. It traveled to Paris, where it was translated into French. A German poet rendered the drama into his own language, and the play was publicized in London. Everywhere people talked about the story of the young Prophet of Shiraz.

"Who can fail to be attracted by the gentle spirit of Mírzá 'Alí-Muḥammad [the Báb]?" wrote the Orientalist Edward Granville Browne.[1] Browne had first learned of the Báb in 1886 from a book he discovered at Cambridge University. Once he started reading, Browne could hardly put the book down. Captivated by the story of the Báb and His Cause, he hungered to learn more. Browne decided he must travel to Persia and there investigate more fully the Báb and His claims.

Of all men in England, Browne seemed best prepared for such a journey. From the time he was a youth of sixteen, he had loved the countries and cultures of the Middle East. Though he studied medicine as a young man, Browne did not forget his first passion. In his spare time he studied Arabic, Persian, and Turkish—all languages spoken in the Middle East—and read whatever books he could find about that part of the world.

When Browne made his journey to Persia in 1887, it was a dream come true for him. For one year the eager young scholar steeped himself in Persian culture. The customs of Persia and its people's ways of living and thinking were as unfamiliar to Europe as the face and figure of a woman behind her veil. Browne was intent on lifting that veil of mystery.

He traveled from city to city, his senses drinking in every new sight, sound, and taste. Because he had learned their language, Browne could talk with the people of Persia and listen to their stories. He was a good observer, too, and he wrote notes about all he experienced that year. Browne was determined to learn everything about Persia, especially about the Báb and His Cause.

What he learned did not disappoint him. The youthful Báb had lived His life with rare "purity of conduct," Browne wrote. He had endured misfortune with "courage and uncomplaining patience."[2]

Browne left Persia with more questions. He was determined to return to the Middle East and this time meet with Bahá'u'lláh. In 1890, as poets in Europe continued to write their verses about the Báb, Browne made his second journey to the Middle East. This journey brought him to the walled city of Acre and, finally, to the mansion of Bahjí. It was April 1890 when Edward Granville Browne prepared to enter the presence of Bahá'u'lláh.

Browne removed his shoes outside the entrance to Bahá'u'lláh's room. His guide drew back the doorway curtain for him to enter, then left. It took a moment before Browne saw, sitting on a couch in the corner of the room, "'a wondrous and venerable figure,'" Bahá'u'lláh.[3]

Browne took notice of every detail, as it was his habit to do. He saw that Bahá'u'lláh wore a felt headdress—a *táj,* with a small white turban wrapped around the base of it. He noticed the jet-black hair and the luxurious beard that grew nearly to Bahá'u'lláh's waist. He noticed, too, the lines of age in Bahá'u'lláh's face. At this time Bahá'u'lláh was seventy-two years old.

But it was the spirit of Bahá'u'lláh that captured Browne's attention. "'The face of him on whom I gazed I can never forget, though I cannot describe it,'" Browne would later write. "'Those piercing eyes seemed to read one's very soul; power and authority sat on that ample brow.'" Browne bowed respectfully. "'No need to ask in whose presence I stood,'" he recalled. This was Bahá'u'lláh—"the Glory of God"—who inspired "'a devotion and love'" among His followers, wrote Browne, "'which kings might envy and emperors sigh for in vain!'"[4]

In a voice mild and dignified, Bahá'u'lláh welcomed the scholar from Cambridge and invited him to be seated. In the course of his interview, Browne listened attentively and later reported these words, which Bahá'u'lláh spoke to him:

> "Praise be to God that thou hast attained! . . . Thou has come to see a prisoner and an exile. . . . We desire but the good of the world and the happiness of the nations; yet they deem us a stirrer up of strife and sedition worthy of bondage and banishment. . . . That all nations should become one in faith and all men as brothers; that the bonds of affection and unity between the sons of men should be strengthened; that diversity of religion should cease, and differences of race be annulled—what harm is there in this? . . . Yet so it shall be; these fruitless strifes, these ruinous wars shall pass away and the 'Most Great Peace' shall come. . . . Do not you in Europe need this also? Is not this that which Christ foretold? . . . Yet do we see your kings and rulers lavishing their treasures more freely on means for the destruction of the human race than on that which would conduce to the happiness of mankind. . . . These strifes and this bloodshed and discord must cease, and all men be as one kindred and one family. . . . Let not a man glory in this, that he loves his country; let him rather glory in this, that he loves his kind. . . ."[5]

Browne spent five days at Bahjí in April of 1890. He was granted four interviews with Bahá'u'lláh before he returned to England. All that he gleaned Browne would share with scholars in the West, lifting a little the veil of mystery from both Persia and the world's newest religion.

Among the "fruitless strifes" and "ruinous wars" of which Bahá'u'lláh spoke were those between indigenous peoples and colonial powers. During Bahá'u'lláh's lifetime many European nations, in their drive to supply their own marketplace with raw materials, subjugated the peoples of whole countries such as India and Indochina. The Maori of New Zealand and the Aborigines of Australia fared even worse as colonial settlers drove them from their best lands and killed large numbers of those who resisted. In the scramble to claim Africa's resources, rival European nations carved up the continent at a conference in Berlin in 1884, giving no consideration to the tribal boundaries of existing African nations. Only Liberia and Ethiopia remained independent.

On the North American continent, in the United States, the story of conflict between settlers of European descent and indigenous Indian tribes was similar to the clash of cultures in other parts of the world. Although American Indian tribes were as distinct from one another in language and custom as were the different nations of Europe, most Indian nations did not divide the land according to fixed boundaries. It was one of many differences that fed the ongoing clash between Indians and non-Indians.

Even before the Civil War, most eastern tribes had been forced from their homelands to less desirable land west of the Mississippi River. The great Cherokee Nation was decimated in the thousand-mile journey west, which they called the "Trail of Tears." Their forced journey in the winter of 1838–39 had been so harsh that an estimated four thousand Cherokees—one in every four men, women, and children—died from hunger, cold, or disease.

As time passed and land west of the Mississippi attracted the interest of settlers, conflict continued to erupt. There were many council meetings and dozens of treaties in which lands were reserved for the Indian nations for "'as long as waters run and the grass shall grow.'"[6] But the discovery of gold on Indian land brought eager miners. Railroads were built that cut through Indian land, and wagon trains traveled along trails such as the Oregon and Santa Fe, bringing non-Indian settlers by the thousands. Many of the new settlers believed that it was their nation's destiny to spread from coast to coast. The American Indians, whom they did not know or understand, seemed only to stand in the way.

The American Indian tribes were herded onto smaller and smaller parcels of land. "It made no difference," said one old Kiowa woman who expressed the feelings of many, "that the land he [the U.S. president] was giving us, and much more besides, was already ours and always had been."[7]

Bitter fighting broke out as various tribes rose up to defend their freedom and to protect their way of life. "Many, if not most, of our Indian wars had their origin in broken promises and acts of injustice," said U.S. President Rutherford B. Hayes.[8] The clash between Indians and government troops continued in every region until the outnumbered Indian peoples were slowly beaten down. The last major battle of the American Indian wars involved a beleaguered remnant of the great Lakota Nation and took place at Wounded Knee, South Dakota, in December 1890.

In an earlier decade, at the end of the bloody American Civil War, another president, Abraham Lincoln, had called for a healing peace: "With malice toward none; with charity for all . . . let us strive on . . . to bind up the nation's wounds," Lincoln had said, ". . . to do all which may achieve and cherish a just and lasting peace among ourselves, and with all nations."[9]

Yet how was it possible to forge "a just and lasting peace" among peoples and nations whose histories were filled with war? The "Most Great Peace" of which Bahá'u'lláh had spoken to Edward Granville Browne in the very year of the battle at Wounded Knee seemed beyond reach, even beyond imagination.

Bahá'u'lláh would write, "It is Our purpose, through the loving providence of God . . . to abolish . . . all disputes, war, and bloodshed, from the face of the earth."[10]

How could so great a change in the workings of the world come to pass?

65

The King of Days

In 1890, when Edward Granville Browne traveled to Bahjí to visit Bahá'u'lláh, people traveled by steamship and railroad. The airplane had not yet been invented. Automobiles were so new and strange that people did not drive them; they went to the circus to see them on display.

In that last decade of the nineteenth century there were no radios or televisions. Antibiotics, which would one day prevent millions of deaths from disease, were unknown. Inventions and discoveries a hundredfold lay asleep in the labyrinth of the human mind. If a man had talked of jets and computers, people would have laughed. How could they believe such fantasies?

Peace, too—a just and lasting peace for all humankind—seemed like an unbelievable utopian fantasy. Too many of the "fruitless strifes" and "ruinous wars" to which Bahá'u'lláh had referred in His meeting with Browne had plagued the peoples of the world for far too long.[1] But the Messenger of God in every age, said Bahá'u'lláh, was a divine Physician Who alone could diagnose the world's sickness and prescribe the remedy to cure it.

Bahá'u'lláh saw the world's conflicts as deadly symptoms of a spiritual disease—the deep division of the human family. The healing cure He prescribed could be summarized in one word: unity. But that unity must be greater unity than the world had ever known. It would require the coming together of all nations and peoples, for peace would not be possible with anything less.

"So powerful is the light of unity that it can illuminate the whole earth," declared Bahá'u'lláh. "This goal excelleth every other goal, and this aspiration is the monarch of all aspirations."[2]

Bahá'u'lláh's call for unity was not a call for uniformity, a suffocating sameness. God had created a world rich in diversity. Its beauty—its very life—thrived on variety. Each culture and every person brought unique gifts to the world. Like the human body with its eyes and heart, hands and feet, every gift was needed for the world to flourish.

But how was this unity of the world's diverse peoples to be achieved? Who would organize the nations of the world to work together in willing cooperation? According to Bahá'u'lláh, the nations themselves must shoulder the responsibility. A great assembly must be held and attended by all the rulers and kings of the earth, said Bahá'u'lláh. There, He instructed, they "must consider such ways and means as will lay the foundations of the world's Great Peace amongst men."[3] Bahá'u'lláh laid out clear steps in His writings to guide them in what they must do.

The rulers must bring their countries together to form a commonwealth of nations. The boundaries of every nation must be agreed upon and permanently fixed. Then, Bahá'u'lláh advised the kings of the earth, "Should any one among you take up arms against another, rise ye all against him, for this is naught but manifest justice."[4]

A world parliament with members elected from every nation must be created. Its decisions and laws must be upheld by one and all and backed by an international force, a force that would only be wielded in the service of justice. A world court must also be created to settle disputes.

Other changes—including the adoption of a single currency to be used by all, and a universal system of weights and measures—would ease trade and travel among nations. But the key to greater understanding was language—the selection of one language to be used by all peoples.

"O members of parliaments throughout the world! Select ye a single language for the use of all on earth," wrote Bahá'u'lláh, "and adopt ye likewise a common script. . . . This will be the cause of unity, could ye but comprehend it, and the greatest instrument for promoting harmony and civilization. . . ."[5]

The chosen language should be taught in the schools of all nations, instructed Bahá'u'lláh. Every child would learn two languages: his own native tongue and the universal language. People from every part of the world would, at last, be able to communicate with one another freely.

"When this is achieved," said Bahá'u'lláh, "to whatsoever city a man may journey, it shall be as if he were entering his own home."[6] Choosing a worldwide language, He said, would be a sign that the human race was coming of age.

Bahá'u'lláh never promised that changing the ways of the world would be easy. Ceaseless endeavor was required to achieve a just and lasting peace, and untold challenges must be conquered. Like a mountain climber who tackles the steepest heights, humanity would need to draw on every strength, overcome every weakness, and replace every doubt with determination.

But what a different world would emerge from the struggle: a world in which hearts would no longer be held captive by hatred, and actions would not be governed by greed; in which science would not be used to construct weapons of war, but to invent, create, and explore; in which all nations would share the abundant resources of the earth, and no peoples would remain deprived.

In the world called for by Bahá'u'lláh, every field of endeavor would find women at work, taking their rightful place as equals with men. Women, who had suffered for centuries when the sons they reared with tenderness were killed in cruel wars, would become the strongest force for peace. The aggressive, masculine strengths that had prevailed in the world needed to be balanced by those strengths in which women excelled—among them the more subtle strengths of mental alertness and intuition, of love and service. As equal education became the right of all and the voices of women were heard in every domain, only then would the climate for peace be created.*

The human race, as it came of age, was in many ways like a young adult whose full range of powers was yet untested. Who could say what was possible? Only God's Messenger knew the truth. Peace had long been the dream of poets and visionaries; now it was the Will of God.

"A new life is, in this age, stirring within all the peoples of the earth; and yet none hath discovered its cause or perceived its motive," wrote Bahá'u'lláh. "In the days to come, ye will, verily, behold things of which ye have never heard before."[7]

Among the nations of the world, one was destined to lead the way to peace. That nation was the United States of America—little more than a century old in 1890 when Browne visited Bahá'u'lláh. In Bahá'u'lláh's lifetime the young country had grown from nineteen states to forty-four, stretching from the eastern Atlantic shore all the way west to the Pacific. Eager to explore and expand its territory, the young nation had not always acted with honor, as witnessed by the American Indians who had appeared to stand in its way. No nation was blameless before God. But the United States was also a nation of great and wonderful powers and capacities.

---

* In October 2000 a United Nations resolution entitled *Women, Peace and Security* and unanimously passed by the UN Security Council called for "increased representation of women at all decision-making levels in . . . the prevention, management, and resolution of conflict." The resolution stated, the "full participation of women in the peace process can significantly contribute to the maintenance and promotion of international peace and security." Reports show that women are in the forefront of peacebuilding efforts throughout the world. To read the complete resolution, see the Web site at www.un.org/events/res_1325.pdf. For current news about women in the world, see the Web site at www.un.org/womenwatch.

In His writings in 1873 Bahá'u'lláh had addressed the rulers of America from His prison cell in Acre: "Hearken ye, O Rulers of America and the Presidents of the Republics therein,* unto that which the Dove is warbling on the Branch of Eternity: 'There is none other God but Me, the Ever-Abiding, the Forgiving, the All-Bountiful.'" He called upon the American rulers to "adorn the temple of dominion" with the "ornament of justice" and "the fear of God" and to adorn its head with "the crown of the remembrance of your Lord, the Creator of the heavens."

"Take ye advantage of the Day of God," He counseled them, ". . . Bind ye the broken with the hands of justice, and crush the oppressor who flourisheth with the rod of the commandments of your Lord, the Ordainer, the All-Wise."[8] The greatness to which Bahá'u'lláh called America required great changes, changes that would be forged in the fires of tests and suffering.

Long ago God had made a promise to His chosen ones and His Prophets: The time would come when warfare would cease and humanity could live in peace. This was the Day, said Bahá'u'lláh, when the promise of God would be kept. This was the "King of days," when the vision of the Hebrew prophet Isaiah recorded in the Bible would come to pass:

> And he [the Lord] shall judge among the nations, and shall rebuke many people: and they shall beat their swords into plowshares, and their spears into pruninghooks: nation shall not lift up sword against nation, neither shall they learn war any more. . . .
>
> . . . For the earth shall be full of the knowledge of the Lord, as the waters cover the sea.[9]

Isaiah had received his vision from God more than 2,500 years before Bahá'u'lláh walked the earth. Other prophets and chosen ones living at different times and places had also received visions of the great changes that lay ahead. God spoke to all of his peoples in a language that each could understand.

---

* While these exhortations of Bahá'u'lláh address the collective nations of the American continents, later Bahá'í writings address more specifically the unique role of the United States in establishing peace.

One of those who had a prophetic vision lived on the plains of North America. His name was Black Elk, of the Oglala Lakota Sioux Indians, and he would grow up to be a holy man among his people. A vision came to him in 1872, when he was a nine-year-old boy and Bahá'u'lláh was a prisoner in Acre. Black Elk saw many things in his vision, which was rich in the language of dreams and filled with sacred mystery. In his vision Black Elk saw his people camped in a circle around a sacred tree. But when he looked again, the tree was dying; its leaves were falling and its birds had flown away. Then he saw the Black Road of conflict, and the hoop that was his nation was broken.

"All of the animals and fowls that were the people ran here and there," Black Elk said later as he told of his vision, "for each one seemed to have his own little vision that he followed, and his own rules; and all over the universe I could hear the winds at war like wild beasts fighting. . . . It was dark and terrible about me, for all the winds of the world were fighting." The sound, he said, was "like women and children wailing and like horses screaming all over the world."[10]

Finally Black Elk, in his vision, stood on the highest mountain and saw the whole hoop of the world. "And I saw that the sacred hoop of my people," he said, "was one of many hoops that made one circle, wide as daylight and as starlight, and in the center grew one mighty flowering tree to shelter all the children of one mother and one father. And I saw that it was holy."[11]

The peoples of many cultures had among their sacred legends those that told of a holy tree. To each culture the holy tree was a many-layered symbol of life cycles and spiritual truths. In Persia, too, there was a legend of a celestial tree whose branches reached to heaven and whose fruit would be for the life of nations. Legend said that it grew in the province of Mázindarán, the birthplace and early home of Bahá'u'lláh. Now, in the teachings of Bahá'u'lláh, divine guidance that clearly marked the road to peace had been given. It was guidance sorely needed by the nations and their peoples. Peace must no longer remain the stuff of dreams; the need for it was as vital as life itself.

From the window of His room at Bahjí, Bahá'u'lláh could see Mount Carmel in the distance. This was "the mountain of the Lord" that Isaiah had praised. To Mount Carmel "all nations shall flow," Isaiah had said.[12] One of the last tasks in Bahá'u'lláh's life would take Him to that ancient and holy mountain.

66

The Holy Mountain and the Martyrs of Yazd

Bahá'u'lláh stood on the gentle slopes of Mount Carmel, halfway up the mountain. From time to time a breeze ruffled His long, black beard. Below Him the port city of Haifa stretched from the base of the mountain to the bright blue waters of the bay. From these slopes Bahá'u'lláh could look across the bay and see, far on the other side, the walled city of Acre.

More than twenty years had passed since He had entered Acre's gates as a prisoner. The sultan who had sentenced Bahá'u'lláh to Acre had been certain He would die there. The Bahá'ís had feared that Bahá'u'lláh would indeed die in that terrible place, but Bahá'u'lláh had consoled them. "'Fear not,'" He had written during those dark days in prison. "'These doors shall be opened. My tent shall be pitched on Mount Carmel, and the utmost joy shall be realized.'"[1]

This visit in the summer of 1891 was Bahá'u'lláh's fourth visit to the ancient and holy mountain. It would not only be His longest visit—lasting three months—but it would also be His last. Today Bahá'u'lláh stood with His faithful son 'Abdu'l-Bahá in the shade of a cluster of cypress trees that grew on the mountainside. Bahá'u'lláh pointed to a rocky place on the slope just below where they stood. That spot, He told 'Abdu'l-Bahá, should be the final resting-place of the Báb.

In July 1850 the Báb had been executed in the public square of Tabríz, and His body had been left in a ditch outside the city. In the dark of night the precious remains of the Báb had been safely recovered. Since then they had been safely hidden—first in one place, then another—

until a final resting-place could be chosen. All was done in secret at the direction of Bahá'u'lláh lest the Báb's remains should be violated by those who would dishonor Him.

One day a building of befitting beauty would entomb the sacred remains of the Báb. In the very spot chosen by Bahá'u'lláh would stand a shrine of pure white stone crowned with a dome of gold. It would call to remembrance the noble Báb, the beauty of His character, and the splendor of His revelation.

Referring to the Báb, Bahá'u'lláh wrote in the Kitáb-i-Íqán (Book of Certitude), "No understanding can grasp the nature of His Revelation, nor can any knowledge comprehend the full measure of His Faith. . . . how great and lofty is His station!"[2]

The lives of the Báb and Bahá'u'lláh and Their revelations from God had been closely intertwined. *"'That so brief a span,'"* wrote Bahá'u'lláh, *"'should have separated this most mighty and wondrous Revelation'"* from that of the Báb *"'is a secret that no man can unravel and a mystery such as no mind can fathom.'"*[3]

The Báb had been the dawn, and the light of His revelation like the first light of day. He had sent His followers to proclaim far and wide the coming of "Him Whom God will make manifest," Who was the "Most Great Light"—Bahá'u'lláh. The revelation of Bahá'u'lláh was like the sun at midday, shining brightly on all from the highest point in the heavens. Who could bear to receive all at once the sun's full measure of heat and brilliance?

Mount Carmel and the land where it stood had cradled the footsteps of many prophets of old. This land was holy to Jews, Christians, and Muslims. Every Messenger of God had called upon the peoples of the world "to embrace the light of God," wrote Bahá'u'lláh. Each Messenger, through the power of God, was able "to scatter the darkness of ignorance."[4]

"As the body of man needeth a garment to clothe it," explained Bahá'u'lláh, "so the body of mankind must needs be adorned with the mantle of justice and wisdom. Its robe is the Revelation vouchsafed unto it by God. Whenever this robe hath fulfilled its purpose, the Almighty will assuredly renew it. For every age requireth a fresh measure of the light of God."[5]

So it was that the Báb—"the Gate"— had prepared the way for "the Glory of God"—Bahá'u'lláh. Their coming had fulfilled many of the prophecies of great expectation given in the world's religions. But many were not aware that so great an event had occurred, even among those who yearned for it.

On this visit to Mount Carmel in 1891 Bahá'u'lláh pitched His tent near a cluster of stone houses nestled at the foot of the mountain. Sunlight glinted off the red rooftops. These houses belonged to a small colony of Christians called "Templers."

Like many Christians with millennial expectations in the mid-nineteenth century, the Templers, who came from Germany, had expected Christ to return close to the year 1844. When they did not see Him in their homeland, the Templers sailed to the Holy Land. It was here, they were convinced, that the Lord Christ would walk among men and establish His spiritual throne. The first Templers reached Haifa in 1863, the year Bahá'u'lláh declared His mission; they established a full-fledged colony by 1868, the very year Bahá'u'lláh entered Acre.

In His writings Bahá'u'lláh extolled Jesus Christ—His life and suffering, His transforming power, and His sacrifice on the cross. "Know thou that when the Son of Man yielded up His breath to God, the whole creation wept with a great weeping," wrote Bahá'u'lláh. "By sacrificing Himself, however, a fresh capacity was infused into all created things. . . . We testify that when He came into the world, He shed the splendor of His glory upon all created things. Through Him the leper recovered from the leprosy of perversity and ignorance. Through Him, the unchaste and wayward were healed. Through His power, born of Almighty God, the eyes of the blind were opened, and the soul of the sinner sanctified."[6]

Bahá'u'lláh upheld the authority of the Gospels and confirmed in the Book of Certitude (Kitáb-i-Íqán) that Muḥammad had also upheld "both the Book and the Cause of Jesus." Muḥammad had "recognized the truth of the signs, prophecies, and words of Jesus," wrote Bahá'u'lláh, "and testified that they were all of God."[7]

Bahá'u'lláh Himself devoted nearly seventy pages of the Book of Certitude to explaining the meanings of several verses in the Gospel. They were verses in which Jesus had made known the signs that would signify the time of His return*—prophecies that had been fulfilled with the coming of Bahá'u'lláh.

* See Matthew 24, also known as Jesus' Olivet Discourse. For a detailed discussion of His words in that chapter and of their interpretation by biblical scholars and by Bahá'u'lláh, see Michael Sours, *The Prophecies of Jesus* (Oxford: Oneworld, 1991).

Now a quarter of a century after the Templers had settled in the Holy Land, Bahá'u'lláh visited them at the foot of Mount Carmel. He was invited to their homes and talked with their leader. Carved in the stone over one Templer doorway were the German words *"Der Herr ist Nahe,"* meaning "the Lord is Nigh."[8] But none among the Templers recognized Bahá'u'lláh as the Promised One they longed to meet.

While His tent was pitched on Mount Carmel in the summer of 1891, Bahá'u'lláh received heartrending news from Persia. On one horrible day in the city of Yazd, seven Bahá'ís had been killed in a bloodthirsty frenzy. The report so saddened Bahá'u'lláh that for nine days He saw no one and refrained from revealing any verses from God.

It happened on a day in May. The mujtahid of Yazd had been the first to stir up trouble against the innocent Bahá'ís. The governor had followed with an order for their deaths. The seven Bahá'ís had met their deaths on May 19, 1891, at the hands of a cruel and beastly mob. Onlookers watched, shouting and rejoicing at the barbaric acts they witnessed.

To the beating of drums and the blaring of trumpets, the Bahá'ís were marched from street to street in the city. At each stop another brave Bahá'í would be killed—strangled, beheaded or their throats cut. With each death the shouting mob grew louder, the throbbing music wilder.

Death alone did not satisfy the ferocious mob. The bodies of those who were killed were dragged through the streets and pelted with stones. Some were even hacked to pieces. One Bahá'í was an eighty-five-year-old man; two were brothers in their early twenties. The headless body of one brother was thrown in front of his mother's house while women pushed their way inside to dance in celebration.

At the end of the day's brutal work, the governor declared a holiday. Shops were closed and the city was lighted for festivities. But the lights in Yazd that night marked a darkness of spirit. The city's true lights had burned in the hearts of those who had been killed. In that long, terrible day not one Bahá'í had denied his faith. The last words of the martyred Bahá'ís were illumined with the love of their Lord.

This was the victory, said Bahá'u'lláh, of the martyrs over their adversaries. The light of their faith and love had not been extinguished, even in the face of brutal death. It was a victory celebrated by the inmates of the highest paradise. When Bahá'u'lláh picked up His pen once more, He praised the steadfast martyrs of Yazd. In His tent on the holy mountain of Carmel, He wrote a tablet that told the story of each one.

In this tablet Bahá'u'lláh also addressed the people who had committed such barbarous acts of injustice, condemning their cruelty. "'The blood of God's lovers hath dyed the earth red, and the sighs of His near ones have set the universe ablaze,'" lamented Bahá'u'lláh. "'. . . At dawn, the gentle breeze of divine compassion hath wafted over charred and cast-out bodies, whispering these exalted words, "Woe, woe unto you, O people of Iran! Ye have spilled the blood of your own friends and yet remain in ignorance of what ye have done. . . . O misguided ones, what sin have the little children committed?"'"[9]

The people of Yazd who killed the seven Bahá'ís had carried out their bloody actions in the name of religion. But such dark deeds were far removed from the divine guidance of any age. "As you wish that men would do to you, do so to them," Jesus had said. It was a command given by God to every Prophet and found in the scripture of every religion. "Not one of you is a believer," the Prophet Muḥammad had taught His followers, "until he loves for his brother what he loves for himself." And Bahá'u'lláh had directed the Bahá'ís, "Lay not on any soul a load which ye would not wish to be laid upon you, and desire not for any one the things ye would not desire for yourselves."[10]

"In truth," Bahá'u'lláh wrote, "religion is a radiant light and an impregnable stronghold for the protection and welfare of the peoples of the world, for the fear of God impelleth man to hold fast to that which is good, and shun all evil. Should the lamp of religion be obscured, chaos and confusion will ensue, and the lights of fairness and justice, of tranquillity and peace cease to shine."[11]

When the robe of religion was cast aside, human nature was perverted, its conduct was degraded, and human institutions—including those related to religion—were corrupted. Intolerance, hatred, lawlessness, and terrorism spread. Families were broken and peace was shattered. The very feelings of joy and hope faded as human hearts were caught in the grip of selfishness, fear, and suspicion.

"How long will humanity persist in its waywardness?" asked Bahá'u'lláh. "How long will injustice continue? How long is chaos and confusion to reign amongst men? How long will discord agitate the face of society? . . . The winds of despair are, alas, blowing from every direction, and the strife that divideth and afflicteth the human race is daily increasing."[12]

The questions remained for humankind to answer. Bahá'u'lláh had fulfilled His part of God's great Covenant, showering the world with divine guidance. A strong, new spirit had taken root. From it, Bahá'u'lláh promised, would come the "Day that shall not be followed by night" and the *"'Springtime which autumn will never overtake.'"*[13] In a tablet revealed on Mount Carmel Bahá'u'lláh would designate that holy mountain as the future world center of His Cause and the visible sign of the majesty of God. It would be the center of a governing system unique in religious annals, a system through which Bahá'u'lláh would keep His promise.

67

A Pattern for the Future

In the summer of 1891, before He left Mount Carmel for the last time, Bahá'u'lláh pitched His tent near a monastery on the mountain. Christian monks had built the monastery centuries earlier. Like the German Templers, they expected to see Christ walk among them one day. Bahá'u'lláh visited the monks, but they, like the Templers, did not recognize in Him the One for Whom they waited.

One day in His tent near the monastery, Bahá'u'lláh summoned His amanuensis. There, on God's holy mountain, He began to reveal a momentous document that He called the Tablet of Carmel. As He revealed the Word of God, Bahá'u'lláh's voice rang out clear and strong: "Render thanks unto thy Lord, O Carmel. . . . Rejoice, for God hath in this Day established upon thee His throne, hath made thee the dawning-place of His signs and the dayspring of the evidences of His Revelation."[1]

So loud and clear was Bahá'u'lláh's voice that the monks inside the monastery could hear every word He uttered. So powerful was the spirit of His revelation that the very earth beneath their feet seemed to tremble.

God had chosen Mount Carmel to show forth His sovereignty and glory, declared Bahá'u'lláh. For the first time in history both the spiritual and administrative centers of God's Cause would be united in one place.

Here, along with the sacred shrine of the Báb, would stand the majestic seat of the Universal House of Justice, the international governing body of the Bahá'í Faith. Here, too, would reside the appointed Guardian of the Bahá'í Faith. These two institutions—the Guardianship and the Universal House of Justice—would be the twin pillars of support for a greater structure: a visible order through which the spirit of Bahá'u'lláh's revelation would flow to every part of the world. The charter for this world center of the Bahá'í Faith was the Tablet of Carmel.

From Mount Carmel, "the Vineyard of God," divine blessings would flow not only to the Bahá'ís of the world but to all humanity. In the fullness of time the revelation of Bahá'u'lláh would become the Ark of salvation for the human race. Just as the prophet Isaiah had foretold, nations and peoples would come here to give homage and honor. Then would the windswept, ancient mountain of Carmel—now covered with scattered patches of tangled brush—bloom with untold beauty.

In the Tablet of Carmel, Bahá'u'lláh voiced His own heart's yearning: "Oh, how I long to announce unto every spot on the surface of the earth, and to carry to each one of its cities, the glad-tidings of this Revelation. . . ."[2] The work of spreading the light of Bahá'u'lláh's glad-tidings into every dark corner of the world would remain for His followers to carry out.

At the heart of Bahá'u'lláh's message of unity was the provision in His Most Holy Book (the Kitáb-i-Aqdas) for a structure—the Bahá'í Administrative Order—that would embody the new spirit released into the world. Its God-given institutions would be distinctly different from anything in the history of religion. The Bahá'ís themselves would be changed through the operation of this new divine Order and become more fit to accomplish their task. The body of this structure would come into being through Bahá'u'lláh's Covenant with His followers.

God's Covenant with humanity was His promise, fulfilled through each Messenger, that He would always bless humanity with His guidance. Within that compass was Bahá'u'lláh's own Covenant with His followers, in which He established an unbroken line of divine authority. Through institutions conceived not by men but by the Messenger of God, humankind would be blessed with a continuous stream of divine guidance far beyond the lifetime of the Messenger Himself. For the first time ever, a religion's unity would be preserved. Bahá'u'lláh's promise of a "Day which shall never be followed by night" would be fulfilled.[3]

People were familiar with ministers and mullás, priests and monks, who had always served as the leaders and teachers of religion. In times past, when many people were illiterate and could not read the Word of God, these leaders guided people in their understanding and practice of divine teachings. The clergy had long held power and authority in society, but now, with the human race at the threshold of its maturity, Bahá'u'lláh had ordained a new system of leadership to replace the old.

The new system would forever change the role of the individual believer and the society in which he lived. The reins of power, the voice of authority, and the mantle of responsibility would no longer rest with a few individuals. The structure conceived by Bahá'u'lláh would rely on rank upon rank of community members. Their talents and energies would flow through two types of institutions—appointed and elected—that would, like two arms, embrace the Bahá'í world.

One arm would consist of institutions whose learned members would be appointed to guide, encourage, and protect the Bahá'í community.* The other arm would consist of elected institutions—the Bahá'í governing bodies at local and national levels—that would be known as "Spiritual Assemblies" or "Houses of Justice."† Both arms would be guided by the twin institutions at their head: the Guardian of the Cause of God—invested with authority to interpret the sacred writings, and the Universal House of Justice—invested with legislative and judicial powers.‡ The

* See chapter 61 for a discussion of teachers and Hands of the Cause of God, who were the first individuals to serve the appointed arm of the Bahá'í Administrative Order.

† In the Kitáb-i-Aqdas the term "House of Justice" is used; for the present, these institutions, because they are as yet in an embryonic stage of development, are referred to as "Spiritual Assemblies."

‡The Universal House of Justice is elected every five years at an international convention by the members of all National Spiritual Assemblies, who are themselves elected annually by delegates elected at the grassroots level. By voting in the election of these delegates, every adult Bahá'í participates indirectly in the election of the National Spiritual Assembly and, by extension, the Universal House of Justice. Guidance from the Universal House of Justice and the Guardian ly:is considered free from error. No other Bahá'í institutions are considered infallible.

Guardian would be appointed, and the Universal House of Justice would be elected by the Bahá'ís of the world.*

Every year each town would elect its Local Spiritual Assembly, and every nation its National Spiritual Assembly. From elections to decision-making, the operation of these elected bodies would be vastly different from the methods and customs of the past.

The election process would be free from nominations, campaigns, and every kind of electioneering, all of which would be strictly prohibited. Instead, Bahá'ís in each community would cast their ballots confidentially in an atmosphere of prayer. The results of this process would be inspired by God, Bahá'u'lláh promised. The nine adults receiving the greatest number of votes would serve on that community's Spiritual Assembly.

Their number would include men and women, old and young, and would represent a diverse selection of the people who lived there. They would serve together side by side, and authority would reside with the Assembly as a body. Outside of Assembly sessions, its individual members would possess no greater authority than any other member of the community.

Each Spiritual Assembly would direct the affairs and develop the resources of its community—organizing, educating, guiding, and assisting. Its decisions and plans would enrich and support individual initiative with collective wisdom, wisdom that would emerge from the divinely inspired process of consultation.

The practice of consultation would involve several steps, from gathering facts and clarifying issues to identifying the spiritual principles that applied to an issue. At the heart of consultation would be frank and open-minded discussion in an atmosphere of courtesy, respect, and humble detachment.

"In all things it is necessary to consult," wrote Bahá'u'lláh, ". . . inasmuch as it is and will always be a cause of awareness and of awakening

---

*For a fuller discussion of the Covenant of Bahá'u'lláh and the Bahá'í Administrative Order, see William S. Hatcher and J. Douglas Martin, *The Bahá'í Faith: The Emerging Global Religion* (Wilmette, IL: Bahá'í Publishing, 2002), pp. 130–68.

and a source of good and well-being." "No welfare and no well-being can be attained except through consultation," He stated clearly. "It is a shining light which, in a dark world, leadeth the way and guideth. . . . The maturity of the gift of understanding is made manifest through consultation."[4]

Consultation should be used by every Bahá'í, Bahá'u'lláh advised, to make sound decisions grounded in spiritual principles. Spiritual Assemblies, which would bear greater responsibility than individuals for investigating truth and determining justice, would particularly need to learn the art of consultation. The tool of consultation would be as indispensable to humanity's coming of age as tools of iron had been in an earlier era.

The worldwide network of Spiritual Assemblies, guided by the Universal House of Justice and the appointed Guardian, would be more than a means of administration. These Spiritual Assemblies would become "the potent sources of the progress of man" and the pattern for future society. 'Abdu'l-Bahá would call them "shining lamps and heavenly gardens, from which the fragrances of holiness are diffused over all regions, and the lights of knowledge are shed abroad over all created things."[6]

All these bestowals of God, bearing infinite possibilities, would bring into being, on the ruins of outdated and expiring institutions, a new civilization. These divine gifts would become the essential tools for the future functioning of a peaceful world. With them humanity would gradually begin to achieve those noble goals that had so long eluded them—the relief of human suffering, the attainment of lasting peace, and all those ideals envisioned by the Prophets of God.

"Mankind's ordered life hath been revolutionized," declared Bahá'u'lláh, "through the agency of this unique, this wondrous System—the like of which mortal eyes have never witnessed."[7]

Gradually, too, a quiet inner transformation would occur—the creation of a new mind. "Ye are My treasury," said Bahá'u'lláh, addressing humanity as the Voice of God, "for in you I have treasured the pearls of My mysteries and the gems of My knowledge."[8] Much in the labyrinth of the human mind and heart remained to be discovered. Prompted by its experience with these new spiritual tools, humanity would make substantial changes and discard the ignorant attitudes of earlier eras. The quiet transformation within each soul would become the spiritual transformation of the human race.

When Bahá'u'lláh returned to Bahjí after His stay at Mount Carmel, He knew that His own work was complete. For forty years—nearly half a century—He had "proclaimed and delivered, in the most eloquent language, before the face of the world" those things which God had revealed to Him. From Baghdad to Bahjí, at every stage in His journey of exile, Bahá'u'lláh had let nothing stand in His way. Neither the schemes of His enemies nor the treachery of the faithless had stopped Him from revealing the Word of God. "Never since the beginning of the world," declared Bahá'u'lláh, "hath the Message been so openly proclaimed."[9]

Now, in His seventy-fourth year, His body was worn to a breath by the tribulations of His life. Though He was a Messenger of God, Bahá'u'lláh had accepted the sufferings heaped upon Him by men. He had exchanged a life of wealth and social privilege for a life of imprisonment and exile. From the cold and gloomy Black Pit of Tehran to the loathsome prison of Acre, Bahá'u'lláh had patiently endured many years of suffering. He had "consented to be bound with chains," He wrote, "that mankind may be released from its bondage." He had "accepted to be made a prisoner . . . that the whole world may attain unto true liberty."[10]

Bahá'u'lláh had survived, with His beloved family, impossible journeys through the cold, snow-laden mountains. He had survived, as well, the coldhearted schemes of His half-brother Mírzá Yaḥyá.* Nothing had caused Bahá'u'lláh to lose courage. He had "drained to its dregs the cup of sorrow," He wrote, so "that all the peoples of the earth may attain unto abiding joy, and be filled with gladness."[11]

Every Messenger of God had endured the cruelest suffering so that humankind might draw closer to its Creator. "This is of the mercy of

* Mírzá Yaḥyá remained on the island of Cyprus, where he lived an unremarkable life until his death in 1912. See Appendix 6 for more details, including Bahá'u'lláh's admonition to Mírzá Yaḥyá in the Kitáb-i-Aqdas.

your Lord, the Compassionate, the Most Merciful," wrote Bahá'u'lláh.[12]

But now Bahá'u'lláh's work in this life was finished. He had fulfilled His mission from God. When He returned from Mount Carmel, He began to put His affairs in order. Already His dear wife Navváb, who had stayed at His side through every exile and borne with Him every trial, had passed away. Mírzá Músá, too, His faithful and devoted brother, had passed from this world to the next.* Now Bahá'u'lláh was ready to join them.

68

The Sun of Bahá Has Set

On May 8, 1892, less than a year after His last visit to Mount Carmel, Bahá'u'lláh became sick with a fever. When the fever abated after a few days, family and friends were relieved. But the fever returned, stronger than before. This time Bahá'u'lláh did not recover. On a Sunday, after He had been ill for two weeks, Bahá'u'lláh asked to see the believers.

All the Bahá'ís who lived near Bahjí, as well as the pilgrims who were visiting, came and gathered around Him. "'*I am well pleased with you all,*'" He said in a gentle and loving voice. "'*Ye have rendered many services, and been very assiduous in your labors. Ye have come here every morning and every evening. May God assist you to remain united. May He aid you to exalt the Cause of the Lord of being.*'"[1] At this the believers could not keep from weeping, for they sensed the end of His earthly life was near.

How much heavier was the heart of 'Abdu'l-Bahá. Day and night he stayed at the bedside of his beloved father. One day Bahá'u'lláh told 'Abdu'l-Bahá to gather all His papers, seals, and other items and put them into two cases. These were the cases Bahá'u'lláh took with Him whenever He left Bahjí to stay elsewhere.

---

* Mírzá Músá—Bahá'u'lláh's kindhearted brother who accompanied Him in exile, helped the family in countless ways over the years, and remained staunchly faithful to the Cause of God—passed away in 1877, a year after the death of Navváb.

'Abdu'l-Bahá obeyed, but his hands trembled and his eyes brimmed with tears. When all was collected, Bahá'u'lláh spoke again. "'These two now belong to you,'" He said.[2] Sharp sorrow pierced 'Abdu'l-Bahá's heart when he heard these words, for he knew that his father's final hour must be near.

On May 29, 1892, when night still lay softly over day, Bahá'u'lláh drew His last breath. It was eight hours after sunset, twenty-one days after He had first fallen ill. For seventy-four years He had blessed the earth with His presence. Now His spirit had departed for those greater worlds of God.

A messenger on horseback was sent at once to Acre. Out of Bahjí and down the road he galloped at full speed. A short time later he rode through the city gates and delivered the news to the leading *muftí* of Acre.

Soon, from the seven minarets of the mosque, the proclamation of Bahá'u'lláh's passing was sounded: "'God is Great. He Giveth Life! He Taketh it Again! He Dieth Not, but Liveth for Evermore!'"[3] Only when a very learned and holy man had passed away—one who was greatly honored—was it proclaimed this way from the mosque.

Word spread through Acre and beyond. The call was proclaimed from mosques throughout the land. A telegram was sent to Sulṭán 'Abdu'l-Ḥamíd. It began with the sorrowful words "the Sun of Bahá has set."[4]

At the mansion, a heartbroken 'Abdu'l-Bahá had the task of preparing his father's body for burial. Two Bahá'ís assisted the grief-stricken Master. One was a doctor; the other was Shaykh Maḥmúd.

How long ago it seemed, that day in Acre, when Shaykh Maḥmúd had first walked angrily into the prison. He had come with a hidden dagger and murderous thoughts, planning to kill Bahá'u'lláh for dishonoring Islam. But nothing was hidden from Bahá'u'lláh, Who, in time, had disarmed the shaykh—not by physical force, but with truth and the majesty of His presence.

Now the devoted Shaykh Maḥmúd lovingly bathed Bahá'u'lláh's sacred remains. The body would be anointed with attar of roses and wrapped in cloth before it was placed in its coffin.* The burial took place on the

* This was the customary way of preparing a body for burial at the time of Bahá'u'lláh, although no details are recorded beyond the washing of the body by the doctor and Shaykh Maḥmúd.

same day as Bahá'u'lláh's passing, a little after sundown. A small house stood next to the mansion of Bahjí. In the ground beneath a room of that house, His body was laid to rest.

'Abdu'l-Bahá wept and wept. For three days and nights his grief allowed him no rest. His beloved father, Who had been the Light of the World, was gone. How could he bear it? No more would he go to Bahjí and see Bahá'u'lláh on the balcony waiting for him. No longer would he be able to tell Him of the people and happenings in Acre, or hear from His lips the loving words *Khaylí-Khúb, Áqá* (Very good, Master).

By the next day a stream of people from Acre and nearby villages made their way to Bahjí. Shaykhs, mullás, and government officials came. Throngs of ordinary people came, too—the rich and the poor, the orphaned and the oppressed. More than five hundred people gathered on the grounds and fields around the mansion. One and all, they mourned the loss of the One they had come to honor.

Who could forget the noble Bahá'u'lláh, Father of the Poor, He Who had lived so simply yet given so generously to those in need? Even as a prisoner in Acre He had helped those who lived there. The aqueduct that carried their water—now fresh and clean from the hills—had been repaired at His request.

At Bahjí, shaykhs chanted prayers. There were poets, too, who wrote poems and chanted songs of praise that glorified Bahá'u'lláh's greatness. He was renowned as a holy one Whose knowledge and wisdom—which eclipsed all others—were matched only by the purity of His deeds; Who had lived a life of sacrifice and honor; Whose love of God had been read, day by day, in His just and loving demeanor toward all who crossed His path. Shaykhs and poets alike lamented the loss of one so wonderful and rare.

Telegrams and tributes came from admirers everywhere. They came from the citizens of other countries—Egypt, Lebanon, Syria. They came from believers of many faiths—Muslims, Christians, Jews, and others. They came from men of learning, from high-ranking officials and religious leaders. They came in different languages. One and all, they lauded Bahá'u'lláh's greatness and lamented His loss.

The telegrams, the tributes to Bahá'u'lláh, and the poetry in His honor—all were sent to 'Abdu'l-Bahá. How often did their praises of

Bahá'u'lláh praise 'Abdu'l-Bahá as well—the shining Exemplar of his father's teachings.

Many who gathered at Bahjí were less eloquent in their sorrow but just as sincere. They could do no more than weep and cry aloud to express their heartfelt sadness. For a full week, mourners gathered at Bahjí to lament the passing of Bahá'u'lláh. Some camped beneath the trees around the mansion while many more encamped in the fields farther out.

Shaykhs brought lamb and rice, sugar and salt, which the family gave to the poor. Those who received these gifts, in the Arab custom, would pray for the soul of the departed one. Each day the family of Bahá'u'lláh gave out food to all those gathered at Bahjí. Each day 'Abdu'l-Bahá gave money to the poor. It was 'Abdu'l-Bahá who, in those grievous days, made certain every detail was attended to.

Now that Bahá'u'lláh was gone, one question remained: Who would lead this young and growing religion? The answer was not long in coming. It lay in the written Will and Testament of Bahá'u'lláh, which He called the *Kitáb-i-'Ahd,* meaning "Book of the Covenant." For two years this important document, written in His own hand and sealed with His seal, lay in a locked box in Acre. Now 'Abdu'l-Bahá sent for the box to be brought to Bahjí.

69

An Excellent and Priceless Heritage

Early on the ninth day after Bahá'u'lláh's passing, in front of nine people chosen from His family and friends, the box containing His will was unlocked. The seal on the document inside was broken, and the will—written entirely in Bahá'u'lláh's own hand—was opened and read. Later that day it was read to the rest of the Bahá'ís who were gathered at Bahjí.

"We have bequeathed to Our heirs an excellent and priceless heritage," Bahá'u'lláh had written. "Earthly treasures We have not bequeathed, nor have We added such cares as they entail."[1]

Among the many provisions in His will, the Book of the Covenant, one provision stood out above all others: Bahá'u'lláh had appointed the Most Great Branch, 'Abdu'l-Bahá, as the Center of His Covenant with His followers and the sole Interpreter of Bahá'u'lláh's writings. Until now every believer had turned to Bahá'u'lláh for authoritative guidance; now all were directed to turn to 'Abdu'l-Bahá. Although 'Abdu'l-Bahá was not a Messenger of God, Bahá'u'lláh had long ago recognized in His eldest son the unique capacity that qualified him for so vital a role. He had prepared His followers little by little over the years for this very time and announcement.

Bahá'u'lláh's appointment of 'Abdu'l-Bahá as His successor in authority—clearly stated in the Book of the Covenant—would be the source of protection for the fledgling faith. In times past divisions had splintered and marred the religion of God, but no longer, for this was the "Day that shall not be followed by night."[2] The priceless heritage bequeathed by Bahá'u'lláh was unity, and this provision—its meaning indisputable and its author undeniable—would be the cornerstone of that foundation.

The revelation of Bahá'u'lláh called all peoples to a greater vision—the unity of humankind. In His writings were the tools to make the vision a reality. Bahá'u'lláh had brought teachings to uplift the human spirit and laws to last for a thousand years. He had ordained a system that was destined to be a fountain of justice and had created a Covenant to protect men from the claws of division.

The gifts of God in the revelation of Bahá'u'lláh were blessings for a new stage in the journey of humankind. The journey would not lead to a new place in the world; it would lead the peoples of the world to a new place of understanding.

"This is not a Cause which may be made a plaything for your idle fancies," Bahá'u'lláh had warned, "nor is it a field for the foolish and faint of heart. By God, this is the arena of insight and detachment, of vision and upliftment, where none may spur on their chargers save the valiant horsemen of the Merciful, who have severed all attachment to the world of being."[3]

Bahá'u'lláh's enemies had plotted to destroy the Bahá'í Faith, but they had not reckoned with the sovereign power of God. *"The Call of God, when raised, breathed a new life into the body of mankind,"* said 'Abdu'l-Bahá, *"and infused a new spirit into the whole creation."*[4]

Once on a late afternoon outside Acre, when Bahá'u'lláh was enjoying the fresh, sweet air in the Garden of Riḍván, He had told the Bahá'ís, "Before long you shall see people of all the nations of the world gathered under the shade of the tent of the Cause of God."[5]

At the time of Bahá'u'lláh's passing, the number of believers had grown far beyond the first few Letters of the Living. The Cause of God had spread beyond the cradle of its birth in Persia to ten countries in Asia and Africa. In little more than a century, as Bahá'u'lláh had foretold, people in every part of the globe would embrace His Cause. Bahá'ís from nearly two hundred countries would come as pilgrims to the Holy Land to pay homage to the Founders of their faith, and every season would see them walk up the gardened slopes of Mount Carmel to the World Center of the Bahá'í Faith.

Every one of them would be cherished by Bahá'u'lláh. "O Lord of all being, and the Desire of all creation!" He had written, "I would love to lay My face upon every single spot of Thine earth, that perchance it might be honored by touching a spot ennobled by the footsteps of Thy loved ones!"[6]

But now the world's handful of Bahá'ís, filled with sorrow, looked to 'Abdu'l-Bahá for solace. Nine days after the reading of Bahá'u'lláh's will, 'Abdu'l-Bahá wrote to the grieving Bahá'ís and urged them to be steadfast. The spirit of Bahá'u'lláh, He said, would assist them from on high, "breathing into their hearts and souls the breath of eternal life."[7]

"Let not your hearts be perturbed, O people, when the glory of My Presence is withdrawn, and the ocean of My utterance is stilled," Bahá'u'lláh had written. "In My presence amongst you there is a wisdom, and in My absence there is yet another, inscrutable to all but God, the Incomparable, the All-Knowing. Verily, We behold you from Our realm of glory, and will aid whosoever will arise for the triumph of Our Cause with the hosts of the Concourse on high and a company of Our favored angels."[8]

The peoples of future centuries would honor Bahá'u'lláh as the "Unifier of the children of men" and the "Establisher of the Most Great Peace." They would remember Bahá'u'lláh—the Glory of God—as the "Proclaimer of the coming of age of the entire human race."[9]

As for 'Abdu'l-Bahá, he would always remember the loving father Who had waited for him in the garden or watched for him on the balcony at Bahjí. Whatever the task he must tackle, whatever troubles lay ahead, 'Abdu'l-Bahá would remember his father's wisdom and courage. And in his heart he would be able to hear Bahá'u'lláh's loving words, *Khaylí-Khúb, Áqá* (Very good, Master).

"O peoples of the earth!" Bahá'u'lláh had addressed humanity, "God, the Eternal Truth, is My witness that streams of fresh and soft-flowing waters have gushed from the rocks, through the sweetness of the words uttered by your Lord, the Unconstrained; and still ye slumber. Cast away that which ye possess and, on the wings of detachment, soar beyond all created things. Thus biddeth you the Lord of creation, the movement of Whose Pen hath revolutionized the soul of mankind."[10]

Appendix 1:

A Brief Chronology of Events in the Life of Bahá'u'lláh

Birth of Bahá'u'lláh	12 November 1817
Birth of the Báb	20 October 1819
Declaration of the Mission of the Báb in Shiraz	23 May 1844
Birth of 'Abdu'l-Bahá	23 May 1844
Departure of the Báb on His pilgrimage to Mecca	c. October 1844
The Báb's Announcement in Mecca	December 1844
Arrival of the Báb in Máh-Kú, Azerbaijan	Summer 1847
The Báb's revelation of the Persian Bayán	1847
Incarceration of the Báb in Chihríq, Azerbaijan	April 1848
Conference of Badasht	June 1848
Interrogation of the Báb in Tabríz, Azerbaijan	July 1848
Death of Muḥammad Sháh; Accession of Náṣiri'd-Dín Sháh	4 September 1848
Beginning of the encounter at Shaykh Ṭabarsí	10 October 1848
Imprisonment of Bahá'u'lláh in Amul	December 1848
End of the encounter at Shaykh Ṭabarsí	10 May 1849
Martyrdom of the Báb	9 July 1850
Attempt on the life of Náṣiri'd-Dín Sháh	15 August 1852
Imprisonment of Bahá'u'lláh in the Black Pit of Tehran	August 1852
Banishment of Bahá'u'lláh to Baghdad	12 January 1853
Withdrawal of Bahá'u'lláh to Kurdistan (and Sulaimaniya)	10 April 1854
Return of Bahá'u'lláh from Kurdistan	19 March 1856
Bahá'u'lláh's revelation of the Hidden Words	1858
Bahá'u'lláh's revelation of the Kitáb-i-Íqán (Book of Certitude)	1862

Public declaration of the mission of Bahá'u'lláh in the
Garden of Riḍván in Baghdád .... 22 April 1863
Departure of Bahá'u'lláh from Garden of
Riḍván for Constantinople .... 3 May 1863
Arrival of Bahá'u'lláh in Constantinople .... 16 August 1863
Departure of Bahá'u'lláh for Adrianople .... 1 December 1863
Arrival of Bahá'u'lláh in Adrianople .... 12 December 1863
Mírzá Yaḥyá's poisoning of Bahá'u'lláh .... c. 1865
Mírzá Yaḥyá claims to be the recipient of a divine
revelation requiring all to turn to him .... c. March 1866
The Most Great Separation .... 10 March 1866
Bahá'u'lláh's revelation of the Tablet to the Kings 1866
Departure of Bahá'u'lláh from Adrianople .... 12 August 1868
Arrival of Bahá'u'lláh in Acre .... 31 August 1868
Badí''s delivery of the Tablet to the Shah .... July 1869
Death of Mírzá Mihdí, the Purest Branch .... 23 June 1870
Bahá'u'lláh's release from the prison barracks
to a house within Acre .... 4 November 1870
Murder of Siyyid Muḥammad and two of his
companions in Acre .... 23 January 1872
Bahá'u'lláh's revelation of the Kitáb-i-Aqdas, the
Most Holy Book 1873
Wedding of 'Abdu'l-Bahá and Munírih Khánum .... 8 March 1873
Death of the King of Martyrs and the Beloved
of Martyrs .... 17 March 1876
Deposal of Sulṭán 'Abdu'l-'Azíz .... 30 May 1876
Bahá'u'lláh's departure from Acre and His occupation
of the Mansion of Mazra'ih .... early June 1877
Bahá'u'lláh's occupation of the Mansion of Bahjí ... September 1879
Visit by Bahá'u'lláh to Haifa 1883
Death of Navváb in Acre 1886

Third visit of Bahá'u'lláh to Haifa .... April 1890
E. G. Browne's visit with Bahá'u'lláh at Bahjí .... 15–20 April 1890
Fourth visit of Bahá'u'lláh to Haifa; identification of the site for the Shrine of the Báb; revelation of the Tablet of Carmel .... Summer 1891
Revelation of Epistle to the Son of the Wolf 1891
Revelation of the Kitáb-i-'Ahd, Bahá'u'lláh's Book of the Covenant 1892
Ascension of Bahá'u'lláh .... 29 May 1892
Unsealing and reading of Bahá'u'lláh's Will, the Book of the Covenant, at Bahjí .... 7 June 1892

Appendix 2:
A Note about the Wives of Bahá'u'lláh and Bahá'í Marriage

Circumstances arose while Bahá'u'lláh still lived in Tehran that led to His taking a second wife. A female relative, Fáṭimih Khánum, had been widowed at a young age. As head of the household after His father's passing, Bahá'u'lláh was obliged to provide for her, as there existed no public system of welfare. To fulfill His obligation, Bahá'u'lláh needed to take her into His household. Under Shia Islamic law, this could only be accomplished through marriage.

Bahá'u'lláh's third marriage was contracted when He lived in Baghdad. Although details are sketchy, it seems that relatives of Bahá'u'lláh arranged the marriage in Káshán, Persia, where the woman, Gawhar Khánum, lived. She was then sent with her brother to Bahá'u'lláh in Baghdad. This arrangement was meant to honor both Bahá'u'lláh and Gawhar Khánum. For Bahá'u'lláh to have refused her hand in marriage would have been highly disrespectful to those involved and especially damaging to the woman's reputation.

Both of these marriages were contracted well within the bounds of Islamic law. Both occurred before Bahá'í marriage law was revealed by Bahá'u'lláh and further elucidated by 'Abdu'l-Bahá.

Bahá'í marriage is defined as a physical and spiritual union between one man and woman, and polygamy is forbidden. Marriage is conditioned upon the consent of both parties and their parents, but the parents may not arrange the marriage. It is also conditioned on both parties' having reached the age of maturity, which Bahá'u'lláh has fixed at fifteen. In the Bahá'í wedding, both parties recite a specifically revealed verse from Bahá'u'lláh: "We will, all, verily, abide by the Will of God."

Because strong, spiritual marriages produce spiritual families, and strong, spiritual families advance the growth and progress of civilization, marriage is strongly recommended but is not obligatory.

Appendix 3:

Islam and Its Two Major Branches, Shia and Sunni

In Arabic *Islam* means complete, trusting surrender to God. The religion of Islam was founded by the Prophet Muḥammad (570–632 A.D.) in Arabia during the seventh century. The Koran—the Muslim holy book, which takes its name from the Arabic *Qur'án*, meaning "reading" or "reciting"—was revealed to Muḥammad over a period of more than two decades. Muslims turn for guidance to the Koran and to the *hadith*, which are stories of Muḥammad's life and sayings that were preserved orally, then written down beginning in the eighth century.

After Muḥammad's death in 632 A.D., there was deep difference of opinion over the issue of who should succeed the Prophet as authoritative head of the religion and bear the responsibility to interpret the Koran and guide the community. Some felt the Muslim community should elect successors, called caliphs. Others were convinced that legitimate succession must be hereditary from the Prophet's family. As a result, the Muslim community split into two major branches: Sunni (favoring the caliphs) and Shia (favoring hereditary succession).

The majority of Muslims—about 80 percent—are Sunni. Sunnis believe that Muḥammad died without appointing a successor. They regard the caliphs who have been elected by the Muslim community to be Muḥammad's legitimate successors and heads of Islam. Caliphs administer the body of rules and regulations called *sharia* and serve for a lifetime. The first caliph, elected by general consensus of a gathering of notable members of Islam, was Abu Bakr, who had been a steadfast friend of the Prophet.

The Shia Muslims, who form the majority of Muslims in Iran, as well as sizable minorities in Iraq and Syria, believe that Muḥammad designated 'Alí, His trustworthy and courageous son-in-law, as His successor. Shiites believe that successors must be direct descendants of Muḥammad through His daughter Fáṭimih and her husband 'Alí. They do not recognize the Sunni caliphs or Sunni legal and political institutions. They give allegiance, instead, to a series of *Imáms* (leaders or guides) beginning with 'Alí and followed by Ḥasan and Ḥusayn, who were the sons of Fáṭimih and 'Alí. Most Shiites acknowledge twelve Imáms, believing the Twelfth Imám will reappear at the Day of Resurrection. (A minority of Shiites recognize only seven Imáms.) The martyrdom of the Imám Ḥusayn at Karbala is commemorated yearly as a symbol of the struggle against oppression.

Despite their differences, Shia and Sunni Muslims agree on the core beliefs and practices of Islam. Central to these are the Five Pillars of Islam: belief in the oneness of God and in Muḥammad as His Prophet, prayer, almsgiving, fasting, and pilgrimage. Fasting is obligatory during the Muslim month of Ramadan, when it commemorates the first revelations of the Koran to Muḥammad.

Jihad, which means "striving," is also enjoined upon all Muslims. It is often mistranslated by non-Muslims and misunderstood by many Muslims themselves to mean "holy war." Muḥammad reportedly said that the Greater Jihad is the struggle against the lower self. It is the battle waged within a person between right and wrong, good and evil. On the outside the Lesser Jihad has to do with protecting the Way of God, which includes one's life, faith, and honor, as well as that of the Muslim community, against the forces of evil. The Prophet Muḥammad reportedly said that "the preferred jihad is a truth spoken in the presence of a tyrant."

Muḥammad taught His followers to respect Jews and Christians as "People of the Book" and to allow them to practice their own religions, asserting that their Prophets and sacred books came from God. The Koran mentions people and stories from Jewish and Christian sacred history, which is also considered part of the history of Islam.

Just as Christianity has its historical roots in Judaism but is recognized as an independent religion and not a sect of Judaism, the Bahá'í Faith has its historical roots in Islam but is regarded as an independent religion.

Appendix 4:
Millennial Christians

A spirit of religious expectation permeated much of the early nineteenth century. The sense that the world was on the threshold of some mighty and wonderful event was widely shared among many Christians, who wondered what the nature of this event might be. This feeling of expectation heightened as the years 1843–44 approached.

The word "millennium"—which comes from the Latin *mille* (thousand) plus *annus* (year) and means a period of one thousand years—came to be applied to the expectation among certain Christians that Jesus Christ would return from heaven in the flesh and reign over the earth for a thousand years. Among Christians there were differing views on the details. Some believed that Christ, on His return, would judge between the righteous and the wicked and then establish a thousand-year reign. Others believed that the faithful must first establish God's Kingdom on earth through "right faith and righteous acts" before Christ would return.[1] Both groups embraced a vision of the future as a paradise free from all suffering and imperfection.

A series of spiritual revivals in early nineteenth-century America infused both perspectives with fresh energy.* The belief that Christ's coming—the advent—was dependent on righteous acts as well as on faith

---

* These revivals were started by Charles Finney (1792–1875), who later became president of Oberlin College. Finney's revivals eventually led to what is referred to as the Second Great Awakening in America, an upsurge in religious fervor similar to that sparked by the sermons of Jonathan Edwards a century before.

led to intense focus on social reform. New reform-minded organizations sprang into being. Among them were the American Education Society (1815), the American Temperance Society (1826), the American Peace Society (1828), and the American Anti-Slavery Society (1833), to name only a few examples.

Millennial beliefs also gained renewed, intense interest among Christians. Such beliefs had a long history with roots in the early Christian church. The book of Daniel in the Old Testament was considered a key source of millennial prophecy, as were the Olivet Discourse of Jesus (Matthew 24–25) and the Revelation of John in the New Testament.

Over the centuries, various Christian scholars made key contributions to the common understanding of the prophecies. Among the most notable scholars were Joachim of Fiore (1130–1202), Joseph Mede of Cambridge (1586–1638), and Sir Isaac Newton (1642–1727). Joachim of Fiore was the first Christian to adopt the formula of Jewish scholars in which a prophetic day equaled an actual year. Joseph Mede coordinated key prophecies of Daniel with those in the Revelation of John. Sir Isaac Newton, who had used mathematics to explain natural phenomena, added a mathematical foundation for calculating prophetic time.

Not everyone accepted a literal understanding of the millennium, including Origen (c. 185–c. 254), an outstanding scholar of the early Greek church, and Saint Augustine (354–430). Nor did all nineteenth-century millennialists agree with the idea of the millennium as a sudden physical event. In particular, George Bush, a professor of Hebrew and Oriental literature at New York University, predicted that 1843 would "mark the beginning of an earthly millennium, with righteousness gaining domination of the world by gradual steps."[2] However, such views remained in the minority.

While historic church creeds had always referred to Christ's role on judgment day,* none referred to a specific time. By the nineteenth century, however, some scholars of biblical prophecy began to attempt to predict the specific year and even the day on which Christ would return.

* The Apostles' Creed, the Nicene Creed, the Athanasian Creed, the Lutheran Augsburg Confession, the Anglican Thirty-Nine Articles, and the Presbyterian Westminster Confession all refer to Christ's role on judgment day. Other church creeds also refer to Christ's return at the end of the world.

Christian millennialists had developed a method of interpreting prophecy called *historicism,* which coordinated all prophecy with specific historical events. Over time there had developed general agreement on the correlation of certain historical events with specific prophecies. Historicism also attempted to anticipate the dates of future events.

In 1812 Timothy Dwight, president of Yale University and a spiritual descendant of Puritans, thought he could "perceive the dawn of the millennium."[3] In that same year a book titled *The Coming of Messiah in Majesty and Glory* was published by a Catholic priest, Manuel de Lacunza, of Chile. By 1820 Archibald Mason in Scotland predicted 1844 as the year of Christ's return. In England, where, by 1820, about three hundred Anglican and six hundred nonconformist clergymen were preaching Christ's return, London's *Christian Observer* predicted Christ's second coming sometime between 1843 and 1847.

But no one was more influential than William Miller (1782–1849), who made his home in Low Hampton, New York. By turns a farmer, peace officer, and soldier, as well as husband and father, William Miller was thirty-four in September 1816 when he had a profound spiritual experience that would change his life and the lives of thousands. He suddenly felt the nearness of Christ as his savior and resolved to join the Baptist Church and make his home a center for Bible study and prayer meetings.

Miller's spiritual experience prompted him to read the Bible with an intense desire to learn. For two years he immersed himself in Bible study and emerged with the firm conviction that its prophecies pointed to sometime between 21 March 1843 and 21 March 1844 as the time for Christ's return.

For more than a decade Miller's belief remained quietly at the center of his personal faith. Not until August 1831 at the age of forty-nine did he begin to preach to others, and then only reluctantly, in response to an invitation from a nearby town. In his first sermon he called listeners to prepare for "Christ's soon return," a claim that he bolstered with proofs of sacred prophecy and secular history.[4] His manner was earnest, his voice strong and mellow, but most of all his proofs were convincing.

He stayed for a week at the request of his hosts to discuss the topic in detail, and more people from neighboring towns came to listen. He returned home to find another invitation to speak to a nearby church, and this time not only was he warmly received but he also succeeded in convincing the minister of the church to accept his views—the first of many ministers who would come to preach Miller's advent message. Those who accepted his views were called "Millerites."

In two years Miller received a Baptist license to preach, and soon he was traveling and preaching his advent message full time. In 1834 he preached thirty-two sermons in twenty-eight days about Christ's imminent return. He wrote a series of articles, which, in 1836, he gathered into a book and published under the title *Evidence from Scripture and History.* The release of the book allowed his message to reach ever widening circles. So influential was his doctrine that the *Boston Times* printed excerpts and reported that Christ would return in five years. A weekly Adventist paper, *Signs of the Times,* was published by a leading Miller supporter. As interest grew, another paper, *The Midnight Cry,* was printed, and ten thousand free copies were distributed each day.

Miller continued traveling and preaching despite generally poor health. His dress was common—he was said to look more like a farmer than a preacher—and he usually paid his own expenses. From October 1839 to April 1841 he traveled an estimated 4,560 miles, preached 627 lectures, and had 5,000 conversions. Though some scoffed at him, unbiased observers saw Miller and his fellow leaders as sincere and respectable.

"'Is the idea itself a vain one?'" asked poet John Greenleaf Whittier. "'Is there no hope that this world-wide prophecy of the human soul, uttered in all climes, in all times, shall yet be fulfilled?'"[5]

Other Millerite ministers were especially successful preaching in a new kind of meeting pioneered by the Methodists—the camp meeting. A camp meeting was a religious service of several days, usually held in a large tent, at which people gathered from far distances. In three years—1842 through 1844—the Millerites held 125 camp meetings, attended by an estimated five hundred thousand persons, with crowds increasing from one thousand to ten thousand as 1843–1844 approached. Whittier, who attended a meeting in New Hampshire, observed that the participants were not fanatical in their behavior but were "sober, intelligent men" and "gentle and pious women."[6]

In twelve years Miller himself gave 4,500 advent lectures to over five hundred thousand people. By May 1844 it was estimated that five million copies of Adventist publications had been distributed. Even so, when the appointed time arrived, the faithful were disappointed in their expectations. Toward the end, many had gathered together on specific dates that had been fixed. Only those who were among the believers could know the depth of their Great Disappointment, as it came to be called.

"Our fondest hopes and expectations were blasted," said Hiram Edson, a prominent Millerite leader, "and such a spirit of weeping came over us as I have never experienced before. The loss of all earthly friends could have been no comparison."[7]

Miller himself remained convinced that Christ would return soon. In consultation with other Adventist leaders he said that much had been learned about the Bible and that the Adventists themselves had learned humility. He died in 1849 still looking for the coming of his Lord.

"If we condemn him (Miller)," wrote Walter Martin, a twentieth-century conservative Christian author, "we must also condemn a large number of internationally known scholars who were among the most highly educated men of their day."[8]

In Bahá'u'lláh's Book of Certitude (Kitáb-i-Íqán), revealed in 1862, several pages are devoted to explaining selected passages of Jesus' prophetic Olivet Discourse. People have often misinterpreted the text of the Bible, Bahá'u'lláh explains, grasping only its literal sense rather than the inner spiritual meanings that were intended. In that same book Bahá'u'lláh declares that His own explanation is no more than "a dewdrop out of the fathomless ocean of the truths treasured" in Jesus' "holy words."[9] In His writings Bahá'u'lláh upholds the truth of the Bible and encourages all to read it. To Muslims He states that its truth is affirmed by the Koran itself.

Appendix 5:
Mírzá Yaḥyá

When Bahá'u'lláh was exiled in 1868, by order of the Ottoman Sulṭán 'Abdu'l-'Azíz, to lifelong imprisonment in the prison-city of Acre, His younger half-brother Mírzá Yaḥyá and a handful of others were sent into confinement in the city of Famagusta on the island of Cyprus. Mírzá

Yaḥyá was later released by the British in 1878 when the island came under their rule. He remained on Cyprus, receiving a pension from the British government. He applied for British citizenship, but his application was denied. Mírzá Yaḥyá died in 1912, having achieved nothing noteworthy. Not one person had converted to his cause, and he was abandoned by those who had initially followed him. His eldest son later sought out 'Abdu'l-Bahá, expressed repentance, and became a Bahá'í, remaining faithful for the rest of his life to the religion his father had striven to extinguish.

Bahá'u'lláh, Who had been so greatly wronged by Mírzá Yaḥyá, addressed him in the Most Holy Book (the Kitáb-i-Aqdas):

> Say: O source of perversion! Abandon thy willful blindness, and speak forth the truth amidst the people. I swear by God that I have wept for thee to see thee following thy selfish passions and renouncing Him Who fashioned thee and brought thee into being. Call to mind the tender mercy of thy Lord, and remember how We nurtured thee by day and by night for service to the Cause. Fear God, and be thou of the truly repentant. Granted that the people were confused about thy station, is it conceivable that thou thyself art similarly confused? Tremble before thy Lord and recall the days when thou didst stand before Our throne, and didst write down the verses that We dictated unto thee—verses sent down by God, the Omnipotent Protector, the Lord of might and power. Beware lest the fire of thy presumptuousness debar thee from attaining to God's Holy Court. Turn unto Him, and fear not because of thy deeds. He, in truth, forgiveth whomsoever He desireth as a bounty on His part; no God is there but Him, the Ever-Forgiving, the All-Bounteous. We admonish thee solely for the sake of God. Shouldst thou accept this counsel, thou wilt have acted to thine own behoof; and shouldst thou reject it, thy Lord, verily, can well dispense with thee, and with all those who, in manifest delusion, have followed thee. Behold! God hath laid hold on him who led thee astray. Return unto God, humble, submissive and lowly; verily, He will put away from thee thy sins, for thy Lord, of a certainty, is the Forgiving, the Mighty, the All-Merciful. (¶184)

Notes

1 / <u>Sh</u>ay<u>kh</u> Maḥmúd's Secret Plan

1. These are not the actual words of the prisoner, but they convey the message He is reported to have given.

2. These are not the actual words of the prisoner, but they convey the message He is reported to have given.

3. Blomfield, *Chosen Highway*, p. 24.

4. Bahá'u'lláh, *Epistle to the Son of the Wolf*, p. 85.

5. Bahá'u'lláh, Súriy-i-Haykal, *Summons of the Lord of Hosts*, ¶192. The shah at this time was Náṣiri'd-Dín <u>Sh</u>áh, who reigned from 1848–96.

6. Ibid., ¶140.

7. Koran 8:30. All references to the Koran are to the Rodwell translation.

2 / The Puppet Show and the Dream

1. See David Ruhe, *Robe of Light*, pp. 29–30.

2. Sources do not agree on Frederick Douglass's date of birth, which is thought to be either 1917 or 1918.

3. <u>Kh</u>adíjih <u>Kh</u>ánum, quoted by 'Abdu'l-Bahá in 'Alí-Akbar Furútan, compiler and editor, *Stories of Bahá'u'lláh*, p. 1.

4. Mírzá Buzurg, quoted by 'Abdu'l-Bahá in I<u>sh</u>ráq-<u>Kh</u>ávarí and 'Abdu'l-Ḥamíd, *Risáliy-i-Ayyám-i-Tis'ih*, pp. 62, 65, 67, in Furútan, *Stories of Bahá'u'lláh*, p. 2.

3 / The Home of Love

1. Nabíl, *Dawn-Breakers*, p. 120.

2. Bahá'u'lláh, quoted by 'Abdu'l-Bahá in Esslemont, *Bahá'u'lláh and the New Era*, p. 35.

3. Ruhe, *Robe of Light*, p. 40.

4. Matthew 24:29, 21. All references to the Bible are to the King James version.

4 / Father of the Poor and Mother of Consolation

1. Crowder, Cootes, and Snellgrove, *Ancient Times*, p. 62.

2. Nabíl, *The Dawn-Breakers*, p. 122.

3. Bahá'u'lláh, *Hidden Words*, Persian, nos. 49, 54.

4. Bahá'u'lláh, the Báb, 'Abdu'l-Bahá, *Bahá'í Prayers*, pp. 39, 42.

5. Quoted by Ḥájí Mírzá Áqásí, in Esslemont, *Bahá'u'lláh and the New Era*, p. 24.

5 / No Time to Lose

1. A. L. M. Nicolas, "Essai sur le <u>Sh</u>ay<u>kh</u>isme," quoted in Périgord, *Translation of French Foot-Notes of the Dawn-Breakers*, p. 1.

2. Bahá'u'lláh, *Gleanings*, p. 66.

3. Nabíl, *Dawn-Breakers,* p. 13.
4. Shaykh Aḥmad, quoted in Nabíl, *Dawn-Breakers,* p. 16.
5. Siyyid Káẓim, quoted in Nabíl, *Dawn-Breakers,* p. 25.
6. Ibid., pp. 41–42.
7. Ibid., pp. 42, 40–41.
8. As reported by Nabíl, *Dawn-Breakers,* p. 44.
9. Siyyid Káẓim, quoted in ibid, p. 45.

6 / The Quest

1. Siyyid Káẓim, quoted in Nabíl, *Dawn-Breakers,* p. 40; see Nabíl, *Dawn-Breakers,* pp. 47–48.
2. Koran 15:46, quoted by the Báb according to Mullá Ḥusayn, as related to Mírzá Aḥmad-i-Qazvíní and recorded in Nabíl, *Dawn-Breakers,* p. 53.
3. Account of Mírzá Ḥusayn as told to Mírzá Aḥmad-i-Qazvíní and recorded in Nabíl, *Dawn-Breakers,* pp. 52–57.
4. Ibid., pp. 59–65.

7 / Witnesses of the Dawn

1. See Nabíl, *Dawn-Breakers,* p. 75.
2. See ibid., p. 79.
3. See ibid., pp. 66–70.
4. See ibid., p. 63; the Báb, quoted in Shoghi Effendi, *God Passes By,* p. 97; the Báb, *Selections from the Writings of the Báb,* p. 168; the Báb, quoted in Shoghi Effendi, *God Passes By,* p. 98.
5. See Nabíl, *Dawn-Breakers,* pp. 86, 92–94.

8 / Noble Descendant of a Noble Father

1. See Gail, *Summon Up Remembrance,* p. 10.
2. Words of Mullá Ḥusayn as recounted by Mullá Muḥammad-i-Mu'allim to Mírzá Músá and recorded in Nabíl, *Dawn-Breakers,* pp. 104–06.
3. See Nabíl, *Dawn-Breakers,* pp. 107–08.

9 / The Mujtahid and the Dervish

1. See Nabíl, *Dawn-Breakers,* pp. 113–17.
2. See ibid., p. 118.
3. Bahá'u'lláh, *Prayers and Meditations,* p. 86.

10 / Awake, Awake!

1. Balyuzi, *The Báb,* p. 71.
2. See Nabíl, *Dawn-Breakers,* pp. 142–43, 85.
3. Account of 'Alíyu'lláhí of the Báb's arrest, as recorded in Nabíl, *Dawn Breakers,* pp. 148–50.
4. See Nabíl, *Dawn-Breakers,* p. 150.

11 / The Scholar and the Governors

1. See Nabíl, *Dawn-Breakers,* pp. 173–75; Koran 7:22.
2. See Nabíl, *Dawn-Breakers,* pp. 176–77.
3. Ibid., pp. 196–97.
4. Ibid., p. 192.
5. Ibid., pp. 212–13.

12 / The Open Mountain and the Grievous Mountain

1. See Koran 79:6–9.
2. See Nabíl, ibid., pp. 260, 262.
3. See ibid., p. 269.

13 / Rage and a Secret Rescue

1. See Nabíl, *Dawn-Breakers,* pp. 81 n2, 273–78, 284.
2. Táhirih, quoted in 'Abdu'l-Bahá, *Memorials of the Faithful,* no. 69.24.

14 / The Blast of the Trumpet

1. See Nabíl, *Dawn-Breakers,* pp. 295–96, 297 n2.
2. Koran, 56:4–6.
3. Abraham Lincoln to A. G. Hodges, letter dated 4 April 1864, reprinted at <http://womhist.binghamton.edu/malesupp/doc4.htm>.
4. Frederick Douglass, "The Rights of Woman," a review of the Woman's Rights Convention held in Seneca Falls, NY, 19–20 July 1848. Originally published in *The North Star,* 28 July 1848. Reprinted at the Women and Social Movements Web site at the State University of New York at Binghamton, <http://womhist.binghamton.edu/malesupp/doc4.htm>.
5. Elizabeth Cady Stanton, quoted by Suzanne Sprague in "From Seneca Falls to Ally McBeal: 150 Years of Women's Rights," aired on KERA 90.1 (Dallas) in March 1999.

15 / The Sermon of Wrath and a Royal Command

1. See Nabíl, *Dawn-Breakers,* pp. 315–16.
2. See ibid., p. 323.

16 / Bandar-Gaz and the Black Standard

1. See Nabíl, *Dawn-Breakers,* p. 324.
2. See ibid., pp. 326–36.
3. Account of Bahá'u'lláh's visit as recounted by Mullá Mírzá Muḥammad-i-Furú<u>gh</u>í and recorded by Nabíl in *Dawn-Breakers,* p. 349.

17 / Danger at Amul

1. See Nabíl, *Dawn-Breakers,* pp. 358–68.
2. See ibid., pp. 369–75, 461.

18 / Courage at Ṭabarsí

1. See Nabíl, *Dawn-Breakers,* pp. 413–14 n2.
2. Account of Mullá Ṣádiq and Mullá Mírzá Muḥammad-i-Furúg͟hí as recorded by Nabíl in *Dawn-Breakers,* pp. 381–82.
3. See ibid., pp. 399–400, 411–12.
4. See ibid., pp. 431–32.
5. Bahá'u'lláh, *Kitáb-i-Íqán,* ¶251.

19 / Embattled

1. See Nabíl, *Dawn-Breakers,* pp. 447–49.
2. Siyyid Káẓim, quoted by Nabíl in ibid., pp. 41–42; the Báb, quoted in Shoghi Effendi, *God Passes By,* pp. 29, 97.
3. Koran 8:30.

20 / No Peace in the City of Tabríz

1. See Nabíl, *Dawn-Breakers,* p. 507, 307–08.
2. See ibid., pp. 509–15.
3. Bahá'u'lláh, *Gleanings,* p. 145; Bahá'u'lláh, *Epistle to the Son of the Wolf,* pp. 119–20.
4. See Nabíl, *Dawn-Breakers,* pp. 556–581; Bahá'u'lláh, *Kitáb-i-Íqán,* ¶250–51.

21 / A Promise Kept in Karbala

1. See Nabíl, *Dawn-Breakers,* p. 591.
2. See ibid., pp. 31–33.

22 / A Plot against the Shah

1. See Nabíl, *Dawn-Breakers,* pp. 599–600 n3.

23 / Prisoner

1. See Nabíl, *Dawn-Breakers,* pp. 602–03.
2. Bahá'u'lláh, *Epistle to the Son of the Wolf,* p. 20.
3. See Nabíl, *Dawn-Breakers,* pp. 607–08.

24 / The Black Pit

1. Words of a household servant as related by Bahíyyih K͟hánum to Lady Blomfield, *Chosen Highway,* pp. 40–41.

2. See Nabíl, *Dawn-Breakers,* pp. 623–26.
3. Ṭáhirih, quoted in Shoghi Effendi, *God Passes By,* p. 75.
4. Sulaymán Náẓim Bey, quoted in Shoghi Effendi, *God Passes By,* p. 76.

25 / Cruel Days

1. Account of Bahá'u'lláh as recorded in Nabíl, *Dawn-Breakers,* pp. 632–634.
2. Account of 'Abdu'l-Bahá as recorded in Balyuzi, *'Abdu'l-Bahá,* p. 11.
3. Account of 'Abdu'l-Bahá as recorded in Nabíl, *Dawn-Breakers,* p. 616.
4. Bahá'u'lláh, *Epistle to the Son of the Wolf,* p. 21.
5. Ibid.

26 / The Mystery of God and His Treasure

1. Bahá'u'lláh, *Epistle to the Son of the Wolf,* p. 22.
2. Bahá'u'lláh, *Summons of the Lord of Hosts,* Súriy-i-Haykal, ¶6.
3. Ibid., ¶6–7.
4. Bahá'u'lláh, *Prayers and Meditations,* p. 21.
5. Ibid., p. 307.
6. The Báb, quoted in Bahá'u'lláh, *Epistle to the Son of the Wolf,* p. 141.
7. See John 16:13.
8. Bahá'u'lláh, *Epistle to the Son of the Wolf,* p. 307.
9. Ruhe, *Robe of Light,* p. 22.
10. Bahá'u'lláh, *Prayers and Meditations,* p. 20.
11. Words of 'Azím as recorded in Nabíl, *Dawn-Breakers,* pp. 634–37.
12. Bahá'u'lláh, quoted in Ruhe, *Robe of Light,* p. 152.
13. Prince Dimitri Dolgorukov, quoted by Bahíyyih Khánum in Lady Blomfield, *Chosen Highway,* pp. 43–44.

27 / Banished

1. See Nabíl, *Dawn-Breakers,* pp. 648–50.
2. Bahá'u'lláh, *Kitáb-i-Íqán,* ¶264.
3. Bahá'u'lláh, *Gleanings,* pp. 121, 110, 111.
4. Ibid., p. 109.

28 / Terrible Journey

1. Bahá'u'lláh, quoted in Shoghi Effendi, *God Passes By,* p. 109.
2. Koran 8:30.
3. Koran 10:26.

29 / Baghdad

1. Nabíl, quoted in Shoghi Effendi, *God Passes By,* p. 113.

30 / Thousands of Oceans of Light

1. Bahá'u'lláh, quoted by Mírzá Áqá Ján in Shoghi Effendi, *God Passes By,* p. 116; Mírzá Áqá Ján, quoted in Shoghi Effendi, *God Passes By,* p. 116.

31 / The Dark Campaign

1. Bahá'u'lláh, quoted in Shoghi Effendi, *God Passes By,* p. 115; Bahá'u'lláh, *Kitáb-i-Íqán,* ¶277.
2. Bahá'u'lláh, *Kitáb-i-Íqán,* ¶277.
3. Shoghi Effendi, *God Passes By,* p. 114.
4. Bahá'u'lláh, *Kitáb-i-Íqán,* ¶277.
5. Bahá'u'lláh, quoted in Shoghi Effendi, *God Passes By,* p. 119.
6. Ibid.
7. Ibid., p. 118.
8. Bahá'u'lláh, *Kitáb-i-Íqán,* ¶278.

32 / Alone in the Wilderness

1. Bahá'u'lláh, quoted in Shoghi Effendi, *God Passes By,* p. 120.
2. Ibid., p. 119.
3. Bahá'u'lláh, *Kitáb-i-Íqán,* ¶278.
4. Bahá'u'lláh, quoted in Shoghi Effendi, *God Passes By,* p. 118.
5. Ibid., pp. 120–21; Bahá'u'lláh, *Kitáb-i-Íqán,* ¶278.

33 / The Nameless One

1. Bahíyyih Khánum, quoted in Lady Blomfield, *Chosen Highway,* p. 54.

34 / A Joyful Naw-Rúz

1. Bahá'u'lláh, *Prayers and Meditations,* p. 243.
2. Bahá'u'lláh, quoted in Shoghi Effendi, *God Passes By,* p. 125.
3. Bahá'u'lláh, quoted in 'Abdu'l-Bahá, *Traveler's Narrative,* p. 41.
4. Bahá'u'lláh, quoted in Balyuzi, *Bahá'u'lláh: The King of Glory,* p. 134.

35 / Purity within Purity

1. 'Abdul-Bahá, quoted in Ruhe, "Pen of Glory" (unpublished manuscript, 2004), chapter 3, p. 15.
2. Áqá Siyyid Mujtahid, quoted by Bahíyyih Khánum in Lady Blomfield, *Chosen Highway,* p. 56.
3. Zaynu'l-'Abidín Khán, quoted in Shoghi Effendi, *God Passes By,* p. 135.
4. Bahá'u'lláh, quoted in Shoghi Effendi, *God Passes By,* pp. 135–136.
5. Bahá'u'lláh, *Tablets of Bahá'u'lláh,* p. 149.
6. Ḥájí Mírzá Ḥaydar-'Alí, quoted in Taherzadeh, *Revelation of Bahá'u'lláh,* 1:29.
7. Siyyid Asadu'lláh-i-Qumí, quoted in ibid., 1:35.

36 / Unlocking the Doors of Heaven

1. Bahá'u'lláh, *Hidden Words,* p. 3.
2. Ibid., Arabic, no. 3.
3. Ibid., Arabic, no. 11.
4. Ibid., Arabic, no. 12.
5. Bahá'u'lláh, *Tablets of Bahá'u'lláh,* pp. 173, 156.
6. Bahá'u'lláh, quoted in Taherzadeh, *Revelation of Bahá'u'lláh,* 1:22–23.
7. Bahá'u'lláh, *Hidden Words,* Arabic, no. 11.
8. Ibid., Persian, no. 32.
9. Ibid., Arabic, no. 22.
10. Ibid., Persian, no. 72.
11. Ibid., Arabic, no. 14.
12. Ibid., Arabic, no. 68.
13. Ibid., Persian, no. 76.
14. Bahá'u'lláh, *Gleanings,* pp. 315–16.
15. Bahá'u'lláh, quoted by Nabíl in Shoghi Effendi, *God Passes By,* p. 137.

37 / The Shaykh and the Assassin

1. Bahá'u'lláh, quoted in Balyuzi, *Bahá'u'lláh: The King of Glory,* p. 148.
2. Bahá'u'lláh, quoted in 'Abdu'l-Bahá, *Some Answered Questions,* p. 29.
3. Ibid.

38 / The Eldest Uncle's Questions

1. Bahá'u'lláh, *Epistle to the Son of the Wolf,* p. 53.
2. Bahá'u'lláh, *Hidden Words,* Persian, no. 80.
3. Bahá'u'lláh, quoted in Balyuzi, *Bahá'u'lláh: The King of Glory,* p. 151.
4. Bahá'u'lláh, quoted by Mírzá Áqá Ján in Shoghi Effendi, *God Passes By,* p. 138.
5. Freedman, *Lincoln: A Photobiography,* pp. 103–04.
6. J. C. Furnas, quoted in Taylor, *Harriet Tubman,* p. 63; Taylor, ibid.

39 / A Paradox Resolved

1. Bahá'u'lláh, *Kitáb-i-Íqán,* ¶109, ¶16.
2. Ibid., ¶67–68, ¶106.
3. Ibid., ¶109, ¶73, ¶109.
4. Bahá'u'lláh, *Gleanings,* p. 66; Bahá'u'lláh, *Kitáb-i-Íqán,* ¶14.
5. Bahá'u'lláh, *Kitáb-i-Íqán,* ¶15, ¶4; Koran 40:5, quoted in Bahá'u'lláh, *Kitáb-i-Íqán,* ¶4.
6. Ibid., ¶114.
7. Ibid., ¶113–14.
8. Ibid., ¶117.
9. Ibid., ¶72, ¶257, ¶262.
10. Mírzá Sa'íd Khán, quoted in Shoghi Effendi, *God Passes By,* p. 146.

11. Shoghi Effendi, *God Passes By,* p. 131.
12. Bahá'u'lláh, quoted in ibid., p. 147.

40 / The Garden of Paradise

1. Bahá'u'lláh, quoted in Shoghi Effendi, *God Passes By,* 149.
2. Bahá'u'lláh, *Gleanings,* pp. 27, 31.
3. Mírzá Áqá Ján, quoted in Shoghi Effendi, *God Passes By,* p. 116.
4. Bahá'u'lláh, *Tablets of Bahá'u'lláh,* p. 78; Bahá'u'lláh, quoted in Shoghi Effendi, *God Passes By,* p. 153.
5. Námiq-Pá<u>sh</u>á, quoted in Shoghi Effendi, *God Passes By,* p. 150; Bahá'u'lláh, quoted in ibid.
6. Bahá'u'lláh, quoted in David Ruhe, "Pen of Glory" (unpublished manuscript, 2004), chapter 3, p. 3.

41 / One Hundred and Ten Days

1. Námiq Pá<u>sh</u>á, quoted by 'Abdu'l-Bahá in Shoghi Effendi, *God Passes By,* p. 150.
2. Bahá'u'lláh, quoted in Balyuzi, *Bahá'u'lláh: The King of Glory,* p. 183.
3. Mírzá Yaḥyá, quoted in Shoghi Effendi, *God Passes By,* p. 155.

42 / The Sultan's Command

1. Adib Taherzadeh, *Revelation of Bahá'u'lláh,* 2:5; Bahá'u'lláh, *Gleanings,* p. 126.
2. Bahá'u'lláh, quoted by Bahíyyih <u>Kh</u>ánum in Lady Blomfield, *Chosen Highway,* p. 59.
3. Words of Bahá'u'lláh as reported by Áqá Riḍá, quoted in Balyuzi, *Bahá'u'lláh: The King of Glory,* p. 202.
4. Bahá'u'lláh, quoted in ibid., p. 203.
5. Words of 'Álí Pá<u>sh</u>á as reported by <u>Sh</u>amsí Big, quoted in Shoghi Effendi, *God Passes By,* p. 160.
6. Bahá'u'lláh, quoted in Shoghi Effendi, *God Passes By,* pp. 160–61.

43 / The Poisoned Cup

1. Bahá'u'lláh, *Summons of the Lord of Hosts,* Súriy-i-Mulúk, ¶81.
2. Bahá'u'lláh, in *Bahá'í Prayers,* p. 309.

44 / The Most Great Separation

1. Mírzá Yaḥyá, quoted in Ustád Muḥammad-'Alíy-i Salmání, *My Memories of Bahá'u'lláh,* p. 51.
2. Ibid.
3. Ustád Muḥammad-'Alíy-i Salmání, *My Memories of Bahá'u'lláh,* p. 52.
4. Ibid., p. 53.
5. Mírzá Yaḥyá, quoted by Ḥájí Mírzá Ḥaydar-'Alí, in Adib Taherzadeh, *Covenant of*

Bahá'u'lláh, p. 86.

6. Bahá'u'lláh, quoted in Shoghi Effendi, *God Passes By,* p. 163.
7. Koran 8:30.

45 / He Who Feareth No One

1. Bahá'u'lláh, quoted in Shoghi Effendi, *God Passes By,* pp. 168–69.
2. The Báb, quoted in Bahá'u'lláh, *Epistle to the Son of the Wolf,* p. 160; see *Selections from the Writings of the Báb,* p. 92.
3. Bahá'u'lláh, quoted in Shoghi Effendi, *God Passes By,* p. 170.

46 / O Kings of the Earth!

1. Bahá'u'lláh, *Summons of the Lord of Hosts,* Súriy-i-Mulúk, ¶1; Bahá'u'lláh, *Kitáb-i-Aqdas,* ¶82.
2. Bahá'u'lláh, *Summons of the Lord of Hosts,* Súriy-i-Mulúk, ¶2.
3. Ibid., ¶4.
4. Ibid., ¶21.
5. Ibid., ¶7.
6. Ibid., ¶8, ¶10.
7. Ibid., ¶11.
8. Ibid., ¶13, ¶14.
9. Ibid., ¶110.
10. Ibid., ¶88.
11. Ibid., ¶12.

47 / Destination Unknown

1. Words of Bahá'u'lláh as reported by Áqá Ḥusayn-i-Á<u>sh</u>chí, quoted in Balyuzi, *Bahá'u'lláh: The King of Glory,* p. 256.
2. Words of Bahá'u'lláh as reported by Áqá Riḍá, quoted in Shoghi Effendi, *God Passes By,* p. 181.
3. Shoghi Effendi, *God Passes By,* p. 186.
4. Bahá'u'lláh, quoted in Shoghi Effendi, *God Passes By,* p. 184.

48 / The Most Great Prison

1. Bahá'u'lláh, quoted in Shoghi Effendi, *God Passes By,* p. 186; Bahá'u'lláh, *Summons of the Lord of Hosts,* Súriy-i-Haykal, ¶140.
2. Bahá'u'lláh, *Summons of the Lord of Hosts,* Lawḥ-i-Ra'ís, ¶4.

50 / For the Healing of all the World

1. Bahá'u'lláh, *Summons of the Lord of Hosts,* ¶158–59.
2. Napoleon III, quoted by Taherzadeh in *Revelation of Bahá'u'lláh,* 3:110.
3. Bahá'u'lláh, *Summons of the Lord of Hosts,* Súriy-i-Haykal, ¶138.

4. Ibid., ¶102, ¶118.
5. Ibid., ¶171, ¶172.
6. Ibid., ¶173.
7. Queen Victoria, quoted in Shoghi Effendi, *Promised Day Is Come,* ¶163.
8. Bahá'u'lláh, *Summons of the Lord of Hosts,* Súriy-i-Haykal, ¶174.
9. Ibid, ¶175.
10. Ibid, ¶176.
11. Bahá'u'lláh, quoted in Taherzadeh, *Revelation of Bahá'u'lláh,* 3:180.
12. Ibid., 3:181.

51 / Into the Mouth of the Serpent

1. Words of Badí' from the account of Ḥájí Sháh-Muḥammad as recorded by Ḥájí Mírzá Ḥaydar-'Alí, quoted in Taherzadeh, *Revelation of Bahá'u'lláh,* 3:183.
2. Words of Badí' from the account of Ḥájí 'Alí as recorded by Ḥájí Mírzá Ḥaydar-'Alí, quoted in Taherzadeh, *Revelation of Bahá'u'lláh,* 3:183–84.
3. Koran 27:22.
4. From the account of Káẓim Khán as recorded by Muḥammad-Valí Khán, quoted in Taherzadeh, *Revelation of Bahá'u'lláh,* 3:187–191.

52 / The Greatest Gift

1. Balyuzi, *Bahá'u'lláh: The King of Glory,* p. 311; Taherzadeh, *Revelation of Bahá'u'lláh,* 3:17.
2. Bahá'u'lláh, quoted in Taherzadeh, *Revelation of Bahá'u'lláh,* 3:207.
3. Words of Bahá'u'lláh and Mírzá Mihdí as recollected by Áqá Ḥusayn, quoted in Balyuzi, *Bahá'u'lláh: The King of Glory,* p. 311.
4. Bahá'u'lláh, quoted in Shoghi Effendi, *God Passes By,* p. 188; words of Bahá'u'lláh as recollected by Áqá Ḥusayn, quoted in Balyuzi, *Bahá'u'lláh: The King of Glory,* p. 311.
5. Bahá'u'lláh, quoted in Taherzadeh, *Revelation of Bahá'u'lláh,* 3:210.
6. Bahá'u'lláh, quoted in Shoghi Effendi, *God Passes By,* p. 188; Bahá'u'lláh, *Prayers and Meditations,* p. 35.

53 / The Whisperings of Satan

1. Bahá'u'lláh, in a tablet translated by Browne, *Materials for the Study of the Bábí Religion,* pp. 53–54, quoted in Balyuzi, *Bahá'u'lláh: The King of Glory,* p. 325.
2. See Bahá'u'lláh, in *Bahá'í Prayers,* "Fire Tablet," pp. 312–18.

54 / The Keys of My Mercy

1. See Shoghi Effendi, *God Passes By,* p. 190.
2. Bahá'u'lláh, quoted in ibid.
3. Bahá'u'lláh, *Tablets of Bahá'u'lláh,* pp. 176, 177.
4. Bahá'u'lláh, quoted in Taherzadeh, *Revelation of Bahá'u'lláh,* 3:279.
5. Bahá'u'lláh, quoted in Shoghi Effendi, *God Passes By,* p. 216; Bahá'u'lláh, *Kitáb-i-Aqdas,* ¶2–3.

6. Bahá'u'lláh, Kitáb-i-Aqdas, ¶5.
7. Ibid., ¶1.
8. Ibid., ¶125, ¶123.
9. Bahá'u'lláh, *Tablets of Bahá'u'lláh,* p. 176.
10. Bahá'u'lláh, quoted by the Universal House of Justice in introduction to Bahá'u'lláh, *Kitáb-i-Aqdas,* p. 6.
11. Bahá'u'lláh, *Kitáb-i-Aqdas,* ¶37; Bahá'u'lláh, *Gleanings,* p. 100.

56 / Two Birds of the Nest of Thy Love

1. See Munírih Khánum, quoted in Lady Blomfield, *Chosen Highway,* pp. 84–85.
2. Khadíjih Bagum, quoted in Taherzadeh, *Revelation of Bahá'u'lláh,* 2:386.
3. Mírzá Músá, quoted by Munírih Khánum in "Episodes in the Life of Munírih Khánum," *The Bahá'í World,* 8:262; Bahá'u'lláh, quoted in ibid.
4. Khájih 'Abbúd, quoted by Munírih Khánum in Lady Blomfield, *Chosen Highway,* p. 88.
5. Khájih 'Abbúd, quoted in Balyuzi, *Bahá'u'lláh: The King of Glory,* p. 348.
6. Munírih Khánum, "Episodes in the Life of Munírih Khánum," *The Bahá'í World,* 8:262.
7. Munírih Khánum, quoted in Lady Blomfield, *Chosen Highway,* p. 89.
8. Bahá'u'lláh, quoted in Balyuzi, *Bahá'u'lláh: The King of Glory,* p. 348.
9. Munírih Khánum, "Episodes in the Life of Munírih Khánum," *The Bahá'í World,* 8:262.
10. 'Abdu'l-Bahá, *Selections from the Writings of 'Abdu'l-Bahá,* ¶92.1, 92.3.
11. See Bahá'u'lláh, *Bahá'í Prayers,* p. 188; Bahá'u'lláh, *Kitáb-i-Aqdas,* Question no. 3, pp. 105–06.

57 / The Hand of God

1. Bahá'u'lláh, quoted by Ḥusayn-i-Áshchí in Taherzadeh, *Revelation of Bahá'u'lláh,* 3:411.
2. Bahá'u'lláh, *Kitáb-i-Aqdas,* ¶84, ¶83.
3. Bahá'u'lláh, quoted in 'Abdu'l-Bahá, *Memorials of the Faithful,* p. 68.
4. Bahá'u'lláh, quoted in Esslemont, *Bahá'u'lláh and the New Era,* p. 35.

58 / Oasis

1. See 'Abdu'l-Bahá, quoted in Esslemont, *Bahá'u'lláh and the New Era,* pp. 35–36.
2. Bahá'u'lláh, *Epistle to the Son of the Wolf,* p. 72; Bahá'u'lláh, quoted in Shoghi Effendi, *God Passes By,* p. 219.

59 / The King of Martyrs and the Beloved of Martyrs

1. Mírzá Ḥasan, quoted in Taherzadeh, *Revelation of Bahá'u'lláh,* 4:76.
2. Bahá'u'lláh, *Tablets of Bahá'u'lláh,* p. 206.

3. Bahá'u'lláh, quoted in Taherzadeh, *Revelation of Bahá'u'lláh,* 4:89.
4. Bahá'u'lláh, *Tablets of Bahá'u'lláh,* pp. 215–216.
5. Ibid., p. 212.
6. Ibid., p. 205.

60 / Blessed Is the Place

1. Bahá'u'lláh, quoted in Taherzadeh, *Revelation of Bahá'u'lláh,* 4:316.
2. Bahá'u'lláh, quoted in Shoghi Effendi, *God Passes By,* p. 193; 'Údí Khammár, quoted in Taherzadeh, *Revelation of Bahá'u'lláh,* 4:104.
3. Isaiah 2:2.
4. Bahá'u'lláh, quoted in Esslemont, *Bahá'u'lláh and the New Era,* p. 38.
5. Bahá'u'lláh, *Epistle to the Son of the Wolf,* pp. 25–26.

61 / To Conquer the Cities of the Hearts

1. 'Abdu'l-Bahá, *Memorials of the Faithful,* p. 16.
2. Ibid., p. 17.
3. Bahá'u'lláh, *Epistle to the Son of the Wolf,* p. 24.
4. Ibid., pp. 25, 55.
5. Bahá'u'lláh, quoted in Taherzadeh, *Revelation of Bahá'u'lláh,* 4:277
6. Bahá'u'lláh, quoted by Ṭubá Khánum in Lady Blomfield, *Chosen Highway,* p. 98.
7. Ibid.

62 / The Master

1. Bahá'u'lláh, quoted by Ḥájí Mírzá Ḥabíbu'lláh-i-Afnán in Taherzadeh, *Covenant of Bahá'u'lláh,* p. 139.
2. Bahá'u'lláh, quoted by Mírzá Maḥmúd-i-Káshání in Taherzadeh, *Covenant of Bahá'u'lláh,* p. 138.
3. Bahá'u'lláh, quoted by Shoghi Effendi in *God Passes By,* p. 242.
4. See account of Ḥájí Mírzá Ḥabíbu'lláh-i-Afnán, quoted in Taherzadeh, *Covenant of Bahá'u'lláh,* pp. 139–40.
5. Bahá'u'lláh, quoted by Ḥájí Mírzá Ḥaydar-'Alí in Taherzadeh, *Revelation of Bahá'u'lláh,* 4:5.
6. See account of Ṭúbá Khánum, in Lady Blomfield, *Chosen Highway,* pp. 100–101.
7. Ibid., p. 101.
8. Bahá'u'lláh, *Tablets of Bahá'u'lláh,* pp. 227–28.
9. See Lady Blomfield, *Chosen Highway,* p. 100.
10. Bahá'u'lláh, quoted in Shoghi Effendi, *World Order of Bahá'u'lláh,* p. 135.
11. Ibid.
12. Ibid.

63 / O Most Exalted Leaf!

1. Bahá'u'lláh, quoted in Shoghi Effendi, *God Passes By,* p. 108.
2. Bahá'u'lláh, quoted in Shoghi Effendi, *This Decisive Hour,* no. 64.14.

3. Ibid., no. 64.13.
4. Ibid., no. 64.16.

64 / These Fruitless Strifes, These Ruinous Wars

1. Edward Granville Browne, "The Bábís of Persia," *Journal of the Royal Asiatic Society,"* 1889, p. 933.
2. Ibid.
3. Edward Granville Browne, quoted in Balyuzi, *Edward Granville Browne and the Bahá'í Faith,* p. 56.
4. Ibid.
5. Bahá'u'lláh, quoted in ibid., p. 57.
6. Freedman, *Indian Chiefs,* p. 4.
7. Ibid., p. 6.
8. *Kingfisher Illustrated History of the World,* p. 620.
9. Abraham Lincoln Online, "Second Inaugural Address," <http://showcase.netins.net/web/creative/lincoln/speeches/inaug2.htm>.
10. Bahá'u'lláh, *Epistle to the Son of the Wolf,* p. 34.

65 / The King of Days

1. Bahá'u'lláh, quoted by Edward Granville Browne in Balyuzi, *Edward Granville Browne and the Bahá'í Faith,* p. 57.
2. Bahá'u'lláh, *Epistle to the Son of the Wolf,* p. 14.
3. Bahá'u'lláh, *Tablets of Bahá'u'lláh,* p. 165.
4. Bahá'u'lláh, *Summons of the Lord of Hosts,* Súriy-i-Haykal, ¶182.
5. Bahá'u'lláh, *Kitáb-i-Aqdas,* ¶189.
6. Bahá'u'lláh, *Tablets of Bahá'u'lláh,* p. 166.
7. Bahá'u'lláh, *Gleanings,* p. 196, 142.
8. Bahá'u'lláh, *Kitáb-i-Aqdas,* ¶88.
9. Bahá'u'lláh, *Summons of the Lord of Hosts,* Súriy-i-Haykal, ¶117; Isaiah 2:4, 11:9.
10. Black Elk, in Niehardt, *Black Elk Speaks,* p. 29.
11. Ibid., p. 33.
12. Isaiah 2:2–3.

66 / The Holy Mountain and the Martyrs of Yazd

1. Bahá'u'lláh, quoted in Esslemont, *Bahá'u'lláh and the New Era,* p. 34.
2. Bahá'u'lláh, *Kitáb-i-Íqán,* ¶272.
3. Bahá'u'lláh, quoted in Shoghi Effendi, *World Order of Bahá'u'lláh,* p. 124.
4. Bahá'u'lláh, *Gleanings,* p. 80.
5. Ibid., p. 81.
6. Ibid., pp. 85, 86.
7. Bahá'u'lláh, *Kitáb-i-Íqán,* ¶20.

8. Ruhe, *Door of Hope,* p. 192.

9. Bahá'u'lláh, quoted in Taherzadeh, *Revelation of Bahá'u'lláh,* 4:349–50.

10. Matthew 7:12; tradition attributed to Muḥammad, <http://www.islamworld.net/nawawi.html#hadith40>; Bahá'u'lláh, *Gleanings,* p. 128.

11. Bahá'u'lláh, *Tablets of Bahá'u'lláh,* p. 125.

12. Ibid., p. 171.

13. Bahá'u'lláh, *Summons of the Lord of Hosts,* Súriy-i-Haykal, ¶63; Bahá'u'lláh, quoted in Shoghi Effendi, *God Passes By,* p. 99.

67 / A Pattern for the Future

1. Bahá'u'lláh, *Tablets of Bahá'u'lláh,* p. 4.

2. Ibid., pp. 4–5.

3. Bahá'u'lláh, *Summons of the Lord of Hosts,* Súriy-i-Haykal, ¶63.

4. Bahá'u'lláh, in *Compilation of Compilations,* 1: nos. 170, 167, 168.

5. Bahá'u'lláh, in *The Local Spiritual Assembly,* p. 6.

6. 'Abdu'l-Bahá, *Selections from the Writings of 'Abdu'l-Bahá,* no. 38.5.

7. Bahá'u'lláh, *Kitáb-i-Aqdas,* ¶181.

8. Bahá'u'lláh, *The Hidden Words,* Arabic, no. 69.

9. Bahá'u'lláh, *Epistle to the Son of the Wolf,* p. 87; Bahá'u'lláh, quoted in Shoghi Effendi, *God Passes By,* p. 212.

10. Bahá'u'lláh, *Gleanings,* p. 99.

11. Ibid.

12. Ibid.

68 / The Sun of Bahá Has Set

1. Bahá'u'lláh, quoted in Shoghi Effendi, *God Passes By,* p. 222.

2. Bahá'u'lláh, quoted in Taherzadeh, *Covenant of Bahá'u'lláh,* p. 149.

3. Munírih Khánum, quoted in Lady Blomfield, *Chosen Highway,* p. 106.

4. 'Abdu'l-Bahá, quoted by Shoghi Effendi in *God Passes By,* p. 222.

5. Bahá'u'lláh, quoted by Ṭúbá Khánum in Lady Blomfield, *Chosen Highway,* p. 100.

69 / An Excellent and Priceless Heritage

1. Bahá'u'lláh, *Tablets of Bahá'u'lláh,* p. 219.

2. Bahá'u'lláh, *Summons of the Lord of Hosts,* Súriy-i-Haykal, ¶63; quoted in Shoghi Effendi, *God Passes By,* p. 99.

3. Bahá'u'lláh, *Kitáb-i-Aqdas,* ¶178.

4. 'Abdu'l-Bahá, quoted in Shoghi Effendi, *World Order of Bahá'u'lláh,* p. 169.

5. Bahá'u'lláh, *Kitáb-i-Aqdas,* ¶38.

6. Bahá'u'lláh, *Epistle to the Son of the Wolf,* p. 44.

7. 'Abdu'l-Bahá, *Selections from the Writings of 'Abdu'l-Bahá,* ¶5.1.

8. Bahá'u'lláh, *Kitáb-i-Aqdas,* ¶53.

9. Shoghi Effendi, *God Passes By,* pp. 93–94.

10. Bahá'u'lláh, quoted by Ṭúbá Khánum in Lady Blomfield, *Chosen Highway,* p. 100.

Appendix 4: Millennial Christians

1. Meister, *Year of the Lord,* p. 19.
2. George Bush, quoted in Meister, *Year of the Lord,* p. 28.
3. Meister, *Year of the Lord,* p. 17.
4. Meister, Ibid., p. 21.
5. John Greenleaf Whittier, quoted in Meister, *Year of the Lord,* p. 18.
6. Ibid., p. 33.
7. Hiram Edson, quoted in Meister, *Year of the Lord,* p. 33.
8. Walter Martin, quoted in Sours, *Prophecies of Jesus,* p. 184 n.
9. Bahá'u'lláh, *Kitáb-i-Íqán,* ¶27.

Glossary

aba. A loose, sleeveless, cloak-like outer garment worn by men.

'Abdu'l-Bahá. *Servant of Bahá:* the title assumed by 'Abbás Effendi (1844–1921), the eldest son and successor of Bahá'u'lláh and the Center of His Covenant.

'Abdu'l-Vahháb. A shopkeeper from Shiraz who embraced the Bábí Cause and was imprisoned with Bahá'u'lláh in the Black Pit of Tehran. Bahá'u'lláh gave him His own shoes to wear on the way to his execution.

ablutions. The washing of one's hands and face before prayer.

Abraham. Considered by Bahá'ís to be a Prophet, or Messenger of God, He is also recognized as the founder of monotheism and the father of the Jewish and Arab peoples. Muḥammad, the Báb, and Bahá'u'lláh are among His descendants.

Acre. Also called 'Akká or Akko. A four-thousand-year-old seaport in northern Israel surrounded by fortress-like walls facing the sea. In the mid-1800s it was a penal colony to which the worst criminals of the Ottoman Empire were sent. In 1868 Bahá'u'lláh and His family and companions were exiled to Acre by Sulṭán 'Abdu'l-'Azíz.

Adrianople. Present-day Edirne, Turkey; designated by Bahá'u'lláh as the "remote prison" when He was exiled there in 1863. It was the furthest point from His homeland that He reached and the first time in known history that a Messenger of God lived on the European continent.

A.H. Abbreviation for *Anno Hegirae,* Latin for "in the year of the Hegira," used to indicate a date reckoned according to the Muslim calendar, which began in 622 A.D. with Muḥammad's emigration from Mecca to Medina. The Muslim calendar is a lunar calendar with twelve months of twenty-nine or thirty days.

Alexander II, Czar. Emperor of Russia from 1855 to 1881. He instigated a number of reforms in his country, including the emancipation of the serfs. He was assassinated after a period of repression that instigated a surge of revolutionary terrorism.

Amru'lláh. Literally *the Cause of God;* also *the Command of God.* Name given to the house in which Bahá'u'lláh lived in Adrianople.

andarún. Private inner rooms where the women of a household resided according to Persian custom.

Anís. Literally *Close Companion.* Surname of Muḥammad-'Alíy-i-Zunúzí, the youth who was martyred with the Báb in 1850.

Áqá. *Master;* an honorific title roughly equivalent to the English "Sir" or "Mister."

Ásíyih Khánum. Wife of Bahá'u'lláh and mother of 'Abdu'l-Bahá, Bahíyyih Khánum, and Mírzá Mihdí. She married Bahá'u'lláh in 1835, accompanied Him throughout all of His exiles, and died in 1886. Bahá'u'lláh addressed her as Navváb (an honorific implying "Grace" or "Highness") and designated her as the "Most Exalted Leaf" and His "perpetual consort in all the worlds of God."

Azalí. Follower of Ṣubḥ-i-Azal, or **Mírzá Yaḥyá.**

'Azím. Literally *Great One;* a title given by the Báb to one of His disciples who later was instrumental in the plot against the shah. He refused to implicate Bahá'u'lláh falsely in the crime, although he knew that his refusal would result in his own death.

Báb, the. Literally *the Gate:* title assumed by Siyyid 'Alí-Muḥammad (20 October 1819–9 July 1850) after declaring His mission in Shiraz in 1844. The Báb's station is twofold: He is a Messenger of God and founder of the Bábí Faith, and He is the herald of Bahá'u'lláh.

Bábí. Follower of the Báb.

Badí'. Literally *unique, wonderful:* title given by Bahá'u'lláh to the seventeen-year-old youth who delivered Bahá'u'lláh's tablet to Náṣiri'd-Dín Sháh. Bahá'u'lláh praised his heroism and gave him the title "Pride of Martyrs."

Bahá'u'lláh. Literally *the Glory of God:* title of Mírzá Ḥusayn-'Alí of Núr (12 November 1817–29 May 1892), founder of the Bahá'í Faith.

Bahíyyih Khánum. (1846–1932) The saintly daughter of Bahá'u'lláh and Ásíyih Khánum who beseeched her father to allow her to remain unmarried in order to devote herself to the service of His Faith. Bahá'u'lláh gave her the title of "the Greatest Holy Leaf," and she was designated as the outstanding heroine of the Bahá'í Dispensation.

Bahjí. Literally *delight:* name of Bahá'u'lláh's last residence and the area northeast of the city of Acre where it is located. Now His shrine, it is the point to which Bahá'ís turn in prayer.

bastinado. A form of corporal punishment in which the soles of the feet are exposed and beaten with a stick.

Bayán. Literally *Explanation, exposition, utterance.* The Persian Bayán, revealed by the Báb in the fortress of Máh-Kú, is His major work. It contains His laws as well as numerous references to "Him Whom God will make manifest" (Bahá'u'lláh).

Beloved of Martyrs, the. Title given to Mírzá Muḥammad-Ḥusayn, who was martyred along with his brother Mírzá Muḥammad-Ḥasan—known as the King of the Martyrs—at the order of Shaykh Muḥammad-Báqir of Isfahan. See also **King of Martyrs.**

bírúní. Outer quarters, or men's quarters, in a Persian home.

Black Elk. (1863–1950) An Oglala Lakota Sioux Indian who was a holy man among the Lakota. He had a prophetic vision about the destiny of his people.

Black Pit. (Síyáh-Chál) The subterranean dungeon of Tehran in which Bahá'u'lláh was imprisoned August–December 1852 and in which He received the first intimations of His divine mission.

Black Standard. According to Islamic tradition, the flag alluded to by Muḥammad that would one day signify the advent of the promised **Mihdí.**

Brown, Edward Granville. The Cambridge scholar who studied and wrote about the Bábí and Bahá'í Faiths and who met Bahá'u'lláh in 1890 at Bahjí.

Buddha. Literally *Enlightened One:* title given to Siddhartha Guatama (c. 6th–c. 4th century B.C.), Whom Bahá'ís consider to be a Prophet, or Messenger of God. He is recognized as the founder of Buddhism.

caravansary. A Middle Eastern inn surrounding a court in which caravans can rest at night.

Christ. (c. 6–4 B.C.–A.D. 30) Recognized by Bahá'ís as a Prophet, or Messenger of God, and the founder of Christianity. The Bahá'í writings often refer to Christ as "the Spirit of God" and "the Son."

circumambulation. Literally *to circle on foot, especially ritualistically.* A Muslim custom by which one expresses devotion for the Prophets of God or other holy souls.

Constantinople. Present-day Istanbul, Turkey.

Covenant. A pact that involves obligations by both parties. According to Bahá'u'lláh, God has always guided and instructed humanity through a succession of Divine Messengers, Whom humanity has the obligation to accept and obey. This is called the *Greater Covenant.* The *Lesser Covenant* is that made between a Messenger and His followers. Bahá'u'lláh instructed His followers in His will and testament to turn to 'Abdu'l-Bahá as the perfect exemplar and sole interpreter of His teachings and provided for a structure of governance.

dervish. Literally *beggar, poor one:* the name given to one of many orders of religious mendicants and Islamic mystics.

Divine Lote-Tree. A reference to the tree beyond which there is no passing—in ancient times, the tree that Arabs planted to mark the end of a road. In Islam, the term symbolizes the point in the heavens beyond which neither humans nor angels can pass in their approach to God, thus delimiting the bounds of divine knowledge as revealed to humankind. In Bahá'í usage it is a reference to the Messenger of God—i.e., Bahá'u'lláh.

Douglass, Frederick. (1817–95) An African-American political leader who was at the forefront of the abolition movement and the women's rights movement.

farmán. An order, command, or royal decree.

Fatḥ'u'lláh. One of three Bábís who together attempted but failed to assassinate the shah in 1852, leading to a wave of persecution against the Bábís and resulting in Bahá'u'lláh's arrest and imprisonment in Tehran.

Fatḥ-'Alí Sh͟áh. A shah of Persia during the Qajar dynasty whose reign lasted from 1798 to 1834. He gave the title *"Buzurg,"* meaning "Great," to Bahá'u'lláh's father.

Garden of Riḍván *(Paradise).* Name given by Bahá'u'lláh to the Garden of Najíbíyyih in Baghdad, where He publicly declared His mission in April 1863. He later gave the same name to the Na'mayn Garden near Acre.

Gabriel. In Muslim belief, the angel who brought God's revelation to the Prophet Muḥammad.

Galilee. A hilly region in northern Israel, the site of Jesus' ministry.

grand vizier. Prime minister.

Greatest Branch. A title given by Bahá'u'lláh to 'Abdu'l-Bahá emphasizing 'Abdu'l-Bahá's station in relation to Bahá'u'lláh's.

Greatest Holy Leaf. See **Bahíyyih Khánum.**

Guardian. The position to which Shoghi Rabbání (1897–1957), great-grandson of Bahá'u'lláh and eldest grandson of 'Abdu'l-Bahá, was appointed by 'Abdu'l-Bahá in his will and testament. Shoghi Rabbání (or "Shoghi Effendi," as he is known to Bahá'ís) assumed the office upon 'Abdu'l-Bahá's passing in 1921. The Guardian's chief functions were to interpret the writings of Bahá'u'lláh, the Báb, and 'Abdu'l-Bahá and to be the permanent head of the Universal House of Justice.

Ḥájí Mírzá Áqásí. (d. 1849) Prime minister of Persia under Muḥammad Sháh, he prevented the meeting of Muḥammad Sháh and the Báb, ordered the successive imprisonments of the Báb in Máh-Kú and Chihríq, and saw to the arrest of Bahá'u'lláh. He fell from power after the death of Muḥammad Sháh and died poor and abandoned.

Ḥájí Sulaymán Khán. A courageous Bábí sent by Bahá'u'lláh to Tabríz to recover the body of the Báb. He was himself martyred in Tehran two years after the Báb.

hajj. Pilgrimage taken by Muslims to Mecca at least once in a lifetime, as instituted in the Koran.

Hands of the Cause of God. Eminent Bahá'ís appointed by Bahá'u'lláh to stimulate the propagation and ensure the protection of the Bahá'í Faith.

House of 'Abbúd. A house in Acre that once belonged to Ilyás 'Abbúd and stands adjacent to the house of 'Údí Khammár (the two connected houses are known today as the House of 'Abbúd). It was occupied by Bahá'u'lláh and His family from late 1873 until June 1877, when He left Acre for Mazra'ih.

howdah. A seat or covered pavilion on the back of a mule or camel.

Ḥusayn-'Alí. See **Bahá'u'lláh.**

He (or Him) Whom God will make manifest. Title that the Báb used to refer to the Promised One Whose advent was imminent—i.e., **Bahá'u'lláh.**

Imam Husayn. In Shia Islam, the third Imám, son of 'Alí and Fáṭimih and grandson of the Prophet Muḥammad. He was martyred at Karbala, Iraq, in 680 A.D., making Karbala a point of pilgrimage for Shiite Muslims.

imám-jum'ih. Chief of the mullás; the Muslim leader who recites the Friday prayers in the mosque.

Isaiah. A Hebrew Prophet of the eighth century B.C.; also a book of the Bible.

Isfandíyár. A loyal servant who refused to abandon Bahá'u'lláh's family while Bahá'u'lláh was imprisoned in Tehran and personally paid their debts during that time.

Islam. Literally *Submission to the Will of God:* The religion of Muḥammad, upheld by Bahá'ís as divine in origin.

Jesus Christ. See **Christ.**

Kaaba. Literally *Cube:* The cube-shaped building in the courtyard of the great Mosque at Mecca that is the goal of Islamic pilgrimage and the point toward which Muslims turn in prayer.

Khadíjih Khánum. The mother of Bahá'u'lláh and the second wife of Mírzá Buzurg.

Khánum. Literally *lady, wife.* When it appears after a woman's given name, it is an honorific meaning "gentlewoman."

King of Martyrs, the. A title referring to Mírzá Muḥammad-Ḥasan, an honored and wealthy citizen of Isfahan who was killed along with his brother at the instigation of the imám-jum'ih of that city. See also **Beloved of Martyrs.**

Kitáb-i-'Ahd. *The Book of the (or My) Covenant:* Bahá'u'lláh's will and testament, written in His own hand. It designates 'Abdu'l-Bahá as His successor and the one to whom all should turn for guidance after Bahá'u'lláh's death.

Kitáb-i-Aqdas. *The Most Holy Book (Kitáb* means "book"; *Aqdas* means "Most Holy"): revealed in Acre in 1873, it is the chief repository of Bahá'u'lláh's laws and is considered by Bahá'ís to be the charter of a future world civilization.

Kitáb-i-Íqán. *The Book of Certitude.* Revealed by Bahá'u'lláh in Baghdad in 1862 in response to questions from the Báb's uncle about the validity of his nephew's claim to be the **Qá'im.**

Koran. Literally *the reading; that which ought to be read:* the holy book of Islam, revealed in Arabic to Muḥammad. It is comprised of 114 suras, or chapters.

Krishna. Considered in Hinduism to be the eighth or ninth avatar, or incarnation, of the God Vishnu. Bahá'ís believe that Bahá'u'lláh is the return of the spirit of Krishna.

Land of Ṭá. Phrase used in the writings of Bahá'u'lláh to refer to Tehran.

Letters of the Living. Refers collectively to the first eighteen individuals who independently recognized and believed in the Báb. The first Letter of the Living was **Mullá Ḥusayn;** the last was **Quddús. Ṭáhirih** was the only female Letter of the Living.

Local Spiritual Assembly. See **Spiritual Assemblies.**

Mahdí. See **Mihdí.**

Maiden. Term used in the Bahá'í writings to refer to the Spirit of God which descended upon Bahá'u'lláh while He was in the Black Pit.

Maitreye. The Buddha of universal fellowship; One Whose appearance is prophesied in Buddhism. Bahá'ís believe Bahá'u'lláh to be the fulfillment of this prophecy.

Maryam. A cousin of Bahá'u'lláh who embraced the Bábí Faith in its early days. She helped take care of Bahá'u'lláh after His release from prison and remained a devoted and loyal follower throughout her life.

Mázindarán. Northern province of Iran bordering the Caspian Sea. Bahá'u'lláh's ancestral home was located there.

Mazra'ih. A mansion situated just north of Acre that 'Abdu'l-Bahá rented for Bahá'u'lláh. Bahá'u'lláh took up residence there in June 1877 and stayed for two years before moving to the mansion of Bahjí.

Messenger. Term used in the Bahá'í writings to refer to a Prophet, or Manifestation of God. Bahá'u'lláh likens the Messenger of God to a perfect mirror reflecting the sun; that is, His life and teachings are a pure reflection of the spiritual light, or attributes, of God, Who is the Source of life. The capacities of a Messenger of God are distinct from those of other humans, according to Bahá'í writings, although the human soul is also created to reflect the attributes of God and is capable of "limitless perfections."

Mihdí. Literally *One Who Is Guided;* term used by Muslims in reference to One Whose appearance they await.

Mírzá. A contraction of *Amír-Zádih,* meaning son of an Amír. When it follows a name, it signifies "prince"; when it precedes, it means simply "Mister."

Mírzá 'Abbás Buzurg. (d. 1839) Also known as Mírzá 'Abbás, he was the father of Bahá'u'lláh. A vizier to a son of Fatḥ-'Alí Sháh and a governor under Muḥammad Sháh, he was respected for his artistic and intellectual abilities as well as his integrity and personal charm.

Mírzá Áqá Ján. (1837–1901) Secretary of Bahá'u'lláh who accompanied Him throughout much of His exiles.

Mírzá Áqá Khán. The prime minister of Persia from 1851 to 1858 under Náṣiri'd-Dín Sháh. He was related to Bahá'u'lláh through the marriage of his niece and made futile efforts to protect Bahá'u'lláh's relatives.

Mírzá Buzurg Khán. The Persian consul-general in Baghdad who, from his arrival there in 1860, allied himself with Shaykh 'Abdu'l-Ḥusayn in an effort to destroy Bahá'u'lláh. After many futile attempts to discredit Bahá'u'lláh and take His life, they eventually succeeded in precipitating His transfer from Baghdad to Constantinople.

Mírzá Mihdí. (1848–70) Son of Bahá'u'lláh and brother of 'Abdu'l-Bahá who died at age twenty-two from injuries received in a tragic accident at the prison-barracks in Acre. Bahá'u'lláh bestowed on him the title of "The Purest Branch."

Mírzá Músá. (d. 1887) Also known as Áqáy-i-Kalím. A younger full brother of Bahá'u'lláh who recognized the station of the Báb and of Bahá'u'lláh and faithfully served Bahá'u'lláh throughout His exiles. He often met with government officials and religious leaders on Bahá'u'lláh's behalf until 'Abdu'l-Bahá assumed that function.

Mírzá Taqí Khán. Prime minister of Persia under Náṣiri'd-Dín Sháh who was involved in persecuting Bábís at the fort of Shaykh Ṭabarsí, at Nayríz, and at Zanján. He was also involved in the execution of the Seven Martyrs of Tehran and ordered the execution of the Báb. He later fell out of favor with the royal court and was killed by royal decree.

Mírzá Yaḥyá. (c. 1831/2–1912) A younger half-brother of Bahá'u'lláh who turned against Him. He was known by the title *Ṣubḥ-i-Azal* (Morn of Eternity) given to him by the Báb, Who appointed him temporary leader of the Bábí community until the appearance of the One foretold by the Báb. He later claimed to be the Báb's successor but was unsuccessful in his ambitions and was eventually exiled to Cyprus.

Mosque of Sulṭán Salím. The site in Adrianople Mírzá Yaḥyá chose for a public debate with and Bahá'u'lláh. The debate, which was suggested and organized by Mír Muḥammad, never took place because Mírzá Yaḥyá did not attend.

Most Great Idol. Title Bahá'u'lláh gave to Mírzá Yaḥyá referring to Mírzá Yaḥyá's pretense in claiming to be a Messenger of God.

Most Great Peace. A condition of permanent peace and world unity founded on spiritual principles and the second of two major stages in which Bahá'ís believe peace will be established. The first stage, the Lesser Peace, refers to political peace established by the nations of the world. The Most Great Peace will then develop in gradual stages.

Most Great Prison. The prison-barracks and prison-city of Acre in which Bahá'u'lláh, His family, and companions were confined from 31 August 1868 until June 1877.

most great separation. Phrase Bahá'u'lláh used to refer to a period of two months, starting 10 March 1866, during which He lived in seclusion from the Bábí community in Adrianople. This period allowed the Bábís, both faithful and unfaithful, to decide where their allegiances lay.

Mott, Lucretia. (1793–1880). A Quaker minister who was active in the movements for peace, women's rights, and the abolition of slavery. She was a primary organizer of the first women's rights convention held in Seneca Falls, New York, in June 1848.

Mount Carmel. The mountain in Israel, called by Bahá'u'lláh "the Hill of God and His Vineyard," that is today the site of the shrine of the Báb and the Bahá'í World Center.

Muḥammad. (A.D. 570–632) Prophet and Founder of Islam. Bahá'ís regard Him as a Messenger of God and His book, the Koran, as holy scripture.

Muḥammad-Qulí. A faithful half-brother of Bahá'u'lláh who accompanied Him in His exiles.

muezzin. A Muslim crier who calls the hour of daily prayers.

muftí. A professional jurist responsible for the interpretation of Islamic law.

mujtahid. The highest rank of divine within Shia Islam. One who has the power to make authoritative decisions on points of law in the name of the Hidden Imám.

mullá. An Islamic cleric, theologian, or judge.

Mullá Ḥusayn. (d. 1849) A leading follower of **Siyyid Káẓim,** he was the first to recognize the Báb as the Promised One, thereby earning the title *Bábu'l-Báb* (Gate of the Gate) and becoming the first of the Báb's eighteen Letters of the Living. He was a leader of the Bábís during the siege at the fort of Shaykh Ṭabarsí, in which he was killed.

Munírih Khánum. (d. 1938) Literally *Illumined:* the name bestowed on Fáṭimih Khánum, who came to Acre at Bahá'u'lláh's invitation to marry 'Abdu'l-Bahá in 1873.

Muslim calendar. See **A.H.**

Mystery of God. A title given by Bahá'u'lláh to 'Abdu'l-Bahá alluding to the unique blend of human nature with a knowledge and perfection beyond the scope of ordinary men that was evident in 'Abdu'l-Bahá.

Najaf. A city in south central Iraq that was the site of the martyrdom of the Imám 'Alí, the cousin and son-in-law of Muḥammad whom Shia Muslims believe to be the Prophet's rightful successor. The shrine of the Imám 'Alí is a place of pilgrimage for Shiites, and the city itself is considered holy.

Napoleon III. Emperor of France from 1852 until 1870. He enjoyed two decades of prosperity until he led his country to defeat in the Franco-Prussian War (1870–71).

Náṣiri'd-Dín Sháh. Shah of Iran, 1848–96. Under his reign the Báb was executed and Bahá'u'lláh was imprisoned and exiled. Bahá'u'lláh addressed him in a tablet delivered by Badí', whose torture and death were consequently ordered by the shah. Called the "Prince of Oppressors" by Bahá'u'lláh, Náṣiri'd-Dín Sháh was assassinated in 1896.

National Spiritual Assembly. See **Spiritual Assemblies.**

Navváb. Literally *Grace, Highness.* A title of great courtesy and respect used by Persian noblemen for their wives. See also **Ásíyih Khánum.**

Naw-Rúz. Literally *New Day:* the Bábí, Bahá'í, Persian, and Zoroastrian New Year's Day. It occurs on the date of the vernal equinox, which, in the Northern Hemisphere, normally falls on 21 March but sometimes on 20 or 22 March.

Núr. A district of Mázindarán in which Bahá'u'lláh's ancestral home was located.

Ottoman Empire. The Turkish dynasty based in Constantinople (modern-day Istanbul) that ruled over regions including Turkey, Iraq, Syria, Palestine, and Arabia during the time of Bahá'u'lláh. Its leaders, Sulṭán 'Abdu'l-'Azíz and Sulṭán 'Abdu'l-Ḥamíd II, were responsible for the imprisonment and banishment of Bahá'u'lláh to Constantinople, Adrianople, and Acre. Both leaders were eventually deposed.

Pope Pius IX. The pope whose reign from 1846 to 1878 was distinguished for his promulgation of the doctrine of papal infallibility.

Pride of Martyrs. See **Badí'.**

Prophet. The Bahá'í writings allude to two distinct types of prophets, the Greater Prophets and the lesser prophets. The Greater Prophets, also called Messengers or Manifestations of God, are the lawgivers and founders of a new religious cycle. The lesser prophets are followers and promoters of the Greater Prophets and include such Old Testament prophets as Solomon, David, and Isaiah. See also **Messenger.**

promised Ḥusayn. The prophesied return of the Imám Ḥusayn anticipated in Shia Islam. Bahá'ís believe Bahá'u'lláh to be the fulfillment of that prophecy.

Promised One(s). A term used to refer to the Messenger(s) of God. Bahá'ís believe the Báb to be the Promised One of Islam (the Qá'im) and Bahá'u'lláh to be the Promised One of the Bayán and of all religions.

Purest Branch, the. See **Mírzá Mihdí.**

Qá'im. Literally *He Who Arises:* in Shia Islam, a reference to the Twelfth Imám, the Mihdí, who was to return in the fullness of time and bring a reign of righteousness to the world. The Báb declared Himself to be the Qá'im and the Gate to a greater Messenger, "Him Whom God shall make manifest"—Bahá'u'lláh.

Qásim. One of three Bábís who together attempted but failed to assassinate the shah in 1852, leading to a wave of persecution against the Bábís and resulting in Bahá'u'lláh's arrest and imprisonment in Tehran.

Qayyúm. Literally *Self-Subsisting, Self-existent, All-Compelling:* A term used in certain Islamic traditions in reference to the One who would come after the appearance of the **Qá'im.** Bahá'ís believe Bahá'u'lláh to be the Qayyúm.

Quddús. (d. 1849) Literally *Most Holy:* title bestowed by the Báb on Ḥájí Muḥammad-'Alíy-i-Bárfurúshí, the last Letter of the Living, who was second only to the Báb in rank. He accompanied the Báb on a pilgrimage to Mecca and attended the Conference of Badasht. He joined the Bábís in the fort at Shaykh Ṭabarsí and afterward was taken to his native town of Bárfurúsh, where he was killed by a mob.

Riḍá. The Turk hired by Mírzá Buzurg Khán to seek out and kill Bahá'u'lláh. More than once Riḍá approached Bahá'u'lláh with the intention of taking His life, but each time he found himself overcome with fear and unable to carry out the task.

Riḍvan. Literally *paradise.* The annual Riḍván Festival, the holiest and most significant of all Bahá'í festivals, commemorates Bahá'u'lláh's declaration of His mission to His companions in the Garden of Riḍván in Baghdad in 1863. It is a twelve-day period celebrated from 21 April to 2 May. During this time, Local and National Spiritual Assemblies are elected and, once every five years, the Universal House of Justice is elected.

Sám Khán. The colonel of the Armenian regiment that was ordered to execute the Báb in 1850. Sám Khán reluctantly carried out his orders and, upon witnessing the miraculous event of his regiment's failed attempt, refused to take any further part in the execution. At the risk of his own life, he ordered his men to leave the barracks.

Sárih. Older sister of Bahá'u'lláh; she remained faithful to His Cause throughout her life and was highly regarded by Him.

Sassanian kings. The kings of the Persian Sassanid dynasty during the third to seventh centuries from whom Bahá'u'lláh was descended through His father.

Seven Martyrs of Tehran. Seven prominent and distinguished Bábís in Tehran, including one of the Báb's uncles, Siyyid 'Alí, who were arrested in 1850 and executed for their beliefs.

Seven Martyrs of Yazd. Seven Bahá'ís of the city of Yazd in southern Persia, who were brutally executed at the hands of a mob on May 19, 1891. Bahá'u'lláh described their unflinching faith as a victory celebrated by the inmates of the highest paradise.

shah. Literally *king,* especially of Persia.

Sháh-Bahrám. The World Savior whose coming was promised by Zoroaster. Bahá'ís believe this prophecy was fulfilled with the coming of Bahá'u'lláh.

shaykh. Title of respect given to old men, men of authority, elders, chiefs, professors, or superiors of a dervish order.

Shaykh 'Abdu'l-Ḥusayn. A mujtahid who became inflamed by the prestige and devotion commanded by Bahá'u'lláh in Baghdad and allied himself with Mírzá Buzurg Khán to destroy Him. Eventually the two succeeded in having Bahá'u'lláh transferred from Iraq to Constantinople by the Ottoman government.

Shaykh Aḥmad. A respected interpreter of Islamic doctrine who attracted many followers in the Shia holy cities of Najaf and Karbala. His teachings, which emphasized the near advent of the Promised One of Islam, and the metaphorical rather than literal interpretation of certain scriptures, prepared the way for the Báb. He chose one of his disciples, Siyyid Káẓim, to carry on his work after his death.

Shaykh Effendi. Name by which Bahá'u'lláh became known outside of the Bahá'í community.

Shaykh Ḥasan. Served as a scribe for the Báb during His imprisonment in Máh-Kú and Chihríq. Later in life he traveled to Karbala at the request of the Báb, where he attained the presence of Bahá'u'lláh.

She-Serpent. Designation Bahá'u'lláh gave to Mír Muḥammad-Ḥusayn, the imám-jum'ih of Isfahan, who instigated the deaths of the two brothers known as the King of Martyrs and the Beloved of Martyrs.

Shia. One of the two major branches of Islam. Its followers view the descendants of 'Alí, son-in-law of the Prophet Muḥammad, as the only rightful successors to Muḥammad, and many await the return of the twelfth Imam.

Shiite. A Muslim of the Shia branch of Islam.

siyyid. Literally *lord, chief, prince:* an honorific title denoting a descendant of the Prophet Muḥammad.

Siyyid 'Alí. The maternal uncle of the Báb who, after the passing of the Báb's father, was responsible for the Báb's upbringing. He recognized his nephew's station and became an ardent follower.

Siyyid Káẓim. The successor of Shaykh Aḥmad who carried on his work and message, preaching the imminent advent of the Qá'im, and who eventually attained the presence of the Báb.

Siyyid Muḥammad. A Bábí of unsavory character who became a companion of Mírzá Yaḥyá, inducing him to oppose Bahá'u'lláh and to claim prophethood for himself. Bahá'u'lláh refers to him in the Kitáb-i-Aqdas as the one who led Mírzá Yaḥyá astray.

Spirit of God. A title used in the Koran and in the Bahá'í writings to refer to Jesus Christ.

Spiritual Assemblies. Bahá'í administrative institutions that operate at the local and national levels and are elected according to Bahá'í principles. They are responsible for coordinating and directing the affairs of the Bahá'í community in their areas of jurisdiction.

Stanton, Elizabeth Cady. (1815–1902) A leader of the American women's rights movement who was a primary organizer of the first women's rights convention (1848) in Seneca Falls, New York. She wrote the *Declaration of Sentiments*—a women's bill of rights with demands for social equality, including the right to vote.

Stowe, Harriet Beecher. (1811–1896) New England author best known today for her novel titled *Uncle Tom's Cabin* (1852), whose human portrayal of slaves galvanized the abolitionist cause just before the American Civil War.

Sunni. The largest of the two major branches of Islam, which accepts the first four caliphs as the rightful successors of Muḥammad and rejects the notion of hereditary successorship to authority over the Muslim community.

Súriy-i-Mulúk. Literally *Súrih of Kings:* tablet revealed by Bahá'u'lláh in Adrianople to the kings of the world. In it He boldly proclaims His station as Messenger of God.

tablet. A term for a sacred epistle containing a revelation from God. The giving of the Law to Moses on tables, or tablets, is mentioned in Koran 7:142: "We wrote for him (Moses) upon tables *(alwah,* pl. of *lauh)* a monition concerning every matter." In Bahá'í scripture the term refers to letters revealed by Bahá'u'lláh, the Báb, and 'Abdu'l-Bahá.

Tablet of Carmel. The charter for the world spiritual and administrative centers of the Bahá'í Faith on Mount Carmel. The tablet was revealed by Bahá'u'lláh in 1890 during one of His visits to Mount Carmel.

Ṭáhirih. (1817–1852) Literally *the Pure One:* title given by the Báb to Fáṭimih Umm-Salamih, also known by the titles *Qurrátu'l-'Ayn* (Solace of the Eyes) and *Zarrín-Táj* (Crown of Gold). Born in the same year as Bahá'u'lláh (1817), she was a woman of learning and the only female Letter of the Living. She was executed in Tehran for her beliefs and is remembered by Bahá'ís as the greatest heroine of the Bábí Dispensation.

Tákur. Village where Bahá'u'lláh's ancestral home was located. Tákur is situated in the district of Núr, in the province of Mázindarán, Iran.

Tehran. Capital of present-day Iran and birthplace of Bahá'u'lláh. Also the site of Bahá'u'lláh's revelation in the underground dungeon known as the Black Pit, where He was falsely imprisoned after the attempted assassination of the shah in 1852.

Templers. Members of the Society of the Temple, founded in the mid 1800s in Germany. They believed that Christ's return was imminent and settled in the Holy Land in anticipation of the event. The first and largest of their settlements was in Haifa at the foot of Mount Carmel, where they built their homes.

Tenth Avatar. The tenth appearance of the God Vishnu, as anticipated in Hinduism.

Truth, Sojourner. (c. 1799–1883) Name taken by Isabella Baumfree, black abolitionist and women's rights advocate from Ulster County, New York, who became the first black woman to speak out publicly against slavery.

Tubman, Harriet. (c. 1820–1913) A leading abolitionist during the American Civil War. She escaped from slavery and led more than three hundred slaves to freedom in the North with the aid of the Underground Railroad.

Universal House of Justice. The supreme governing and legislative body of the Bahá'í Faith. Elected every five years at an international Bahá'í convention, it is the institution invested by Bahá'u'lláh with authority to legislate on matters not covered in His writings. In his will and testament 'Abdu'l-Bahá elaborates on its functions and affirms that it is infallibly guided.

Vaḥíd. *Peerless:* Title given by the Báb to a leading Muslim clergyman, Siyyid Yaḥyá (d. 1850), an erudite, eloquent, and influential emissary of Muḥammad Sháh. He was sent by the shah to interrogate the Báb but was instead converted and became one of the most learned and influential of His followers. He died in the upheaval at Nayríz.

vizier. A high executive officer in various Muslim countries and especially of the Ottoman Empire.

Wolf, the. Name given by Bahá'u'lláh to Shaykh Muḥammad-Báqir, a divine of Isfahan who in 1879 ordered the death of the two brothers known as the **King of Martyrs** and the **Beloved of Martyrs.**

Zagros Mountains. A mountain range in southern and southwestern Iran bordering Iraq, Turkey, and the Persian Gulf.

Zoroaster. (c. 628 B.C.–c. 551 B.C.) Regarded by Bahá'ís as a Messenger of God and founder of the Zoroastrian religion. He predicted the coming of a World Redeemer, the Sháh-Bahrám, Who would create an era of world peace. Bahá'ís believe the figure referred to in this prophecy is Bahá'u'lláh, Who is also a descendant of Zoroaster.

Bibliography

Works of Bahá'u'lláh

Epistle to the Son of the Wolf. 1st pocket-size ed. Translated by Shoghi Effendi. Wilmette, IL: Bahá'í Publishing Trust, 1988.

Gleanings from the Writings of Bahá'u'lláh. 1st pocket-size ed. Translated by Shoghi Effendi. Wilmette, IL: Bahá'í Publishing Trust, 1983.

The Hidden Words. Translated by Shoghi Effendi. Wilmette, IL: Bahá'í Publishing, 2002.

The Kitáb-i-Aqdas: The Most Holy Book. 1st pocket-size ed. Wilmette, IL: Bahá'í Publishing Trust, 1993.

The Kitáb-i-Íqán: The Book of Certitude. Translated by Shoghi Effendi. Wilmette, IL: Bahá'í Publishing, 2003.

Prayers and Meditations. Translated by Shoghi Effendi. 1st pocket-size ed. Wilmette, IL: Bahá'í Publishing Trust, 1987.

The Summons of the Lord of Hosts: Tablets of Bahá'u'lláh. Haifa, Israel: Bahá'í World Centre, 2002.

Tablets of Bahá'u'lláh revealed after the Kitáb-i-Aqdas. Compiled by the Research Department of the Universal House of Justice. Translated by Habib Taherzadeh et al. Wilmette, IL: Bahá'í Publishing Trust, 1988.

Works of the Báb

Selections from the Writings of the Báb. Compiled by the Research Department of the Universal House of Justice. Translated by Habib Taherzadeh et al. Haifa: Bahá'í World Centre, 1976.

Works of 'Abdu'l-Bahá

Memorials of the Faithful. New ed. Translated by Marzieh Gail. Wilmette, IL: Bahá'í Publishing Trust, 1996.

Selections from the Writings of 'Abdu'l-Bahá. Compiled by the Research Department of the Universal House of Justice. Translated by a Committee at the Bahá'í World Center and Marzieh Gail. Wilmette, IL: Bahá'í Publishing Trust, 1997.

Some Answered Questions. Compiled and translated by Laura Clifford Barney. 1st pocket-size ed. Wilmette, IL: Bahá'í Publishing Trust, 1984.

A Traveler's Narrative Written to Illustrate the Episode of the Báb. Translated by Edward G. Browne. New and corrected ed. Wilmette, IL: Bahá'í Publishing Trust, 1980.

Works of Shoghi Effendi

God Passes By. New ed. Wilmette, IL: Bahá'í Publishing Trust, 1974.

The Promised Day Is Come. 3rd ed. Wilmette, IL: Bahá'í Publishing Trust, 1980.

The World Order of Bahá'u'lláh: Selected Letters. 1st pocket-size ed. Wilmette, IL: Bahá'í Publishing Trust, 1991.

Compilations

Bahá'u'lláh, the Báb, and 'Abdu'l-Bahá. *Bahá'í Prayers: A Selection of Prayers Revealed by Bahá'u'lláh, the Báb, and 'Abdu'l-Bahá.* Wilmette, IL: Bahá'í Publishing Trust, 2002.

Other Works

The Bahá'í World: A Biennial International Record, Volume VIII, 1938–1940. Compiled by the National Spiritual Assembly of the Bahá'ís of the United States and Canada. Wilmette, IL: Bahá'í Publishing Committee, 1942.

Bahíyyih Khánum: The Greatest Holy Leaf. Compiled by the Research Department at the Bahá'í World Centre. Haifa: Bahá'í World Centre, 1982.

Balyuzi, H. M. *'Abdu'l-Bahá: The Centre of the Covenant of Bahá'u'lláh.* London: George Ronald, 1971.

———. *The Báb: The Herald of the Day of Days.* Oxford: George Ronald, 1973.

———. *Bahá'u'lláh: The King of Glory.* Oxford: George Ronald, 1980.

Blomfield, Lady (Sitárih Khánum), *The Chosen Highway.* Wilmette, IL: Bahá'í Publishing Trust, n.d.; reprinted 1975.

Brekus, Catherine A. "Harriet Livermore, the Pilgrim Stranger: Female Preaching and Biblical Feminism in Early-Nineteenth-Century America." *Church History* 65 (September 1996): 389–404.

Brown, Dee. *Wounded Knee: An Indian History of the American West.* Adapted by Amy Ehrlich. New York: Henry Holt & Company, 1993.

Browne, Edward Granville. *A Year Amongst the Persians.* London: Century Publishing, 1984.

Cameron, Glenn, with Wendi Momen. *A Basic Bahá'í Chronology.* Oxford: George Ronald, 1996.

Crowder, M., R. J. Cootes, and L. E. Snellgrove. *Ancient Times: A Junior History of Africa.* London: Longman Group Limited, 1970.

Dickinson, Mary B., ed. *National Geographic Picture Atlas of Our World.* Washington, D. C.: National Geographic Society, 1993.

Eller, David B. "Livermore, Harriet." *American National Biography* 13 (1999): 758–59.

Esslemont, J. E. *Bahá'u'lláh and the New Era: An Introduction to the Bahá'í Faith.* 5th rev. ed. Wilmette, IL: Bahá'í Publishing Trust, 1980.

Fernea, Elizabeth W. *Guests of the Sheik: An Ethnography of an Iraqi Village.* New York: Anchor Books, 1989.

Fisher, Mary Pat. *Living Religions.* 5th ed. Upper Saddle River, NJ: Prentice-Hall, 2002.

Freedman, Russell. *Indian Chiefs.* New York: Holiday House, 1987.

———. *Lincoln: A Photobiography.* New York: Clarion Books, 1987.

Furútan, 'Alí-Akbar, comp. *Stories of Bahá'u'lláh.* Translated by Katayoon and Robert Crerar. Oxford: George Ronald, 1986.

Gail, Marzieh. *Summon up Remembrance.* Oxford: George Ronald, 1987.

Hatcher, William S., and J. Douglas Martin. *The Bahá'í Faith: The Emerging Global Religion.* New edition. Wilmette, IL: Bahá'í Publishing, 2002.

The Kingfisher Illustrated History of the World. Charlotte Evans, general ed. 1st American ed. New York: Larousse Kingfisher Chambers Inc., 1993

Lyle, Garry. *Let's Visit Iran*. London: Burke Publishing Limited, 1977.

Ma'ani, Baharieh Rouhani. *Ásíyih Khánum: The Most Exalted Holy Leaf*. Oxford, U.K.: George Ronald, 1993.

Marks, Geoffry W., comp. *Call to Remembrance: Connecting the Heart to Bahá'u'lláh*. Wilmette, IL: Bahá'í Publishing Trust, 1992.

Maxwell, W. S. "The Passing of Munírih Khánum, the Holy Mother: Episodes in the Life of Munírih Khánum." *The Bahá'í World* 8 (April 1938–1940 A.D.): 262.

Mehrabkhani, Ruhu'llah. *Mullá Ḥusayn: Disciple at Dawn*. Los Angeles: Kalimát Press, 1987.

Meister, Charles W. *Year of the Lord*. Jefferson, NC: McFarland & Company, 1983.

Momen, Moojan. *Selections from the Writings of E. G. Browne on the Bábí and Bahá'í Religions*. Oxford: George Ronald, 1987.

Momen, Wendi, ed. *A Basic Bahá'í Dictionary*. Oxford: George Ronald, 1989.

Nábil-i-A'ẓam [Muḥammad-i-Zarandí]. *The Dawn-Breakers: Nabíl's Narrative of the Early Days of the Bahá'í Revelation*. Translated and edited by Shoghi Effendi. Wilmette, IL: Bahá'í Publishing Trust, 1932.

Périgord, Emily McBride. *Translation of French Foot-notes of the Dawn-Breakers*. Wilmette, IL: Bahá'í Publishing Trust, 1939.

Perkins, Mary. *Day of Glory: The Life of Bahá'u'lláh*. Oxford: George Ronald, 1992.

———. *Hour of the Dawn: The Life of the Báb*. Oxford: George Ronald, 1987.

Ruhe, David S. *Door of Hope: A Century of the Bahá'í Faith in the Holy Land*. Oxford: George Ronald, 1983.

———. "Pen of Glory." Photocopy, unpublished manuscript, 1995.

———. *Robe of Light: The Persian Years of the Supreme Prophet Bahá'u'lláh 1817–1853*. Oxford: George Ronald, 1994.

Ruhe-Schoen, Janet. *The Nightingale, Bahá'u'lláh*. Place: Publisher, forthcoming.

Salmání, Ustád Muḥammad-'Alíy-i. *My Memories of Bahá'u'lláh*. Translated by Marzieh Gail. Los Angeles: Kalimát Press, 1982.

Sears, William. *Release the Sun*. New ed. Wilmette, IL: Bahá'í Publishing, 2003.

———. *Thief in the Night: Or The Strange Case of the Missing Millenium*. Oxford: George Ronald, 1980.

Smith, Sammireh Anwar, trans. *Munírih Khánum: Memoirs and Letters*. Los Angeles: Kalimát Press, 1986.

Sours, Michael. *The Prophecies of Jesus*. Oxford: Oneworld Publications, 1991.

Taherzadeh, Adib. *The Covenant of Bahá'u'lláh*. Oxford: George Ronald, 1992.

———. *The Revelation of Bahá'u'lláh: Adrianople 1863–68*. Oxford: George Ronald, 1977.

———. *The Revelation of Bahá'u'lláh: 'Akká, The Early Years 1868–77*. Oxford: George Ronald, 1983.

———. *The Revelation of Bahá'u'lláh: Baghdád 1853–63*. Rev. ed. Oxford: George Ronald, 1976.

———. *The Revelation of Bahá'u'lláh: Mazra'ih & Bahjí 1877–1892*. Oxford: George Ronald, 1987.

Taylor, M. W. *Harriet Tubman*. New York, New York: Chelsea House Publishers, 1991.

Wilber, Donald N. *Iran: Past and Present*. Princeton: Princeton University Press, 1975.

Periodicals

Hickey, Neil. "125 years later, why we're still riveted by the Civil War." *TV Guide*, September 22, 1990.

Collins, William. "Millenialism, the Millerites, and Historicism." *World Order* 30, no. 1 (fall 1998): 9–26.

Milani, Leila Rassekh. "Women as Decision Makers: A Case for Inclusion." *World Order* 32, no. 4 (summer 2001): 11–18.

Online Resources

Bucko, Rev. Ray A. "Other Sites" relating to things Lakota. http://puffin.creighton.edu/lakota/index_other_sites.html.

Douglass, Frederick. "The Rights of Woman," a review of the Woman's Rights Convention held in Seneca Falls, NY, 19–20 July 1848. Originally published in *The North Star*, 28 July 1848. Reprinted at the *Women and Social Movements* Web site by the State University of New York, Binghamton. http://womhist.binghamton.edu/malesupp/doc4.htm.

Harriet Beecher Stowe House and Library. "Harriet's Life and Times." *Harriet Beecher Stowe Center: The Harriet Beecher Stowe Center and Library*. http://www.harrietbeecherstowecenter.org/life/.

Kennedy, Ira. *American Indian Prophecies: A Brief History on the Future of America*. http://www.texfiles.com/features/prophecies.htm.

Lincoln, Abraham. Letter to A. G. Hodges, 4 April 1864. Reprinted at "American Treasures of the Library of Congress." *The Library of Congress*. http://www.loc.gov/exhibits/treasures/trt027.html.

———. "Second Inaugural Address," quoted from *The Collected Works of Abraham Lincoln*, edited by Roy P. Basler. Reprinted at *Abraham Lincoln Online*. http://showcase.netins.net/web/creative/lincoln/speeches/inaug2.htm.

National Cable Satellite Corporation. "Harriet Beecher Stowe." *C-Span American Writers: A Journey Through History*. http://www.americanwriters.org/writers/stowe.asp.

"Native American Prophecies," *Rainbow Family of Living Light Unofficial Home Page*. http://www.welcomehome.org/rainbow/prophecy/prophecies.html.

Niehardt, John G. *Black Elk Speaks: Being the Life Story of a Holy Man of the Oglala Sioux*, 21st century electronic edition. Reprinted at *Black Elk's World*. University of Nebraska Press, n.d. http://www.blackelkspeaks.unl.edu/index2.htm.

Public Broadcasting Service. "Islam, Empire of Faith." *pbs.org*.
http://www.pbs.org/empires/islam/index.html.

Yahia bin Sharaful-Deen An-Nawawi. *An-Nawawi's Forty Hadiths*. Published by the International Islamic Federation of Students Organizations and translated by Ezzeddin

Ibrahim and Denys Johnson-Davies. Reprinted at http://www.islamworld.net/nawawi.html#hadith40.

Broadcast Resources

Sprague, Suzanne. "From Seneca Falls to Ally McBeal: 150 Years of Women's Rights," aired on KERA 90.1 (Dallas), March 1999.

Index

Note: Middle Eastern names of the nineteenth century did not include surnames; therefore, such names have been indexed according to the initial part of the name and without regard to honorifics such as Bagum, Effendi, Ḥájí, Khán, Khánum, Mír, Mírzá, Sháh, Shaykh, Siyyid, and Sulṭán.

A

aba, definition of, 141n, 319
'Abbás Buzurg, Mírzá (father of Bahá'u'lláh), 8
  character of, 11
  death of, 16
  dream of, 9–11
  title of, 322
  wife of, 8, 324
'Abbás Effendi. *See* 'Abdu'l-Bahá
'Abbúd, house of
  'Abdu'l-Bahá in, 252, 253, 258–59
  Bahá'u'lláh in, 233–34
  See also 'Abbúd, Ilyás
'Abbúd, Ilyás (neighbor of Bahá'u'lláh in Acre)
  barricades house against Bahá'u'lláh, 223
  as friend to Bahá'u'lláh, 227–28
  gives room to 'Abdu'l-Bahá and Munírih Khánum, 232
  moves out of Acre, 233
  See also 'Abbud, house of
'Abdu'l-Aḥad (Bahá'í in Acre), 200–201
'Abdu'l-'Azíz, Sulṭán (ruler of Ottoman Empire)
  Bahá'u'lláh reveals tablet to, 177–78
  banishes Bahá'u'lláh from Adrianople to Acre, 193, 195, 236, 300, 319, 329
  banishes Bahá'u'lláh from Baghdad to Constantinople, 166, 236, 329
  banishes Bahá'u'lláh from Constantinople to Adrianople, 176–77, 236, 329
  downfall of, 236, 292
'Abdu'l-Bahá ('Abbás Effendi; son of Bahá'u'lláh)
  in Acre, 218–19, 255–57, 258–59
  as Áqá, 158, 254, 262
  and Baghdad, 113–14, 158
  and Bahá'u'lláh, love between, 214, 254–55, 257–58, 290
  at Bahá'u'lláh's passing, 284–89
  and Bahjí, 246, 257
  birth of, 32, 291
  and Black Pit, 103
  as a boy, taunted, 103–4
  care of, for poor, 227, 253, 255–57
  as Center of the Covenant, 288, 322, 324

'Abdu'l-Bahá *(continued)*
characteristics of, 202, 214, 254–55, 261, 328
children of, 253
as "Father of the Poor," 227
as Greatest Branch, 254, 323
as "Lord of Generosity," 256
marriage of, 232–33, 292
as the Master, 227, 232n, 254
and Mazra'ih, mansion of, 238–39
and Mírzá Mihdí, mourning for, 217
as Mystery of God, 255, 328
recognizes Bahá'u'lláh, 112
title of, 257
transcribes Bahá'u'lláh's writings, 160
wife of (Munírih Khánum), 228–33, 259, 292, 328
will and testament of, 323, 334
'Abdu'l-Ghaffár, forced to go to Cyprus with Mírzá Yaḥyá, 196
'Abdu'l-Ḥamíd II, Sulṭán (ruler of Ottoman Empire), 285, 329
'Abdu'l-Ḥamíd Khán (chief constable of Ḥusayn Khán), 46–47
'Abdu'l-Ḥusayn, Shaykh (mujtahid), plots against Bahá'u'lláh, 153–58, 160, 166, 167, 326
'Abdu'l-Vahháb (Bábí shop-keeper), death of, 101–2
'Abdu'r-Raḥmán Páshá (governor of Acre), 234–35
abolitionists, 61, 162
Aborigines of Australia, 266
Abraham, Prophet, 148–49, 163, 319
Abu Bakr, as first Muslim caliph, 295
Abu'l-Qásim (servant of Bahá'u'lláh), 130–31, 139
Acre
'Abdu'l-Bahá in, 252–53, 255–57
aqueduct of, 228
Bahá'u'lláh in, 4–6, 195, 197, 198–208, 212, 213, 228, 232–35, 237–39, 252, 292, 319
governor of, devoted to Bahá'u'lláh, 228
history of, 198
Most Great Prison in, 198–218, 327
Adrianople (Edirne, Turkey) and Bahá'u'lláh, 179–81, 193–95, 292
Africa, resources of, 266
Aḥmad, Shaykh (Muslim scholar)
prepares the way for the Báb, 17–20, 165
Ṭáhirih studies writings of, 55
Aḥmad Big Tawfíq (governor of Acre), 228, 234
Aḥmad (son of the Báb), 28
'Akká. *See* Acre

'Alí, Ḥájí, Mírzá Yaḥyá as, 174
'Alí, Imám (son-in-law of Prophet Muḥammad)
as Muḥammad's successor, 295, 331
shrine of, 86n, 328
'Alí, Siyyid (uncle of the Báb)
martyrdom of, 77, 330
raises the Báb, 27
'Alí Khán, (prison warden), guards the Báb, 51–52
'Alí-Muḥammad, Siyyid. *See* Báb, the
'Alí-Muḥammad (son of Bahá'u'lláh), 260n
'Álí Páshá (grand vizier to the sultan of the Ottoman Empire), 204, 235–36
"Alláh-u-Abhá" (God is All-Glorious), 189
Alláh-yár, Ḥájí, retrieves the Báb's remains, 84
amanuensis
of the Báb (Siyyid Ḥusayn), 81–83
of Bahá'u'lláh (*see* Áqá Ján, Mírzá)
Ambassador of Persia, 192
Ambassador of Russia (Prince Dimitri Dolgorukov), 95, 109, 204
America
rulers of, Bahá'u'lláh addresses, 271
Second Great Awakening in, 296n
United States of, destiny of, 270–71
American Anti-Slavery Society, 297
American Education Society, 297
American Indians, 107, 266–67, 270, 272
American Peace Society, 297
American Temperance Society, 297
Amru'lláh, house of, Bahá'u'lláh in, 180, 184
Amul, Bahá'u'lláh in, 70–72, 291
angel Gabriel, 106, 322
Anís (Bábí youth)
death of, 81–84
remains of, 84, 87
Apostles of Bahá'u'lláh, 212n
Áqá, 'Abdu'l-Bahá as, 158, 254, 262
Áqá Ján, Mírzá (amanuensis of Bahá'u'lláh), 138, 181, 183
recognizes Bahá'u'lláh, 125–26
transcription of revelation, 147–48, 190
Áqá Khán, Mírzá (grand vizier of Persia)
Bábís of Káshán help, 90, 91
orders arrest of Bábís, 94
orders killing of Bábís to be stopped, 111
surrenders Bahá'u'lláh to the shah, 95
welcomes Bahá'u'lláh to Tehran, 90
Áqásí, Ḥájí Mírzá (grand vizier of Persia)
downfall of, 65

Áqásí, Ḥájí Mírzá *(continued)*
plots against the Báb, 49, 50, 53, 62–64
aqueduct of Acre, 228
Ásíyih Khánum (wife of Bahá'u'lláh). *See also* Navváb
Assemblies, Spiritual, 280–82, 330, 332
Augustine, Saint, 297
"Azalís," definition of, 189, 320
'Azím (disciple of the Báb), 91–92, 108–9
'Azíz (uncle of Bahá'u'lláh), 36–37

B

Báb, the (Siyyid 'Alí-Muḥammad)
Bahá'u'lláh and, 35, 40, 50, 60, 79, 274
and the Bayán, 51, 291, 321
birth of, 27, 291
character of, 28
in Chihríq, fortress of, 53, 62–64, 291, 323
childhood of, 27–28
death of, 80–84, 291
declaration of, 26, 291
disciples of (Letters of the Living), 26–27, 29–31, 42, 75, 325
and Fort Ṭabarsí martyrs, 75
Ḥájí Mírzá Áqásí plots against, 49, 50, 53, 62–64
and "Him Whom God Will Make Manifest," 51, 80, 89, 106, 125, 170, 323
Ḥusayn Khán plots against, 43, 46–47
in Isfahan, 48–49
in Máh-Kú, fortress of, 51–53, 291, 323
marriage of, 28
in Mecca, 291
and Mullá Ḥusayn, 24–27
plays about, 263
as Qá'im and Promised One, 26, 41–42, 63, 329
remains of, 84, 87, 273–74
in Shiraz, 47–48
shrine of, 273–74, 293
son of (Aḥmad), 28
in Tabríz, interrogation of, 62–64, 81–84, 291
torture of, 63, 71
uncle of (*see* 'Alí, Siyyid)
uncle of, eldest (*see* Muḥammad, Ḥájí Mírzá Siyyid)
and Vaḥíd, 44–46
wife of (Khadíjih Bagum), 28, 48, 230–31
Bábís
of Baghdad, 123, 138, 142–44, 152–53, 168–69
Bahá'u'lláh guides, 142–43, 151–52
Bahá'u'lláh secludes himself from, 130–40, 184–85, 220, 291, 327
in Black Pit, 98, 100–102
death of, 74–78, 111
definition of, 36, 320
at Fort Ṭabarsí, 68, 69, 72–76
of Karbala, 87–88, 89, 124–25, 138

of Káshán, 90, 91
Mírzá Taqí Khán plots against, 76–77
Mírzá Yaḥya as leader of, 87, 92, 104, 123, 129, 327
of Nayríz, 78
of Qazvín, 53–54
of Tehran, 113–14
of Zanján, 78–79, 85
"Bábíyyih" (House of the Bábís), 66
Bábu'l-Báb ("the Gate of the Gate")
Mullá Ḥusayn as, 26, 52, 328
See also Ḥusayn, Mullá
Badasht, Conference of (1848), 53, 57–60, 291
Badí' (Áqá Buzurg)
Bahá'u'lláh's tablet to, 209
death of, 211–12, 328
delivers tablet to the shah, 204, 208, 209–11, 292, 328
father of, death of, 213
title of, 212
transformation of, 207–8
visits Bahá'u'lláh, 204, 208
Baghdad
Bábís of, 123, 138, 142–44, 152–53, 168–69
Bahá'u'lláh exiled and journeys to, 111–18, 291
Bahá'u'lláh in, 140–41, 142–45, 148–49, 152–54, 159–60, 166–72
life in, 141–42
Bahá, definition of, 58, 79
Bahá'í Administrative Order, 226, 279–82
Bahá'í Faith, 288
Administrative Order of, 226, 279–82
and Christianity, 275
and Islam, 296
laws of, 224–26
marriage in, 233, 294
spread of, 245–46, 289
teaching of, 245–46, 251–52
World Center of, 327
See also Bahá'ís
Bahá'ís
conduct of, 251
definition of, 189
visit Bahá'u'lláh, 201–4, 219, 237, 240, 249–50, 254
See also Bahá'í Faith
Bahá'í World Center, 327
Bahá'u'lláh (Mírzá Ḥusayn-'Alí)
and 'Abdu'l-Bahá, love between, 214, 254–55, 257–58, 290
in Acre, 4–6, 195, 197, 198–208, 212, 213–28, 232–35, 237–39, 252, 292, 319
in Adrianople, 177, 179–81, 193–95, 292, 319
in Amul, 70–72, 291
ancestral home of, 272, 325, 329, 333
ancestry of, 9, 330
the Báb and, 35, 40, 50, 60, 79, 84, 87, 273–74
and Baghdad, 111–18, 123, 140–41, 142–45, 148–49, 152–54, 159–60, 166–72, 291

Bahá'u'lláh *(continued)*
in Bahjí, mansion of, 246–50, 252, 292
in Bandar-Gaz, 65
birth of, 8, 291
in Black Pit, 96–98, 100–103, 104–7, 109, 111–12, 291, 321, 333
character of, 12, 249
childhood of, 7–9
children of (*see* 'Abdu'l-Bahá; 'Alí-Muḥammad; Bahíyyih Khánum; Káẓím; Mihdí, Mírzá; Ṣádiq)
and Conference of Badasht, 53, 57–60
in Constantinople, 166, 175–78, 292
and the countryside, 12, 238, 248–49
as Darvísh Muḥammad, 135–37, 143
death of, 284–87, 293
declaration of, 170, 292, 322
education of, 8–9
as "Father of the Poor," 4, 15, 96, 260
and government position, 16–17
grandchildren of, 253
and Haifa, 196, 292, 293
in Karbala, 87–90, 124–25
marriages of, 14, 293–94
in Mazra'ih, mansion of, 239–41, 325
and Mírzá Mihdí, death of, 216–17
and Mírzá Yaḥyá (*see* Yaḥyá, Mírzá)
in Most Great Prison, 198–208, 212, 213–18, 327
and Mount Carmel, 273, 275, 278, 279, 327, 333
and mullás' challenge, 156–57
parents of (*see* 'Abbás Buzurg, Mírzá; Khadíjih Khánum)
poetry of, 137
poisoning of, 108, 181–82, 292
as Qayyúm and Promised One, 89, 107, 170, 183, 329, 330
revelation of, process of, 147–48, 190
revelation received, from Maiden, 105–6, 112, 123, 325
as Shaykh Effendi, 331
simple life of, 152, 249
sufferings and torture of, 4, 71, 95–97, 103, 158, 283
in Sulaimaniya, 131–32, 135–37, 139, 140, 291
in Ṭabarsí, 68
teaches Faith, 36–39, 251–52
and Tehran, 86–87, 90, 95–96, 111–14, 333
title of, 8, 58, 79, 222n
will and testament of (Book of the Covenant), 287–88, 293, 322, 324
withdraws himself, 130–40, 184–85, 220, 291, 327

wives of, 293–94
(*see also* Navváb)
writings of (*see* writings of Bahá'u'lláh)
Bahíyyih Khánum (daughter of Bahá'u'lláh)
character of, 214, 261
faints in Most Great Prison, 198
hardships of, 133–34
travels to Baghdad, 113, 114
Bahjí, Bahá'u'lláh in, 246–50, 252, 292
Bandar-Gaz, port city of, 65
Báqir, Mírzá (scribe), 190
Báqir, Shaykh ("the Wolf"; Muslim leader in Isfahan), 242–45, 321, 334
Báqir (Bábí), troublesome conduct of, 143
Barfurush, town of
mullá of, plots against Bábís, 67
Quddús in, 74–75
bastinado
the Báb tortured by, 63, 71
Badí' tortured by, 211–12
Bahá'u'lláh tortured by, 4, 71, 95
Bayán, the Persian
the Báb reveals, 51, 291
Beloved of the Martyrs (Mírzá Ḥusayn), 230n
martyrdom of, 241–44, 292
Bernhardt, Sarah, 263
Bible
book of Daniel, 297
Jesus' Olivet Discourse, 275n, 297, 300
Revelation of John, 297
truth of, 300
Biela's Comet, 107
Black Elk, 272, 321
Black Pit (Síyáh-Chál)
Bábís in, 98, 100–102
Bahá'u'lláh in, 96–98, 100, 104–7, 109, 111–12, 291, 321, 333
Black Standard, 66–67, 321
Black Stone, 41
Book of Certitude (Kitáb-i-Íqán), 162–63
Gospels explained in, 275, 300
and Messengers, 163–66
revelation of, 161, 291
book of Daniel, 297
Book of the Covenant (Kitáb-i 'Ahd; Will and Testament of Bahá'u'lláh), 287–88, 293, 322, 324
Browne, Edward Granville (Orientalist), 263–65, 293, 321
Brussels, conference in, 61
Buddhists, await Maitreye, 106, 325
Burning Bush, 106
Bush, George (professor), 297
Buzurg Khán, Mírzá (consul-general from Persia), plottings against Bahá'u'lláh, 154–55, 331

C

calendar, Muslim, 319
Carmel, Mount
Bahá'u'lláh on, 273, 275, 278
and Prophet Isaiah, 248, 273

Carmel, Mount *(continued)*
revelation of tablet on, 278–79, 333
significance of, 274
Carmel, Tablet of. *See* Tablet of Carmel
Center of the Covenant, 'Abdu'l-Bahá as, 288, 322, 324
Cherokee Nation, 266
Chihríq, fortress of, 53, 62–64, 291, 323
Christ, 164
Bahá'u'lláh extolls, 275
Dove appears to, 106
Muḥammad recognizes, 275
Olivet Discourse of, 275n, 297, 300
return of, 13, 21–23, 106, 275, 296–300
as Spirit of God, 107, 332
Christianity
and Bahá'í Faith, 275
and Islam, 275, 295–96
Christian Observer (London), 298
Christians, Millennial, 296–300
Christians, Templar, 275, 276, 333
circumambulation of mansion of Bahjí, 246–49
Civil War, 161, 267
coffeehouses
Bahá'u'lláh visits, 159–60
closing of, 171
comets, 17, 18, 107–8
Coming of Messiah in Majesty and Glory, The (de Lacunza), 298
Communist Manifesto, The (Marx), 60
Conference of Badasht (1848), 53, 57–60, 291
Constantinople (Istanbul,Turkey)
Bahá'u'lláh in, 166, 175–78, 292
location and history of, 175
consultation, 281–82
countryside, Bahá'u'lláh and, 12, 238, 248–49
Covenant, 279, 322
creeds, church, 297
Cyrus the Great (king of Persia), 13
Czar of Russia, 205

D

Daniel, book of, 297
Darvísh Muḥammad
Bahá'u'lláh as, 135–37, 144
See also Bahá'u'lláh
"Dawn-Breakers," 31
Declaration of Sentiments, 61–62, 332
de Lacunza, Manuel, 298
dervish
Bahá'u'lláh as, 135, 144
Mírzá Yaḥyá as, 122, 127
Dhabíḥ (Bábí), devotion of, toward Bahá'u'lláh, 153
Dolgorukov, Prince Dimitri (ambassador of Russia), 95, 109, 204
Douglass, Frederick, 61, 162, 322
Dove, appears to Jesus, 106
dreams
of Arab shepherd, 20–21
of Bahá'u'lláh, 167, 231
of Mírzá Buzurg, 9–11
of Munírih Khánum, 229–30
Dwight, Timothy, 298

E

Edwards, Jonathan, 296n
1890s, the world during, 267–68
election process, Bahá'í, 281
Epistle to the Son of the Wolf, 293
Europe
  revolution in, 60
  stories of the Báb spread to, 263
Evidence from Scripture and History (Miller), 299

F

fasting, in Islam, 295
Fatḥ'u'lláh (Bábí) attempts to assassinate the shah, 92–94, 109
Fáṭimih (daughter of Prophet Muḥammad), 295
Fáṭimih Khánum (Munírih Khánum; wife of 'Abdu'l-Bahá), 228–33, 259, 292, 328
Fáṭimih Khánum (wife of Bahá'u'lláh), 293
Finney, Charles, 296n
fish, Mírzá Buzurg's dream of, 9–11
Fort of Shaykh Ṭabarsí, 68, 69, 72–76, 291
Furúsh, Ḥájí
  Mírzá Yaḥyá as, 122, 127
  See also Yaḥyá, Mírzá

G

Gabriel, angel, 106, 322
Gallipoli, port city of, 195, 196
Garden of Najíbíyyih. *See* Riḍván, Garden of, in Baghdad
Garden of Na'mayn. *See* Riḍván, Garden of, in Acre
Gawhar Khánum (wife of Bahá'u'lláh), 293
glory, true, 191–92
God
  Covenant with humanity, 279, 322
  love for creation, 149, 150–51
  turning toward, 150–51
Gospels, explanation of, 275
Great Disappointment, The, 300
Greatest Branch. *See* 'Abdu'l-Bahá
Great Redeemer, American Indians await, 107
Guardianship, institution of, 279, 280

H

Ḥabíb, Siyyid (coffeehouse owner), 159–60, 171
hadith, 294
Haifa, 196, 292, 293
Hands of the Cause of God, role of, 252
Ḥasan, Ḥájí (Bábí), 143
Ḥasan, Ḥájí Mullá (mujtahid), 156–57
Ḥasan, Imám, 295
Ḥasan, Mírzá. *See* King of the Martyrs
Ḥasan, Shaykh (scribe of the Báb), recognition of Bahá'u'lláh by, 88–89, 125
Ḥasan Khán, Mírzá (brother of grand vizier), the Báb's execution and, 80–81

Hayes, President Rutherford B., 267
Hazart, definition of, 137
heavenly signs
announce Messengers, 13, 18, 163, 165
comets, 17, 107–8, 165
meteor shower, 13
Hidden Words, revelation of, 149–51, 291
"Him Whom God will make manifest," 51, 80, 89, 106, 125, 170, 323
Hindus, await Tenth Avatar, 106, 333
historicism, 298
Holy Spirit, 106
house of 'Abbúd. *See* 'Abbúd, house of
Houses of Justice. *See* Spiritual Assemblies; Universal House of Justice
Ḥujjat (Bábí), in fort of Zanján, 79
humanity, oneness of, 151
Ḥusayn, Imám
death of, 18n, 86n, 295, 324
return of (Twelfth Imám), 17n, 80n, 107, 295, 329, 331
Ḥusayn, Mírzá. *See* Beloved of the Martyrs
Ḥusayn, Mullá
and the Báb in Máh-Kú, 52
as Bábu'l-Báb, 26, 52, 328
courage of, 52, 73
death of, 73–74, 75
fights mob, 67–68
at Fort Ṭabarsí, 68, 72–73
as Letter of the Living, 325, 328
and Promised One, search for, 23–27
teaches Faith, 28–31, 32–33, 66
Ḥusayn, promised (return of Imám Ḥusayn; Twelfth Imám), 17n, 80n, 107, 295, 329, 331
Ḥusayn, Siyyid (amanuensis of the Báb), 81–83
Ḥusayn-'Alí, Mírzá. *See* Bahá'u'lláh
Ḥusayn Khán, Mírzá (Persian ambassador to Constantinople), 176, 178
Ḥusayn Khán (governor of Shiraz), 43, 46–47

I

imám-jum'ih, definition of, 242, 324
India, subjected people of, 266
Indians, American, 107, 266–67, 270, 272
Indonesia, subjected people of, 266
Inn of the Pillars (caravansary), 218
institutions of Bahá'í Faith. *See* Bahá'í Administrative Order; Spiritual Assemblies; Universal House of Justice
Isaiah, Prophet
and Mount Carmel, 248, 273
vision of, 271

Isfahan
the Báb in, 48–49
brothers of
(*see* Beloved of the Martyrs; King of the Martyrs)
Isfandíyár (faithful servant of Bahá'u'lláh), 103, 113, 324
Islam
and Bahá'í Faith, 296
Black Standard, 66–67, 321
calendar of, 319
and Christianity, 275, 295–96
Five Pillars of, 295
founding of, 294
and Mahdí, 107, 326
marriage laws of, 293–94
split of, into two branches, 294
See also Shia Islam; Sunni Islam

J

Ja'far, Mullá (sifter of wheat), 32
Ja'far-Qulí Khán (brother of grand vizier), 90, 94
Jamál Effendi, teaches Bahá'í Faith, 245–46
Jeans, James, 17
Jesus Christ. *See* Christ
Jews
and King of Glory, 106
Muḥammad's teachings about, 295–96
jihad, explanation of, 295
Joachim of Fiore, 297
John, Revelation of, 297

K

Kaaba (holiest shrine of Islam), 41
Karbala, 18
Bábís of, 87–88, 89, 124–25, 138
Bahá'u'lláh in, 87–90, 124–25
death of Imam Ḥusayn at, 18n, 86n, 295, 324
Káshán, Bábís of, help Mírzá Áqá Khán, 90, 91
Káẓim, Siyyid, 331
prepares the way for the Báb, 19–21, 165
Káẓim (son of Bahá'u'lláh), 16, 260n
Khadíjih Bagum (wife of the Báb), 28, 48, 230–31
Khadíjih Khánum (mother of Bahá'u'lláh), 8, 324
Khammár, 'Údí, 219, 246–48, 323
Khánum, definition of, 8n, 324
Khurusan, 53
King of Glory, Jews await, 106
King of the Martyrs (Mírzá Ḥasan), 230n, 331, 334
death of, 241–44, 292
Kings, Tablet to the (Súriy-i-Mulúk), 190–92, 226, 292, 332
kings and rulers, Bahá'u'lláh's tablets to, 190–93, 204–7, 226, 236, 271, 292, 332
Kirmanshah, town of, 115–16
Kitáb-i-'Ahd (Book of the Covenant; Will and Testament of Bahá'u'lláh), 287–88, 293, 322, 324

Kitáb-i-Aqdas. *See* Most Holy Book
Kitáb-i-Íqán. *See* Book of Certitude
Koran, 296, 300
    revelation of, 294
    Súrih of Kaw<u>th</u>ar, 45
    Súrih of Joseph, 25–26
Kulayn, village of, 50
Kurdistan, Bahá'u'lláh in, 131–32,
    135–36, 291

L

Lakota vision, 272, 321
Land of Ṭá, 113
    See also Tehran
language, universal, 269
laws of Bahá'u'lláh, 224–26
Letters of the Living, 26–27,
    29–31, 75
    Mullá Ḥusayn as, 325, 328
    Quddús as, 30, 325
    Ṭáhirih as, 29, 325, 333
    teaching Bábí Faith, 42
Lincoln, Abraham, 61, 161, 162,
    267
Livermore, Harriet, 22
Louis-Philippe,
    King (of France), 60

M

Mahdí, Muslims await, 17n, 107,
    326, 329
Máh-Kú, castle fortress of, 51–53,
    291, 323
Maḥmúd, <u>Sh</u>ay<u>kh</u> (Muslim leader
    in Acre), 3–6, 197, 203–
    4, 216, 285
Maiden, appearance to
    Bahá'u'lláh, 105–6, 112,
    123

Maitreye, awaited by Buddhists,
    106
Majíd (husband of Bahá'u'lláh's
    sister), 95
Manifestations of God. *See*
    Messengers of God
al-Manṣúr, Abu-Ja'far (Muslim
    caliph), 118n
Manú<u>ch</u>ihr <u>Kh</u>án (governor of
    Isfahan), recognizes the
    Báb, 48–49
Maori of New Zealand, 266
marriage, Bahá'í, 233, 294
Marx, Karl, 60
Maryam (cousin of Bahá'u'lláh),
    care of Bahá'u'lláh by,
    112
Mason, Archibald, 298
Mázindarán, province of, 132
    and legend of holy tree, 107,
    272
Mazra'ih, mansion of, 238–41,
    325
Mecca, the Báb in, 40–42, 291
Mede, Joseph, 297
Mendès, Catulle, 263
Messengers of God
    Covenant of, 279, 322
    heavenly signs of, 13, 18,
    163–65
    oneness of, 163–66
    role of, 18
    suffering of, 164
meteor shower, 13
Mihdí, Mírzá (son of Bahá'u'lláh)
    in Baghdad, 158
    characteristics of, 214
    death and sacrifice of,
    215–17, 218, 292

remains of, 262n
in Tehran, 87, 113
Millennial Christians, 296–300
Miller, William, 298–300
miracle, Bahá'u'lláh asked to perform, 156–57
Mírzá, definition of, 8n, 326
Morse, Samuel F. B., 31–32
Moses, Burning Bush and, 106
mosque of Sulṭán Salím, 187–88, 327
"Most Great House" (Baghdad), 145
"Most Great Idol," Mírzá Yaḥyá as, 189
"Most Great Peace," 265, 267, 327
Most Great Prison, Bahá'u'lláh in, 190–218
"most great separation," 185, 292, 327
Most Holy Book (Kitáb-i-Aqdas)
Bahá'í Administrative Order in, 226, 279
laws of, 225, 233
Mírzá Yaḥya addressed in, 301
revelation of, 224, 292
Mosul, city of, 174
Mott, Lucretia, 61–62, 327
Mount Carmel. *See* Carmel, Mount
Muḥammad, Darvísh
Bahá'u'lláh as 135–37, 144
See also Bahá'u'lláh
Muḥammad, Ḥájí Mírzá Siyyid (eldest uncle of the Báb), 160–61, 165, 324
Muḥammad, Mír (Bábí caravan-driver), 186–88, 327
Muḥammad, Mullá (husband of Ṭáhirih), 55–56
Muḥammad, Mullá (mujtahid of Núr), denies Bábí Faith, 36–38
Muḥammad, Mullá (student), delivers scroll to Bahá'u'lláh, 33–35
Muḥammad, Prophet, 164
and angel Gabriel, 106, 322
recognizes Jesus, 275, 295–96
successor of, 294–95, 331, 332
teachings of, 295–96
Muḥammad, Siyyid (Bábí)
death of, 221, 292
expelled from Bábí community, 185
as jealous of Bahá'u'lláh, 89–90
plots against Bahá'u'lláh, 126–29, 175, 177, 178, 181, 184–86, 193, 201, 219–20
Muḥammad-'Alí, Mírzá (father of Munírih Khánum), 230
Muḥammad-'Alí, Ustád (barber), 182–83
Muḥammad-Báqir, Shaykh ("the Wolf"; Muslim leader in Isfahan), 242–45, 321, 334
Muḥammad Big (chief courier of the shah), 49, 50
Muḥammad-Hádí (bookbinder and artist), as devoted to Bahá'u'lláh, 237
Muḥammad-Ḥusayn, Mír ("the She Serpent"; chief Muslim leader in Isfahan), 242–45, 331

Muḥammad-Qulí (half-brother of
        Baháʼuʼlláh), 112, 327
Muḥammad Sẖáh (ruler of Persia)
        asks to meet the Báb, 49
        asks Vaḥíd to investigate the
                Báb, 43–44, 46
        death of, 65, 291
        orders Baháʼuʼlláhʼs execu-
                tion, 64
mujtahid, definition of, 146, 328
Munírih Khánum (Fátimih
        Khánum; wife of ʻAbduʼl-
        Bahá), 228–33, 259,
        292, 328
Músá, Mírzá (brother of
        Baháʼuʼlláh)
        the Bábʼs remains and, 87
        in Baghdad, 114
        death of, 284
        helps Baháʼuʼlláhʼs family,
                97, 104, 112, 121, 184
        recognizes the Báb, 35
        uses herbs and plants, 181
Muslim calendar, 319
Muslims
        and Mahdí, 107, 326
        See also Islam; Shia Islam;
                Sunni Islam
Muṣṭafá (dervish), meets
        Baháʼuʼlláh, 39
"Mystery of God," 255, 328
        See also ʻAbduʼl-Bahá

                        N
Nabíl-i-Akbar, recognizes
        Baháʼuʼlláh, 146
Nabíl-i-Aʻẓam, visits Badíʻ, 207
Najaf, city of, 86n, 328
Najíb Pásẖá (wealthy man)

garden of, 168–70
        See also Riḍván, Garden of,
                in Baghdad
Námiq Pásẖá (governor of
        Baghdad), 166, 167, 171,
        173
Napoleon III (emperor of France)
        Baháʼuʼlláhʼs tablet to, 205
        downfall of, 236
Náṣiriʼd-Dín Sẖáh (king of Persia)
        accession of, 291
        army of, fights Bábís at Fort
                Ṭabarsí, 68–69, 73–74
        attempted assassination of,
                91–94, 291
        Badíʻ delivers tablet to, 204,
                208, 209–11, 292
        Baháʼuʼlláhʼs tablet to, 192–
                93, 207
Native Americans (American
        Indians), 107, 266–67,
        270, 272
Naʻúm (sick woman), ʻAbduʼl-
        Bahá cares for, 256
Navváb (Ásíyih Khánum; wife of
        Baháʼuʼlláh)
        and Baháʼuʼlláhʼs imprison-
                ment, 97, 102–3
        character of, 259–63
        death of, 261–63, 292
        and journey to Baghdad,
                112–13, 114–15
        life in Baghdad, 121, 132–34
        and loss of children, 217,
                260
        marriage of, 14–16
        as "Mother of Consolation,"
                15, 115, 260
        remains of, 262n

sews aba for Bahá'u'lláh, 140–41
in Tehran, 87
Naw-Rúz (New Year), 52n, 116–17, 166–67, 329
Nayríz, Bábís of, 78
Newton, Isaac, 297
New Year (Naw-Rúz), 52n, 116–17, 166–67, 329
"nine, year," Qayyúm revealed in, 80, 106

O

Oglala Lakota Sioux Indians, 272, 321
Olivet Discourse of Jesus, 275n, 297, 300
Origen (scholar of Greek church), 297

P

parliaments of the world, 206–7
peace, 265, 267, 268–71, 327
Persia
Ambassador of, 192
days of glory in, 13
legend of tree in, 107, 272
teaching in, 252
Pius IX, Pope, Bahá'u'lláh's tablet to, 205–6
Promised One
the Báb as, 26, 41–42, 63, 329
Bahá'u'lláh as, 89, 107, 125, 170, 183, 323, 329
preparing for, 17–23, 80, 106
Prophets. *See also* Messengers of God

Q

Qá'im ("He Who Shall Arise")
the Báb as, 41
definition of, 17
signs of, 19
Qará-Guhar (Big and Heavy), 97
Qásim (Bábí), attempts of, to assassinate the shah, 92–94, 109
Qayyúm ("The All-Compelling")
Bahá'u'lláh as, 89, 330
definition of, 17, 330
revealed in "year nine," 80, 106
Qazvín, murder in, 53–54, 56
Quddús
arrest of, in Sárí, 66–68
death of, 75
at Fort of Shaykh Ṭabarsí, 74
as Letter of the Living, 30, 325
recognizes the Báb, 29–30
title of, 58
travels with the Báb, 40–42
Qur'án. *See* Koran

R

Ramadan, Muslim month of, 295
religion, purpose of, 277
revelation, Bahá'u'lláh's process of, 147–48, 190
Revelation of John, 297
Riḍá Big, house of, 184
Riḍá-Qulí, Mírzá (half-brother of Bahá'u'lláh), 112
Riḍá (Turk), attempt of, to assassinate Bahá'u'lláh, 155

Riḍván
Festival of, 170, 330
Garden of, in Acre (Garden of Na'mayn), 240–41, 248, 253, 254, 292, 322
Garden of, in Baghdad (Garden of Najíbíyyih), 168–71, 292, 322, 330
Russia
ambassador of, 95, 109, 204
Czar of, Bahá'u'lláh's tablet to, 205

S

Ṣádiq (Bábí), attempts to assassinate shah, 92–93, 109
Ṣádiq (son of Bahá'u'lláh), 16, 260n
Salásil (Iron Chains), 97
Salmán, Shaykh (courier), 250–51
Sám Khán and execution of the Báb, 82–83
Sar-Galú, mountain of, Bahá'u'lláh at, 131–32
Sárih (sister of Bahá'u'lláh), 14, 330
Sassanian kings, 9, 330
Sayyáh (Bábí), makes pilgrimage to Ṭabarsí, 75
Second Great Awakening in America, 296n
self, discovery of, 150–51
Seneca Falls, New York, 61, 327
Sermon of Wrath (the Báb's letter to grand vizier), 64
Seven Martyrs of Tehran, 77, 326, 330
Seven Martyrs of Yazd, 276–77, 331
Sháh-Bahrám, 106, 331, 334
Shaykh Effendi
Bahá'u'lláh as, 180
See also Bahá'u'lláh
shepherd, Arab, dream of, 20–21
"She-Serpent, the" (Mír Muḥammad-Ḥusayn), 242–45, 331
Shia Islam
favors hereditary succession, 294–95
and return of Imám Ḥusayn, 17n, 80n, 107, 295, 329, 331
Shiraz
the Báb leaves, 47–48
declaration of the Báb in, 291
Mullá Ḥusayn in, 24
Síyáh-Chál. *See* Black Pit
siyyid, definition of, 46n, 108n, 332
slavery, 61, 161–62
Spirit of God (Jesus Christ), 17, 107, 332
Spiritual Assemblies, 280–82, 330, 332
Stanton, Elizabeth Cady, 61–62, 332
stars, 13, 18, 165
Stowe, Harriet Beecher, 162, 332
Sulaimaniya, Bahá'u'lláh in, 131, 135–37, 139, 140, 291
Sulaymán Khán, Ḥájí (Bábí), and the Báb's remains, 84
Sulaymán N'Azím Bey (Turkish poet), 100
Sulṭán, Shaykh (father-in-law of Mírzá Músá), 139, 140

Sunni Islam
and descent of "Spirit of God," 17n, 107
favors caliphs, 294–95
Sura of Joseph, the Báb's commentary on, 25–26, 55
Sura of Kawthar (Paradise), the Báb's commentary on, 45
Súriy-i-Mulúk (Tablet to the Kings), 190–92, 226, 292, 332

T

Ṭabarsí, Shaykh, Fort of, 68, 69, 72–76, 291
Tablet of Carmel, revelation of, 278–79, 293
Tablet to the Kings (Súriy-i-Mulúk), 190–92, 226, 292, 332
tablets of Bahá'u'lláh
to Bábís of Baghdad, 169
to Badí', 209
to kings and rulers, 190–93, 204–7, 226, 271, 292, 332
to Mírzá Yaḥyá, 183, 188
to Seven Martyrs of Yazd, 277
Tabríz, the Báb in, 62–63, 81–84, 291
Ṭáhirih
arrest of, 78, 98–99
Bahá'u'lláh protects, 56–57
characteristics of, 54–55
death of, 100
husband of (Mullá Muḥammad), 55–56
as Letter of the Living, 29, 54, 325
recognizes the Báb, 29, 55
title of, 58
veil of, 58–59, 62
Tákur, village of
burning of, 104
mansion in, 12, 14
Taqí, Mullá (father-in-law of Ṭáhirih), murder of, 54, 56
Taqí Khán, Mírzá (grand vizier of Persia)
downfall of, 90
orders Bahá'u'lláh to leave Tehran, 86
plots against Bábís, 76–77
teaching the Bahá'í Faith, 245–46, 251–52
Tehran (Persia)
Bábís of, 113–14
Badí' in, 209–10
and Bahá'u'lláh, 90, 95–96, 111–14, 333
Black Pit of (*see* Black Pit)
as Land of Ṭá, 325
life in, 6, 10
Seven Martyrs of, 77, 326, 330
telegraph, invention of, 31–32
Templars (Christian), 275, 276, 333
Tenth Avatar, 106, 333
Tigris River, 124, 148–50
"Trail of Tears," 266
tree
in Black Elk's vision, 272
Divine Lote-Tree, 322
Persian legend of, 107, 272
trumpet blasts, 17
Truth, Sojourner, 161–62, 333
Tubman, Harriet, 161, 333

Twelfth Imám
(return of Imám Ḥusayn), 17n, 80n, 107, 295, 329, 331
twin duties of human beings, 225

U

Uncle Tom's Cabin (Stowe), 162, 332
Underground Railroad, 61, 161, 333
United States of America, destiny of, 270–71
unity, 268
universal auxiliary language, 269
Universal House of Justice
election of, 280n, 281, 330
establishment of, 226
powers of, 226, 280
seat of, 279

V

Vaḥíd (Siyyid Yaḥyá), 44–46, 57, 78, 334
Victoria, Queen, 206

W

wealthy, instructions to, 16
wedding vows, Bahá'í, 233
Will and Testament of Bahá'u'lláh (*Kitáb-i-'Ahd;* Book of the Covenant), 287–88, 293, 322, 324
"Wolf, the" (Shaykh Báqir), 242–45, 321, 334
women
peace and, 270
rights of, convention for (1848), 61–62, 327, 332
Women, Peace and Security (UN resolution), 270n
World Anti-Slavery Convention (1840), 61
world court, 269
world parliament, 269
writings of Bahá'u'lláh
cast into river, 160
as distinct, 146–48
revelation of, process of, 147–48, 190
uphold truth of Bible and Koran, 300
See also Book of Certitude; Book of the Covenant; Epistle to the Son of the Wolf; Hidden Words; Most Holy Book; Tablet of Carmel; tablets of Bahá'u'lláh; Tablet to the Kings

Y

Yaḥyá, Mírzá (half-brother of Bahá'u'lláh), 69
as Bábí leader, 87, 92, 104, 123, 129, 327
in Baghdad, 116, 122, 133–34, 173
Bahá'u'lláh addresses, 183, 188, 301
Bahá'u'lláh breaks ties with, 184, 188–89
Bahá'u'lláh raises, 87, 129
in Constantinople, 174–75
in Cyprus, 195, 300
debate with Bahá'u'lláh, 186–88, 327

downfall and death of, 301
followers of *("Azalís")*, 189, 320
as Ḥájí 'Alí, 174
as Ḥájí Furú<u>sh</u>, 122, 127
hides from Bábís, 104, 122, 124, 126–27, 138, 180
as Most Great Idol, 189, 327
plots against Bahá'u'lláh, 126–29, 138, 174, 177, 181–86, 193, 292
in Tehran, 87
titles of, 92, 129, 188

Yaḥyá, Siyyid (Vaḥíd), 44–46, 57, 78, 334

Yaḥyá <u>Kh</u>án (the Báb's prison warden), 62

Yazd, Seven Martyrs of, 276–77, 331

"year nine," Qayyúm revealed in, 80, 106

Yúsif, Mírzá (husband of Navváb's great-aunt), 97, 98

Z

Zagros Mountains, 114, 116, 131, 334

Zanján, Bábís of, 78–79, 85

Zoroaster, 64, 334

Zoroastrians, and <u>Sh</u>áh-Bahrám, 106, 331, 334

For more information about the Bahá'í Faith,
or to contact the Bahá'ís near you, visit
www.us.bahai.org
or call
1-800-22-UNITE

Bahá'í Publishing and the Bahá'í Faith

Bahá'í Publishing produces books based on the teachings of the Bahá'í Faith. Founded nearly 160 years ago, the Bahá'í Faith has spread to some 235 nations and territories and is now accepted by more than five million people. The word "Bahá'í" means "follower of Bahá'u'lláh." Bahá'u'lláh, the Founder of the Bahá'í Faith, asserted that He is the Messenger of God for all of humanity in this day. The cornerstone of His teachings is the establishment of the spiritual unity of humankind, which will be achieved by personal transformation and the application of clearly identified spiritual principles. Bahá'ís also believe that there is but one religion and that all the Messengers of God—among them Abraham, Zoroaster, Moses, Krishna, Buddha, Jesus, and Muḥammad—have progressively revealed its nature. Together, the world's great religions are expressions of a single, unfolding divine plan. Human beings, not God's Messengers, are the source of religious divisions, prejudices, and hatreds.

The Bahá'í Faith is not a sect or denomination of another religion, nor is it a cult or a social movement. Rather, it is a globally recognized independent world religion founded on new books of scripture revealed by Bahá'u'lláh.

Bahá'í Publishing is an imprint of the National Spiritual Assembly of the Bahá'ís of the United States.

Other Books Available from Bahá'í Publishing

The Hidden Words

by Bahá'u'lláh

A collection of lyrical, gem-like verses of scripture that convey timeless spiritual wisdom "clothed in the garment of brevity," the Hidden Words is one of the most important and cherished scriptural works of the Bahá'í Faith.

Revealed by Bahá'u'lláh, the founder of the religion, the verses are a perfect guidebook to walking a spiritual path and drawing closer to God. They address themes such as turning to God, humility, detachment, and love, to name but a few. These verses are among Bahá'u'lláh's earliest and best-known works, having been translated into more than seventy languages and read by millions worldwide. This edition will offer many American readers their first introduction to the vast collection of Bahá'í scripture.

The Kitáb-i-Íqán: The Book of Certitude

by Bahá'u'lláh

The Book of Certitude is one of the most important scriptural works in all of religious history. In it Bahá'u'lláh gives a sweeping overview of religious truth, explaining the underlying unity of the world's religions, describing the universality of the revelations humankind has received from the Prophets of God, illuminating their fundamental teachings, and elucidating allegorical passages from the New Testament and the Koran that have given rise to misunderstandings among religious leaders, practitioners, and the public. Revealed in the span of two days and two nights, the work is, in the words of its translator, Shoghi Effendi, "the most important book written on the spiritual significance" of the Bahá'í Faith.

Advancement of Women: A Bahá'í Perspective

by Janet A. Khan and Peter J. Khan

Advancement of Women presents the Bahá'í Faith's global perspective on the equality of the sexes, including:

- The meaning of equality
- The education of women and the need for their participation in the world at large
- The profound effects of equality on the family and family relationships
- The intimate relationship between equality of the sexes and global peace
- Chastity, modesty, sexual harassment, and rape

The equality of women and men is one of the basic tenets of the Bahá'í Faith, and much is said on the subject in Bahá'í writings. Until now, however, no single volume created for a general audience has provided comprehensive coverage of the Bahá'í teachings on this topic. In this broad survey, husband-and-wife team Janet and Peter Khan address even those aspects of equality of the sexes that are usually ignored or glossed over in the existing literature.

Tactfully treating a subject that often provokes argumentation, contention, polarization of attitudes, and accusations, the authors elevate the discussion to a new level that challenges all while offending none.

The Bahá'í Faith: The Emerging Global Religion

by William S. Hatcher and J. Douglas Martin

Explore the history, teachings, structure, and community life of the worldwide Bahá'í community—what may well be the most diverse organized body of people on earth—through this revised and updated comprehensive introduction (2002).

Named by the *Encylopaedia Britannica* as a book that has made "significant contributions to knowledge and understanding" of religious thought, *The Bahá'í Faith* covers the most recent developments in a Faith that, in just over 150 years, has grown to become the second most widespread of the independent world religions.

An excellent introduction. [*The Bahá'í Faith*] offers a clear analysis of the religious and ethical values on which Bahá'ism is based (such as all-embracing peace, world harmony, the important role of women, to mention only a few)."—Annemarie Schimmel, past president, International Association for the History of Religions

"Provide[s] non-Bahá'í readers with an excellent introduction to the history, beliefs, and sociopolitical structure of a religion that originated in Persia in the mid-1800s and has since blossomed into an international organization with . . . adherents from almost every country on earth."—*Montreal Gazette*

The Challenge of Bahá'u'lláh: Does God Still Speak to Humanity Today?

by Gary L. Matthews

One person examines the astonishing claims made by the prophet who founded the Bahá'í religion.

Author Gary Matthews documents why he believes that the Revelation of Bahá'u'lláh is divine in origin, representing a unique summons of unequaled importance to humanity. The book contains discussions of Bahá'í prophecies concerning historical events and scientific discoveries. Among the events and discoveries discussed are the fall of the Ottoman Empire, the worldwide erosion of ecclesiastical authority, the Holocaust, and the development of nuclear weapons. A new and updated edition. The previous edition (George Ronald, ISBN 0-85398-360-7) was a limited release and not offered to the U.S. trade/consumer market.

Close Connections: The Bridge between Physical and Spiritual Reality

by John S. Hatcher

Examines the bonds between physical and spiritual reality and their implications for science.

Close Connections will appeal to anyone interested in spirituality and its link to everyday life. For more than twenty-five years John Hatcher has studied the nature and purpose of physical reality by exploring the theological and philosophical implications of the authoritative Bahá'í texts. His latest book explains how the gap between physical and spiritual reality is routinely crossed and describes the profound implications that result from the interplay of both worlds.

God Speaks Again: An Introduction to the Bahá'í Faith

by Kenneth E. Bowers

The Bahá'í Faith is a recognized independent world religion attracting increasing attention—and a growing number of followers—in the U.S. and around the globe as people from all walks of life search for practical spiritual direction and confident hope for the future. *God Speaks Again* tells the story of this thoroughly inclusive religion and describes how the history and teachings of the Bahá'í Faith center around the inspiring person of its Prophet and Founder, Bahá'u'lláh (1817–1892), Whom Bahá'ís around the world regard as the Messenger of God for this day. The cornerstone of Bahá'u'lláh's teachings is the establishment of the unity of humankind, which Bahá'ís believe will be achieved by the application of clearly identified spiritual principles revealed by Bahá'u'lláh. Bahá'ís also believe that there is but one religion, and that all the Messengers of God—among them Abraham, Zoroaster, Moses, Krishna, Buddha, Jesus, and Muḥammad—have progressively revealed its nature. Together, the world's great religions are expressions of a single, unfolding Divine plan. Human beings, not God's Messengers, are the source of religious divisions, prejudices, and hatreds.

It's Not Your Fault: How Healing Relationships Change Your Brain & Can Help You Overcome a Painful Past

by Patricia Romano McGraw

Simply put, you can't think your way to happiness if you're suffering the effects of trauma or abuse. Yet every day, millions receive this message from a multi-billion-dollar self-help industry. As a result, many think it's their fault when their efforts to heal themselves fail. Far too many sincere, intelligent, and highly motivated people who have followed popular advice for self-healing still feel depressed, anxious, unloved, and unlovable. Why is this? If popular pathways for self-healing don't work, what does? How can those who suffer begin to find relief, function better, and feel genuinely optimistic, relaxed, loved, and lovable? This engaging and highly readable book, based on the author's professional experience in treating those who suffer from the devastating effects of emotional trauma, offers hope for those who suffer and those who care about them. McGraw describes how trauma affects the brain and, therefore, one's ability to carry out "good advice"; explains the subtle and largely hidden processes of attunement and attachment that take place between parents and children, examining their impact on all future relationships; tells what is needed for healing to occur; discusses the profound health benefits of spirituality and a relationship with God in assisting and accelerating the healing process; and suggests how members of the helping professions can begin to tap the deepest, most authentic parts of themselves to touch the hearts of those they seek to help.

Marriage beyond Black and White: An Interracial Family Portrait

by David Douglas and Barbara Douglas

A powerful story about the marriage of a Black man and a White woman, *Marriage beyond Black and White* offers a poignant and sometimes painful look at what it was like to be an interracial couple in the United States from the early 1940s to the mid-1990s. Breaking one of the strongest taboos in American society at the time, Barbara Wilson Tinker and Carlyle Douglas met, fell in love, married, and began raising a family. At the time of their wedding, interracial marriage was outlawed in twenty-seven states and was regarded as an anathema in the rest.

Barbara began writing their story to record both the triumphs and hardships of interracial marriage. Her son David completed the family chronicle. The result will uplift and inspire any reader whose life is touched by injustice, offering an invaluable perspective on the roles of faith and spiritual transformation in combating prejudice and racism.

Prophet's Daughter: The Life and Legacy of Bahíyyih Khánum, Outstanding Heroine of the Bahá'í Faith

by Janet A. Khan

The first full-length biography of a member of Bahá'u'lláh's family, an important woman in world religious history.

A biography of a largely unknown yet important woman in world religious history—the eldest daughter of Bahá'u'lláh, founder of the Bahá'í religion—who faithfully served her family and the early followers of a then completely new faith through nearly seven decades of extreme hardship. During the mid-nineteenth and early twentieth centuries, when women in the Middle East were largely invisible, deprived of education, and without status in their communities, she was an active participant in the religion's turbulent early years and contributed significantly to its emergence as an independent world religion. The example of her life, and her remarkable personal qualities, have special relevance to issues confronting society today.

The Reality of Man

compiled by Terry J. Cassiday, Christopher Martin, and Bahhaj Taherzadeh

An important new collection of Bahá'í writings on the spiritual nature of human beings.

This compilation provides a sample of the Bahá'í religion's vast teachings on the nature of man. Topics include God's love for humanity; the purpose of life; our spiritual reality; the nature of the soul; how human beings develop spiritually; and immortality and life hereafter. The writings are from Bahá'u'lláh and His appointed successor, 'Abdu'l-Bahá.

"Men at all times and under all conditions stand in need of one to exhort them, guide them and to instruct and teach them. Therefore He hath sent forth His Messengers, His Prophets, and chosen ones that they might acquaint the people with the divine purpose underlying the revelation of Books and the raising up of messengers, and that everyone may become aware of the trust of God, which is latent in the reality of every soul." —Bahá'u'lláh

"The mission of the Prophets, the revelation of the Holy Books, the manifestation of the heavenly teachers and the purpose of divine philosophy all center in the training of the human realities so that they may become clear and pure as mirrors and reflect the light and love of [God]. . . . Otherwise, by simple development along material lines man is not perfected. At most, the physical aspect of man, his natural or material conditions, may become stabilized and improved, but he will remain deprived of the spiritual or divine bestowal.He is then like a body without a spirit, a lamp without the light. . . ." — 'Abdu'l-Bahá

Refresh and Gladden My Spirit: Prayers and Meditations from Bahá'í Scripture

Introduction by Pamela Brode

Discover the Bahá'í approach to prayer with this uplifting collection of prayers and short, inspirational extracts from Bahá'í scripture. More than 120 prayers in *Refresh and Gladden My Spirit* offer solace and inspiration on themes including spiritual growth, nearness to God, comfort, contentment, happiness, difficult times, healing, material needs, praise and gratitude, and strength, to name only a few. An introduction by Pamela Brode examines the powerful effects of prayer and meditation in daily life, outlines the Bahá'í approach to prayer, and considers questions such as "What is prayer?" "Why pray?" "Are our prayers answered?" and "Does prayer benefit the world?"

Release the Sun

by William Sears

Millennial fervor gripped many people around the world in the early nineteenth century. While Christians anticipated the return of Jesus Christ, a wave of expectation swept through Islam that the "Lord of the Age" would soon appear. In Persia, this reached a dramatic climax on May 23, 1844, when a twenty-five-year-old merchant from Shíráz named Siyyid 'Alí-Muḥammad, later titled "the Báb," announced that he was the bearer of a divine Revelation destined to transform the spiritual life of the human race. Furthermore, he claimed that he was but the herald of another Messenger, who would soon bring a far greater Revelation that would usher in an age of universal peace. Against a backdrop of wide-scale moral decay in Persian society, this declaration aroused hope and excitement among all classes. The Báb quickly attracted tens of thousands of followers, including influential members of the clergy—and the brutal hand of a fearful government bent on destroying this movement that threatened to rock the established order.

Release the Sun tells the extraordinary story of the Báb, the Prophet-Herald of the Bahá'í Faith. Drawing on contemporary accounts, William Sears vividly describes one of the most significant but little-known periods in religious history since the rise of Christianity and Islam.

Seeking Faith: Is Religion Really What You Think It Is?

by Nathan Rutstein

What's your concept of religion? A 2001 Gallup Poll on religion in America found that while nearly two out of three Americans claim to be a member of a church or synagogue, more than half of those polled believe that religion is losing its influence on society. *Seeking Faith* examines today's concepts of religion and the various reasons why people are searching in new directions for hope and spiritual guidance. Author Nathan Rutstein explores the need for a sense of purpose, direction, and meaning in life, and the need for spiritual solutions to global problems in the social, economic, environmental, and political realms. Rutstein also discusses the concept of the Spiritual Guide, or Divine Educator, and introduces the teachings of Bahá'u'lláh and the beliefs of the Bahá'í Faith.

A Wayfarer's Guide to Bringing the Sacred Home

by Joseph Sheppherd

What's the spiritual connection between self, family, and community? Why is it so important that we understand and cultivate these key relationships? *A Wayfarer's Guide to Bringing the Sacred Home* offers a Bahá'í perspective on issues that shape our lives and the lives of those around us: the vital role of spirituality in personal transformation, the divine nature of child-rearing and unity in the family, and the importance of overcoming barriers to building strong communities—each offering joy, hope, and confidence to a challenged world. Inspiring extracts and prayers from Bahá'í scripture are included. This is an enlightening read for anyone seeking to bring spirituality into their daily lives.

Visit your favorite bookstore today to find or request these titles from Bahá'í Publishing.